A MACMILLAN
ILLUSTRATED ENCYCLOPEDIA

ANIMALS

VOLUME 1
MAMMALS

A MACMILLAN ILLUSTRATED ENCYCLOPEDIA

ANIMALS

EDITED BY PHILIP WHITFIELD

VOLUME 1
MAMMALS

MACMILLAN LIBRARY REFERENCE • NEW YORK

First published as three volumes in 1999 by Macmillan Library Reference USA

Macmillan Library Reference USA
1633 Broadway, 7th Floor
New York, New York 10019

Consultant Editor: **Dr. Philip Whitfield**
Biology Department, King's College, University of London
This edition updated by **Richard Walker**
Consultants:
Mammals: **Professor D. M. Stoddart,**
Zoology Department, University of Tasmania, Hobart, Australia
Birds: **I. C. J. Galbraith,**
Ornithology Department, British Museum (Natural History), Tring, Hertfordshire
Reptiles and Amphibians: **Professor Barry Cox,**
Biology Department, King's College, University of London
Fishes: **Alwyne Wheeler,**
British Museum (Natural History), London

Artists:
Mammals: **Graham Allen**
Dick Twinney
Birds: **Michael Woods**
Malcolm Ellis
Keith Brewer
Reptiles and Amphibians: **Alan Male**
Fishes: **Colin Newman**

1 2 3 4 5 6 7 8 9 10

ISBN
0-02-865417-X (Volume 1)
0-02-865418-8 (Volume 2)
0-02-865419-6 (Volume 3)
0-02-865420-X (3 Volumes)

Manufactured by Imago, Singapore

Cataloging-in-Publication Data available

This paper meets the requirements of ANSI/NISO Z39.48-1992 (Permanence of Paper).

CONTENTS

14 **Volume One: Mammals**
18 Echidnas, Platypus
20 Opossums, Shrew Opossums, Colocolo
22 Dasyurid Marsupials
24 Numbat, Bandicoots, Marsupial Mole, Wombat
26 Koala, Phalangers, Pygmy Possums, Possums
28 Kangaroos
30 Kangaroos, Rat Kangaroos
32 Anteaters, Sloths
34 Armadillos, Pangolins
36 Pikas, Rabbits, and Hares
38 Rabbits and Hares
40 Squirrels
44 Pocket Gophers, Pocket Mice
46 Mountain Beaver, Beavers, Spring Hare, Scaly-tailed Squirrels
48 New World Rats and Mice
50 Hamsters, Mole Rats
52 Crested Rat, Spiny Dormice, and relatives
54 Voles and Lemmings
56 Gerbils
58 Climbing Mice, Pouched Rats, Old World Rats and Mice
60 Old World Rats and Mice
62 Dormice, Jumping Mice, Jerboas, Gundis
64 Porcupines
66 Cavies, Capybara, Agoutis, and Pacas
68 Chinchillas, Hutias, Coypu, Octodonts, Tuco-tucos, and Chinchilla-rats
70 Spiny Rats, Cane Rats, Dassie Rat, and Mole-rats
72 Elephant Shrews, Tenrecs
74 Golden Moles, Hedgehogs
76 Shrews
78 Solenodons, Moles, Flying Lemurs
80 Tree Shrews
82 Mouse-lemurs, Lemurs, Aye-aye
84 Lorises, Tarsiers
86 Marmosets, Tamarins
88 New World Monkeys
92 Old World Monkeys
100 Gibbons
102 Apes
104 Fruit Bats

106 Mouse-tailed Bats, Sheath-tailed Bats
108 Hog-nosed Bat, Slit-faced Bats, False Vampire Bats
110 Horseshoe Bats
112 Fisherman Bats, Mustached Bats, Free-tailed Bats, New World Leaf-nosed Bats
114 New World Leaf-nosed Bats
116 Evening Bats
118 Funnel-eared Bats, Smoky Bats, Disc-winged Bats, Sucker-footed Bat, Short-tailed Bats
120 Dogs
124 Bears
126 Pandas, Raccoons
128 Mustelids
134 Civets
136 Civets, Mongooses
138 Mongooses
140 Hyenas
142 Cats
148 Sea Lions, Fur Seals, Walrus
150 Seals
154 Aardvark, Pigs
156 Peccaries, Hippopotamuses
158 Camels
160 Mouse Deer, Musk Deer, Deer
162 Deer
164 Deer, Giraffes, Pronghorn
166 Bovids
184 River Dolphins, Dolphins
186 Dolphins
188 Sperm Whales, White Whales
190 Beaked Whales
192 Gray Whale, Rorquals, Right Whales
194 Horses, Tapirs
196 Rhinoceroses, Hyraxes
198 Elephants, Dugong, Manatees

200 **Volume Two: Birds**
204 Ratites
206 Tinamous, Megapodes, Curassows
208 Pheasants
212 Grouse, Turkeys, Guineafowl, New World Quails
214 Screamers, Magpie Goose, Whistling Ducks, Ducks
216 Ducks

218 Buttonquail, Honeyguides, Woodpeckers
220 Woodpeckers
222 Woodpeckers, Asian Barbets, African Barbets
224 Toucans
226 Jacamars, Puffbirds, Hornbills
228 Ground-hornbills, Hoopoes, Wood-hoopoes, Trogons
230 Rollers, Ground-rollers, Cuckoo-rollers, Motmots, Bee-eaters
232 Kingfishers
234 Mousebirds, Cuckoos
236 Cuckoos
238 Parrots
244 Swifts, Crested Swifts
246 Hummingbirds
248 Turacos, Barn Owls, Typical Owls
250 Typical Owls
252 Owlet-nightjars, Frogmouths, Oilbirds, Potoos
254 Nightjars
256 Pigeons
258 Sunbittern, Bustards, Cranes, Trumpeters
260 Limpkin, Finfoot, Sungrebe, Seriemas, Kagu, Mesites
262 Rails
264 Sandgrouse, Seedsnipes, Plainswanderer, Painted Snipe, Jacanas
266 Sandpipers, Woodcock, Snipe
268 Sheathbills, Thick-knees, Pratincoles
270 Oystercatchers, Avocets, Plovers
272 Skuas, Skimmers, Gulls
274 Auks
278 Hawks
280 Hawks, Secretarybird
282 Falcons
284 Grebes, Tropicbirds, Gannets
286 Anhingas, Cormorants
288 Herons
290 Hammerkop, Flamingos, Ibises, Pelicans
292 New World Vultures, Storks
294 Frigatebirds, Penguins, Divers
296 Petrels
298 Albatrosses, Storm Petrels
300 New Zealand Wrens, Pittas, Broadbills, Asities

302 Tyrant Flycatchers
306 Tyrant Flycatchers, Sharpbill, Plantcutters
308 Cotingas, Manakins
310 Typical Antbirds, Ground Antbirds
312 Ovenbirds
314 Woodcreepers, Gnateaters, Tapaculos, Australian Treecreepers
316 Lyrebirds, Bowerbirds, Fairy Wrens, Grass Wrens
318 Scrub Birds, Honeyeaters
320 Pardalotes, Australasian Robins, Leafbirds
322 Shrikes, Vireos
324 Whipbirds, Quail Thrush, Apostlebird, Sitellas, Shrike Tits, Whistlers
326 Crows
328 Birds of Paradise, Butcherbirds, Australian Magpie, Currawongs
330 Cuckoo Shrikes and Minivets
332 Wood Swallows, Orioles, Fantails
334 Monarchs, Magpie Lark, Silktail
336 Drongos, Iora, Bush-shrikes
338 Helmet Shrikes, Vangas, New Zealand Wattlebirds
340 Rockfowl, Waxwings, Silky Flycatchers, Dippers
342 Thrushes
344 Thrushes, Old World Flycatchers
346 Old World Flycatchers, Chats
348 Starlings
350 Mockingbirds, Nuthatches, Wallcreepers
352 Wrens, Treecreepers
354 Gnatcatchers, Penduline Tits, Titmice, Long-tailed Tits
356 Swallows
358 Bulbuls
360 Bulbuls, Kinglets, Hypocolius, African Warblers
362 White-eyes, Leaf Warblers
364 Leaf Warblers, Grass Warblers, Laughingthrushes
366 Babblers
368 Babblers, Wrentit, Typical Warblers
370 Larks
372 Sunbirds
374 Flowerpeckers, Sugarbirds, Berrypeckers, Dunnocks
376 Pipits, Wagtails
378 Sparrows, Weavers
380 Grass Finches, Parasitic Whydahs
382 Finches, Buntings, Tanagers

396 **Volume Three: Reptiles, Amphibians, and Fish**
400 Emydid Turtles
402 Land Tortoises
404 Softshell Turtles, River Turtles, Mud Turtles
406 Leatherback, Marine Turtles
408 Snapping Turtles, Greaved Turtles, Matamatas
410 Tuataras, Iguanas
412 Iguanas
414 Agamid Lizards
416 Chameleons
418 Geckos
420 Geckos, Scaly-foot Lizards
422 Burrowing Lizards, Teiid Lizards
424 Lacertid Lizards, Night Lizards
426 Skinks
430 Girdled and Plated Lizards
432 Crocodile Lizards, Alligator and Legless Lizards
434 Monitors, Gila Monster
436 Amphisbaenians
438 Thread Snakes, Blind Snakes, Pipe Snakes, Shieldtail Snakes, Sunbeam Snakes
440 Pythons and Boas, Wart Snakes
442 Burrowing Asps, Colubrid Snakes
444 Colubrid Snakes
448 Cobras and Sea Snakes
450 Vipers
452 Pit Vipers
454 Crocodiles, Alligators and Caimans, Gavial
456 **Amphibians**
460 Tailed Frogs, New Zealand Frogs, Discoglossid Frogs, Pipid Frogs
462 Mexican Burrowing Toad, Parsley Frog, Spadefoot Toads, Glass Frogs, Ghost Frogs
464 Bufonid Toads, Gold Frog
466 Treefrogs, Mouth-brooding Frog
468 Leptodactylid Frogs, Myobatrachid Frogs, Sooglossid Frogs, Poison Dart Frogs, Reed Frogs
470 Narrow-mouthed Frogs, True Frogs
472 True Frogs, Rhacophorid Treefrogs
474 Sirens, Congo Eels, Olms, Mudpuppies
476 Lungless Salamanders
478 Mole Salamanders, Dicamptodontid Salamanders
480 Newts, Salamanders
482 Caecilians

484 **Fishes**
488 Hagfish, Lampreys, Sharks
490 Sharks
494 Skates, Rays and Chimaeras
496 Bichirs, Sturgeons, Gars, Bowfin
498 Osteoglossiform Fishes, Elopiform Fishes, Bonefish and Spiny Eels
500 Eels, Snipe-eels and Gulper Eels
502 Herrings
504 Gonorynchiform Fishes, Cypriniform Fishes
506 Cypriniform Fishes
512 Siluriform Fishes
518 Gymnotiform Fishes, Pikes, Osmeriform Fishes, Salmon
520 Salmon, Stomiiform Fishes
522 Aulopiform Fishes, Lanternfishes, Trout-perches
524 Ophidiiform Fishes, Codfishes
526 Codfishes
528 Toadfishes, Angler Fishes
530 Beloniform Fishes
532 Cyprinodontiform Fishes
534 Cyprinodontiform Fishes, Atheriniform Fishes
536 Lampridiform Fishes, Whalefishes, Beryciform Fishes
538 Beryciform Fishes, Zeiform Fishes
540 Gasterosteiform Fishes
542 Swamp Eels, Flying Gurnards, Scorpaeniform Fishes
544 Scorpaeniform Fishes
546 Perchlike Fishes
570 Perchlike Fishes, Flatfishes
572 Flatfishes
576 Tetraodontiform Fishes
580 Coelacanth, Lungfishes

FOREWORD

The value of a natural history such as this, so concise and beautifully illustrated, can hardly be overestimated, both as a reference work for identification and as a teaching tool. I sometimes think that we in the West are somewhat complacent about magnificent books like this – we tend to take them for granted. We should not. When I was in Madagascar, probably one of the most interesting areas, biologically speaking, in the world, I was horrified to find that the only means of identification of some of their unique fauna available to the ordinary Malagasy was a series of blurred and not very well-drawn pictures of lemurs on the backs of matchboxes.

It is a sobering thought that within the next 80 to 100 years, many of the fascinating creatures so beautifully described here will vanish unless world governments start thinking in terms of conservation and not desecration. It is the appearance of books like this that, hopefully, will help stem the tide of extermination now sweeping the world.

With its fine illustrations and its careful and unusual layout, this is an excellent encyclopedia. It really is a sort of who's who of the animal world showing who is related to whom. It is so deftly written and arranged that it will be of immense value to both the professional and amateur naturalist, and certainly every school should have a copy.

I am delighted to recommend it to all who have an interest in and who value the fascinating planet we live on.

This foreword was written for the first edition of The Animal Encyclopedia by the late Gerald Durrell, world-famous naturalist and founder of The Jersey Wildlife Preservation Trust.

INTRODUCTION

HUMAN BEINGS ARE VERTEBRATE ANIMALS, AS ARE ALL OUR ESSENTIAL DOMESTICATED CREATURES AND MOST OF THE DOMINANT LARGE ANIMALS IN EVERY EARTHLY ECOSYSTEM. THE FEW SUCCESSFUL, LARGE, INVERTEBRATE ANIMALS THAT DO EXIST, GIANT SQUID FOR EXAMPLE, SERVE TO EMPHASIZE BY THEIR VERY RARITY THE PRE-EMINENT POSITION OF VERTEBRATES. BETWEEN THEM, THE MAMMALS, BIRDS REPTILES, AMPHIBIANS AND FISHES RULE THE SEA AND THE LAND. IN RIVERS, LAKES, SWAMPS AND EVEN IN THE AIR, IT IS VERTEBRATE ANIMALS THAT PROVIDE THE OBVIOUS ANIMAL SEGMENT OF LIVING COMMUNITIES.

One particular feature links creatures as diverse as lampreys, sharks, salmon, frogs, alligators, eagles and chimpanzees and makes them a natural grouping – an organic and interrelated assemblage. All vertebrates have vertebrae, that is, a longitudinal series of skeletal elements along their main nerve tract, the spinal cord. Not all, however, have a back-bone exactly like ours, consisting of distinct, bony blocks, although all the higher, most recently developed types do. These latter animals include the bony fishes, amphibians, reptiles, birds and mammals. The cartilaginous fishes – sharks, rays and skates, for example – have vertebrae, but these consist of cartilage rather than bone; and the even more primitive lampreys have only simple rudiments of vertebral structures, close to the spinal cord.

When compared with invertebrate groups, such as corals, flatworms, worms, mollusks, crustaceans, spiders and insects, there is little doubt that the vertebrate type of body organization provides the potential for the most intricate and sophisticated animals. Animals have been called the most exquisite and complicated machines in the known universe, and, if this is so, the higher vertebrates are the most complex and subtle of these already remarkable entities. In the light of this perspective, zoology, which might sometimes appear to be an esoteric speciality, becomes one of the most demanding and vital disciplines – the attempt to understand these extraordinary machines.

This book sets out to provide a comprehensive catalog of the staggering range of animal types within the vertebrate group.

From the 45,000 or so species of living vertebrates, a selection has had to be made to represent their diversity to best effect. It is clearly impossible to be comprehensive at the species level, so we have looked at a higher level in the classification hierarchy and organized the book at family level, at which it is possible to be comprehensive.

The classification of animals into groups often seems a mystifying or intimidating exercise, as does the scientific naming of animals that goes with it. But both are merely an attempt to organize the creatures into recognizable groups which show their relationships. The Latin- or Greek-based names are enormously useful because of their stability: the scientific name of a creature remains the same all over the world, but it may have dozens of common names. An animal species is a group of animals that can, at least potentially, successfully breed with one another. This is a natural grouping based on the intrinsic attributes and activities of the animals themselves. Each species is given a unique, two-part name in which the second component is specific to that species. The tiger, for example, is called *Panthera tigris*. *Panthera* is its generic name – the genus *Panthera* contains 5 different species of big cat – while *tigris* is its specific name, which refers only to the tiger. The generic and specific names are always printed in italic.

The species names are only the first two rungs of a taxonomical ladder of hierarchy. Many more rungs are required in order to encompass the patterns of similarity which exist. In ascending order, the most commonly used levels are species, genus, family, order, class and phylum; ultimately all animals are grouped together in the Kingdom (classification began in pre-republican days) Animalia.

To return to the tiger, this animal and all other cats belong to the cat family, Felidae, and all have certain physical and behavioral characteristics in common. This family is grouped with other families of related animals, such as dogs, viverrids and mustelids, in the Order Carnivora, and this and all other orders of mammals belong to the Class Mammalia. It is at the vital, family level that this book is comprehensive. A résumé of the major characteristics of each family is accompanied by a number of representative examples of the family, so that although each species cannot be shown, a close relative of it will be. Each order is also mentioned. Some of the larger families, such as the Rodent Family Muridae, which includes old world rats and mice, are split up into many subfamilies, since this facilitates the description of the various groups and avoids gross generalization.

Only in the Fish section has this level of comprehensiveness had to be changed. Here, because of the enormous number of families – many of them little known – it has not been possible to deal with fish diversity in terms of a comprehensive analysis of all fish families. Instead, every order of fish is described, and, where relevant, important families are considered separately.

In something so complex as taxonomy, there is bound to be argument, and there are many areas of disagreement in the ordering and grouping of particular species and families; in this book the consultants have followed what they believe to be the best guidelines. Where there is particular controversy over the placing of a particular species, this is mentioned in the text.

The tiger is a species of cat, and everyone knows – or thinks they know – what a tiger looks like. However, species do not consist of identical individuals. Enormous genetic diversity exists within a species, as a cursory examination of our own species, *Homo sapiens*, reveals. In many animal species it is possible to identify groupings, known as subspecies or races. These often represent geographically localized forms of a species that show characteristic differences from one another. This accounts, for example, in the birds for the sometimes quite striking differences in plumage between individuals of the same species. The tiger, too, has half a dozen geographically distinct subspecies, which vary in size and in fur coloration and patterning. Subspecies of a species can still interbreed. All subspecies, however, are human-defined and they are essentially arbitrary, unlike the species themselves, which correspond more or less precisely to actual interbreeding groups of animals.

This book is a catalog and, as with any catalog, part of its organization emphasizes similarities. Similar animals are grouped into their family assemblages and this format enables the shared habits and structures of related animals to be easily grasped. Ultimately though, there is another way of responding to the patterns of animal organization delineated here. Instead of emphasizing the shared characteristics, one can marvel at the almost infinite inventiveness of the life-styles and physical structure of vertebrate animals that is a joy in itself. There is space and opportunity enough in this book to savor the amazing diversity of mammals, birds, reptiles, amphibians and fishes and to find fascination in the contrasts, even between members of the same family.

Philip Whitfield

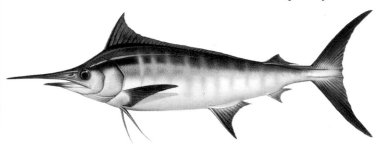

CLASSIFICATION AND EVOLUTION

Classification enables biologists to make sense of the diversity of vertebrate animals and other groups of living organisms. We have already seen how species, such as the tiger, are identified and named and then collected together in progressively larger groups with other species that share similar characteristics. This hierarchy of groupings – or taxa – ranges from the smallest, at species level, through genus, family, order, class and phylum, to the largest taxon at the level of the kingdom. This system has its roots in the work of the Swedish naturalist Carolus Linnaeus (1707–78). When Linnaeus drew up his classification scheme, species were regarded as unchanging. His system was essentially a static one that pigeonholed species and organized them, much as a librarian would place books in a library.

The widespread acceptance of Charles Darwin's theory of evolution in the latter part of the nineteenth century brought a new significance to classification. Evolution means that species change over time, with some species dying out and others appearing. A classification system based on similarities between species may, in addition to providing an organizational framework, also indicate natural patterns within the living world – how species are related through descent from a common ancestor, an ancient extinct organism from which they inherited shared characteristics. Once the theory of evolution was accepted, a dynamic classification system that indicates phylogeny or evolutionary history could be created.

What characteristics do biologists use when classifying animals? Traditionally, taxonomists – the biologists who specialize in classification – have used information based on anatomy, physiology and embryology. More recently, taxonomists have been able to use biochemical data including the similarities of genetic material. This includes using analysis of genetic material – DNA and RNA – and of proteins as a means to determine the relatedness of species: the more similar the structure of these chemicals, the more closely related the species. However, certain pitfalls are placed in the taxonomist's way. For example, common characteristics shared by different species may not indicate a relation but instead be caused by convergent evolution. This is the evolution of similar characteristics in unrelated organisms that have independently evolved the same adaptations to similar ways of life. An extreme example of this is the "fishlike" body shape shared by both sharks and whales, two completely unrelated species. Characteristics used in classification should be homologous; that is, have the same evolutionary origin.

The problem for the taxonomist is to determine which characteristics are most important in relatedness. The "weight" that is attached to different characteristics underpins the differences between systems of classification.

There are two major methods of classification, or systematics, in use today. Traditional systematics groups organisms using both ancestral and derived characteristics in order to show their phylogenetic relationships. It produces the traditional classification found in many textbooks. It may include groups called clades that are monophyletic – a group of living things that have a single common ancestor – as well as groups called grades – a group of related species that do not share a single common ancestor. Phylogenetic systematics, or cladistics, is a method used by many modern taxonomists which is thought to be the most natural means of classification. The only groups recognized in cladistics are clades, the members of which share unique derived characteristics. Clades are arranged in a branching diagram, or cladogram, that shows which clades are more closely related than others, thereby indicating their phylogeny. Only clades can be given names. This contrasts with traditional systematics where, for example, groups with different ancestry are "lumped" together in a grade called "reptiles".

While the grouping of vertebrates in the Animal Encyclopedia is based on more traditional systematics in order to make the book easier to use, the sequence of groups within the book reflects the phylogeny of vertebrates indicated by cladistics.

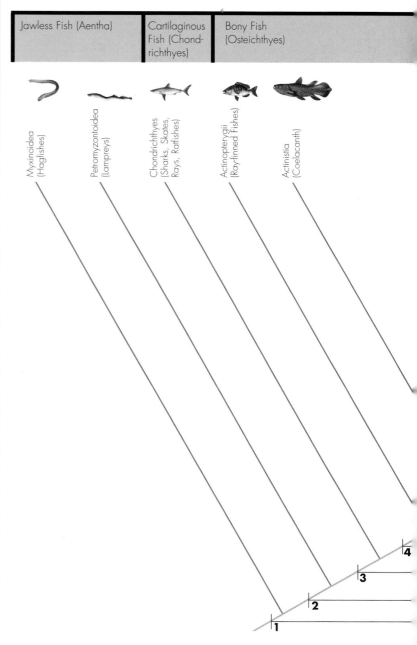

| Jawless Fish (Aentha) | | Cartilaginous Fish (Chond-richthyes) | Bony Fish (Osteichthyes) | |

Cladogram showing possible phylogenetic relationships among living vertebrates. The cladogram shows how the major vertebrate groups are related. All the vertebrates found above a certain branch point on the cladogram are related by shared derived characters. The process of producing a cladogram generates groups within groups, an arrangement known as a nested structure.

On the left of the cladogram is the most inclusive group, while on the right is the least inclusive. For example, the name Tetrapoda includes all vertebrates with four limbs: that is, every group to the right of number 7. By contrast, the name Mammalia, at the right of the diagram, includes only those vertebrates with hair and mammary glands. The numbers below the cladogram identify some of the derived characteristics that distinguish groups. The traditional classification at the top of the cladogram is included by way of comparison.

KEY TO CLADISTICS

1 Distinct head region; brain consisting of three regions
2 Vertebrae
3 Jaws; paired fins
4 Swim bladder or lung derived from gut
5 Fins with supporting skeleton
6 Connection between nasal and oral cavities
7 Paired front and rear limbs
8 Eggs with protective internal membranes
9 Shell encloses body trunk
10 Skull with two openings: one in cheek and one in roof
11 Opening in skull in front of eye
12 Feathers, endothermy (warm-bloodedness)
13 Hair, mammary glands, endothermy (evolved independently from birds)

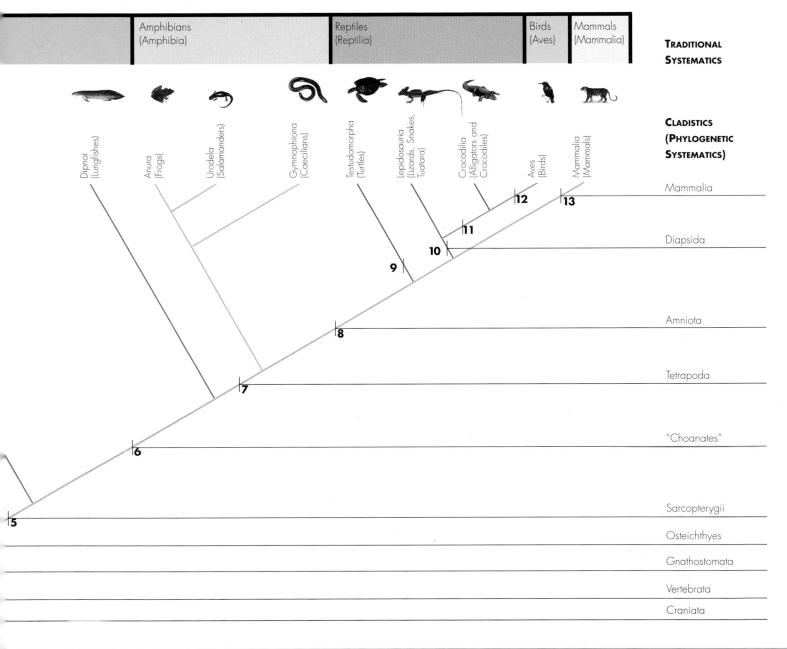

ANIMALS UNDER THREAT

The living world is a dynamic entity. In all habitats, from the Arctic to the Sahara Desert, and from tropical rainforests to coral reefs, there is constant competition for resources both within and between species. The struggle to survive in these competitive conditions favors some individuals more than others. Such selection is the force behind evolution, the gradual change of species over time as they adapt to changing requirements and conditions. The process of evolution has ensured that, as the millennia pass, some species become extinct, while new species emerge.

In recent centuries, however, the rate of extinctions has accelerated far beyond that which should be occurring naturally. Many of the world's animal species are in danger of extinction or are becoming rare. And the number of animals becoming extinct or threatened with extinction is increasing year by year. The World Conservation Union (IUCN) estimates that, as far as vertebrates are concerned, the following are threatened with extinction:
- 25 per cent of mammal species
- 11 per cent of bird species
And of those species that have been evaluated in these groups:
- 20 per cent of reptile species
- 25 per cent of amphibian species
- 34 per cent of fish species (mainly freshwater fish)

More often than not, the main threat to animal species is posed by human pressures. Human population numbers have risen exponentially in recent centuries. Increasing demands for living space, agricultural land, water, and raw materials, have led to extensive habitat loss, including the destruction of vast tracts of forest. Deforestation still continues, most notably in the felling of the tropical rainforests that are the most species-rich of all habitats, and within which species are becoming extinct before they can be identified. The diversity of the unique endemic fauna found on oceanic islands is being depleted by human population pressure and the introduction of alien species such as cats, dogs, and rats. Pollution, road building and urban sprawl are also taking their toll worldwide.

Extinction of a species does not simply mean removing a name from a long list. Life forms are interdependent, and interact with each other in complex ways often too subtle for human comprehension. Any significant decrease in species numbers, or the loss of a species, has a knock-on effect on other species in its ecosystem.

It is important to maintain biodiversity because it underpins the dynamism and success of ecosystems, and ultimately of the entire biosphere.

The work of IUCN and other organizations in listing threatened animals is vital in order to pinpoint the habitats and species most at risk, and to provide the hard information necessary for both governments and non-governmental bodies to devise workable conservation strategies, and to make governments aware of the effects of their policies on the future of the world's biological resources. Conservation strategies have removed some vertebrates that were listed as threatened in the first edition of the Animal Encyclopedia from the at-risk list; unfortunately, this second edition also sees a greater number of other vertebrate species attaining threatened status.

HOW TO USE THIS BOOK

NAMES

Common and scientific names are given for each species. Common names tend to vary greatly, but the most generally accepted version is used. In some instances, where there are two names of equal importance, both are given thus: Common/Brown Noddy.

RANGE AND HABITAT

The normal range of a species is explained as fully as possible, given the limitations of space. The animal's particular habitat helps to clarify its precise occurrence within a large range. In some instances, where a species has been introduced outside its native range by man, accidentally or deliberately, this is added.

SIZE

Sizes are given as approximate total lengths unless otherwise stated; in birds this is the length from bill tip to tail tip; in turtles and tortoises the length of the shell is given. Exceptions are made where individual circumstances demand: for example, where a bird has an exceptionally long tail, this measurement may be given separately. In the Mammals section, two separate measurements are given: head and body length, and tail length. The vast range of sizes of the animals has meant that the drawings cannot be to a single scale.

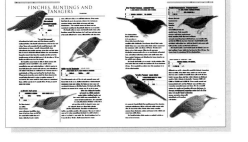

Purple Honeycreeper *Cyanerpes caeruleus*

RANGE Trinidad; N. South America to Bolivia, Paraguay, Brazil

HABITAT Rainforest, forest edge, mangroves, plantations

SIZE 4 in (10 cm)

Groups of purple honeycreepers frequent flowering trees in many different types of wooded areas. Fruit, especially bananas, and insects are important foods, but these birds also perch by flowers and suck nectar from them with their long, curved bills. Male and female differ in plumage; the male is largely bluish-purple and black, with yellow legs, while the female is rich green, with buff and blue patches on the head and breast.

The female builds a cup-shaped nest in the fork of a tree or bush and lays 2 eggs, which she incubates for 12 to 14 days. The young leave the nest about 14 days after hatching.

CONSERVATION STATUS

Many of the world's vertebrate animals are monitored by the World Conservation Union (IUCN) and associated organizations to determine whether individual species are at risk or are becoming rare. Species that are threatened are listed in the Red List of Threatened Animals that is produced by the IUCN.

Whether a species is at risk is determined using quantitative criteria that include its present and projected population size, its distribution, and the viability of its population if small and shrinking. The Red List uses specific categories to describe the degree of threat, and these are the categories used in this book. The meaning of the symbols and the categories of threat are given below.

Threatened Species

Species in these three categories are collectively termed "threatened".

CRITICALLY ENDANGERED (CR)

Species faces an extremely high risk of extinction in the wild.

ENDANGERED (EN)

Species faces a very high risk of extinction in the wild in the near future.

VULNERABLE (VU)

Species faces a high risk of extinction in the wild in the medium-term future.

Lower Risk Species

These are species that are at risk but do not fit into the "threatened" categories. The Lower Risk (LR) category is divided into three subcategories.

LOWER RISK: conservation dependent (LR:cd)

Species which is the focus of a conservation program. If this program stopped, the species would qualify for one of the threatened categories within five years.

LOWER RISK: near threatened (LR:nt)

Species which are not the subject of a conservation program and are close to qualifying for VULNERABLE status.

LOWER RISK: least concerned (LR:lc)

Species which appeared in earlier Red Lists but have been removed.

Extinct or Near-Extinct Species

EXTINCT IN THE WILD (EW)

Species that has been wiped out in its natural habitat.

EXTINCT (EX)

According to available evidence, the last individual of that species has died.

DATA DEFICIENT (DD)

Used when too little is known about an animal to assess its population numbers or conservation status.

MAMMALS

The peak of vertebrate adaptability.

THERE ARE ABOUT 4,000 SPECIES OF MAMMAL, WHICH ARE THE MOST ADAPTABLE AND DIVERSE GROUP OF VERTEBRATES ON OUR PLANET TODAY. WHALES, DOLPHINS AND SEALS ARE IMPORTANT MEMBERS OF THE ANIMAL COMMUNITY IN THE SEAS, WHILE FORMS SUCH AS OTTERS AND BEAVERS ARE SUCCESSFUL IN FRESHWATER HABITATS. ON DRY LAND, A HUGE DIVERSITY OF MAMMAL TYPES PROSPERS UNDERGROUND, ON THE LAND SURFACE AND IN TREES AND OTHER VEGETATION. MAMMALS HAVE EVEN TAKEN TO THE AIR IN THE FORM OF BATS, THE NIGHT-FLYING INSECTIVORES. IN ALL THESE NICHE TYPES, MAMMALS REVEAL A STARTLING VARIABILITY IN FEEDING STRATEGIES: SOME FEED ONLY ON PLANT MATERIAL, OTHERS ON SMALL INVERTEBRATES. MANY KILL AND EAT OTHER VERTEBRATES, INCLUDING MAMMALS, WHILE SOME EAT ALMOST ANYTHING. TO BEGIN TO UNDERSTAND THE REASONS FOR THE ADAPTABILITY AND SUCCESS OF MAMMALIAN LINES OF EVOLUTION, IT IS NECESSARY TO LOOK AT WHAT A MAMMAL IS, HOW IT IS CONSTRUCTED, HOW IT OPERATES PHYSICALLY AND BEHAVIORALLY AND WHAT ITS ANCESTORS WERE LIKE.

Tree Anteater

A mammal is an endothermic (warm-blooded), four-limbed, hairy vertebrate (an animal with a backbone). Male mammals inseminate females internally, using a penis, and females, typically, retain their developing fetuses within the uterus, where the bloodstreams of mother and offspring come close together (but do not fuse) in a placenta. The time spent in the womb by the developing fetus is known as the gestation period and varies from group to group. Some mammals, such as rabbits, rodents and many carnivores, are born naked, blind and helpless; while others, such as cattle and deer, are small, but fully formed and capable, versions of the adult. Mothers produce milk for their young from skin-derived mammary glands.

The vast majority of mammals possess these characteristics, but a few exceptions, real and apparent, must be taken into account. Whales and their relatives and manatees have only forelimbs. There is no doubt, however, from their skeletal structure, that these highly modified aquatic

Indri

animals are derived from four-legged ancestors. However, the monotremes – the platypus and echidnas – are highly uncharacteristic mammals. They have retained the egg-laying habits of their reptilian ancestor and do not form placentas. The pouched mammals, or marsupials, also have a method of reproduction that differs from that of the placenta-forming mammals. Kangaroos, wallabies and their relatives retain a thin shell around the developing young inside the mother's body, but it breaks down before the offspring emerges to crawl into the pouch and attach itself to a milk-delivering nipple. Some species do have a primitive placenta. The marsupial young is born in a far less advanced state than most mammals and finishes its development in the pouch.

Knowledge of the ancestry of mammals is based largely on the study of fossil remains of parts of skeletons. Mammals evolved from reptiles about 220 million years

Golden Lion Tamarind

ago. During the "age of dinosaurs" between 230 and 65 million years ago, mammals remained small and were shrewlike in appearance and lifestyle. When the dinosaurs became extinct 65 million years ago, the mammals adapted to the wide range of habitats and niches vacated by the extinct reptiles. The mammals have continued their explosive expansion into different types of life and environment to become the dominant group of land-dwelling vertebrates and an important part of aquatic life.

Apart from reproductive sophistication, mammals are remarkable in a number of ways. They have large, complex brains, and acute and well-integrated sensory systems. They employ a range of vocal, visual and olfactory means of communication with other species and with members of their own species – communication with the latter is important in the organization of family and social groupings. The keratinous hairs that grow out of mammalian skin insulate the body and are part of a complex of temperature-regulation mechanisms with which mammals maintain a constant, high body temperature, irrespective of external climatic conditions. Metabolic heat, especially that produced by brown fat in the body, can be used to offset heat losses and can be transferred around the body via the circulatory system, which is powered by the four-chambered heart. The body can be cooled by the evaporation of sweat secretions at the body surface. All this temperature-control "machinery" is under the control of the hypothalamus in the brain. When temperature control becomes energetically impossible, for example in low temperatures, some mammals are able to hibernate.

During the hibernatory sleep, the animal's body temperature drops to close to that of the surroundings, and its heart and respiration slow dramatically so that it uses the minimum of energy. Thus it is able to survive for as long as several months on stored fat.

The astonishing diversity of present day mammals is illustrated in the following pages, which review each living family and describe representative examples. Briefly, the range of types is as follows. The primitive monotremes and the marsupials – the majority of which are found in Australia – have already been mentioned. Australia separated from the southern continents before it could receive any eutherian mammals. Thus the marsupial mammal fauna was able to radiate into a diverse range of forms which mirrors the types of placental mammals found in the rest of the world. There are burrowing, tree-dwelling, ant-eating, herbivorous and predatory marsupials, and marsupial analogues exist or have existed for almost all placental mammals except bats, whales and seals.

The placental mammals form a diverse and successful group that includes the insectivores such as shrews, hedgehogs and moles, bats, sloths, anteaters,

Gorilla

armadillos, pangolins, primates (to which humans belong), rodents, rabbits, whales, dolphins and porpoises, carnivores (cats, dogs, mustelids and bears), seals, aardvark, elephants, hyraxes, manatees and the dugong, uneven-toed hoofed mammals such as tapirs, horses and rhinoceroses, and the even-toed (cloven-hoofed) hoofed mammals such as pigs, peccaries, camels, deer, cattle, sheep and goats.

The evolutionary success of the mammals is hard to

Lion

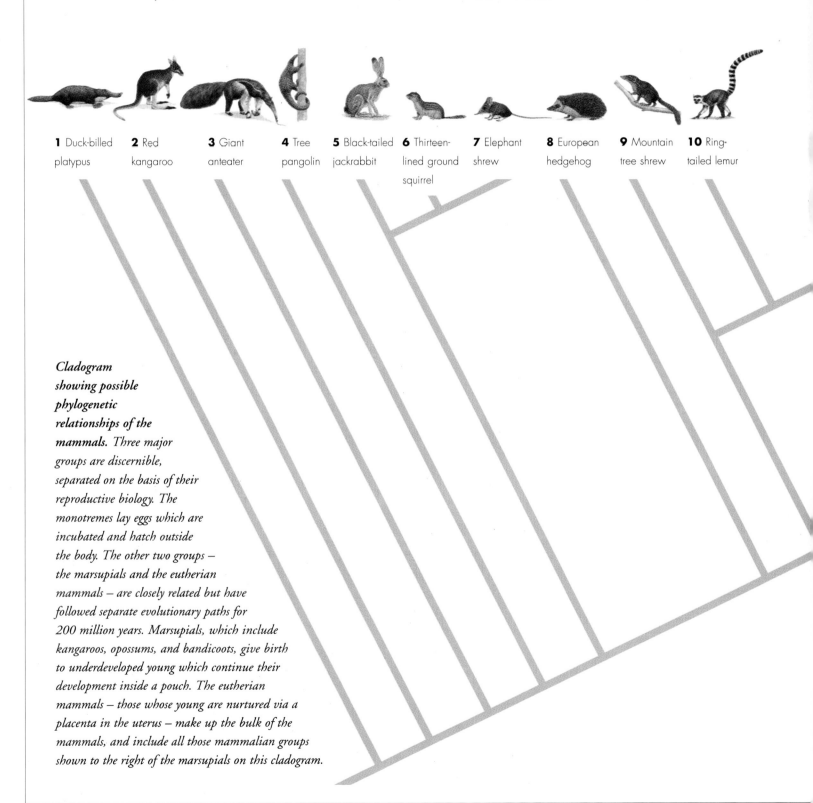

1 Duck-billed platypus   **2** Red kangaroo   **3** Giant anteater   **4** Tree pangolin   **5** Black-tailed jackrabbit   **6** Thirteen-lined ground squirrel   **7** Elephant shrew   **8** European hedgehog   **9** Mountain tree shrew   **10** Ring-tailed lemur

Cladogram showing possible phylogenetic relationships of the mammals. Three major groups are discernible, separated on the basis of their reproductive biology. The monotremes lay eggs which are incubated and hatch outside the body. The other two groups — the marsupials and the eutherian mammals — are closely related but have followed separate evolutionary paths for 200 million years. Marsupials, which include kangaroos, opossums, and bandicoots, give birth to underdeveloped young which continue their development inside a pouch. The eutherian mammals — those whose young are nurtured via a placenta in the uterus — make up the bulk of the mammals, and include all those mammalian groups shown to the right of the marsupials on this cladogram.

evaluate. As measured by the dominance of a particular group or its species diversity, success must be the result of an amalgam of intrinsic biological merit and chance. But no other major class of vertebrates has ever conquered such a variety of habitats so completely. The advent of modern humans has probably increased the rate of mammalian

Capybara

extinctions in some groups, but others, such as the rodents, are evolving into new ecological niches created by man's activities. At the present time, the mammals are an overwhelmingly successful group, and it may be true that its most dominant species – man – holds the future of the planet in his hands.

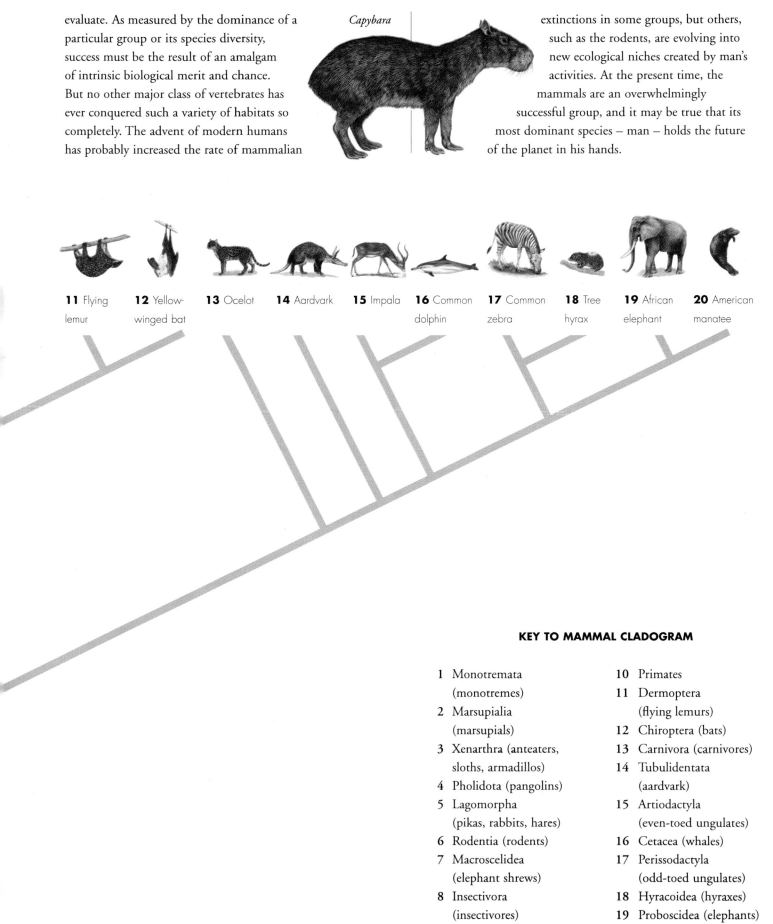

11 Flying lemur

12 Yellow-winged bat

13 Ocelot

14 Aardvark

15 Impala

16 Common dolphin

17 Common zebra

18 Tree hyrax

19 African elephant

20 American manatee

KEY TO MAMMAL CLADOGRAM

1 Monotremata (monotremes)
2 Marsupialia (marsupials)
3 Xenarthra (anteaters, sloths, armadillos)
4 Pholidota (pangolins)
5 Lagomorpha (pikas, rabbits, hares)
6 Rodentia (rodents)
7 Macroscelidea (elephant shrews)
8 Insectivora (insectivores)
9 Scandentia (tree shrews)

10 Primates
11 Dermoptera (flying lemurs)
12 Chiroptera (bats)
13 Carnivora (carnivores)
14 Tubulidentata (aardvark)
15 Artiodactyla (even-toed ungulates)
16 Cetacea (whales)
17 Perissodactyla (odd-toed ungulates)
18 Hyracoidea (hyraxes)
19 Proboscidea (elephants)
20 Sirenia (sea cows)

ECHIDNAS AND PLATYPUS

ORDER MONOTREMATA

Two families with a combined total of only 3 living species make up this order. Although well-adapted for their environments, monotremes are considered primitive mammals in that they retain some reptilian characteristics of body structure and they lay eggs. However, they also possess the essential mammalian characteristics of body hair and mammary glands. Monotremes are probably a parallel development, rather than a stage in the evolution of mammals. A problem in understanding the origins of this order is that no fossil monotremes have been found.

TACHYGLOSSIDAE: ECHIDNA FAMILY

There are 2 species of echidna, previously known as spiny anteater. Both are covered with coarse hairs, and their backs are set with spines. They have elongated, slender snouts and strong limbs and are powerful diggers. Echidnas, like other anteating species have no teeth and very weak jaws. Termites, ants and other small arthropods are swept into the mouth by a long, sticky tongue, which can reach well beyond the tip of the snout. The insects are then crushed between the tongue and the roof of the mouth.

Long-beaked Echidna *Zaglossus bruijni*

RANGE New Guinea

HABITAT Forest

SIZE Body: 17–30 in (45–77 cm) Tail: vestigial

The long-beaked echidna is larger than the short-beaked and has fewer, shorter spines scattered among its coarse hairs. The snout is two-thirds of the head length and curves slightly downward. There are five digits on both hind and forefeet, but on the former, only the three middle toes are equipped with claws. Males have a spur on each of the hind legs. This echidna is primarily a nocturnal animal that forages for its insect food on the forest floor.

The breeding female has a temporary abdominal brood patch, in which her egg is incubated and in which the new born young remains in safety, feeding and developing. Little is known

about the life of this rarely seen animal, but it is believed to have similar habits to those of the short-beaked echidna.

There were once thought to be 3 species in this genus, but now all are believed to be races of this one species. The population of echidnas in New Guinea is declining because of forest clearance and overhunting, and the animal is much in need of protection.

Short-beaked Echidna *Tachyglossus aculeatus*

RANGE Australia, Tasmania, S.E. New Guinea

HABITAT Grassland, forest

SIZE Body: 13¾–19¾ in (35–50 cm) Tail: 3½ in (9 cm)

The short-beaked echidna has a compact, round body, closely set with spines. At the end of its naked snout is a small, slitlike mouth, through which its long tongue is extended 6 to 7 in (15 to 18 cm) beyond the snout. The tongue is coated with sticky saliva, so that any insect it touches is trapped. Echidnas have no teeth but break up their food between horny ridges in the mouth. Termites, ants and other small invertebrates form their main diet.

Echidnas have five digits, all equipped with strong claws, on both hind and forefeet. Males also have spurs on each hind leg which may be used in defense. They are excellent diggers and, if in danger, they will rapidly dig themselves into the ground. However, they do not live in burrows, but in hollow logs or among roots and rocks. The echidnas' capacity for temperature regulation is poor, and in cool weather they hibernate.

On her abdomen, the breeding female has a temporary patch, or groove, which develops at the start of the breeding season. When she has laid her leathery-shelled egg, she transfers it to the patch, where it incubates for between 7 and 10 days. The egg is coated with sticky mucus which helps it to stay in the groove. When the young echidna hatches, it is only ½ in (1.25 cm) long and helpless, so it must remain on the mother's abdomen while it develops.

The female produces plenty of milk from mammary glands but she has no nipples, so the baby feeds by sucking on specially adapted areas of abdominal skin through which the milk flows. Once the spines develop, at about 3 weeks, the young is no longer carried by its mother.

ORNITHORHYNCIDAE: PLATYPUS FAMILY

The single species of this family is an extraordinary animal in appearance, due to the strange combination of a beak, fur and webbed feet, but it is perfectly adapted for its way of life.

The platypus was discovered 200 years ago, and when the first specimen arrived at London's Natural History Museum, scientists were so puzzled by it that they believed the specimen to be a fake.

Platypuses are now protected by law and are quite common in some areas.

Platypus *Ornithorhynchus anatinus*

RANGE Australia, Tasmania

HABITAT Lakes, rivers

SIZE Body: 18 in (46 cm)
Tail: 7 in (18 cm)

The platypus is a semi-aquatic animal, and many of its physical characteristics are adaptations for its life as a freshwater predator.

Its legs are short but powerful, and the feet are webbed, though the digits retain large claws, which are useful for burrowing. On the forefeet the webs extend beyond the claws and make efficient paddles. On land, however, the webbing can be folded back in order to free the claws for digging.

On each ankle the male platypus has a spur which is connected to poison glands in the thighs. These spurs are used against an attacker or against a competing platypus, but they are never used against prey. The poison is not fatal to man, but does cause intense pain.

The platypus's eye and ear openings lie in furrows, which are closed off by folds of skin when the animal is submerged. Thus, when hunting under water, the platypus relies on the sensitivity of its leathery bill – which is sensitive to both touch and electric currents produced by prey – to find its prey. The nostrils are toward the end of the upper bill but can only function when the platypus's head is in air. Young platypuses have teeth, but adults have horny, ridged plates on both sides of the jaws which are used for crushing prey.

The platypus feeds mainly at the bottom of the water, making dives lasting for a minute or more in order to probe the mud with its bill for crustaceans, aquatic insects and larvae. It also feeds on frogs and other small animals and on some plants. Platypuses have huge appetites, consuming up to 2¼ lb (1 kg) of food each night.

Short burrows, dug in the river bank above the water level, are used by the platypus for refuge or during periods of cool weather. In the breeding season, however, the female digs a burrow 40 ft (12 m) or more in length, at the end of which she lays her clutch of 2 or 3 eggs on a nest of dry grass and leaves; the rubbery eggs are cemented together in a raft. She plugs the entrance to the burrow with moist plant matter, and this prevents the eggs from drying out during the 7- to 14-day incubation period.

When the young hatch, they are only about 1 in (2.5 cm) long and helpless. Until they are about 5 months old, they feed on milk, which issues from slits in the mother's abdominal wall. Unlike echidnas, they do not draw up tucks of skin into pseudonipples, but simply lap and suck the milk off their mother's abdominal fur.

OPOSSUMS AND COLOCOLO

INFRACLASS METATHERIA

MARSUPIAL MAMMALS

There are 260 species of marsupial mammals in North and South America and in Australasia east of Wallace's line (an imaginary line drawn between Borneo and Sulawesi, and Bali and Lombok). Marsupials evolved at about the same time as the true (placental) mammals, but were replaced by them over much of their range. Australia has only marsupial mammals because it separated from the ancient southern continents of Gondwanaland after it had been populated by early marsupials, but before placental mammals arrived. In Australia marsupials have realized their true potential and have adapted to a variety of ecological niches and have exploited all available habitats.

The principal characteristic of marsupial mammals is their reproduction. Instead of retaining young inside the uterus until they are well developed, as in placental mammals, the gestation period is extremely short – as brief as 11 days – and the young finish their development inside a pouch on the mother's belly.

ORDER DIDELPHIMORPHA

DIDELIPHIDAE: OPOSSUM FAMILY

This order contains the opossum family only. There are more than 70 species of opossum and they are found from the southern tip of South America northward to southeast Canada. Opossums are all basically rat-shaped animals, with scaly almost hairless tails and rather unkempt fur. Some species possess a proper pouch, while others carry their young between two flaps of skin on the belly.

Most opossums are forest dwellers, although one exceptional species has taken to an aquatic way of life. They feed on leaves, shoots, buds and seeds, and insects may also be eaten.

Pale-Bellied Mouse Opossum   *Marmosa robinsoni*

RANGE Belize to N.W. South America; Trinidad, Tobago, Grenada

HABITAT Forest, dense scrubland

SIZE Body: 6½–7¼ in (16.5–18.5 cm) Tail: 10¼–11 in (26–28 cm)

The mouse opossum has a long, pointed nose and huge eyes, which indicate its nocturnal way of life. This opossum is more shrewlike than mouselike in appearance. It makes no permanent home, but constructs temporary daytime nests in tree holes or old birds' nests.

An agile climber, the mouse opossum uses its long, prehensile tail as a fifth limb.

Mouse opossums breed two or three times a year, and litters of up to 10 young are born after a gestation period of 17 days. The young must cling to the mother's fur as she moves around, since mouse opossums do not have proper pouches.

Virginia Opossum   *Didelphis virginiana*

RANGE S.E. Canada through USA to Central America: Nicaragua

HABITAT Forest, scrubland

SIZE Body: 12¾–19¾ in (32.5–50 cm)
Tail: 10–21 in (25.5–53.5 cm)

The only marsupial found north of Mexico and the largest of the opossum family, the Virginia opossum may weigh up to 12 lb (5.5 kg). It is a successful creature, which has adapted to modern life, scavenging in refuse tips and bins. Should this creature be threatened, by a dog, bobcat, eagle or mink for example, it may react by feigning death. This habit of "playing possum" may result in the predator losing interest or give the opossum vital seconds to make its escape.

In Canada, opossums breed once a year, in spring, but in the south of the range, two or even three litters of 8 to 18 young may be produced in a year. Usually only about 7 of a litter survive pouch life. In the southern USA, opossums are trapped by man for their fur and flesh.

Water Opossum/Yapok   *Chironectes minimus* **LR:nt**

RANGE Mexico, south through Central and South America to Argentina

HABITAT Freshwater lakes and streams

SIZE Body: 10½–12¾ in (27–32.5 cm) Tail: 14¼–15¾ in (36–40 cm)

The water opossum, or yapok, is the only marsupial to have adapted to aquatic life. It lives in bankside burrows, emerging after dusk to swim and search for fish, crustaceans and other invertebrates, which it carries to the riverbank to eat. The opossum's long tail helps to control its movement through water.

It uses its broadly webbed hind feet to propel itself through the water. Its fur is oily and water repellant.

In December, water opossums mate, and produce a litter of about 5 young, born some 2 weeks later. The fur-lined pouch is closed by a strong ring of muscle and fatty secretions create a water-tight seal so that the young inside remain quite dry, even when the mother is totally immersed in water. It is not known how the young obtain sufficient oxygen in their hermetically sealed environment.

Short-tailed Opossum *Monodelphis brevicaudata*

RANGE Venezuela and The Guianas to N. Argentina

HABITAT Forest

SIZE Body: 4–5 in (11–14 cm) Tail: 1¼–2½ in (4.5–6.5 cm)

Although the short-tailed opossum lives in forested country, it is a poor climber and tends to stay on the forest floor. During the day it shelters in a leafy nest, which it builds in a hollow log or tree trunk. It emerges at night to feed on seeds, shoots and fruit, as well as on insects, carrion and some small rodents, which it kills with a powerful bite to the back of the head.

Litters of up to 14 young are born at any time of year and cling to their mother's nipples and the surrounding fur, since she has no pouch. When they are older, they ride on her back.

ORDER PAUCITUBERCULATA

CAENOLESTIDAE: SHREW OPOSSUM FAMILY

There are only 7 known species of shrew opossum, which belong to the only family in this order. All live in inaccessible forest and grassland regions of the High Andes. None is common, and the family is poorly known. Shrew opossums are small, shrewlike animals, with thin limbs, a long, pointed snout and slender, hairy tail. Their eyes are small, and they seem to spend much of their lives in underground burrows and on surface runways. It is likely that there are more species yet to be discovered.

Shrew Opossum *Caenolestes obscurus*

RANGE Colombia, Venezuela

HABITAT Montane forest

SIZE Body: 3½–5in (9–13 cm)

Tail: 3½–4¾ in (9–12 cm)

The shrew opossum lives on the forest floor and shelters in hollow logs or underground chambers during the day. At dusk, it emerges to forage around in the surface litter for small invertebrate animals and fruit.

Shrew opossums may be far more common than is generally thought, but their inhospitable habitat makes studying them difficult. Nothing is known of their reproductive habits.

ORDER MICROBIOTHERA

MICROBIOTHERIIDAE: COLOCOLO FAMILY

There is a single family in this order, and a single species in this family, which appears to be closely related to the opossums.

Colocolo *Dromiciops gliroides* **VU**

RANGE Chile, W. Argentina

HABITAT Forest

SIZE Body: 4¼–5 in (11–12.5 cm)

Tail: 3½–4 in (9–10 cm)

The colocolo occurs in high-altitude and lowland forest, especially in areas where Chilean Bamboo grows. It feeds mainly on insects and other invertebrates, but may also eat vegetation. It makes nests using bamboo leaves. In the colder parts of the range, colocolos hibernate in winter, but in more temperate regions, they remain active all year round.

Colocolos breed in spring. Litters contain up to 5 young which cling to the mother's fur, because there is no true pouch.

DASYURID MARSUPIALS

ORDER DASYUROMORPHA

This order includes two families of carnivorous and insectivorous marsupials that are found in Australia, Tasmania, and New Guinea.

DASYURIDAE: DASYURID MARSUPIAL FAMILY

This family of approximately 58 species contains a wide variety of marsupials, from tiny mouse-sized creatures, which live on the forest floor, to large, aggressive predators. Many zoologists regard it as the least advanced family of Australian marsupials because all members have fully separated digits – fused digits are a characteristic of advanced families of marsupials. Yet its success is undoubted, for representatives are found in all habitats, from desert to tropical rain forest.

Most of the dasyurids have poorly developed pouches and resort to carrying their small, underdeveloped young about underneath them, either clinging to the mother's fur or dangling from her teats like bunches of grapes. Unlike the American opossums, which carry older young on their backs, the dasyurids deposit their offspring in nests when they become too large to carry around with them.

Brown Antechinus *Antechinus stuartii*

RANGE E. seaboard of Australia

HABITAT Forest

SIZE Body: 3¾–4¼ in (10–12 cm) Tail: 4–4¾ in (10–12 cm)

The brown antechinus is a secretive, nocturnal animal, that is common in the forests surrounding Australia's major cities. It climbs well and probably searches for insect food in Eucalyptus and Acacia trees.

Mating, which is a violent procedure in this species that can last about 5 hours, occurs in August. A litter of 6 or 7 young is born after a gestation period of 30 to 33 days. The babies cling to the nipples on the mother's belly until they become so large that they impede her movements. They are then left in an underground nest while the mother hunts for food. The offspring reach sexual maturity and breed almost a year after birth. As a result of a hormone imbalance, the males of the species can mate only once before they die.

Pygmy Planigale *Planigale maculata*

RANGE N. and E. Australia

HABITAT Arid bush and scrub

SIZE Body: 2–2½ in (5–5.5 cm) Tail: 2¼ in (5.5 cm)

The pygmy planigale shelters in a burrow during the day and emerges at night to search for food. Although it is smaller than a white mouse, it feeds on large insects, such as grasshoppers (which it kills by biting off the head) and small birds. In one night, a pygmy planigale may eat its own weight in food.

Little is known of the reproduction and social organization of these animals. They appear to be solitary and to give birth to up to 12 young between December and March.

Mulgara *Dasycercus cristicauda* **Vu**

RANGE C. Australia

HABITAT Desert, spinifex bush

SIZE Body: 5–8½ in (12.5–22 cm) Tail: 2¼–5 in (7–13 cm)

The mulgara is perfectly adapted for life in one of the world's most inhospitable, hot, dry environments. It protects itself from the extreme heat of the desert by remaining in its burrow until the heat of the day has passed. Even when it leaves its underground home it tends to stay in places that have been in shadow.

The staple diet of the mulgara consists mainly of insects, but lizards, newborn snakes and mice are also eaten. This creature never drinks. It derives all of its liquid requirements from its prey and in order to preserve water its kidneys are highly developed to excrete extremely concentrated urine.

Mulgaras breed from June to September and the usual litter contains 6 or 7 young. The pouch is little more than two lateral folds of skin.

Kowari *Dasyuroides byrnei*

RANGE C. Australia

HABITAT Desert, grassland

SIZE Body: 6½–7 in (16.5–18 cm)
Tail: 5–5½ in (13–14 cm)

The kowari lives, either singly
or in small groups, in underground burrows. At night, it
emerges to search among the grass tussocks for insects, lizards
and various small birds.

Kowaris breed in winter, from May to October, and produce
litters of 5 or 6 young after a gestation period of 32 days.

Fat-tailed Dunnart *Sminthopsis crassicaudata*

RANGE W. Australia, E. to W. Queensland, W. New South Wales and
W. Victoria

HABITAT Woodland, heath, grassland

SIZE Body: 3–3½ in (8–9 cm) Tail: 2¼–3½ in (5.5–8.5 cm)

The fat-tailed dunnart stores fat in special cells at the base of its
tail. In the wet season, when the food supply of insects and spiders
is abundant, the dunnart builds up its fat reserves. During the dry
season it lives off these reserves and its tail gradually slims. If the
drought persists longer than usual, the dunnart's body temperature
falls and it enters a state of torpor so that its fat reserve lasts longer.

Dunnarts start to breed when they are about 4 months old
and produce litters about every 12 weeks. Courtship is aggressive
and males indulge in vicious fights for females on heat.

Quoll *Dasyurus viverrinus* **LR:nt**

RANGE S.E. Australia and Tasmania

HABITAT Forest

SIZE Body: 13¾–17¾ in
(35–45 cm) Tail: 8¼–11¾ in
(21–30 cm)

The quoll is one of 6 species of
cat-sized predatory dasyurid,
specialized for life as carnivores. At
one time quolls were ruthlessly destroyed
by poultry keepers, but they are now known to do as

much good as harm, by killing rodents, rabbits and invertebrate
pests and helping to maintain the ecological balance. Quolls make
their homes in rock piles or in hollow logs and emerge only at
night in order to search for food.

The breeding season lasts from May to August. The
quoll is one of the few marsupials known in which
the litter size at birth is far higher than the
number that can be supported by the mother – a
phenomenon known as superfetation. Up to
18 young are born after a gestation period of about
20 days, but within 48 hours of birth 10 or more of the babies
will die. The young quolls spend the early weeks of their lives in
the mother's well-developed pouch and later emerge to clamber
all over her, clinging to her fur as she feeds. They are weaned at
4½ months.

Tasmanian Devil *Sarcophilus harrisii*

RANGE Tasmania

HABITAT Dry forest

SIZE Body: 20½–31½ in (52.5–80 cm) Tail: 9–11¾ in (23–30 cm)

This powerfully built marsupial has the reputation of being a
vicious killer of sheep and as a result great numbers were once
hunted by farmers. Numbers have now recovered. In fact, the
Tasmanian devil is more of a scavenger of dead sheep than a
killer of live ones. Its massive head and enormous jaws,
resembling those of the hyena, allow it to smash through bones.
Before the Tasmanian wolf became extinct, Tasmanian devils
lived almost exclusively on the carcasses discarded by the wolf.

Tasmanian devils live in dens in rock piles and under tree
stumps and are normally nocturnal. Sometimes, however, they
emerge during the day to bask in the sun. Tasmanian devils
can live for up to 8 years. They breed in the second
year, producing a litter of about 4 young in early
winter (May or June). The babies remain
inside the mother's well-developed
pouch for 15 weeks. They
are weaned at about
20 weeks old.

NUMBAT, MARSUPIAL MOLE, BANDICOOTS AND WOMBATS

MYRMECOBIIDAE: NUMBAT FAMILY

The single species in this Australian family is a small marsupial, which is adapted to the ecological niche that is filled by anteaters in other parts of the world. It was formerly called the banded anteater and feeds in a similar manner to anteaters.

Numbat *Myrmecobius fasciatus* **VU**

RANGE S.W. Australia

HABITAT Forest

SIZE Body: 6¾–10¾ in (17.5–27.5 cm) Tail: 5–6¾ in (13–17cm)

The numbat is active during the day. It feeds mainly on termites, although ants and some other small invertebrates are also eaten. Its sticky tongue, which is about 4 in (10 cm) long, is used to sweep insects into its mouth, where they are crushed by the numbat's poorly developed teeth. A captive numbat was observed to eat 10 to 20 thousand termites daily.

Between January and May, the female numbat produces a litter of 4 young. The mother has no pouch. The young cling to her nipples and she drags them around as she searches for food.

ORDER PERAMELEMORPHA

This order includes about 21 species of omnivorous marsupials which are found in Australia and New Guinea. There are two families in the order – the bandicoots and bilby; and the New Guinean bandicoots.

PERAMELIDAE: BANDICOOT FAMILY

There are about 12 species of bandicoot, widely distributed over Australia in a range of habitats, from desert to rain forest. The family includes the Bilby or Rabbit Bandicoot. Most of the bandicoots use their strong, clawed front feet to dig for insects larvae and plant roots and tubers.

Eastern Barred Bandicoot

Perameles gunnii **VU**

RANGE Australia S. Victoria; Tasmania

HABITAT Woodland, heathland

SIZE Body: 9¾–15¾ in (25–40 cm) Tail: 3–7 in (7.5–18 cm)

Like most bandicoots, the eastern barred bandicoot is a very aggressive, belligerent creature, which lives alone. The males occupy large territories and consort with females for only as long as is necessary for mating.

Primarily a nocturnal animal, it emerges from its nest at dusk to forage for earthworms and other small invertebrates. Probing deep into the soil with its long nose, the bandicoot digs eagerly when food is located.

Although the female bandicoot has 8 nipples, she seldom produces more than 4 or 5 young. The gestation period of 11 days is one of the shortest of any mammal and is followed by 8 weeks in the pouch.

Brown Bandicoot *Isoodon obesulus*

RANGE S. Australia, Queensland; Tasmania

HABITAT Scrub, forest

SIZE Body: 11¾–13¾ in (30–33 cm) Tail: 3–7 in (7.5–18 cm)

The brown bandicoot occurs in areas of dense ground cover and can survive in quite dry places, as long as it has somewhere to hide from eagles and foxes. It appears to locate prey, such as earthworms and beetle larvae, by scent and leaves small conical marks with its long nose as it forages about. Ant larvae and subterranean fungi are also eaten, as well as scorpions, which it nips the tails off before consuming them.

Reproduction is closely linked to the local rainfall pattern, and many brown bandicoots breed all year round. A litter of up to 5 young is born after an 11-day gestation and is weaned at 2 months.

Rabbit-bandicoot
Macrotis lagotis **EN**

RANGE C. and N.W. Australia

HABITAT Woodland, arid scrub

SIZE Body: 7¾–21½ in
(20–55 cm)
Tail: 4½–10¾ in (11.5–27.5 cm)

The rabbit-bandicoot lives alone in a burrow
system, which it digs with its powerful forepaws.
The burrow descends 2m (6ft) or more, and the bandicoot is
thus protected from the heat of the day. After dark, when the air
is cool, the rabbit-bandicoot emerges to feed on termites and
beetle larvae, which it digs from the roots of wattle trees. It may
also eat some of the fungi that grow around the roots.

Courtship is brief and aggressive, as with most bandicoots.
The litter of 3 young is born between March and May and the
young spend 8 weeks in the mother's pouch.

ORDER NOTORYCTEMORPHA

NOTORYCTIDAE: MARSUPIAL MOLE FAMILY

The two species in this Australian marsupial family have a clear
resemblance to the placental moles and lead a similar existence.

Southern Marsupial Mole *Notoryctes typhlops* **EN**

RANGE S.W. Australia

HABITAT Desert

SIZE Body: 3½–7 in (9–18 cm) Tail: ½–1 in (1.25–2.5 cm)

The marsupial mole is superbly adapted to a burrowing way of
life. It has large, shovellike forepaws, no eyes and silky fur, which
helps it move easily through the sandy soil.

Marsupial moles do not dig permanent burrows for as they
travel through the soft sand the tunnel falls in immediately
behind them. They feed on earthworms and other underground
invertebrates, such as beetle larvae, and come to the surface
quite frequently, although they move awkwardly on land.

Nothing is known of the reproductive habits of the
marsupial mole, but since the female's pouch contains only two
nipples, presumably only 2 young are born at a time.

The testes of the male
never descend into
a scrotum, but
remain in the body,
close to the
kidneys.

ORDER DIPROTODONTA

More than half of the Australian marsupials, including
the koala, kangaroos, and possums, belong to this
order. Most diprotodonts are primarily plant eaters, but
many also eat insects. Some species feed on
nectar or other plant secretions.

VOMBATIDAE: WOMBAT FAMILY

The 3 species of wombat all live in Australia, 1 in Tasmania also.
They are strong, powerfully built marsupials, which superficially
resemble badgers. With their long, bearlike claws, they excavate
vast burrow systems and tear up underground roots and tubers
for food. They are strictly vegetarian and often raid cultivated
fields to feed on the soft, developing ears of corn.

Common Wombat *Vombatus ursinus*

RANGE E. Australia, Tasmania

HABITAT Forest, scrub

SIZE Body: 27½ in–4 ft (70cm–1.2 m) Tail: vestigial

This wombat is a common forest animal along Australia's eastern
seaboard and is often found at high altitudes in the Snowy
Mountains.

It digs burrows that may stretch for more than 42 ft (13 m)
from the entrance and go down more than 6 ft (2 m). It is not
known whether wombats are gregarious below ground, but the
number of burrows occurring together suggests that they may
be. Above ground, the wombat follows regularly used pathways
through the forest.

The female gives birth in late autumn, usually to a single
young, which remains in the pouch, where there are two
nipples, for about 3 months. Once out of the pouch, it forages
with its mother for several months before living independently.
It is not unusual for wombats to live for more than 20 years.

KOALA, HONEY POSSUM, PHALANGERS, GLIDING POSSUMS AND RINGTAILS

PHASCOLARCTIDAE: KOALA FAMILY

The single species in this family is one of Australia's best-known marsupials and also the species most specialized and adapted for life in the trees.

During the first three decades of this century, koalas were hunted for their skins, and in 1924 alone, over 2 million were exported. Today the koala is no longer threatened, and following strict conservation measures, populations are increasing throughout its range.

Koala *Phascolarctos cinereus* **LR:nt**

RANGE E. Australia

HABITAT Dry forest

SIZE Body: 23½–33½ in (60–85 cm) Tail: vestigial

The arboreal koala rarely leaves the safety of the trees. It comes down to the ground only in order to pass from one tree to another. Its diet is limited, consisting of the leaves and shoots of a few species of Eucalyptus. An adult will consume just over 20 lb (1 kg) of leaves a day.

Koalas live singly or in small groups, consisting of a single male with a harem of females. They breed in summer, and each female produces a single young after a gestation of about a month. The tiny koala enters the pouch, which opens backward, and remains there for 5 or 6 months. After this period of pouch life it rides on its mother's back. After weaning, the mother feeds her young on semidigested leaves.

Many koalas suffer from the infectious fungal disease cryptococcosis, which causes lesions or abscesses in the lungs, joints and brain. The disease can be transferred to man, often with fatal results. It is thought that the source of the fungal infection is soil, which koalas regularly eat, apparently as an aid to digestion.

TARSIPEDIDAE: HONEY POSSUM FAMILY

The only member of its family, the honey possum is a zoological enigma because it has no obvious close relatives. In general appearance it resembles the other small possums, but its feet are quite different. The second and third digits on each hind foot are totally fused with two tiny claws at the tip of the fused digit.

Honey Possum *Tarsipes rostratus*

RANGE S.W. Australia

HABITAT Heathland with bushes and trees

SIZE Body: 2¾–3¼ in (7–8.5 cm) Tail: 3½–4 in (9–10 cm)

Occasionally the honey possum will eat small insects, but it mainly feeds on the pollen and nectar of the flowers of the Banksia, a flowering shrub. The honey possum's tongue, with its bristly tip, resembles that of a hummingbird or nectar-feeding bat and can be extended about 1 in (2.5 cm) beyond the tip of the nose. The teeth are poorly developed. Tough ridges on the palate are used to scrape nectar and pollen off the tongue.

The honey possum often hangs upside down while feeding, using its prehensile tail as a fifth limb. In midwinter, the honey possums mate, and females give birth to 2 young after a gestation of about 4 weeks. The young remain in the pouch until they are about 4 months old.

PHALANGERIDAE: PHALANGER FAMILY

The 18 species in this family occur in Australia, New Guinea and Sulawesi. The totally Australian species are known as possums, those from the islands are known as phalangers. All are nocturnal and arboreal and use their prehensile tails as a fifth limb when climbing. Leaves, gum from wattle trees and insects are the main foods, but small birds and lizards may also be eaten.

Brush-tailed Possum
Trichosurus vulpecula

RANGE Australia, Tasmania; introduced into New Zealand

HABITAT Forest, woodland

SIZE Body: 12½–22¾ in (32–58 cm)
Tail: 9½–13¾ in (24–35 cm)

The brush-tailed possum is the only native marsupial to have benefited from man's encroachment on virgin land, for it has become adapted to living on man's buildings and to feeding on refuse. In natural conditions, it eats young shoots, flowers, leaves and fruit, with some insects and young birds.

Breeding occurs once or twice a year, normally with 1 young in each litter. The gestation period is 17 days, and the young possum then stays in the pouch for about 5 months.

ACROBATIDAE: PYGMY GLIDING POSSUM FAMILY

There are 7 species of these tiny, mouse-sized possums in Australia and New Guinea. All are arboreal.

Pygmy Glider *Acrobates pygmaeus*

RANGE E. and S.E. Australia

HABITAT Dry forest

SIZE Body: 2¼–3¼ in (6–8.5 cm)
Tail: 2¼–3¼ in (6.5–8.5 cm)

The pygmy glider lives at the top of tall forest trees. Its flight membrane – flaps of skin between wrists and heels – enables it to glide from tree to tree. The tail gives directional stability. The tips of its digits are broad and deeply furrowed, to help it grip when landing. The pygmy glider eats insects, gum, nectar and pollen. A litter of 2 to 4 young is born in July or August.

PETAURIDAE: STRIPED AND LESSER GLIDING POSSUM FAMILY

There are about 9 species in this family found in Australia and New Guinea. All species are tree-dwellers and some glide from branch to branch.

Sugar Glider *Petaurus breviceps*

RANGE E. and N. Australia; New Guinea

HABITAT Woodland

SIZE Body: 4¼–6 in (11–15 cm)
Tail: 4¾–7 in (12–18 cm)

The sugar glider feeds on the sugary sap that oozes from wounds on the bark of wattle and gum trees, returning to the same tree for several days. Sugar gliders live in groups of up to 20, in holes in trees. They use their gliding membranes to leap up to 180 ft (55 m) between trees.

A litter of 2 or 3 is born after a 21-day gestation. The young leave the mother's pouch at 3 or 4 months old.

PSEUDOCHEIRIDAE: RING-TAILED AND GREATER GLIDING POSSUM FAMILY

This family includes 14 tree-living species. Their prehensile tails are used to grip while climbing.

Greater Glider *Petauroides volans*

RANGE E. Australia

HABITAT Forest

SIZE Body: 11¾–18¾ in (30–48 cm) Tail: 17¾–21½ in (45–55 cm)

The greater glider is the largest of Australia's gliding marsupials, weighing up to 3 lb (1.4 kg). It lives in holes, high in the trees, and feeds on leaves and shoots. This animal can glide 330 ft (100 m) or more, from tree to tree, using its long tail to steer.

In midwinter, the female gives birth to 1 young, which spends 4 months in the pouch.

KANGAROOS

MACROPODIDAE: KANGAROO FAMILY

There are about 46 species of kangaroo, and the family is regarded by most authorities as the most advanced of all the 18 surviving families of marsupials, because both the teeth and feet are greatly modified. The hind feet are extremely large – the origin of the family's scientific name – and the thumb is totally absent. Digits 2 and 3 are slender and bound together by skin; digit 4 is massive and armed with a long, tough claw, and digit 5 is only a little smaller. Males and females generally look alike, except for the pouch structure of the female. In some of the larger species of kangaroo, the male is slightly larger than his mate.

A kangaroo has fewer teeth than other marsupials, and these are high-crowned and deeply folded. They are similar to those of the placental mammals of the family Bovidae (sheep and cattle). Kangaroos eat only plant matter. Some are browsers, while others are grazers.

The main characteristic of kangaroos is their method of moving on two legs. They make a series of great bounds, during which the long hind legs propel the body forward with considerable force. A long, powerful tail acts as a counterbalance, providing stability on landing. Although hopping may seem an awkward form of locomotion, at speeds of more than 12 mph (20 km/h) it is more efficient in terms of energy use than quadrupedal running. Kangaroos often have to travel long distances to find food, so speed and efficiency are important, and selective pressures for fast movement are great.

Members of the kangaroo family occur in Australia and New Guinea and also in Tasmania and the Bismarck Islands. Some are forest-dwellers, but others live in hot, arid areas and during the worst of the day's heat they seek the shade of a rocky outcrop and regularly salivate over their upper arms to cool themselves. If intense drought continues for so long that the females can no longer make milk for their young, the sucklings are expelled from the pouch and perish. When the rains arrive and food supplies return, a reserve embryo, which has been held in a suspended state of development, is implanted in the uterus and a new pregnancy begins without the female having to mate again. In this way, kangaroos cope successfully with their harsh environment. Most kangaroos produce only 1 young at a time.

Red-legged Pademelon
Thylogale stigmatica

RANGE Australia: E. Queensland, E. New South Wales

HABITAT Wet forest

SIZE Body: 20¾–24½ in (53–62 cm) Tail: 12½–17¾ in (32–45 cm)

The red-legged pademelon is one of 4 pademelon species, all of which are solidly built forest-dwellers, slightly heavier in the hindquarters than the graceful kangaroos of the open plains. Pademelons are adaptable creatures that can occupy a variety of habitats, provided that there is plenty of cover. They sometimes occur in herds, but there are also solitary individuals. At dusk, pademelons emerge to forage for leaves, buds, shoots and fruit.

Usually a single young is produced, although twins do occur.

Spectacled Hare-wallaby *Lagorchestes conspicillatus* **LR:nt**

RANGE N. and C. Australia

HABITAT Desert grassland

SIZE Body: 15¾–19¾ in (40–50 cm) Tail: 13¾–17¾ in (35–45 cm)

There are 4 species of small hare-wallaby inhabiting the arid and desert grasslands of Australia. They build themselves rough, grassy nests among the tough spinifex vegetation. If disturbed, the hare-wallaby behaves much like a hare – leaping off in a zigzag manner.

Spectacled hare-wallabies lead solitary lives, only coming together with each other for mating. This isolation is necessary because of the extreme difficulty of eking out an existence in the inhospitable desert environment.

The young are produced singly at any time of year and become sexually mature at about a year old.

Yellow-footed Rock Wallaby *Petrogale xanthopus* **LR:nt**

RANGE C. and E. Australia

HABITAT Rocky outcrops, boulder piles

SIZE Body: 19¾–31½ in (50–80 cm) Tail: 15¾–27½ in (40–70 cm)

The yellow-footed, or ring-tailed rock wallaby is the most handsomely marked of the rock wallabies. It has long been exploited for its high-quality fur and is now found in a few isolated areas only.

All rock wallabies live in the most inhospitable regions of the outback. They are remarkably agile and their feet are adapted for scrambling around on rocks, with broad, soft pads and strong claws. Unlike true kangaroos the rock wallaby's long tail does not have a thickened base and is not used for support.

Rock wallabies feed on whatever plant material they can find. Breeding takes place throughout the year, but if drought conditions persist too long, the rock wallabies sacrifice any young in their pouches.

Quokka *Setonix brachyurus* **Vu**

RANGE S.W. Australia

HABITAT Dense vegetation

SIZE Body: 18¾–23½ in (47.5–60 cm) Tail: 9¾–13¾ in (25–35 cm)

The quokka was once widespread over the southwest of Australia, but shooting for sport quickly reduced the population to a low level. Today the quokka occurs in only a few swampy valleys in the Darling Range, near Perth, but it is abundant on Rottnest and

Bald Islands, just off the coast. Quokkas have a good nose for fresh water, and on Rottnest Island travel as far as 1½ miles (2.5 km) to find it. They have learned to scavenge on refuse dumps for food in times of drought and sparse plant supply, and are also able to supplement their protein intake by utilizing urea, a urinary waste product. In this respect, they resemble desert mammals.

The female quokka gives birth to 1 tadpole-sized young after a gestation period of 17 days and mates again the following day. The embryo resulting from this second mating is held free in the uterus and will implant and start development only after the earlier offspring has left the pouch. Quokkas first breed when they reach about 2 years old.

It is to be hoped that the development of Rottnest Island as an important recreational site for the people of Perth can be achieved without destroying the habitat of this intelligent little wallaby.

Lumholtz's Tree Kangaroo

Dendrolagus lumholtzi **LR:nt**

RANGE Australia: N.E. Queensland

HABITAT Rain forest

SIZE Body: 20½–31½ in (52–80 cm) Tail: 16½–36½ in (42–93 cm)

Only 7 species of kangaroo, 2 of which occur in Australia and 5 in New Guinea, have taken to life in the trees. Unlike most arboreal mammals, they have few adaptations for this specialized way of life; their hind feet are singularly undeveloped for climbing, but their front feet are better adapted for grasping than those of other kangaroos. They are, however, remarkably agile in trees, and their long tails, although not prehensile, give considerable stability. Grass, leaves and fruit are their main foods, and they frequently climb backward down trees to the ground to graze.

Small groups live together and sleep in the same tree. Little is known of their breeding habits other than that they produce 1 young at any time of year. Tree kangaroos are not rare, but their secretive way of life and the denseness of their forest habitat make them hard to observe.

KANGAROOS CONTINUED

Red Kangaroo *Macropus rufus*

RANGE C. Australia

HABITAT Grassy arid plains

SIZE Body: 3¼–5¼ ft (1–1.6 m) Tail: 3–3½ ft (90 cm–1.1 m)

The red kangaroo is the largest living marsupial. An old male can attain a weight of about 154 lb (70 kg). The male has a deep russet-red coat, the female has a bluish-gray coat and is often referred to as the "blue flier".

Red kangaroos live on the arid grassland of the desert in small herds, which consist of an adult male and several females. During the heat of the day, they shelter by rocky outcrops or in the shade of trees and emerge in the evening to feed and drink. Weight for weight, kangaroos eat as much as sheep, but they convert their food more efficiently.

Breeding occurs throughout the year, and the gestation lasts 30 to 40 days. A few hours before the birth, the mother starts to clean and nuzzle at her pouch. Sitting back, with her tail bent forward between her hind legs, and holding the pouch open with her forelimbs, she licks it inside and out, often continuing until the moment of birth.

The newborn offspring weighs only ¹⁄₄₀ oz (0.75 g) and is ¹⁄₃₀,₀₀₀ of its mother's weight. The tiny baby has well-developed front claws, which it uses to clamber up into the pouch. Once safely inside, it takes a nipple into its mouth. The nipple grows with the baby to reach 4 in (10 cm) long at the time of weaning. The mother's milk changes as the baby grows, becoming richer and more fatty during the later phase of lactation.

The young kangaroo spends about 240 days in the mother's pouch and then accompanies her for a further 120 days. During this period the young "joey" will occasionally put its head into the pouch to suckle, even though the pouch may already contain a younger sibling.

During intense drought conditions, most pouch young die, but the loss will be made up from a stock of "reserve" embryos carried in the mother's uterus.

Until recently, red kangaroos were hunted on a massive scale, but this practise is now subject to strict government controls.

New Guinea Forest Wallaby *Dorcopsis veterum*

RANGE New Guinea

HABITAT Lowland rain forest

SIZE Body: 19¼–31¼ in (49–80 cm) Tail: 11¾–21½ in (30–55 cm)

In most respects, the New Guinea forest wallaby appears to resemble the Australian pademelons, but very little is known of this retiring species. The tip of the forest wallaby's tail is armed with a few broad, tough scales, the function of which remains a mystery. Whenever possible, forest wallabies feed on grass, but they also eat a variety of other plant foods. They are seldom observed by day and may lie up in leafy nests until dusk. Little is known of their breeding habits, except that only 1 young is carried at a time.

Bridled Nail-tailed Wallaby *Onychogalea fraenata* **EN**

RANGE Australia: C. Queensland

HABITAT Thick scrub

SIZE Body: 17¾–26¼ in (45–67 cm) Tail: 13–26 in (33–66 cm)

The 2 species of nail-tailed wallaby derive their name from a scale, like a small fingernail, hidden in the thick hair at the tip of the long, thin tail. Its function is unknown. In the middle of the nineteenth century, the bridled nail-tailed wallaby was abundant over much of eastern and southeastern Australia, but in this century, it was unrecorded for several decades until a population was discovered in central Queensland, in 1974. Competition by rabbits for food, predation by red foxes and hunting are major causes of its decline. Conservation measures are in hand and will need to be applied for many years if this species is to survive in the wild.

Thick scrub is used for food and cover by nail-tailed wallabies. Nothing is known of their breeding habits except that they usually produce 1 young at a time.

Swamp Wallaby *Wallabia bicolor*

RANGE E. and S.E. Australia

HABITAT Dense thickets, rocky gullies

SIZE Body: 25½–35½ in (65–90 cm) Tail: 25¼–33¾ in (64–86 cm)

Swamp wallabies occur in small herds but are often hard to see because of their habit of lying down when danger threatens. Only when the danger is imminent do the wallabies break cover and scatter in different directions with explosive speed. Their diet is varied, and they readily switch from one plant species to another. This flexibility means that they can become pests of agricultural crops, and some measure of control is often necessary locally.

Breeding takes place throughout the year, and the female produces 1 young, which stays in her pouch for about 300 days. It continues to feed for 60 days after leaving the mother's pouch.

POTOROIDAE RAT-KANGAROO FAMILY

There are 10 species of rat kangaroo found in Australia. They are smaller than their close relatives the kangaroos. They have long tails and elongated hind feet which, in most species, are used for bipedal hopping movement. As well as feeding on vegetation, some rat-kangaroos also eat insects and other invertebrates.

Musky Rat-kangaroo *Hypsiprymnodon moschatus*

RANGE Australia: N.E. Queensland

HABITAT Rain forest

SIZE Body: 9¼–13¼ in (23.5–33.5 cm) Tail: 5–6¾ in (13–17 cm)

The musky rat-kangaroo is unique in two ways. It has a well-formed first digit, or thumb, on each hind foot and it is the only kangaroo to regularly give birth to twins. The young are usually born in the rainy season (February to May), but this can vary.

The musky rat-kangaroo is also unusual in that it often moves around on four legs in the manner of a rabbit. Little is known of the social habits of this species, but they seem to move singly or in pairs. Both the male and female produce a pungent musky odor, but the reason for this is not known.

Their diet includes a wide range of plant matter, from palm berries to root tubers, and they also eat insects and earthworms.

Potoroo *Potorous tridactylus*

RANGE E. Australia, S.W. corner of W. Australia; Tasmania

HABITAT Low, thick, damp scrub

SIZE Body: 11¾–15¾ in (30–40 cm) Tail: 6–9½ in (15–24 cm)

Despite its small size and rabbitlike appearance, the potoroo has all the characteristics of reproduction of the larger kangaroos and moves with a similar gait. Although it may occasionally move on all fours, it usually bounds along on its strong hind legs, covering 12 to 18 in (30 to 45 cm) with each hop. It is nocturnal, emerging at dusk to forage for plants, roots, fungi and insects.

Potoroos breed at any time of year, and the single young spends 17 weeks in the pouch.

Rufous Rat-kangaroo *Aepyprymnus rufescens*

RANGE E. Australia: Queensland to C. New South Wales

HABITAT Grassland, woodland

SIZE Body: 15–20½ in (38–52 cm) Tail: 13¾–15¾ in (35–40 cm)

The largest of the rat-kangaroos, the rufous rat-kangaroo builds a grassy nest in which it shelters from the heat of the day. It has little fear of humans and will enter foresters' camps and even feed from the hand. This lack of fear makes the animals vulnerable to attack by dogs and red foxes, and while their populations are in no immediate danger, the future survival of these little kangaroos is a cause for concern.

They breed slowly – a maximum of 2 young a year – but nothing more is known of their breeding habits.

ANTEATERS AND SLOTHS

ORDER XENARTHRA

This order includes 4 families of mammals all of which have gone along the evolutionary track of tooth reduction or loss in connection with their specialized diet of insects, such as ants and termites. The families are the anteaters, the three-toed sloths, the two-toed sloths, and the armadillos.

MYRMECOPHAGIDAE: AMERICAN ANTEATER FAMILY

There are 4 species of American anteater found in Mexico and Central and South America as far south as northern Argentina. They normally inhabit tropical forests, but also occur in grassland. All forms have extremely elongate snouts and no teeth. Their tongues are long and covered with a sticky salivary secretion, which enables them to trap insects easily. The anteaters break into ant or termite nests by means of their powerful clawed forefeet, each of which has an enlarged third digit. The largest species, the giant anteater, is ground-dwelling, while the other, smaller species are essentially arboreal.

Giant Anteater *Myrmecophaga tridactyla* **VU**

RANGE Central America, South America to N. Argentina

HABITAT Forest, savanna

SIZE Body: 3¼–4 ft (1–1.2 m) Tail: 25½–35¼ in (65–90 cm)

The remarkable giant anteater is the largest of its family. It has a long snout, a distinctive black stripe across its body and a bushy, long-haired tail. Using its powerful foreclaws, the anteater breaks open ant or termite mounds and feeds on huge quantities of the insects and their eggs and larvae. Its long tongue can be extended as much as 24 in (61 cm) and is covered

with sticky saliva, that traps insects. As it wanders in search of food supplies, the anteater walks on its knuckles, thus protecting its sharp foreclaws. Unlike other anteaters, this species does not climb trees, although it readily enters water and can swim. Except for females with young, giant anteaters usually live alone. In areas far from human habitation, the giant anteater is active in the daytime, but near people it is only active at night.

The female produces 1 young after a gestation period of about 190 days. The offspring is carried on the mother's back and stays with her until her next pregnancy is well advanced.

Northern Tamandua *Tamandua mexicana*

RANGE S. Mexico, through Central and South America, N.W. Venezuela and N.W. Peru

HABITAT Forest

SIZE Body: 21¼–22¾ in (54–58 cm) Tail: 21½–21¾ in (54.5–55.5 cm)

This anteater is a tree dweller. It is smaller than its giant relative and has a prehensile tail, which it uses as a fifth limb. The underside of the tail is naked to improve its grip. On the ground, the northern tamandua moves slowly and clumsily.

It is active mainly at night, when it breaks open the nests of tree-living ants and termites and feeds on the insects. Like all anteaters, it has a long, protrusible tongue, which is covered with sticky saliva, enabling it to trap its prey.

If attacked, the northern tamandua strikes out at its adversary with its powerful foreclaws. The female gives birth to 1 young. The length of the gestation is unknown. The youngster is carried on its mother's back but may be set down on a branch while she feeds.

Silky Anteater *Cyclopes didactylus*

RANGE S. Mexico, Central and South America to Bolivia and Brazil

HABITAT Forest

SIZE Body: 6–7 in (15–18 cm) Tail: 7–7¾ in (18–20 cm)

The silky anteater is an arboreal animal that climbs with agility. It has a prehensile tail and long feet with special joints, which enable the claws to be turned back under the foot when grasping branches so that they do not become blunted. This anteater rarely comes down to the ground, but sleeps in a hollow tree or on a branch during the day and is active at night, searching for ants and termites. Like its relatives, it uses its sharp, powerful foreclaws to break into ant and termite nests and its long, sticky tongue for gobbling up the insects. Silky anteaters are often attacked by large birds of prey.

Little is known about the silky anteater's breeding habits. The female produces 1 young, which both parents feed on regurgitated insects.

BRADYPODIDAE: THREE-TOED SLOTH FAMILY

There are five species, and two families, of sloth that all live in the tropical forests of Central and South America. These highly adapted mammals are so specialized for life in the trees that they are unable to walk normally on the ground. Most of their life is spent among the branches, where they hang upside-down by means of their curved, hooklike claws. They feed on leaves and other plant material. The three species of three-toed sloths have three digits on both their front and hind feet.

Three-toed Sloth *Bradypus tridactylus*

RANGE S. Venezuela, The Guianas, N. Brazil

HABITAT Forest

SIZE Body: 19¾–23½ in (50–60 cm) Tail: 2½–2¾ in (6.5–7 cm)

The three-toed sloth is so well adapted to living upside down, hanging from branches by its hook-like claws, that its hair grows in the opposite direction from that of other mammals and points downward when the sloth is hanging in its normal position. Each of the outer hairs is grooved, and green algae grow in these grooves giving the sloth a greenish tinge, which helps to camouflage it amid the foliage of its habitat.

This sloth's head is short and broad. It has two more neck vertebrae than is normal for mammals, giving a greater range of head movement. It climbs slowly, moving one limb at a time, and swims quite well. On the ground it drags its body forward with its hooked limbs. The three-toed sloth descends about once a week to defecate in a hole that it digs with its tail.

Leaves and tender buds, particularly those of Cecropia trees, are the three-toed sloth's main food. The sloth's sight and hearing are poor, and it depends on smell and touch to find food.

The female produces 1 young after a gestation of 120 to 180 days. She even gives birth hanging in the trees. The offspring is suckled for about a month and then fed on regurgitated food.

MEGALONYCHIDAE: TWO-TOED SLOTH FAMILY

The two species of sloth in this family have two clawed digits on their front feet and three on their hind feet.

Two-toed Sloth *Choloepus didactylus* **DD**

RANGE Venezuela, N. Brazil, Guyana, Suriname, French Guiana

HABITAT Forest

SIZE Body: 23½–25¼ in (60–64 cm) Tail: absent or vestigial

The two-toed sloth eats, sleeps and gives birth while hanging upside down in the trees. Each forefoot has two digits, closely bound together with skin, each of which bears a large, curved claw. Although all its movements are extremely slow, the two-toed sloth can strike out quickly to defend itself and inflict a serious wound with its claws. On the ground, it can only drag itself along, but it swims easily. The two-toed sloth sleeps during the day, keeping still to avoid detection by enemies and to conserve energy. It becomes active at night when it feeds on leaves, twigs and fruit.

The female gives birth to a single baby after a gestation of at least 263 days. The young sloth clings to its mother while she hangs in the trees.

ARMADILLOS AND PANGOLINS

DASYPODIDAE: ARMADILLO FAMILY

The 20 species of armadillo all occur in the New World, from the southern states of the USA through Central and South America to Chile and Argentina.

Armadillos are digging animals, that are usually active at night. They have short, powerful limbs with strong, curved claws. They can dig burrows rapidly and some species do this as a means of escaping predators. When they are not active, armadillos rest underground in their burrows. Their skin is dramatically modified to form extremely tough, articulated plates – made of bone covered by horn – which cover the top of the tail, the back, sides, ears and front of the head. This provides the animal with excellent protection. Two armadillo species can curl themselves up into a ball so that their limbs and vulnerable underparts are protected by the armor.

Nine-banded Armadillo *Dasypus novemcinctus*

RANGE S. USA, through Central and South America to Peru and N. Argentina

HABITAT Arid grassland, semidesert

SIZE Body: 17¾–19¾ in (45–50 cm) Tail: 9¾–15¾ in (25–40 cm)

This is the most common and widespread armadillo species. It usually has 9 bands of horny plates across its body, though this can range from 8 to 11. It has powerful, clawed forefeet.

The nine-banded armadillo spends the daylight hours in a burrow, which may house several individuals, and emerges at night to root about in search of food, investigating holes and crevices with its tapering snout for insects, spiders, small reptiles, amphibians and eggs.

The female nearly always gives birth to a litter of 4 identical young of the same sex, which she suckles for about 2 months.

Giant Armadillo *Priodontes maximus* **En**

RANGE Venezuela to N. Argentina

HABITAT Forest

SIZE Body: 29½ in–3¼ ft (75 cm–1 m) Tail: 19¾ in (50 cm)

The largest of its family, the giant armadillo may weigh up to 132 lb (60 kg). Its body is armored with movable horny plates, and there are only a few hairs on the skin between the plates. It may have as many as 100 small teeth, but these are gradually shed with age. The claws on its forefeet are particularly long – those on the third digits measuring up to 7¾ in (20 cm). A fairly agile animal, the giant armadillo can support itself on its hind legs and tail, while digging or smashing a termite mound with its powerful forelimbs. It feeds on ants, termites, other insects and also on worms, spiders, snakes and carrion. If attacked, it can only partially roll itself up and is more likely to flee.

The breeding habits of this armadillo are little known. The female produces 1 or 2 young.

Pink Fairy Armadillo *Chlamyphorus truncatus* **En**

RANGE C. W. Argentina

HABITAT Dry sandy plains

SIZE Body: 5–6 in (12.5–15 cm) Tail: 1 in (2.5 cm)

This tiny armadillo, with its pale pink armor, emerges from its burrow at dusk to feed on ants in particular, but also on worms, snails and plant material. It digs with its forefeet and supports its rear on its rigid tail, thus freeing its hind limbs for kicking away earth. It has five claws on each foot.

This species has proved difficult to keep in captivity, and its breeding habits remain unknown.

ORDER PHOLIDOTA

MANIDAE: PANGOLIN FAMILY

The pangolin family is the only one in its order. The family contains 7 species of nocturnal ant-eating and termite-eating mammals, found in Africa and south and Southeast Asia. The typical pangolin has the same general body shape as that of the American giant anteater, but is covered with enormous overlapping scales, like the bracts of a pinecone. The scales are movable and sharp edged and are probably developed from modified hairs (like the horn of a rhinoceros). The pangolin has no teeth in its elongate head but it does have an extremely long, protrusible tongue, which it uses to catch its prey.

Giant Pangolin *Manis gigantea*

RANGE Africa: Senegal, east to Uganda, south to Angola

HABITAT Forest, savanna

SIZE Body: 29½–31½ in (75–80 cm) Tail: 19¾–25½ in (50–65 cm)

The giant pangolin is the largest of the family. The female is smaller than the male. This species sleeps by day in a burrow and is active mainly between midnight and dawn, when it searches for ants and termites. Its powerful foreclaws can break into nests above or below ground.

Though the pangolin's movements are slow and deliberate, it can walk on its hind limbs – using its tail for balance – as well as on all fours. It can also swim.

When threatened, this species rolls into a ball, which protects it from most enemies. It may also lash out with its sharp-scaled tail and spray urine and anal gland secretions.

The single baby is born in an underground nest after a gestation period of about 5 months. The newborn pangolin's soft scales harden in about 2 days. After a month or so, the youngster accompanies its mother on feeding trips sitting on the base of her tail. It is weaned at about 3 months.

Tree Pangolin *Manis tricuspis*

RANGE Africa: Senegal to W. Kenya, south to Angola

HABITAT Rain forest

SIZE Body: 13¾–17¾ in (35–45 cm) Tail: 19¼–23½ in (49–60 cm)

The tree pangolin has distinctive scales on its back. Each scale has three pronounced points on its free edge. In older animals the points of the scales become worn. An adept climber, the tree pangolin has a very long prehensile tail, with a naked pad on the underside of the tip that helps it to grip.

During the day, it sleeps on the branch of a tree or in a hole, which it digs in the ground, and emerges at night to feed on tree-dwelling ants and termites, which it detects by smell. It tears open arboreal nests with its powerful forelimbs and sweeps up the insects with deft movements of its long tongue. Like all pangolins, it shows a strong preference for particular species of ant and termite and will reject others. The food is ground down in the pangolin's muscular, horny-surfaced stomach.

The female gives birth to a single young after a gestation period of 4 to 5 months. Its scales harden after a couple of days, and at 2 weeks of age, it starts to go on feeding trips with its mother.

PIKAS, RABBITS AND HARES

ORDER LAGOMORPHA

There are 2 families and about 68 species in this order: the pikas, and the rabbits and hares. For many years, these herbivores were regarded as a subgroup of the rodents, but a detailed examination of their structure, dentition and chewing mechanisms suggests that the two groups are distinct but related.

OCHOTONIDAE: PIKA FAMILY

There are about 21 species of pika, all in the same genus. They live in north and central Asia and 2 species also occur in North America. Pikas are smaller than rabbits and have short, rounded ears and no visible tail.

Northern Pika *Ochotona alpina*
RANGE Siberia, Mongolia, N.E. China, Japan: Hokkaido
HABITAT Rocky mountain slopes, forest
SIZE Body: 7¾–9¾ in (20–25 cm)

A small, short-legged animal, this pika cannot run fast like a rabbit, but moves in small jumps, rarely venturing far. It lives in family groups and takes shelter in a den, made among rocks or tree roots. Grass and slender plant stems are its main food, and, like all pikas, it gathers extra food in late summer and piles it in heaps like little haystacks to use in the winter. If they run short of food in winter, pikas tunnel through the snow to reach their stores.

There may be up to three litters a year, depending on the region. Each litter contains 2 to 5 young, born after a gestation period of 30 or 31 days.

LEPORIDAE: RABBIT AND HARE FAMILY

Found in forest, shrubby vegetation, grassland, tundra and on mountain slopes in the Americas, Europe, Asia and Africa, the rabbits and hares are an extremely successful family of small herbivorous mammals. The common rabbit has been introduced in Australia and New Zealand, where it has proved itself to be remarkably adaptable. Compared with pikas, the 47 or so species of rabbit and hare have become highly adapted for swift running, with disproportionately well-developed hind limbs. They also have long, narrow ears and small tails. Their teeth are adapted for gnawing vegetation – they have chisel-shaped upper incisors (which grow throughout life) for biting and large cheek teeth for chewing.

Brown Hare
Lepus europaeus
RANGE Europe (not Iceland or northern Scandinavia), N. Iran, N.E. China; introduced in North and South America, Australia and New Zealand
HABITAT Open country, farmland, woodland
SIZE Body: 17¼–30 in (44–76 cm)
Tail: 2¾–4¼ in (7–11 cm)

A fast-running hare, with long hind limbs, the brown, or European hare is mainly active at dusk and at night. During the day it remains in a shallow depression in the ground, known as a form, which is concealed among vegetation. It feeds on leaves, buds, roots, berries, fruit, fungi, bark and twigs. It is usually a solitary animal.

The female may have several litters a year, each of between 1 and 6 young, which are born in the form, fully furred and active, with their eyes open. They are suckled for about 3 weeks and leave their mother about a month after birth.

Black-tailed Jack Rabbit *Lepus californicus*
RANGE USA: Oregon, east to South Dakota and Missouri, south to N. Mexico; introduced in some eastern states of USA
HABITAT Prairie, cultivated land, arid scrub
SIZE Body: 18¼–24¾ in (46.5–63 cm) Tail: 2–4½ in (5–11.5 cm)

Identified by its long ears and large black-striped tail, this jack rabbit has powerful, elongate hind limbs and moves with a fast, bounding gait. For short periods, it may attain speeds of up to 35 mph (56 km/h) and tends to run rather than to take cover if

threatened. In summer it eats green plants and grass, and more woody vegetation in winter. This rabbit, like all lagomorphs, eats its feces. It is thought to obtain additional nutrients when the material passes through its digestive system a second time.

Several litters of 1 to 6 young may be born each year. The gestation period is 43 days on average. The young are born fully furred, with their eyes open, in a shallow depression on the ground.

Snowshoe Hare *Lepus americanus*

RANGE Alaska, Canada, N. USA

HABITAT Forest, swamps, thickets

SIZE Body: 14¼–20½ in (36–52 cm) Tail: 1–2¼ in (2.5–5.5 cm)

Also known as the varying hare, this animal has a dark-brown coat in summer that turns white in winter, except for a black edging on the ear tips. This coat is of undoubted camouflage value, although in fact it is a yellowish-buff, with only the visible tips of the hairs pure white. Usually active at night and in the early morning, the snowshoe hare feeds on juicy green plants and grass in summer and twigs, shoots and buds in winter. The population of these hares fluctuates tremendously on a roughly 10-year cycle, due to food availability and predator interactions. Breeding begins in March, and there may be two or three litters, each of 1 to 7, young, which are born well furred, with open eyes.

Greater Red Rockhare *Pronolagus crassicaudatus*

RANGE Africa: E. South Africa

HABITAT Stony country with scattered vegetation, forest edge

SIZE Body: 16½–19¾ in (42–50 cm) Tail: 2¼–5½ in (6–14 cm)

The greater red rockhare lives alone in a small territory and is usually active at dusk and at night, feeding on grass and green-leaved plants. During the day, it rests in a shallow depression, or form, near cover of grass or rocks, and if alarmed, it darts into a rock crevice or hole. Like all hares, its hearing is acute and its sight and sense of smell are also good.

The female gives birth to 1 or 2 fully haired young after a gestation period of about a month.

Volcano Rabbit *Romerolagus diazi* **EN**

RANGE Mexico: S.E. of Mexico City

HABITAT Slopes of volcanoes

SIZE Body: 11¼–12¼ in (28.5–31 cm) Tail: vestigial

This unusual rabbit, with its extremely restricted distribution, is now rare and strictly protected. It has short, rounded ears and trots, rather than hops, on its short legs as it moves along the runways it makes in the grass. Mainly active at night and at dusk, it feeds on grass and young shoots. Volcano rabbits live in colonies and dig burrows for shelter.

The wild population of this species may be as low as 1,300, but a captive colony exists in the zoo on Jersey in the Channel Islands.

Hispid Hare *Caprolagus hispidus* **EN**

RANGE Bangladesh, India, Nepal

HABITAT Forest, grassy bamboo thickets

SIZE Body: about 18½ in (47 cm) Tail: 1 in (2.5 cm)

Also known as the bristly or Assam rabbit, the hispid hare has an unusual coat of coarse, bristly fur; its ears are short and broad and its legs stout. It lives alone or in pairs and digs a burrow for shelter. Grass shoots, roots and bark are its main foods.

RABBITS AND HARES CONTINUED

Swamp Rabbit

Sylvilagus aquaticus

RANGE S. C. USA: Georgia to Texas

HABITAT Marshland, swamps, wet woodland

SIZE Body: 17¾–21½ in (45–55 cm) Tail: 2¼ in (6 cm)

The robust, large-headed swamp rabbit takes to water readily and is an expert swimmer and diver. It swims to avoid danger when pursued and also to reach islets or other new feeding areas. With its large, splayed toes, it also moves easily on damp, muddy land.

Mainly nocturnal, the swamp rabbit emerges from its shelter beneath a log or in a ground hollow at any time of the day after heavy rain and feeds on grass, herbs and aquatic vegetation. It may also forage in grain fields, where these are near swamps. Although usually docile, rival males will attack each other in ferocious, face-to-face fights, sometimes inflicting serious wounds.

A litter of 1 to 6 young, usually 2 or 3, is born, after a gestation period of about 40 days, in a shallow depression in the ground lined with grass and fur. The young are born furred, and their eyes open a few days after birth. There are thought to be two litters a year.

Brush Rabbit *Sylvilagus bachmani*

RANGE W. coast of N. America: British Columbia to Baja California

HABITAT Chaparral, thick brush or scrub

SIZE Body: 10½–13 in (27–33 cm) Tail: ¾–1½ in (2–4 cm)

The small, brown brush rabbit has a tiny tail and rounded ears. The rabbits living in hot inland regions to the south of the range tend to have longer ears than those living on the cooler, humid northern coast.

Presumably this is because sound does not travel as well in hot, dry air as in moist, cool air and so they need the larger ears to pick up sounds more effectively. This shy elusive rabbit stays hidden in cover of dense undergrowth for much of the time, venturing out for only short distances to feed on a wide variety of green plants and taking almost anything within reach. It moves along well-trodden runways through the vegetation, but does not make a burrow.

There are three or four litters a year, between January and June. Each litter contains 3 to 5 young, born after a gestation of about 27 days in a shallow hollow in the ground, which is lined with grass and fur. The young are born blind, but with a covering of fine fur.

Desert Cottontail *Sylvilagus audubonii*

RANGE USA: California to Montana, south to Arizona and Texas; N. Mexico

HABITAT Open plains with scattered vegetation, wooded valleys, sagebrush

SIZE Body: 11¾–15 in (30–38 cm) Tail: 2–3 in (5–7.5 cm)

The desert cottontail is distinguished from the brush rabbit, with which it overlaps in the south of its range, by its larger size and ears and by its grayish coat.

Often abroad at any time of day, it is, however, most active in the late afternoon and at night, when it feeds on grass, leaves of various plants including cultivated plants, and fruit. It can do much damage to gardens and crops. Never far from some form of cover, it darts for safety if alarmed, the white underside of its tail momentarily revealed as it is flicked up. A burrow or a shallow depression in the ground is used for shelter.

Breeding takes place in spring or throughout the year, depending on the area. A litter of between 1 and 5 blind, helpless young is born after a gestation period of between 26 and 30 days.

Pygmy Rabbit *Brachylagus idahoensis* **LR:nt**

RANGE N.W. USA: Oregon, Idaho, Montana, Utah, Nevada, N. California

HABITAT Arid areas with sagebrush

SIZE Body: 9–11½ in (23–29 cm) Tail: ¾–1¼ in (2–3 cm)

The only member of its genus, this small rabbit has thick, soft fur and short hind legs. It lives in a burrow that it excavates itself and does not often venture far from its home. During much of the day, it rests up in the burrow, emerging at dusk to feed on sagebrush and any other available plant matter. Its main enemies are coyotes and owls, and if alarmed, the pygmy rabbit takes refuge in its burrow, which usually has 2 or 3 entrances.

Litters of 5 to 8 young are born between May and August.

European Rabbit

Oryctolagus cuniculus

RANGE Europe (except far north and east), N.W. Africa; introduced in many countries including New Zealand, Australia, Chile

HABITAT Grassland, cultivated land, woodland, grassy coastal cliffs

SIZE Body: 13¾–17¾ in (35–45 cm) Tail: 1½–2¾ in (4–7 cm)

The ancestor of the domestic rabbit, this species has been introduced into many areas outside its native range and has been so successful as to become a major pest in some places. Smaller than a hare, with shorter legs and ears, the common rabbit is brownish on the upperparts, with buffy-white underneath. The feet are equipped with large, straight claws.

Gregarious animals, these rabbits live in burrows, which they dig near to one another, and there may be a couple of hundred rabbits in a colony, or warren. They are most active at dusk and during the night, but may emerge in the daytime in areas where they are undisturbed. Grass and leafy plants are their main foods, but rabbits also eat vegetable and grain crops and can damage young trees. In winter, they eat bulbs, twigs and bark if more succulent foods are unavailable. As a warning of approaching danger, a rabbit may thump the ground with its hind foot.

There may be several litters a year, born in the spring and summer in Europe. There are 3 to 9 young in a litter, and the gestation period is 28 to 33 days. Young are born naked, blind and helpless in a specially constructed burrow, lined with vegetation and fur, which the mother plucks from her belly. They do not emerge from the burrow until about 3 weeks old. The female is on heat again 12 hours after the birth, but not all pregnancies last the term, and many embryos are resorbed. Only about 40 per cent of litters conceived are born. On average a female will produce 11 live young in a year.

Sumatran Short-eared Rabbit *Nesolagus netscheri* **CR**

RANGE S.W. Sumatra

HABITAT Forested mountain slopes at 2,000–4,600 ft (600–1,400 m)

SIZE Body: 14¼–15¾ in (36–40 cm) Tail: ½ in (1.5 cm)

The only member of its family to have a definitely striped coat, the Sumatran rabbit has buffy-gray upperparts with brown stripes and a line down the middle of its back, from nose to tail. The tiny tail and the rump are reddish, while the limbs are grayish-brown.

This unusual rabbit is now extremely rare, even in areas where it was once abundant, because of large-scale clearance of its forest habitat for cultivation.

Primarily nocturnal, the Sumatran rabbit spends the day in a burrow, but it is believed to take over an existing hole, rather than to dig its own. It feeds on leaves and stalks of plants in the forest undergrowth.

SQUIRRELS

ORDER RODENTIA

The largest of the mammalian orders, Rodentia contains at least 1800 species in 28 families.

SCIURIDAE: SQUIRREL FAMILY

There are about 260 species of squirrel and generally they are alert, short-faced animals. Some have taken to burrowing and live in vast subterranean townships (prairie dogs); others run and hop about over logs and stones (chipmunks); and many have taken to life in the trees (tree and flying squirrels). Most forms are active by day and are among the most brightly-colored of all mammals. Their eyes are large and vision, including color vision, good. The few nocturnal species, such as the flying squirrels, are more drab in appearance. Males and females generally look alike.

Squirrels have a wide distribution, occurring in all parts of the world except for southern South America, Australia, New Zealand, Madagascar and the deserts of the Middle East. In temperate climates they undergo periods of dormancy in cold weather. Dormancy differs from true hibernation in that the creature wakes every few days for food. True hibernation occurs in a limited number of squirrel species. Squirrels are social animals and have evolved a complex system of signaling with their bushy tails. They are also quite vocal, and most can make a variety of sounds.

European Red Squirrel *Sciurus vulgaris* **LR:nt**
RANGE Europe, east to China, Korea and Japan: Hokkaido.
HABITAT Evergreen forest
SIZE Body: 7¾–9½ in (20–24 cm) Tail: 6–7¾ in (15–20 cm)

Until the arrival of the North American gray squirrel in Britain at the beginning of this century, the only European species was the red squirrel. Populations are now declining in Britain, but red squirrels are still abundant in Europe and Asia. Conifer cones are their main food, although in summer they also eat fungi and fruit. The length of the breeding season is dictated by local climate. In a good year

a female may produce two litters of about 3 young each. The young are born in a tree nest, called a drey, which also doubles as winter quarters.

Gray Squirrel *Sciurus carolinensis*
RANGE S.E. Canada, E. USA; introduced in Britain and South Africa
HABITAT Hardwood forest
SIZE Body: 9–11¾ in (23–30 cm) Tail: 8¼–9 in (21–23 cm)

The gray squirrel's natural home is the oak, hickory and walnut forests of eastern North America, where its numbers are controlled by owls, foxes and bobcats. It feeds on seeds and nuts. An adult squirrel takes about 2¾ oz (80g) shelled nuts each day. It will also eat eggs, young birds and insects. Occasionally gray squirrels strip the bark from young trees to gain access to the nutritious sap beneath.

Two litters are produced each year, in early spring and summer. There are up to 7 young in a litter, but usually only 3 or 4 survive. Males are excluded from the nest and take no part in rearing the young. In Great Britain, the introduced gray squirrel is ousting the native red squirrel.

African Giant Squirrel *Protoxerus stangeri*
RANGE W. Africa, east to Kenya; Angola
HABITAT Palm forest
SIZE Body: 8½–13 in (22–33 cm) Tail: 9¾–15 in (25–38 cm)

Sometimes called the oil-palm squirrel, this species feeds primarily on nuts from the oil palm. In regions where calcium is scarce, it has been observed to gnaw bones and ivory. The African giant squirrel is a secretive creature, and its presence is usually only detected by a booming call, which it utters when disturbed. Little is known of its breeding habits, but it probably breeds throughout the year.

Indian Striped Palm Squirrel *Funambulus palmarum*

RANGE C. and S. India, Sri Lanka

HABITAT Palm forest

SIZE Body: 4½–7 in (11.5–18 cm)
Tail: 4½–7 in (11.5–18 cm)

With their distinctive stripes, these little squirrels superficially resemble chipmunks. They are highly active animals, foraging by day for palm nuts, flowers and buds. They may damage cotton trees by eating the buds, but when they feed on the nectar of the silky oak flowers, they do good by pollinating the flowers that they investigate.

Males are aggressive and fight for females, but once mating has taken place, they show no further interest in females or young. About three litters, each containing about 3 young, are born during the year. The gestation period is 40 to 45 days. Young females are sexually mature at 6 to 8 months old.

Black Giant Squirrel *Ratufa bicolor*

RANGE Myanmar to Indonesia

HABITAT Dense forest

SIZE Body: 11¾–17¾ in (30–45 cm) Tail: 11¾–19¾ in (30–50 cm)

The 4 species of giant squirrel are, as their name implies, very large, and they can weigh up to 6½ lb (3 kg). Black giant squirrels are extremely agile, despite their size, and can leap 20 ft (6 m) or more through the trees; as they do so, their tails trail down like rudders. They feed on fruit, nuts, bark and a variety of small invertebrate animals. Singly or in pairs, they shelter in nests in tree holes. In the breeding season a huge nest is made in which the female produces 1, sometimes 2, young after a gestation of about 4 weeks.

African Palm Squirrel

Epixerus ebii **LR:nt**

RANGE Ghana, Sierra Leone

HABITAT Dense forest; near swamps

SIZE Body: 9¾–11¾ in (25–30 cm)
Tail: 11–11¾ in (28–30 cm)

The African palm squirrel is one of the rarest rodents on record. Forest clearance and swamp-draining activities present an intolerable disturbance to this species, from which it may not recover. However, the inaccessibility of its habitats affords it a measure of protection in some parts of its range. It is believed to feed largely on the nuts of the *Raphia* swamp palm, but it probably eats other foods as well. Nothing is known of its breeding habits nor the reasons for its rarity.

Prevost's Squirrel *Callosciurus prevostii*

RANGE S.E. Asia

HABITAT Forest

SIZE Body: 7¾–11 in (20–28 cm) Tail: 6–9¾ in (15–25 cm)

The sharp contrast of colors in the coat of Prevost's squirrel makes it one of the most distinctive members of the family (the generic name means "beautiful squirrel").

These squirrels forage by day for seeds, nuts, buds, shoots and, occasionally birds' eggs and insects. They live singly or in pairs. Shortly before giving birth, the female leaves her normal nest in a hollow tree and builds a nest of sticks and leaves high up in the branches. Here, safe from the attentions of ground-living predators, she gives birth to a litter of 3 or 4 young. It is not known how many litters each female produces in a year, but in some parts of the range there may be as many as four.

SQUIRRELS CONTINUED

African Ground Squirrel

Xerus erythropus

RANGE Africa: Morocco to Kenya

HABITAT Forest, scrub, savanna

SIZE Body: 8½–11¾ in (22–30 cm) Tail: 7–10½ in (18–27 cm)

Rather like that of its North American counterpart, the fur of the African ground squirrel is harsh and smooth, with practically no underfur. It lives in extensive underground burrow systems, which it digs with its strong forepaws. Very tolerant of humans, it carries out its routine of searching for seeds, berries and green shoots by day. These squirrels are a social species and greet one another with a brief "kiss" and a flamboyant flick of the tail.

Mating occurs in March or April and litters of 3 or 4 young are born after a gestation of about 4 weeks. In some areas, African ground squirrels are thought to inflict a poisonous bite; the basis for this mistaken belief is that their salivary glands contain streptobacilli, which cause septicaemia.

Thirteen-lined Ground Squirrel

Spermophilus tridecemlineatus

RANGE S.C. Canada, C. USA

HABITAT Short, arid grassland

SIZE Body: 6¾–11½ in (17–29 cm) Tail: 2¼–5½ in (6–14 cm)

These strikingly marked little rodents are active during the day and are often seen in considerable numbers, although their social groups are far looser than those of prairie dogs.

Like other ground squirrels, they have keen eyesight and frequently rear up on their haunches to survey the scene, searching for predators such as hawks, bobcats and foxes. If danger threatens, the squirrels disappear into their burrows. Although some squirrels live among piles of boulders, most dig burrows which vary in size and complexity. Large squirrels may dig tunnels, which are 200 ft (60 m) or more in length, with side chambers. Younger individuals make smaller, shallower burrows. Seeds, nuts, fruit, roots and bulbs form the main bulk of the diet of these squirrels, but they sometimes eat insects, birds' eggs and even mice. In winter, they hibernate, having gained layers of body fat to sustain them through the winter. Their body temperature falls to about 35.6°F (2°C) and their hearts beat only about 5 times a minute, compared to 200 to 500 times in active animals.

After hibernation the squirrels mate; the gestation period is about 4 weeks, and a litter of up to 13 blind, helpless young is born in early summer. The eyes of the young open at about 4 weeks. They are independent of the mother at about 6 weeks.

Black-tailed Prairie Dog *Cynomys ludovicianus*

RANGE C. USA

HABITAT Grassland (prairie)

SIZE Body: 11–12½ in (28–32 cm) Tail: 3¼–3¾ in (8.5–9.5 cm)

The prairie dog derives its common name from its stocky, terrierlike appearance and from its sharp, doglike bark, which it utters to herald danger. One of the most social rodent species, prairie dogs live in burrows called townships, containing several thousands of individuals. They emerge by day to graze on grass and other vegetation and can damage cattle ranges. Feeding is interspersed by socializing, accompanied by chattering.

Females give birth to litters of up to 10 young from March to May, after a 4-week gestation period. After being weaned at 7 weeks, the young disperse to the edge of the township. Prairie dogs are most commonly preyed on by eagles, foxes and coyotes.

Eastern Chipmunk *Tamias striatus*

RANGE S.E. Canada, E. USA

HABITAT Forest

SIZE Body: 5¼–7½ in (13.5–19 cm) Tail: 3–4½ in (7.5–11.5 cm)

The chipmunk is one of the best-known small mammals in North America, for its lack of fear of man and its natural curiosity make it a frequent sight at camping and picnic sites. Chipmunks dig burrows under logs and boulders, emerging in the early morning to forage for acorns, cherry stones, nuts, berries and seeds. Occasionally they are sufficiently numerous to cause damage to crops.

During the autumn chipmunks store food supplies for use during the winter; they do not truly hibernate, but just become somewhat lethargic during winter.

A single litter of up to 8 young is born each spring. Although weaned at 5 weeks, the young stay with their mother for some months. They have a lifespan of about 5 years.

Woodchuck *Marmota monax*

RANGE Alaska, Canada, S. to E. USA

HABITAT Forest

SIZE Body: 17¾–24 in (45–61 cm) Tail: 7–9¾ in (18–25 cm)

The woodchuck, or ground hog as it is called in some regions, is a heavily built, rather belligerent rodent. Woodchucks feed in groups, and, ever fearful of the stealthy approach of a mountain lion or coyote, one member of the group keeps watch while the others search for edible roots, bulbs, tubers and seeds.

The young – 4 or 5 in a litter – are born in late spring and grow very quickly. By autumn they have achieved adult size and are forced away from the parental nest by the aggression of the male. Woodchucks may live for as long as 15 years.

Red Giant Flying Squirrel *Petaurista petaurista*

RANGE Asia: Kashmir to S. China; Sri Lanka, Java, Borneo

HABITAT Dense forest

SIZE Body: 15¾–22¾ in (40–58 cm) Tail: 17–25 in (43–63 cm)

The broad membrane that joins the ankles to the wrists of this handsome creature does not allow true flight, but the squirrel can glide up to 1,500 ft (450 m). Gliding enables the squirrel to move from one tall tree to another without having to descend to the ground each time. By day, these squirrels rest in hollow trees, coming out at dusk to search for nuts, fruit, tender twigs, young leaves and flower buds to eat. They live singly, in pairs or in family groups.

Little is known of the reproductive habits of these squirrels, but they appear to have just 1 or 2 young in each of 2 or 3 litters a year. Because the young are not seen to ride on the mother's back, it is assumed that they are deposited in a safe refuge while the mother feeds. These substantial rodents are hunted by local tribespeople for their flesh.

Northern Flying Squirrel *Glaucomys sabrinus*

RANGE Alaska, Canada, N. and W. USA, Appalachian mountains

HABITAT Forest

SIZE Body: 9¼–10½ in (23.5–27 cm) Tail: 4¼–7 in (11–18 cm)

By stretching out all four limbs when it jumps, the flying squirrel opens its flight membrane, which extends from wrists to ankles, and is able to glide from one tree to another. Speeds of as much as 360 ft/min (110 m/min) may be achieved.

Normally the squirrels forage about in the treetops for nuts, living bark, lichens, fungi, fruit and berries, only taking to the air should an owl or other predator appear. In autumn, stocks of nuts and dried berries are laid up in hollow trees, for the flying squirrels do not hibernate in winter.

At any time from April onward, young are born in a softly lined nest in a hollow tree. There are normally between 2 and 6 young in a litter, and they suckle for about 10 weeks, an unusually long period for small rodents. It is thought that this is because an advanced level of development is necessary before gliding can be attempted.

The northern flying squirrel is threatened in the southernmost parts of its range.

POCKET GOPHERS AND POCKET MICE

GEOMYIDAE: POCKET GOPHER FAMILY

There are some 32 species of pocket gopher distributed throughout North America, from 54° North to Panama and from coast to coast. They spend most of their lives underground, in complex and wide-ranging burrow systems which they dig with their chisellike incisor teeth and strong, broad paws. Gophers occur wherever the soil is soft and supports rich vegetation – roots and tubers form the main diet.

The burrowing activities of these animals tend to be detrimental to grassland and great efforts are made to exterminate pocket gophers, which reproduce at a prodigious rate.

Plains Pocket Gopher *Geomys bursarius*

RANGE	C. USA: Canadian border to S.C. USA
HABITAT	Sandy soil in sparsely wooded areas
SIZE	Body: 7–9½ in (18–24 cm) Tail: 4–5 in (10–12.5 cm)

Pocket gophers get their common name from the two deep, fur-lined cheek pouches, which can be crammed full of food to transport back to the nest. They lead solitary lives, the male leaving its burrow only to find a female during the breeding season. After mating, he returns to his burrow. A litter of 2 or 3 young is born after a gestation of 18 or 19 days. The young are weaned at 28 days but stay in their mother's burrow until they are about 2 months old. They are sexually mature at 3 months.

Although ranchers consider pocket gophers pests, their burrowing does aerate the soil and thus, in the long term, improves the productivity of the pastureland.

Northern Pocket Gopher *Thomomys talpoides*

RANGE	S.W. Canada to Colorado, USA
HABITAT	Grassland and open forest to altitudes of 13,000 ft (4,000 m)
SIZE	Body: 9¾–11¾ in (25–30 cm) Tail: 2¼–3¾ in (6–9.5 cm)

The northern pocket gopher often lives in areas which experience intense winter weather, but it does not hibernate. It builds up huge piles of roots and bulbs in underground larders and survives during the winter on these stores. Pairs mate in early spring. Litters of up to 10 young are born after a gestation of 18 days. Females may mate again almost immediately, giving birth a few days after the first litter is weaned.

HETEROMYIDAE: POCKET MOUSE FAMILY

There are about 60 species of pocket mouse and kangaroo rat, with considerable variations in external appearance. Some are mouselike and live in dense forest, others have long hind legs, bound along like kangaroos and live in deserts and arid plains. They eat seeds, as well as insects and other invertebrates, and have deep, fur-lined cheek pouches in which food can be transported. They are fertile animals, some species producing three or four litters a year. The family occurs in North, Central and South America.

Silky Pocket Mouse *Perognathus flavus*

RANGE	USA: Wyoming, south to Texas; Mexico
HABITAT	Low arid plains
SIZE	Body: 2¾–3½ in (6–9 cm) Tail: 2–4 in (5–10 cm)

The silky pocket mouse has dense, soft fur which it keeps in immaculate condition. Although nocturnal, when it emerges from its burrows the sand is still hot, and to prevent the soles of its feet from burning they are covered by thick pads of soft fur, which also act like snowshoes, spreading the body weight more evenly. It moves on all fours or on its hind legs only.

Breeding seasons are from April to June and August to September, and there are normally 4 young in a litter. They are born deep in the burrow system and first emerge to forage for seeds at about 3 weeks old.

Californian Pocket Mouse *Chaetodipus californicus*

RANGE USA: California; south to Mexico: Baja California

HABITAT Arid sandy plains

SIZE Body: 3–5 in (8–12.5 cm) Tail: 4–5¾ in (10–14.5 cm)

Californian pocket mice dig extensive burrow systems in the sandy soil of their habitat. The entrance is usually sited underneath a small shrub or bush to provide some shade and protection from predators. The mice feed largely on seeds, transporting them back to the burrow in their cheek pouches. They also eat green plants on occasion. Their bodies are adapted to survive without drinking. The breeding season lasts from April to September, but there is a marked decline in activity during the hottest part of the summer. Up to 7 young are born in each litter, after a gestation of about 25 days.

Pale Kangaroo-mouse *Microdipodops pallidus*

RANGE USA: W. C. Nevada

HABITAT Wind-swept sand-dunes

SIZE Body: 2½–3¼ in (6.5–8 cm) Tail: 2½–4 in (6.5–10 cm)

This rodent covers great distances in order to find food in its barren habitat. It has powerful hind legs for bounding, with broad flat feet, fringed with stiff hairs. As the mouse hops, its long tail is used as a counterbalance and gives it the appearance of a small kangaroo.

Kangaroo-mice are long-lived and breed more slowly than other members of their family. In particularly hot, dry summers, they do not breed at all.

Desert Kangaroo-rat *Dipodomys deserti*

RANGE USA: Nevada, south to Mexico

HABITAT Arid brush and grassland

SIZE Body: 12–15 in (10–20 cm)
Tail: 7–8½ in (18–21.5 cm)

Desert kangaroo-rats dig their burrows in well-drained, easily

dug soils. They are nocturnal and travel great distances in search of food. Since their kidneys are four times more efficient than a human's, they can live their whole lives without ever drinking.

Breeding occurs in any month of the year. Litters of up to 5 young are born after a gestation period of about 30 days.

Mexican Spiny Pocket Mouse *Liomys irroratus*

RANGE USA: S.W. tip of Texas; Mexico

HABITAT Arid woodland

SIZE Body: 4–5¼ in (10–13.5 cm) Tail: 3¾–6¾ in (9.5–17 cm)

The coat of the Mexican spiny pocket mouse bears stiff, grooved hairs, which form a protective shield around the body, helping to deter some of its predators.

This mouse prefers lush, succulent vegetation to eat, but it also forages for seeds and roots, which it carries back to its burrow in its cheek pouches.

Breeding takes place at any time of year, and litters usually contain about 4 young.

Forest Spiny Pocket Mouse

Heteromys anomalus

RANGE Colombia, Venezuela; Trinidad

HABITAT Tropical rain forest

SIZE Body: 5–6¼ in (12.5–16 cm)
Tail: 5–7¾ in (13–20 cm)

This shy, nocturnal rodent lives in burrows on the forest floor. It collects seeds, buds, fruit, leaves and shoots and carries them back to its burrows for eating.

Litters of about 4 young are born at any time of the year, but mostly in spring and early summer.

MOUNTAIN BEAVER, BEAVERS, SPRINGHARE, AND SCALY-TAILED SQUIRRELS

APLODONTIDAE: MOUNTAIN BEAVER FAMILY

This rodent family contains a single species, the mountain beaver. Its common name is particularly inappropriate because this heavy-bodied, burrowing animal is neither a beaver nor associated with high country. Indeed, its ancestry and evolution are poorly understood despite the fact that the fossil record suggests that the family is an ancient one.

Mountain Beaver/Aplodontia *Aplodontia rufa*

RANGE N.W. USA

HABITAT Moist forest

SIZE Body: 11¾–17 in (30–43 cm) Tail: 1 in (2.5 cm)

The mountain beaver is a solitary creature, and each adult digs its own burrow system of underground nest and tunnels. Although it climbs poorly, rarely going up trees, almost any plant material, including bark and twigs, is eaten by the mountain beaver, and it makes stores of food to keep it going through the winter months.

In spring, beavers produce a litter of 2 or 3 young, which are born in a nest lined with dry vegetation.

CASTORIDAE: BEAVER FAMILY

The 2 species of beaver both lead semiaquatic lives and are excellent swimmers. Their hind feet are webbed and they have broad, flat, hairless tails. Males and females look alike, but males tend to have larger anal scent glands. These glands produce a musky-smelling secretion, which is probably used for marking territory boundaries.

Beavers are always found near waterways surrounded by dense growths of trees, such as willow, poplar, alder and birch. They feed on the bark, twigs, roots and leaves of these trees and use their enormous incisor teeth to fell trees for use in the construction of their complex dams and lodges.

Beavers make dams to create their desired living conditions. A pair starts by damming a stream with branches and mud to create a lake, deep enough not to freeze to the bottom in winter, in which to hoard a winter food supply of branches. A shelter with sleeping quarters is made of branches, by the dam or on an island or bank, or a burrow is dug in the river bank. When beavers have felled all the available trees in their territory, they dig canals into the woods to float back trees from farther afield. Most of the beavers' activity takes place at night.

American Beaver *Castor canadensis*

RANGE N. America: Alaska to Texas

HABITAT Rivers, lakes, with wooded banks

SIZE Body: 28¾ in–4¼ ft (73 cm–1.3 m) Tail: 8¼–11¾ in (21–30 cm)

One of the largest rodents, the American beaver weighs up to 60 lb (27 kg) or more. It is well adapted for its aquatic habits: the dense fur provides both waterproofing and insulation and its ears and nostrils can be closed off by special muscles when it is under water allowing it to stay submerged for up to 15 minutes.

A beaver colony normally consists of an adult pair and their young of the present and previous years. Two-year-old young are driven out to form their own colonies. Autumn is a busy time for the beavers, when they must make repairs to the lodge and dam and stockpile food for the winter. They mate in midwinter and the young, usually 2 to 4, are born in the spring. The young are well developed at birth and are able to swim and feed themselves after about a month.

Eurasian Beaver *Castor fiber* **LR:nt**

RANGE Now only in parts of Europe, Russia and China

HABITAT Rivers, lakes, with wooded banks

SIZE Body: 28¾ in–4¼ ft (73 cm–1.3 m) Tail: 8¼–11¾ in (21–30 cm)

The largest European rodent, this beaver has the same habits and much the same appearance as the American beaver, and they are considered by some experts to be one species. Like its American counterpart, this beaver builds complex dams and lodges but, where conditions are right, may simply dig a burrow in the river bank which it enters under water. It feeds on bark and twigs in the winter and on all kinds of vegetation in summer.

Females are thought to mate for life, but the male in a pair may mate with other females. Litters of up to 8 (usually 2 to 4) young are born in spring.

PEDETIDAE: SPRINGHARE FAMILY

This African rodent family contains a single species, the springhare. Its forelegs are short but the hind legs are relatively long and powerful, and it leaps along in hops of at least 10 ft (3 m). The long bushy tail acts as a counterbalance.

Springhare *Pedetes capensis* **VU**

RANGE Kenya to South Africa

HABITAT Dry open country

SIZE 13¾–17 in (35–43 cm) Tail: 14½–18½ in (37–47 cm)

When alarmed or traveling distances, springhares bound along like kangaroos, but when feeding, they move on all fours. A nocturnal animal as a rule, the springhare spends the day in its burrow. It feeds on bulbs, roots, grain and sometimes insects. Several burrows occur together, some occupied by individuals, others by families. There is probably only one litter a year of 1 or 2 young.

ANOMALURIDAE: SCALY-TAILED SQUIRREL FAMILY

The 7 species of scaly-tailed squirrel are all tree-dwelling rodents found in the forests of west and central Africa. Apart from a single "non-flying" species, they all have broad membranes at the sides of the body which can be stretched out to allow the animal to glide through the air. Scaly-tailed squirrels are not closely related to true squirrels (*Sciuridae*).

Beecroft's Flying Squirrel

Anomalurus beecrofti

RANGE W. and C. Africa

HABITAT Forest

SIZE Body: 11¾–16 in (30–40.5 cm)
Tail: 9–17 in (23–43 cm)

Beecroft's flying squirrel travels from tree to tree, rarely descending to the ground. With flight membranes extended, it leaps off one branch and glides up to 300 ft (90 m), to land on another tree. It finds all its food up in the trees and feeds on berries, seeds and fruit, as well as on some green plant material. Most of its activity takes place at night. These rodents generally live singly or in pairs and make dens in tree holes. They produce two litters a year of 2 or 3 young each.

Zenker's Flying Squirrel *Idiurus zenkeri* **LR:nt**

RANGE Cameroon, Zaire

HABITAT Forest

SIZE Body: 2¼–4 in (6–10 cm) Tail: 3–5 in (7.5–13 cm)

This small flying squirrel has an unusual tail with long hairs projecting from each side, giving it a feathery appearance. Like its relatives, Zenker's squirrel is mainly nocturnal and feeds on berries, seeds and fruit. A gregarious species, it lives in holes in trees in groups of up to a dozen.

NEW WORLD RATS AND MICE

SIGMODONTINAE: NEW WORLD RATS AND MICE SUBFAMILY

This is one of the 17 subfamilies of the huge rodent family Muridae which contains rats, mice, voles, gerbils, hamsters and others. There are about 400 species in this subfamily. Members occur in all habitats, from deserts to humid forests. These undistinguished but abundant little rodents are of immense importance as the primary consumers in their range and occupy a basic position in a number of food chains.

Baja California Rice Rat *Oryzomys peninsulae*

RANGE Mexico: tip of Baja California

HABITAT Damp land in dense cover

SIZE Body: 9–13 in (22.5–33 cm) Tail: 4¼–7 in (11–18 cm)

There are about 50 species of rice rat, all looking much like the Baja California species and leading similar lives. They feed mostly on green vegetation, such as reeds and sedges, but also eat fish and invertebrates. They can become serious pests in rice fields and can cause severe damage to the plants. They weave grassy nests on reed platforms above water level or, in drier habitats, excavate burrows in which they breed throughout the year, producing up to 7 young in each litter.

Spiny Rice Rat *Neacomys guianae*

RANGE Colombia, east to Guyana

HABITAT Dense humid forest

SIZE Body: 2¾–4 in (7–10 cm)
Tail: 2¾–4 in (7–10 cm)

This species is distinguished by the spiny coat, which grows thickly on the rat's back, but sparsely on its flanks. Little is known of these rodents, which live on the floors of the most impenetrable forests, but it is believed that they probably breed the year round, producing litters of 2 to 4 young.

American Climbing Mouse *Rhipidomys venezuelae*

RANGE W. Venezuela

HABITAT Dense forest

SIZE Body: 3¼–6 in (8–15 cm) Tail: 7–9¾ in (18–25 cm)

This secretive, nocturnal mouse lives in the deepest forest. Although it makes its nest in a burrow beneath the roots of a tree, it spends much of its life high in the treetops, feeding on lichens, small invertebrates and plants such as bromeliads. Equipped with strong, broad feet and long, sharp claws, it is an agile climber, and its long tail acts as a counterbalance when it jumps from one branch to the next. Climbing mice breed throughout the year, and the usual litter is 2 to 5 young.

Western Harvest Mouse *Reithrodontomys megalotis*

RANGE USA: Oregon, south to Panama

HABITAT Grassland

SIZE Body: 2–5½ in (5–14 cm) Tail: 2¼–3½ in (6–9 cm)

Harvest mice tend to prefer overgrown pastures to cultivated farmland. In summer, they weave globular nests, up to 7 in (17.5 cm) in diameter, attached to stalks of vegetation.

Litters of about 4 young are born in these nests after a gestation period of about 23 days.

Deer Mouse *Peromyscus maniculatus*

RANGE Canada to Mexico

HABITAT Forest, grassland, scrub

SIZE Body: 4¾–8½ in (12–22 cm)
Tail: 3¼–7 in (8–18 cm)

Deer mice are agile, running and hopping with ease through dense bush. They construct underground nests of dry vegetation and may move house several times a year. They have a catholic diet, consisting almost equally of plant and animal matter. Young deer mice start to breed at 7 weeks, and litters of up to 9 young are born after a gestation of between 3 and 4 weeks.

Golden Mouse
Ochrotomys nuttalli

RANGE S.E. USA

HABITAT Brushy and thicketed scrub

SIZE Body: 3¼–3¾ in (8–9.5 cm) Tail: 2¾–3¾ in (7–9.5 cm)

The golden mouse spends most of its life among the vines of wild honeysuckle and greenbrier. It weaves a nest, which may hold a family or a single mouse. It also builds rough feeding platforms, where it sits to eat seeds and nuts. Golden mice breed from spring to early autumn. The gestation period is about 4 weeks, and there are usually 2 or 3 young in a litter.

Northern Grasshopper Mouse *Onychomys leucogaster*

RANGE S. Canada to N. Mexico

HABITAT Semiarid scrub and desert

SIZE Body: 3½–5 in (9–13 cm) Tail: 1¼–2¼ in (3–6 cm)

This mouse is largely carnivorous. Grasshoppers and scorpions are its main prey, but it may even eat its own kind. These mice nest in burrows, which they dig themselves or find abandoned, and breed in spring and summer, producing litters of 2 to 6 young after a 33-day gestation.

South American Field Mouse *Akodon reinhardti*

RANGE Brazil

HABITAT Woodland, cultivated land

SIZE Body: 4½–5¾ in (11.5–14.5 cm) Tail: 2–4 in (5–10 cm)

There are about 43 species of South American field mice. They are active day and night, although most above-ground activity takes place at night. They feed on a wide range of plant matter. Usually two litters are produced each year, in November and March, with up to 7 young in each. The pregnant and nursing females use special breeding chambers situated in the burrows.

Arizona Cotton Rat *Sigmodon arizonae* **EN**

RANGE USA: S.E. California, Arizona, south to Mexico

HABITAT Dry grassland

SIZE 5–7¾ in (12.5–20 cm) Tail: 3–5 in (7.5–12.5 cm)

Cotton rats are so abundant that they are sometimes declared a plague. They normally feed on plants and small insects, but when populations are high they take the eggs and chicks of bobwhite quail as well as crayfish and fiddler crabs. The female produces her first litter of up to 12 young when just 10 weeks old. This species is now endangered because of the destruction of its habitat.

White-throated Woodrat *Neotoma albigula*

RANGE USA: California to Texas, south to Mexico

HABITAT Scrub, lightly forested land

SIZE Body: 11–15¾ in (28–40 cm) Tail: 3–7¼ in (7.5–18.5 cm)

A group of up to 100 of these rats will build a nest up to 6½ ft (2 m) across from any readily available material, usually in a pile of rocks or at the base of a tree. The rats forage for shoots, fruit and other plant food. Litters contain between 1 and 4 young.

Fish-eating Rat *Ichthyomys stolzmanni*

RANGE E. Ecuador, Peru

HABITAT Near rivers and lakes

SIZE Body: 5¾–8¼ in (14.5–21 cm) Tail: 5¾–7½ in (14.5–19 cm)

Fish-eating rats have partially webbed feet and swim strongly. The upper incisor teeth are simple, spikelike structures, used to spear fish, which is then dragged ashore for consumption. The rats produce one or two litters of young each year.

HAMSTERS AND MOLE-RATS

CRICETINAE: HAMSTER SUBFAMILY

The true hamsters are small burrowing rodents, found in the Old World from Europe eastward through the Middle East and central Asia. There are 18 species known, all of which are characterized by a body shape similar to that of a thickset rat with a short tail.

All species have capacious cheek pouches, which are used for carrying food back to the burrow. When full, the cheek pouches may extend back beyond the level of the shoulder blades.

Common Hamster *Cricetus cricetus*

RANGE W. Europe to C. Russia

HABITAT Grassland, cultivated land

SIZE Body: 8½–11¾ in (22–30 cm) Tail: 1¼–2¼ in (3–6 cm)

The common hamster occupies a burrow system with separate chambers for sleeping and food storage. It feeds on seeds, grain, roots, potatoes, green plants and insect larvae. In late summer it collects food for its winter stores. Grain is a particularly favoured food source, and up to 22 lb (10 kg) may be hoarded. From October to March or April, the hamster hibernates, waking periodically in order to feed on its stores.

During the summer, females usually produce two litters, each of 6 to 12 young, which themselves bear young when they are just 2 months old.

Golden Hamster *Mesocricetus auratus* **EN**

RANGE N.W. Syria

HABITAT Steppe

SIZE Body: 6¾–7 in (17–18 cm) Tail: ½ in (1.25 cm)

Golden hamsters are primarily nocturnal creatures, but they may be active at times during the day. Adults live alone in burrow systems which they dig for themselves. They are omnivorous, feeding on

vegetation seeds, fruit and even small animals. Their cheek pouches are large and, when filled are double the width of the animal's head and shoulders.

Golden hamsters are highly aggressive and solitary creatures, and females must advertise clearly when they are sexually receptive. They do this by applying a specific vaginal secretion to rocks and sticks in their territories, and cease to mark as soon as the receptive phase of the estrous cycle is over. The usual litter contains 6 or 7 young, and there may be several litters a year.

The domesticated strain of the species makes a popular pet.

Dwarf Hamster *Phodopus sungorus*

RANGE Kazakstan, Mongolia, N. China

HABITAT Arid plains, sand dunes

SIZE Body: 2–4 in (5–10 cm) Tail: absent

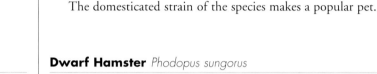

This small, yet robust, hamster is active at night and at dawn and dusk. Little is known about it, but its habits seem to be similar to those of other hamsters. It feeds on seeds and plant material and fills its cheek pouches with food supplies to carry back to its burrow.

Dwarf hamsters are more sociable than their golden cousins and may occur in quite large colonies. They are so well adapted to their cool habitat that they do not breed well at room temperature. Litters usually contain 2 to 6 young, which are weaned at 21 days. Females mate again immediately after giving birth, so they can produce litters at three-weekly intervals.

SPALACINAE: BLIND MOLE-RAT SUBFAMILY

This small subfamily of highly specialized burrowing rodents probably contains only the 8 species found in the eastern Mediterranean area, the Middle East, Ukraine and northern Africa. They are heavy-bodied rodents, with short legs, small feet and a remarkable absence of external projections – there is no tail, external ears are not apparent, and there are no external openings for the tiny eyes that lie buried under the skin.

Lesser Mole-rat *Spalax leucodon* **VU**

RANGE S.E. Europe; Ukraine, Turkey

HABITAT Grassland and cultivated land

SIZE Body: 6–12 in (15–30.5 cm) Tail: absent

Mole-rats live in complex burrow systems, with many chambers and connecting tunnels, which they dig with their teeth and heads, rather than with their feet. They feed underground on roots, bulbs and tubers but may occasionally venture above ground at night to feed on grasses, seeds and even insects.

One litter of 2 to 4 young is born in early spring, after a gestation of about 4 weeks.

MYOSPALACINAE: EASTERN ASIATIC MOLE-RAT SUBFAMILY

There are 6 species in this subfamily, found in Russia and China. These mole-rats are stocky, burrowing rodents, well equipped with heavily clawed limbs for digging. They do not have external ears, but their tiny eyes are apparent, and there is a short, tapering tail.

Common Chinese Zokor *Myospalax fontanierii* **VU**

RANGE China: Szechuan to Hopei Provinces

HABITAT Grassland, steppe

SIZE Body: 6–10½ in (15–27 cm) Tail: 1¼–2¾ in (3–7 cm)

The zokor lives in long burrows, which it digs with amazing speed among the roots of trees and bushes, using its long, sharp claws. As it goes, it leaves behind a trail of "mole hills" on the surface. Grain, roots and other underground parts of plants form the main part of its diet.

The zokor ventures above ground only occasionally at night, because it runs the risk of being caught by an owl.

RHYZOMYINAE: MOLE AND BAMBOO RAT SUBFAMILY

There are 6 species in this subfamily, which fall into two closely related groups – 2 species of East African mole-rats and 4 species of Southeast Asian bamboo rats. All species are plant-eating, burrowing rodents.

Giant Mole-rat *Tachyoryctes macrocephalus*

RANGE Africa: Ethiopia

HABITAT Montane grassland

SIZE Body: 7–10 in (18–25.5 cm) Tail: 2–3 in (5–8 cm)

The giant mole-rat has a stout, molelike body and small, yet functional eyes. It is a powerful burrower, equipped with short, strong limbs and claws. When a pile of soil has built up behind it, the animal turns and pushes the soil to the surface with the side of its head and one forefoot.

It is active both during the day and at night and feeds on plant material both above and below ground. Surprisingly for such a common species, nothing is known of the breeding habits of this mole-rat.

Bamboo Rat *Rhizomys sumatrensis*

RANGE Indo-China, Malaysia, Sumatra, Thailand, Myanmar

HABITAT Bamboo forest

SIZE Body: 13¾–18¾ in (35–48 cm) Tail: 4–6 in (10–15 cm)

The bamboo rat has a heavy body, short legs and a short, almost hairless tail. Its incisor teeth are large and strong, and it uses these and its claws for digging. It burrows underground near clumps of bamboo, the roots of which are its staple diet. It also leaves its burrow to feed on bamboo, plants, seeds and fruit.

The usual litter is believed to contain between 3 and 5 young, and there may be more than one litter a year.

CRESTED RAT, SPINY DORMICE AND RELATIVES

LOPHIOMYINAE: CRESTED RAT SUBFAMILY

A single species is known in this group – the crested or maned rat is found in dense mountain forests in East Africa. The animal's general appearance is not at all ratlike, for it is about the size of a guinea pig and has long, soft fur and a thick, bushy tail. The female is generally larger than the male.

Crested Rat *Lophiomys imhausi*

RANGE E. Africa

HABITAT Forest

SIZE Body: 10–14¼ in (25.5–36 cm)
Tail: 5½–7 in (14–18 cm)

Crested rats are skilled climbers, leaving their daytime burrows at night to collect leaves, buds and shoots among the trees.

Along the neck, back and part of the tail is a prominent mane of coarse hairs which can be erected when the animal is excited or alarmed. The raised crest exposes a long scent gland running down the back, which produces a stifling odor to deter predators. The hairs lining the gland have a unique, wicklike structure to help broadcast the odor.

Another curious feature of these rodents is the reinforced skull, the significance of which is not known.

NESOMYINAE: MADAGASCAN RAT SUBFAMILY

This subfamily includes 11 species, of which 10 are found only in Madagascar and 1 occurs in South Africa. It is a varied group, and the species seem to have become adapted to fill different ecological niches, although they share some common features.

It has been suggested of this subfamily, however, that they are not all of common ancestry and that a considerable amount of evolutionary convergence has occurred.

Madagascan Rat *Nesomys rufus*

RANGE Madagascar

HABITAT Forest

SIZE Body: 7½–9 in (19–23 cm) Tail: 6¼–7½ in (16–19 cm)

This species of Madagascan rat is mouselike in appearance, with long, soft fur and a light-colored belly. Its hind feet are long and powerful, and the middle three toes are elongated. It seems likely that the Madagascan rat is an adept climber, using its sharp claws to grip smooth bark.

Although little is known of this creature's habits, it is probable that its diet is made up of small invertebrates, buds, fruit and seeds. Nothing is known of its breeding cycle.

White-tailed Rat *Mystomys albicaudatus*

RANGE South Africa

HABITAT Grassland, arid plains

SIZE Body: 5½–7 in (14–18 cm) Tail: 2–3 in (5–8 cm)

The white-tailed rat is the only member of its group to occur outside Madagascar. It is a nocturnal creature and spends the day in an underground hole, emerging at dusk to feed on seeds and other plant material. It is said that the strong smell of these rodents repels mammalian predators, such as suricates and mongooses, but they are caught by barn, eagle and grass owls.

White-tailed rats appear to breed throughout the year, producing litters of 4 or 5 young. A curious feature of the early development of these rats is that the young become firmly attached to the female's nipples and are carried about by her. They only detach themselves when about 3 weeks old.

PLATACANTHOMYINAE: SPINY DORMOUSE SUBFAMILY

There are 2 species in this subfamily. Their common name originates from the flat, pointed spines that are intermixed with the fur, particularly on the back.

Spiny dormice are well adapted for tree-climbing, for their feet are equipped with sharp claws and padded soles, and the digits spread widely.

Malabar Spiny Dormouse *Platacanthomys lasiurus*

RANGE S. India

HABITAT Forest, rocks

SIZE Body: 5–8¼ in (13–21 cm) Tail: 3–4 in (7.5–10 cm)

The Malabar spiny dormouse lives in trees and feeds on seeds, grain and fruit. The long tail, with its dense, bushy tip, is used as a balancing aid when the animal is moving in trees. A nest of leaves and moss is made for shelter in a hole in a tree or among rocks.

This rodent sometimes becomes an agricultural pest because of its diet, and it has been known to destroy quantities of crops such as ripe peppers.

Although spiny dormice are not uncommon, nothing is known of the breeding habits of these secretive rodents. The other species of the subfamily, the Chinese pygmy dormouse, *Typhlomys cinereus*, lives in forest in southeast China.

OTOMYINAE: AFRICAN SWAMP RAT SUBFAMILY

There are about 11 species in this group, all found in Africa, south of the Sahara to Cape Province. They inhabit a wide variety of habitats and climatic zones, including mountains, arid regions and swampy areas. All members of the subfamily are competent swimmers.

A characteristic of the group is that the members have only two pairs of mammary glands, situated in the lower abdomen.

Swamp Rat *Otomys irroratus*

RANGE Zimbabwe to South Africa

HABITAT Damp grassland, swamps

SIZE 5–7¾ in (13–20 cm) Tail: 2–6¾ in (5–17 cm)

A plump-bodied rodent, the African swamp rat has a rounded, volelike head and small ears. Characteristic features are the grooves on each side of the incisor teeth.

Active day and night, this rat feeds on seeds, berries, shoots and grasses. It will enter water readily and even dive to escape danger. Its nest is usually above ground and is made of plant material, although in some areas swamp rats make use of burrows discarded by other species.

Young females reach sexual maturity at 10 weeks of age, males about 3 weeks later. Although swamp rats seldom damage man's crops, their parasites do transmit tick-bite fever and possibly bubonic plague. Swamp rats are an important food source for many larger predators.

Karroo Rat *Parotomys brantsii*

RANGE South Africa: Cape Province

HABITAT Sandy plains

SIZE Body: 5¼–6¾ in (13.5–17 cm) Tail: 3–4¾ in (7.5–12 cm)

Karroo rats are gregarious animals which live in colonies. They dig burrows and sometimes also build nests of sticks and grass above the burrows. They are nervous, wary animals and stay near their shelters most of the time.

Leaves of the saltbush tree provide the bulk of their diet, and they generally feed during the day. Every 3 or 4 years, their population increases dramatically, and they feed on agricultural crops, causing considerable damage.

Karroo rats are believed to breed about four times a year, producing litters of 2 to 4 young.

VOLES AND LEMMINGS

ARVICOLINAE: VOLE AND LEMMING SUBFAMILY

There are about 120 species in this group of rodents, found in North America, northern Europe and Asia; lemmings tend to be confined to the more northerly regions. All species are largely herbivorous and they usually live in groups or colonies. Many dig shallow tunnels, close to the ground surface, and clear paths through the grass within their range. Others are partly aquatic and some species climb among low bushes.

Local populations of voles and lemmings are subject to cyclical variation in density, with boom years of greatly increased population occurring every few years.

surface, where they keep the grass cut and trimmed; little piles of cuttings punctuate these runways. Bog lemmings are active day and night. They have powerful jaws and teeth and feed largely on plant material.

Breeding continues throughout the spring and summer, and females produce two or three litters a year of 1 to 4 young each.

Norway Lemming
Lemmus lemmus

RANGE Scandinavia

HABITAT Tundra, grassland

SIZE Body: 5–6 in (13–15 cm) Tail: ¾ in (2 cm)

The boldly patterned Norway lemming is active day and night, alternating periods of activity with short spells of rest. Grasses, shrubs and particularly mosses make up its diet; in winter it clears runways under the snow on the ground surface in its search for food. These lemmings start to breed in spring, under the snow, and may produce as many as eight litters of 6 young each throughout the summer.

Dramatic population explosions occur every three or four years or so. It is not known what causes these, but a fine, warm spring following two or three years of low population usually triggers an explosion that year or the next. As populations swell, lemmings are forced into surrounding areas. More and more are driven out. Many are eaten by predators, and more lose their lives crossing rivers and lakes, but they do not "commit suicide".

Southern Bog Lemming *Synaptomys cooperi*

RANGE N.E. USA; S.E. Canada

HABITAT Bogs, meadows

SIZE Body: 3¼–4¼ in (8.5–11 cm) Tail: ¾ in (2 cm)

Sociable animals, southern bog lemmings live in colonies of up to about 30 or so. They make burrows just under the ground surface and also clear a network of paths, or runways, on the

Sagebrush Vole *Lemmiscus curtatus*

RANGE W. USA

HABITAT Arid plains

SIZE Body: 3¾–4¼ in (9.5–11 cm) Tail: ½–1¼ in (1.5–3 cm)

As its common name suggests, this pale-colored vole is particularly common in some areas of arid plains where the sagebrush is abundant. It makes shallow burrows near the ground surface and is active at any time of the day and night. This vole feeds on the sagebrush, after which it was named, and on other green vegetation and produces several litters a year of 4 to 6 young each.

Southern Mole-vole *Ellobius fuscocapillus*

RANGE C. Asia

HABITAT Grassy plains

SIZE Body: 4–6 in (10–15 cm) Tail: ¼–¾ in (0.5–2 cm)

The mole-vole is a more habitual burrower than other voles and lemmings and is more specifically adapted for underground life. Its snout is blunt, its eyes and ears small to minimize damage from the soil, and it has short, strong legs. It probably uses its teeth to loosen the soil when burrowing, for while its incisors are stronger than is usual in

voles, its claws, although adequate, are not as strong as those of other burrowing rodents.

Mole-voles feed on roots and other underground parts of plants. Like moles, they make shallow tunnels in which to search for food and deeper, more permanent tunnels for nesting. They breed at any time of year (the timing is probably dictated by the availability of food) and produce 3 or 4 young in each litter.

Bank Vole *Clethrionomys glareolus*

RANGE Europe (not extreme north or south), east to C. Asia

HABITAT Woodland

SIZE Body: 3¼–4¼ in (8–11 cm) Tail: 1¼–2½ in (3–6.5 cm)

The bank vole feeds on softer plant material than most voles. It will climb on bushes to find its food, eating buds, leaves and fruit, as well as some insects. It is active night and day,  with several rest periods, and, like other voles, it clears well-defined runways in the grass and makes shallow tunnels. Nests are usually made under logs or among treeroots, and in summer females produce several litters of 3 to 5 young each.

Meadow Vole *Microtus pennsylvanicus*

RANGE Canada, N. and W. USA, N. Mexico

HABITAT Grassland, woodland, often near water

SIZE Body: 3½–5 in (9–12.5 cm) Tail: 1¼–2½ in (3.5–6.5 cm)

The meadow vole is a highly adaptable species. It is found in a wide range of habitats. It is a social animal, but each adult has its own territory. The voles move along runways which they clear in the grass and keep trimmed. They feed on plant material, such as grass, seeds, roots and bark. A nest of grass is made in the ground or in a shallow burrow under the runways.

The female is a prolific breeder, producing at least three and often as many as twelve or thirteen litters a year of up to 10 young each. The gestation period is 3 weeks, and females start to breed at only 3 weeks old.

Muskrat *Ondatra zibethicus*

RANGE Canada, USA; introduced in Europe

HABITAT Marshes, freshwater banks

SIZE Body: 9¾–14¼ in (25–36 cm) Tail: 7¾–11 in (20–28 cm)

The muskrat is an excellent swimmer and in fact this large rodent spends much of its life in water. It has webbed hind feet and a long, naked, vertically flattened tail which it uses as a rudder. It feeds on aquatic and land vegetation and occasionally on some mussels, frogs and fish. It usually digs a burrow in the bank of a river, but where conditions permit, it builds a lodge from plant debris in shallow water and inside it constructs a dry sleeping platform above water level. The lodge may shelter as many as 10 animals.

At the onset of the breeding season, the muskrats' groin glands enlarge and produce a musky secretion, believed to attract male and female to one another. They breed from April to August in the north, and throughout the winter in the south of their range. Two or three litters of 3 or 4 young are born after a gestation of 29 or 30 days.

European Water Vole *Arvicola terrestris*

RANGE Europe, east to E. Siberia and Mongolia

HABITAT Freshwater banks, grassland

SIZE Body: 5½–7½ in (14–19 cm) Tail: 1½–4 in (4–10 cm)

Although competent in water, the European water vole is less agile than the more specialized muskrats and beavers. It makes a burrow in the bank of a river or stream or burrows into the ground, if far from water. Grasses and other plant material are its main food. Water voles breed in summer, producing several litters of 4 to 6 young.

GERBILS

GERBILLINAE: GERBIL SUBFAMILY

There are some 87 or so members of this subfamily of rodents, all of which come from central and western Asia and Africa. They are all well adapted for arid conditions and many occur only in apparently inhospitable deserts. Chief among their adaptations is a wonderfully efficient kidney, which produces urine several times more concentrated than in most rodents, thus conserving moisture. Water loss from the lungs is a major problem for desert-dwelling animals, and all gerbils have specialized nose bones which act to condense water vapour from the air before it is expired. This essential water is then reabsorbed into the system.

To keep their bodies as far as possible from the burning sand, gerbils have long hind legs and feet, the soles of which are insulated with dense pads of fur. Their bellies are pure white in order to reflect radiated heat. Finally, gerbils adapt to desert life by being strictly nocturnal, never emerging from their burrows until the heat of the day has passed.

Gerbils are all seed-eaters and make large stores of food during the brief periods when the desert blooms. Gerbils never occur in great densities, although they are abundant enough to be an important source of food for predators such as fennec foxes and snakes.

Large North African Gerbil *Gerbillus campestris*

RANGE Africa: Morocco to Somalia

HABITAT Sandy desert

SIZE Body: 4–5½ in (10–14 cm)
Tail: 4¼–4¾ in (11–12 cm)

There are about 35 species in the genus *Gerbillus*, all found from Morocco eastward to Pakistan. All occupy the driest deserts and eke out their existence in the most inhospitable environments. The large North African gerbil occurs in groups of 12 or more, living in simple, poorly made burrows, dug in the sand. The gerbils remain hidden by day, emerging at dusk to search for insects, seeds and windblown vegetation. They never drink, but derive all the water they need from the fats contained in seeds. This gerbil breeds throughout the year, producing litters of up to 7 young after a gestation of 20 or 21 days.

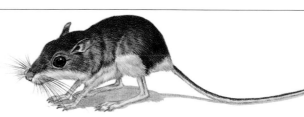

South African Pygmy Gerbil *Gerbillurus paeba*

RANGE S. Africa: S.W. Angola to Cape Province

HABITAT Desert

SIZE Body: 3½–4¾ in (9–12 cm) Tail: 3¾–6 in (9.5–15 cm)

Of the 4 species of pygmy gerbil which are found in the southwestern corner of Africa, *Gerbillurus paeba* appears to be the most widespread.

It constructs simple burrows in sandy or gravelly soil, usually with one entrance higher than the other to improve ventilation. Pygmy gerbils feed on whatever plant and animal food is available. When the desert plants bloom, the gerbils lay in stores of seeds and fruit in underground larders.

They usually breed about twice a year, but in times of abundant food supplies may breed up to four times in a year. The young are fed by their mother for up to a month.

Greater Short-tailed Gerbil *Dipodillus maghrebi*

RANGE Africa: N. Morocco

HABITAT Upland, arid semidesert

SIZE Body: 3½–5 in (9–12.5 cm)
Tail: 2½–2¾ in (6.5–7 cm)

Among the many gerbil species in North Africa, the greater short-tailed gerbil occupies a specific and specialized ecological niche. It inhabits the foothills and mid-regions of the Atlas mountains and lives among boulder fields and rock scree. Like all gerbils, it is an active animal, emerging at night to forage among the sparse vegetation for seeds, buds and insects. It may have to travel considerable distances each night to find food.

The female gives birth to a litter of about 6 young in undeground brood chambers.

Great Gerbil *Rhombomys opimus*

RANGE Iran, east to Mongolia and China

HABITAT Arid scrubland

SIZE Body: 6¼–7¾ in (16–20 cm)
Tail: 5–6¼ in (13–16 cm)

The great gerbil occupies a wide range of habitats, from the cold central Asiatic mountains to the Gobi desert, with its high summer temperatures. It is an adaptable animal, which changes its behavior to suit its environment. In winter, its activity is in inverse proportion to the depth of snow, and in some colonies the gerbils come to the surface only rarely. Large colonies can do much damage to crops and irrigation channels and great gerbils are considered pests in parts of central Asia.

They are herbivorous animals and build up stores of 130 lb (60 kg) or more of plant material in their burrows on which to live in winter. During the winter, huge numbers of these gerbils are preyed on by owls, stoats, mink and foxes. In spring, however, their rapid breeding soon replenishes the colonies.

Indian Gerbil *Tatera indica*

RANGE W. India, Sri Lanka

HABITAT Plains, savanna, arid woodland

SIZE Body: 6–7½ in (15–19 cm) Tail: 7¾–9¾ in (20–25 cm)

The Indian gerbil is a sociable animal, living communally in deep burrow systems with many entrances. Often these entrances are loosely blocked with soil to discourage the entry of predatory snakes and mongooses. Sometimes the populations of this species increase to such an extent that the animals leave their normal habitat and invade fields and gardens in search of bulbs, roots, green vegetation, insects and even eggs and young birds.

Indian gerbils breed throughout the year, producing litters of up to 8 young. It is thought that these animals are a reservoir of bubonic plague.

Fat-tailed Gerbil *Pachyuromys duprasi*

RANGE Africa: Algerian Sahara to S.W. Egypt

HABITAT Sandy desert

SIZE Body: 4¼–5¼ in (10.5–14 cm) Tail: 1¾–2¼ in (4.5–6 cm)

This little gerbil derives its name from its habit of storing fat in its stubby tail. During periods when food is abundant, the tail enlarges in size and may even become too fat to be carried. In lean times, the fat is used up and the tail decreases again. These gerbils spend their days in underground burrows, emerging at night to search for whatever seeds and grubs they can find in the scant vegetation. They have enormous ear bones and very acute hearing, which may help them to locate underground insects. Litters of about 6 young are produced throughout the year and the gestation period is 19 to 22 days. The young gerbils are independent at about 5 weeks old.

Fat Sand Rat *Psammomys obesus*

RANGE Libya, east to Saudi Arabia

HABITAT Sandy desert

SIZE Body: 5½–7¼ in (14–18.5 cm) Tail: 4¾–6 in (12–15 cm)

The fat sand rat overcomes the problem of the unpredictability of desert food supplies by laying down a thick layer of fat all over its body when food is abundant. It then lives off this fat when food is short.

Active day and night, this gerbil darts about collecting seeds and other vegetation which it carries back to its burrow. In early spring, a brood chamber is made and lined with finely shredded vegetation, and the first litter of the year is born in March.

There are usually 3 to 5 young in a litter and the breeding season continues until late summer.

CLIMBING MICE AND POUCHED RATS

DENDROMURINAE: AFRICAN CLIMBING MOUSE SUBFAMILY

There are about 21 species of climbing mice, all of which occur in Africa, south of the Sahara. They are linked by certain skull and tooth characteristics, but otherwise they are quite a varied group. Most are agile climbers and have an affinity for tall vegetation, but some species are ground-living. Many forms have extremely long tails which they wrap around stems and twigs for extra stability. Although abundant, these rodents do not occur in the large groups characteristic of mice and voles. Many species live in extremely dense forest.

One climbing mouse, *Dendroprionomys rousseloti*, is known only from four specimens caught in Zaire, but this may indicate the degree of research effort rather than rarity.

African Climbing Mouse *Dendromus mesomelas*

RANGE Cameroon to Ethiopia, south to South Africa

HABITAT Swamps

SIZE Body: 2¼–4 in (6–10 cm) Tail: 2¾–4¾ in (7–12 cm)

The most striking feature of this little rodent is its prehensile tail, which acts as a fifth limb when the mouse climbs the stems of plants. Climbing mice are strictly nocturnal and are always on the alert for owls, mongooses and other predators. They feed on berries, fruits and seeds, and occasionally search for lizards and the eggs and young of small birds. Sometimes they manage to climb into the suspended nests of weaver finches, and there are records of them establishing their own nests in these secure hammocks, although they usually build nests of stripped grass at the base of grass stems.

Climbing mice breed throughout the year, producing litters of 3 to 5 young.

Fat Mouse *Steatomys krebsii*

RANGE Angola, Zambia, south to South Africa

HABITAT Dry, open, sandy plains

SIZE Body: 2¾–4 in (7–10 cm) Tail: 1½–1¾ in (4–4.5 cm)

Fat mice are adapted for life in the seasonal parts of southern Africa. In the rainy season, when seeds, bulbs and insects are abundant, the mice gorge, becoming quite fat. In the dry season, when plant growth stops, they live off their stores of fat. They live singly or in pairs in underground burrows, breeding in the wet season and produce litters of 4 to 6 young.

CRICETOMYINAE: AFRICAN POUCHED RAT SUBFAMILY

There are about 6 species of African pouched rat, all with deep cheek pouches for the transportation of food. They occur south of the Sahara and occupy a range of habitats, from sandy plains to the densest forests. One species has taken to living close to human refuse dumps, scavenging for a living.

Normally African pouched rats live alone in underground burrows, which they construct or take over from other species. The burrows include separate chambers for sleeping, excreting and, if the rat is female, breeding. Larder chambers are used as food stores for the dry season. Pouched rats move every few weeks to a new burrow.

Giant Pouched Rat *Cricetomys emini*

RANGE Sierra Leone to Malawi

HABITAT Dense forest

SIZE Body: 9¾–17¾ in (25–45 cm)
Tail: 14¾–18 in (36–46 cm)

As its name implies, the giant pouched rat is a substantial rodent, weighing up to about

2½ lb (1 kg). It lives in dark forests or areas of dense scrub. It emerges from its burrow at night in order to forage for roots, tubers, fruit and seeds. Some of the food is eaten where it is found, but much is taken back to the burrow in the rat's capacious cheek pouches.

Giant rats live singly, associating only briefly with others for mating, which occurs at all times of the year. Litters contain 2 or 3 young, born after a gestation period of about 6 weeks.

Long-tailed Pouched Rat *Beamys hindei* **VU**

RANGE Kenya, Tanzania

HABITAT Forest

SIZE Body: 5–7½ in (13–19 cm) Tail: 4–6 in (10–15.5 cm)

The long-tailed pouched rat occurs in a restricted part of central Africa, although the related *Beamys major* extends as far south as northern Zimbabwe.

This rat seems to spend much of its life underground in a complex burrow system which it constructs. It feeds mainly on the underground storage organs of plants – tubers and bulbs – although the presence of seeds in its food stores suggests that it spends some time above ground searching for food.

Groups of up to two dozen rats live together, breeding at all times of the year. Litters contain 1 to 5 young, which are mature at about 5½ months.

MURINAE: OLD WORLD RATS AND MICE SUBFAMILY

This subfamily of almost 500 species of rodents contains some of the world's most successful mammals. They are highly adaptable and extremely tolerant of hostile conditions.

Many of this subfamily are pests, wreaking havoc on stored grain and root crops, while others act as reservoirs for diseases. Rats and mice occur throughout the world and have followed man across the world, even to the remote polar regions and to the tops of mountain ranges.

Australian Water Rat *Hydromys chrysogaster*

RANGE Tasmania, Australia, New Guinea; Aru, Kai and Bruni Islands

HABITAT Swamps, streams, marshes

SIZE Body: 7¾–13¾ in (20–35 cm) Tail: 7¾–13¾ in (20–35 cm)

There are about 17 species of water rats, most of which inhabit rivers and swamps in Australia, New Guinea and its associated islands, and the Philippines.

This imposing rodent has a sleek, streamlined appearance, and is well suited to its aquatic habits. Its partially webbed hind feet enable it to perform complex maneuvers in the water. It feeds on small fish, frogs, crustaceans and water birds which it pursues and captures. Catches are often taken to a special food store for later consumption.

In the south of their range, water rats breed in early spring, producing a litter of 4 or 5 young; farther north they may breed all year round.

Eastern Shrew Mouse *Pseudohydromys murinus* **CR**

RANGE N.E. New Guinea

HABITAT Montane forest

SIZE Body: 3¼–4 in (8.5–10 cm) Tail: 3½–3¾ in (9–9.5 cm)

The Eastern shrew mouse, or false water rat, is known from a few specimens taken at between 6,900 and 9,000 ft (2,100 and 2,700 m) in dense forest. Little is known about the natural history of this animal, but since it does not have webbed feet, it probably does not have an aquatic lifestyle. Its long, strong tail may aid in climbing, and it probably spends much of its time seeking food in the shrub layer of the rain forest.

OLD WORLD RATS AND MICE

Harvest Mouse
Micromys minutus **LR:nt**

RANGE   Europe, E. Russia, Korea, S. China, N. India

HABITAT   Hedgerows, reedbeds

SIZE   Body: 2¼–3 in (5.5–7.5 cm) Tail: 2–3 in (5–7.5 cm)

These mice are among the smallest rodents. A fully grown male weighs about ½ oz (7 g). Harvest mice build tennis-ball-sized nests of finely stripped grass among reed stems or grass heads where the litter of up to 12 young is born and reared. Adults feed on seeds and small insects. They are the only Old World mammals to have truly prehensile tails.

Wood Mouse *Apodemus sylvaticus*

RANGE   Ireland, east to C. Asia

HABITAT   Forest edge

SIZE   Body: 3¼–5¼ in (8–13 cm) Tail: 2¾–3¾ in (7–9.5 cm)

The wood mouse is one of the most common European small rodents. Wood mice emerge from their nests under the roots of trees in the evening and often forage in pairs for seeds, insects and seasonal berries. They usually breed between April and November, but may continue through the winter, if food supplies are abundant.

Rough-tailed Giant Rat *Hyomys goliath*

RANGE   New Guinea

HABITAT   Forest

SIZE   Body: 11½–15¼ in (29–39 cm) Tail: 9¾–15 in (25–38 cm)

This rat derives its common name from the thick overlapping scales covering the underside of its tail. The scales are often worn down, and it is thought that they prevent the tail from slipping when it is used as a brace for climbing. This shy, secretive species is poorly studied, but it appears to feed on epiphytic plants on the branches of trees and on insects.

African Grass Rat *Arvicanthis abyssinicus*

RANGE   W. Africa to Somalia and Zambia

HABITAT   Savanna, scrub, forest

SIZE   Body: 4¾–7½ in (12–19 cm) Tail: 3½–6¼ in (9–16 cm)

The grass rat is a highly social rodent, living in colonies which sometimes number up to a thousand. The rats dig burrows in the earth or, alternatively, may establish themselves in a pile of rocks. Their staple food is probably grass seeds, but they also eat sweet potatoes and cassava. They breed throughout the year.

Four-striped Grass Mouse *Rhabdomys pumilio* **DD**

RANGE   C. Africa, south to the Cape of Good Hope

HABITAT   Grass, scrub

SIZE   Body: 33½–5¼ in (9–13 cm) Tail: 3¼–5 in (8–12.5 cm)

This common rodent lives in a burrow that opens into thick vegetation. It feeds on a wide variety of plant and animal food. In central Africa, these mice breed through the year, producing up to six litters annually, with 4 to 12 young per litter. In the south, the breeding season is limited to September through to May, and four litters are born.

Black Rat/House Rat *Rattus rattus*

RANGE   Worldwide (originally native to Asia)

HABITAT   Associated with humans

SIZE   Body: 7¾–10¼ in (20–26 cm) Tail: 7¾–9½ in (20–24 cm)

The house, or ship, rat, carrying with it such diseases as bubonic plague, typhus and rabies is sometimes said to have altered human destiny more than any man or woman. Wherever man has gone, and in all his activities, the rat has been his persistent, but unwanted companion.

The success of this species is due to its

extremely wide-ranging diet and its rapid rate of reproduction. Litters of up to 10 young are born every 6 weeks or so.

rainy season – November to April – and produce litters of up to 4 young. They are active climbers and often rest up in pandanus trees in nests made of finely shredded grass and leaves.

Brown Rat/Norway Rat *Rattus norvegicus*

RANGE Worldwide (originally native to E. Asia and Japan)

HABITAT Associated with humans

SIZE Body: 9¾–11¾ in (25–30 cm) Tail: 9¾–11¾ in (25–32 cm)

The brown rat is a serious pest, living alongside man wherever he lives and feeding on a wide range of food. Brown rats carry *Salmonella* and the bacterial disease tularaemia, but rarely the plague. They breed throughout the year, and the gestation period is 21 days.

Stick-nest Rat *Leporillus conditor* **VU**

RANGE S. C. Australia; Franklin Island, South Australia

HABITAT Arid grassland

SIZE Body: 5½–7¾ in (14–20 cm)
Tail: 5¼–7 in (13–18 cm)

Stick-nest rats build huge nests of sticks and debris, each inhabited by a pair or by a small colony of rats. The rats are vegetarian but may occasionally eat insects. They breed during the wet season, producing litters of 4 to 6 young.

Mosaic-tailed Mouse *Melomys cervinipes*

RANGE N. E. Australia

HABITAT Forest, usually near water

SIZE Body: 3½–6¾ in (9–17 cm) Tail: 4¼–6¾ in (11–17 cm)

The scales on the tails of most rats and mice are arranged in rings, but in this species they resemble a mosaic. These mice breed during the

House Mouse *Mus musculus*

RANGE Worldwide

HABITAT Fields; associated with man

SIZE Body 2½–3¾ in (6.5–9.5 cm) Tail: 2¼–4¼ in (6–10.5 cm)

Mice eat relatively little, but they spoil vast quantities of stored food such as grain. Wild mice are nocturnal and feed on grass seeds and plant stems and, occasionally, on insects.

Hopping Mouse *Notomys alexis*

RANGE C. Australia

HABITAT Dry grassland, spinifex scrub

SIZE Body: 3½–7 in (9–18 cm)
Tail: 4¾–9 in (12–23 cm)

The Australian counterpart of the kangaroo rats of North Africa and North America, this rodent emerges from its cool, humid burrows only at night. It feeds on seeds, roots and any green vegetation. Hopping mice breed during the winter months, producing litters of 2 to 5 young.

Greater Bandicoot Rat *Bandicota indica*

RANGE India to S. China; Taiwan, Sumatra, Java

HABITAT Forest, scrub; often near man

SIZE Body: 6¼–14¼ in (16–36 cm) Tail: 6¼–10¼ in (16–26 cm)

These rodents are serious pests in agricultural areas because they not only spoil grain but also steal quantities of food for their own underground larders. They breed throughout the year and bear litters of 10 to 12 young.

DORMICE, JUMPING MICE AND JERBOAS

MYOXIDAE: DORMOUSE FAMILY

There are about 21 species of dormouse found in Africa, Europe, northern Asia and Japan. These nocturnal rodents resemble short, fat squirrels and most have bushy tails. In late summer and autumn, most dormice build up their body fat reserves and then hibernate during the winter. They wake periodically to feed on the fruit and nuts that they store for winter consumption.

Fat Dormouse/Edible Dormouse *Glis glis*

RANGE Europe, Asia

HABITAT Forest

SIZE Body: 6–7 in (15–18 cm)
Tail: 5¼–6¼ in (13–16 cm)

The largest of its family, the fat dormouse has a long bushy tail and rough pads on its paws which help to facilitate climbing. It feeds on nuts, seeds, berries and fruit and occasionally catches insects and small birds. In summer, it makes a nest of plant fiber and moss up in a tree, but its winter hibernation nest is usually made nearer the ground in a hollow tree or in an abandoned rabbit burrow. The female produces a litter of 2 to 6 young in early summer.

Japanese Dormouse *Glirurus japonicus*

RANGE Japan (except Hokkaido)

HABITAT Montane forest

SIZE Body: 2½–3¼ in (6.5–8 cm) Tail: 1½–2 in (4–5 cm)

A tree-dwelling, nocturnal rodent, the Japanese dormouse spends its days in a tree hollow or in a nest built in the branches. It feeds at night on fruit, seeds, insects and birds' eggs. In winter it hibernates in a hollow tree or even in a man-made shelter, such as an attic or nesting box. After hibernation, the dormice mate, and the female gives birth to 3 to 5 young in June or July. Occasionally a second litter is produced in the month of October.

African Dormouse *Graphiurus murinus*

RANGE Africa, south of the Sahara

HABITAT Varied, forest, woodland

SIZE Body: 3¼–6½ in (8–16.5 cm)
Tail: 3¼–5¼ in (8–13 cm)

African dormice are agile creatures which move swiftly over bushes and vegetation in search of seeds, nuts, fruit and insects. They shelter in trees or rock crevices and, although primarily nocturnal, may be active by day in dense dark forests. Up to three litters of 2 to 5 young are born in summer.

Desert Dormouse *Selevinia betpakdalaensis* **EN**

RANGE S.E. Kazakhstan

HABITAT Desert

SIZE Body: 2¾–3¼ in (7–8.5 cm) Tail: 2¾–3¾ in (7–9.5 cm)

This species was discovered in 1938. The desert dormouse digs a burrow for shelter in which it is believed also to hibernate. It feeds largely on insects, but also eats plants and makes winter food stores of plant material in its burrow. It moves with short jumps on its hind legs. In late spring, the mice mate and produce litters of up to 8 young.

DIPODIDAE: JUMPING MOUSE AND JERBOA FAMILY

The 49 species in this family are small mouse-shaped rodents, with long hind limbs used for jumping. Some species can leap up to 6½ ft (2 m). Jumping mice live in open and forested land and swamps, throughout eastern Europe, Asia and North America. Jerboas live in deserts, semi-arid zones and steppe country in North Africa and Asia, where they construct complex burrow systems.

Meadow Jumping Mouse *Zapus hudsonius*

RANGE Canada, N.E. and N.C. USA

HABITAT Open meadows, woodland

SIZE Body: 2¾–3¼ in (7–8 cm)
Tail: 4–6 in (10–15 cm)

Meadow jumping mice feed on seeds, fruit and insects for which they forage on the ground, bounding along in a series of short jumps. They are primarily nocturnal, but in wooded areas may be active day and night under cover of the vegetation. In summer they make nests of grass and leaves on the ground, in grass or under logs; but in winter, they dig burrows or make small nests just above ground in which to hibernate.

They do not store food but, prior to hibernation, gain a substantial layer of body fat that sustains them. From October to April, the jumping mouse lies in its quarters in a tight ball, its temperature only just above freezing, and its respiration and heart rates greatly reduced to conserve energy.

Meadow jumping mice produce two or three litters a year. Most mate for the first time shortly after emerging from hibernation. The 4 or 5 young are born after about 18 days.

Northern Birch Mouse *Sicista betulina*

RANGE N. and C. Europe, E. Siberia

HABITAT Woodland

SIZE Body: 2–2¾ in (5–7 cm) Tail: 3¼–4 in (8–10 cm)

This rodent is easily distinguished by the dark stripe down its back and by its tail, which is about one and a half times the length of its body. It spends the day in its burrow, emerging at night to search for insects and small invertebrates to eat. It also feeds on seeds and fruit. It hibernates from October to April. Females produce a litter of 3 to 5 young in May or June, after a gestation of 4 or 5 weeks.

Northern Three-toed Jerboa *Dipus sagitta*

RANGE C. Asia: Caucasus to N. China

HABITAT Sand dunes, steppe, pine forest

SIZE Body: 4–5¼ in (10–13 cm)
Tail: 6–7½ in (15–19 cm)

The northern three-toed jerboa feeds on plants, seeds and insects. It needs very little water and is able to survive on the water contained in its food. In summer, it spends its days in a shallow burrow and emerges in the evening to travel to its feeding grounds, leaping along on its powerful hind limbs.

In autumn, it digs a deeper burrow and hibernates from November to March. Jerboas mate soon after awakening and may have two litters of 2 to 5 young in a season.

Great Jerboa *Allactaga major*

RANGE Ukraine, east to China

HABITAT Steppe, semidesert

SIZE Body: 3½–6 in (9–15 cm) Tail: 6¼–8½ in (16–22 cm)

The great jerboa and 10 of the 11 other species in the genus *Allactaga* have five toes on each hind foot. Great jerboas feed on seeds and insects, which they find by combing through the sand with the long slender claws on their front feet. They are nocturnal, spending the day in burrows; they also hibernate in burrows. One or two litters are produced each year.

CTENODACTYLIDAE: GUNDI FAMILY

The 5 species of gundi are found in Africa. They are extremely agile and can climb almost vertical rock faces. All members of the family are highly vocal and can utter a range of birdlike trills and twitters.

Gundi *Ctenodactylus gundi*

RANGE Africa: Sahara

HABITAT Rocky outcrops

SIZE Body: 6¼–7¾ in (16–20 cm) Tail: ½–¾ in (1–2 cm)

Shy animals, gundis feed only at night on a range of plant material which they usually take back to the safety of a rock crevice to consume. The gestation period of gundis is about 40 days, and the usual litter size is 1 or 2 young, which are able to run about immediately after birth.

PORCUPINES

HYSTRICIDAE: OLD WORLD PORCUPINE FAMILY

The 11 species in this family are all large rodents, unmistakable in their appearance, with long spines, derived from hairs, covering back, sides and parts of the tail. Porcupines live in desert, forest and savanna regions of Africa, parts of Asia and Indonesia, and the Philippines. Most are primarily ground living creatures; they move in a clumsy, shuffling manner which rattles their spines. They are generally nocturnal animals and live in burrows, which they dig, or in holes or crevices. They feed on plant material, such as roots, bulbs, tubers, fruit and bark, and on some carrion. Males and females look alike.

Indonesian Porcupine *Thecurus sumatrae*

RANGE Sumatra

HABITAT Forest

SIZE Body: 21¼ in (54 cm) Tail: 4 in (10 cm)

The Indonesian porcupine's body is covered with flattened spines, interspersed with short hairs. The spines are longest on the back and sides, becoming smaller on the tail; on the underside of the body, the spines are rather more flexible than those elsewhere. The specialized "rattling" quills on the tail expand near the tips; these expanded portions are hollow so that the quills rattle when they are vibrated together as a warning to potential enemies.

Crested Porcupine *Hystrix africaeaustralis*

RANGE Africa: Senegal to Cape Province

HABITAT Forest, savanna

SIZE Body: 28–33 in (71–84 cm) Tail: up to 1 in (2.5 cm)

The crested porcupine is a stout-bodied rodent, with sharp spines up to 12 in (30 cm) long on its back. Specialized hollow quills on the tail can be rattled in warning when the tail is vibrated. If, despite its warnings, a porcupine is still threatened, it will charge backward and drive the sharp, backward-curving spines into its enemy. The spines detach easily from the porcupine but cannot actually be "shot" as was once believed. Crested porcupines are slow-moving animals that rarely climb trees. They dig burrows in which they spend the day, emerging at night to feed. They are thought to produce two litters a year of 2 to 4 young each. The young are born with soft spines and remain in the nest until their spines harden, when they are about 2 weeks old.

Asian Brush-tailed Porcupine *Atherurus macrourus*

RANGE S.E. Asia: Assam to the Malay Peninsula

HABITAT Forest, often near water

SIZE Body: 15¾–21½ in (40–55 cm) Tail: 6–9¾ in (15–25 cm)

The slender, ratlike brush-tailed porcupine, has a distinctive long tail, tipped with a tuft of bristles. The spines of this species are flattened and grooved and most are short.

During the day, the brush-tailed porcupine shelters in a burrow, among rocks or even in a termite mound and emerges at night to hunt for food, mostly plants, roots, bark and insects. An agile creature, it will climb trees and runs well. It has partially webbed feet and is able to swim. Groups of up to 8 individuals shelter and forage together.

There are 3 other species of brush-tailed porcupine in this genus, all with similar appearance and habits.

Long-tailed Porcupine *Trichys fasciculata*

RANGE S.E. Asia: the Malay Peninsula, Sumatra, Borneo

HABITAT Forest

SIZE Body: 11–18½ in
(28–47 cm)
Tail: 6¾–9 in (17–23 cm)

The spines of the long-tailed porcupine are flattened and flexible, but shorter and less well developed than those of other species. The long tail breaks off easily, and many adults are found in this condition.

These porcupines are good climbers and have broad paws, with strong digits and claws for holding on to branches.

ERITHIZONTIDAE: NEW WORLD PORCUPINE FAMILY

The 10 species of New World porcupine are generally similar in appearance to the Old World species and have the same coarse hair and specialized spines. Unlike the Old World porcupines, they are largely tree-living, and the feet are adapted for climbing, with wide soles and strong digits and claws. Six of the species have prehensile tails – a prehensile tail is one equipped with muscles which allow it to be used as a fifth limb, for curling around and grasping branches. Males and females look alike.

New World porcupines are generally, but not exclusively, nocturnal and spend their days in hollows in trees or in crevices in the ground. Both males and females mark their home range with urine. The family occurs throughout North, Central and South America.

North American Porcupine

Erithizon dorsatum

RANGE Canada; USA: Alaska, W. states, south to New Mexico, some N.E. states.

HABITAT Forest

SIZE Body: 18–22 in (46–56 cm)
Tail: 7–9 in (18–23 cm)

A thickset animal, this porcupine has spines on its neck, back and tail and some longer spines, armed with minute barbs at their tips. It is slow and clumsy, but climbs trees readily in order to feed on buds, twigs and bark. In summer, it also feeds on roots and stems of flowering plants and even on some crops. It does not hibernate.

The porcupines mate at the beginning of winter, and the courting male often sprays the female with urine before mating, perhaps to prevent other males attempting to court her. After a gestation period of 7 months, the young, usually only 1, is born in the late spring. It is well developed at birth, with fur, open eyes and soft quills which harden within an hour. A few hours after birth, the young porcupine can climb trees and feed on solid food.

Tree Porcupine

Coendou prehensilis

RANGE Bolivia, Brazil, Venezuela

HABITAT Forest

SIZE Body: 11¾–24 in (30–61 cm)
Tail: 13–17¾ in (33–45 cm)

The body of the tree porcupine is covered with short, thick spines. Its major adaptation to arboreal life is its prehensile tail, which it uses to grasp branches when it is feeding. The tail lacks spines and the upper part of its tip is naked, with a callused pad to give it extra grip. The hands and feet, too, are highly specialized for climbing, with long curved claws on each digit.

Tree porcupines are mainly nocturnal, and slow but sure climbers. They feed on leaves, stems and some fruits. Females seem to produce only 1 young a year.

Upper Amazon Porcupine *Echinoprocta rufescens*

RANGE Colombia

HABITAT Forest

SIZE Body: 18 in (46 cm) Tail: 4 in (10 cm)

The Upper Amazon porcupine has a short, hairy tail that is not prehensile. Its back and sides are covered with spines which become thicker and stronger toward the rump. It is an arboreal animal and generally inhabits mountainous areas over 2,600 ft (800 m). Little has been discovered about the breeding habits and biology of this species of porcupine.

GUINEA PIGS, CAPYBARA, PACARANAS, PACAS AND AGOUTIS

CAVIIDAE: GUINEA PIG/CAVY FAMILY

There are about 14 species in this interesting and entirely South American family of ground-living rodents. Within the group are forms known as guinea pigs or cavies, mocos or rock cavies, and the Patagonian "hares", locally called "maras". Cavies and rock cavies have the well-known chunky body shape of domestic guinea pigs, with short ears and limbs, a large head and a tail which is not externally visible. Maras have a more harelike shape, with long legs and upstanding ears.

Cavies feed on plant material, and their cheek teeth continue to grow throughout life to counteract the heavy wear caused by chewing such food. Most live in small social groups of up to 15 or so individuals; sometimes they join in larger groups of as many as 40. They do not hibernate, even in areas which experience low temperatures.

Cavy/Guinea pig *Cavia tschudii*

RANGE Peru to N. Argentina

HABITAT Grassland, rocky regions

SIZE Body: 7¾–15¾ in (20–40 cm) Tail: no visible tail

These nocturnal rodents usually live in small family groups of up to 10 individuals, but may form larger colonies in particularly suitable areas. Although their sharp claws are well suited for digging burrows, they often use burrows made by other species or shelter in rock crevices. They feed at dawn and dusk, largely on grass and leaves.

Cavies breed in summer, or throughout the year in mild areas, producing litters of 1 to 4 young after a gestation of 60 to 70 days. The young are well developed at birth and can survive alone at 5 days old. This species is the probable ancestor of the domestic guinea pig, which is kept as a pet and also widely used in scientific research laboratories. Cavies are still kept by upland Indians as a source of fine, delicate meat.

Rock Cavy

Kerodon rupestris

RANGE N.E. Brazil

HABITAT Arid rocky areas

SIZE Body: 7¾–15¾ in (20–40 cm) Tail: no visible tail

Similar in build to the cavy, the rock cavy has a longer, blunter snout and longer legs. It shelters under rocks or among stones and emerges in the afternoon or evening to search for leaves to eat. It will climb trees to find food. The female rock cavy is believed to produce two litters a year, each of 1 or 2 young.

Mara *Dolichotis patagonum* **LR:nt**

RANGE Argentina

HABITAT Open arid land

SIZE Body: 27¼–29½ in (69–75 cm)

Tail: 1¾ in (4.5 cm)

The mara has long, slender legs and feet, well adapted for running and bounding along at speeds as great as 181 mph (30 km/h) in the manner of a hare or jack rabbit. Indeed, the mara fills the niche of the hare in an area where this group is absent.

On each hind foot there are three digits, each with a hoof-like claw; each forefoot bears four digits, armed with sharp claws. Maras are active in the daytime and feed on any available plant material. They dig burrows or take existing ones over from other animals, and the litter of 2 to 5 young is born in a nest made in the burrow.

HYDROCHAERIDAE: CAPYBARA FAMILY

This family contains only 1 species, the capybara, which is the largest living rodent. It resembles a huge guinea pig, with a large head and square muzzle, and lives in dense vegetation near lakes, rivers or marshes.

Capybara *Hydrochaeris hydrochaeris*

RANGE Panama to E. Argentina

HABITAT Forest, near water

SIZE Body: 3¼–4¼ ft (1–1.3 m) Tail: vestigial

The capybara spends much time in water and is an excellent swimmer and diver, it has partial webs between the digits of both its hind and forefeet. When swimming, only its eyes, ears and nostrils show above the water. Capybaras feed on plant material, including aquatic plants, and their cheek teeth grow throughout life to counteract the wear and tear of chewing. They live in family groups and are active at dawn and dusk. In areas where they are disturbed, capybaras may be nocturnal.

Males and females look alike, but the scent gland on the nose is larger in the male. They mate in spring, and 2 well-developed young are born after a gestation of 15 to 18 weeks.

DINOMYIDAE: PACARANA FAMILY

This South American family contains 1 apparently rare species, the false paca, or pacarana, so called because its striking markings are similar to those of the paca.

Pacarana *Dinomys branickii* **En**

RANGE Colombia to Bolivia

HABITAT Forest

SIZE Body: 28¾–31 in (73–79 cm) Tail: 7¾ in (20 cm)

The pacarana is slow-moving and docile with short, strong limbs and powerful claws. It feeds on leaves, stems and fruit, and sits on its haunches to examine and eat its food. Its cheek teeth grow continuously. It is probably nocturnal. Little is known of its breeding habits but 2 young normally seem to be born in a litter.

AGOUTIDAE: PACA FAMILY

The two species in this family are found in Central and South America. Pacas are large, nocturnal, ground-dwelling rodents that have limbs well-adapted to running.

Paca *Agouti paca*

RANGE S. Mexico to Suriname, south to Paraguay

HABITAT Forest, near water

SIZE Body: 23½–31 in (60–79 cm)
Tail: 1 in (2.5 cm)

The nocturnal paca is usually a solitary animal. It spends its day in a burrow, which it digs in a riverbank, among tree roots or under rocks, emerging after dark to feed. It swims readily. It is believed to produce two litters a year of 1, rarely 2, young.

DASYPROCTIDAE: AGOUTI FAMILY

The 13 species in this family are medium to large ground-living rodents found in Central and South America. They split naturally into two groups: the daytime-active agoutis, and the acouchis, about which less is known. The members of this family have legs adapted for walking, running, or galloping. Most species have been hunted. They eat leaves, fruit, roots, and stems, all of which may be hoarded in underground stores.

Agouti *Dasyprocta leporina*

RANGE Venezuela, E. Brazil; Lesser Antilles

HABITAT Forest, savanna

SIZE Body: 16–24½ in (41–62 cm) Tail: ½–1¼ in (1–3 cm)

Agoutis are social animals and are active in the daytime. They are good runners and can jump up to 6½ ft (2 m) vertically, from standing. Agoutis dig burrows in riverbanks or under trees or stones, and tread well-defined paths from burrows to feeding grounds. They mate twice a year and bear litters of 2 to 4 young.

CHINCHILLAS AND RELATIVES

CHINCHILLIDAE: VISCACHA AND CHINCHILLA FAMILY

There are about 6 species in this family which is found only in South America. All species have dense, beautiful fur and the importance of the chinchillas, in particular to the fur trade has led to their becoming relatively endangered as a wild species.

The hind limbs of the Chinchillidae are longer than their forelimbs and they are good at running and leaping; they are also good climbers. They feed on plants, including roots and tubers, and their cheek teeth grow throughout life. Social animals, they live in small family groups which are part of larger colonies. Where the ground is suitable, they dig burrows, but otherwise they shelter under rocks.

Plains Viscacha
Lagostomus maximus

RANGE	Argentina
HABITAT	Grassland
SIZE	Body: 18½–26 in (47–66 cm)
	Tail: 6–7¾ in (15–20 cm)

The plains viscacha is a robust rodent with a large head and blunt snout. Males are larger than females. Colonies of plains viscachas live in complex burrows, with networks of tunnels and entrances. They are expert burrowers, digging mainly with their forefeet and pushing the soil with their noses – their nostrils close off to prevent soil from entering them.

Females breed once a year or sometimes twice in mild climates. There are usually 2 young, born after a gestation period of 5 months.

Chinchilla *Chinchilla laniger* **VU**

RANGE	N. Chile
HABITAT	Rocky, mountainous areas
SIZE	Body: 8¾–15 in (22.5–38 cm)
	Tail: 3–6 in (7.5–15 cm)

Chinchillas are attractive animals, with long ears, large eyes and bushy tails. They live in colonies of 100 or more, sheltering in holes and crevices in rocks. They feed on any available vegetation, sitting up on their rear haunches to eat and holding their food in their front paws.

Female chinchillas are larger than males and are aggressive toward one another. They breed in winter, usually producing two litters of 1 to 6 young. The gestation period is 111 days, and the young are suckled for 6 to 8 weeks.

The chinchilla's exceedingly soft, dense coat is the cause of its present extreme rarity in the wild, although it is now farmed all over the world for its valuable fur.

CAPROMYIDAE: HUTIA FAMILY

There are now about 12 living species in this family – several other species have become extinct relatively recently. All the surviving species are found on West Indian islands.

Hutia *Geocapromys ingrahami* **VU**

RANGE	Bahamas
HABITAT	Forest
SIZE	Body: 11¾–19¾ in (30–50 cm) Tail: 6–11¾ in (15–30 cm) **E**

The hutia feeds mostly on fruit and leaves, but it occasionally eats small invertebrates and reptiles. It is a good climber and seeks some of its food in the trees. Active in the daytime, it shelters in a burrow or rock crevice at night. It is believed to breed all year round, provided that the temperature stays above 60°F (15°C), and produces litters of 2 to 9 young.

Hutias have been unable to cope with man's introduction of mongooses and dogs to the West Indies, and as a result many species may be heading for imminent extinction.

MYOCASTORIDAE: COYPU FAMILY

The single species in this family – the coypu or nutria – is a semi-aquatic rodent that is a native of South America.

Coypu/Nutria *Myocastor coypus*

RANGE Bolivia and S. Brazil to Chile and Argentina; introduced in North America, Europe and Asia

HABITAT Near marshes, lakes, streams

SIZE Body: 17–24¾ in (43–63 cm)
Tail: 9¾–16½ in (25–42 cm)

The semiaquatic coypu is a skilled swimmer and diver and looks like a beaver with a rat's tail. Its hind feet are webbed and it has dense fur. Coypus feed on aquatic vegetation and possibly on mollusks. They dig burrows in river banks, clear trails in their territory and are extremely destructive to plants and crops. By escaping from the farms where they are bred for their fur, these animals have colonized new areas all over the world, and are sometimes considered pests because of the damage that they are capable of doing.

Two to three litters of up to 10 young are produced during the year, and the gestation period is 132 days. Young coypus can swim only a few hours after birth.

OCTODONTIDAE: OCTODONT RODENT FAMILY

The 9 species of octodont rodent all occur in South America. Most resemble rats with round noses and long furry tails. They are all good burrowers and feed on plant material.

Degu *Octodon degus*

RANGE W. Peru, Chile

HABITAT Mountains, coastal regions

SIZE Body: 5–7½ in (12.5–19.5 cm) Tail: 4–6¼ in (10–16 cm)

The degu is a stout, short-legged rodent with a large head for its size. Active during the day, it feeds on plants, bulbs and tubers. It is thought to breed all year round and may produce several litters a year of 2 young each.

CTENOMYIDAE: TUCO-TUCO FAMILY

This family of 38 species, all found in South America, is believed by some authorities to be a group of relatives of the octodont rodents which has become highly specialized for an underground existence.

Tuco-tuco *Ctenomys talarum*

RANGE E. Argentina

HABITAT Grassland

SIZE Body: 6¾–9¾ in (17–25 cm)
Tail: 2¼–4¼ in (6–11 cm)

Tuco-tucos look very much like North American pocket gophers (*Geomyidae*) and lead similar lives in complex burrow systems. Their front teeth are enormous relative to body size and are used, when burrowing, to loosen the soil. Tuco-tucos spend nearly all their lives underground and feed on roots, tubers and stems.

In winter and spring, the tuco-tucos mate, and a single litter of 2 to 5 young is born after a gestation of about 15 weeks.

ABROCOMIDAE: CHINCHILLA-RAT FAMILY

There are 2 species only of chinchilla-rat, both native to South America. As their common name suggests, their fur resembles that of the chinchilla, although it is of poorer quality, and they have a ratlike body shape.

Chinchilla-rat *Abrocoma bennetti*

RANGE Chile

HABITAT High coastal plains

SIZE Body: 7½–9¾ in (19–25 cm)
Tail: 5¼–7 in (13–18 cm)

A resident of cold, bleak mountain regions, the chinchilla-rat is a little-known creature. It feeds on plant food and its cheek teeth grow throughout life. Mainly a ground-dweller, it can also climb trees in search of food. Chinchilla-rats live in burrows or rock crevices.

SPINY RATS, CANE RATS AND RELATIVES

ECHIMYIDAE: AMERICAN SPINY RAT FAMILY

The 63 or so species of American spiny rat are found from Nicaragua in the north to central Brazil in the south. Most are robust, ratlike creatures with a more or less spiny coat of sharp hairs. They are herbivorous, feeding on a variety of plant material. Most prefer to live close to rivers and streams.

Like many South American rodents, spiny rats have a long gestation and give birth to well-developed young which can run around when only a few hours old.

Gliding Spiny Rat *Diplomys labilis*

RANGE Panama

HABITAT Forest

SIZE Body: 9¾–19 in (25–48 cm) Tail: 7¾–11 in (20–28 cm)

Well adapted for arboreal life, the gliding spiny rat has long, strong toes and sharp, curved claws with which it can grip the smoothest of bark. Its common name derives from its habit of leaping from branch to branch, spreading its limbs to utilize its gliding membrane as it does so.

Gliding spiny rats make their nests in hollows in trees near water. They breed throughout the year, producing litters of 2 young after a gestation period of about 60 days. The young are able to clamber around among the branches only a few hours after they are born.

Armored Rat *Hoplomys gymnurus*

RANGE Nicaragua, south to Colombia and Ecuador

HABITAT Rain forest, grassy clearings

SIZE Body: 8¾–12½ in (22–32 cm) Tail: 6–9¾ in (15–25 cm)

The most spiny of all the spiny rats, the armored rat has a thick coat of needle-sharp hairs along its back and flanks. These

rodents live in short, simple burrows in the banks of streams and emerge at night to forage for food. They breed throughout the year, producing litters of 1 to 3 young.

THRYONOMYIDAE: CANE RAT FAMILY

The 2 species of cane rat are found throughout Africa, south of the Sahara. They are substantial rodents, weighing up to 15½ lb (7 kg), and they are the principal source of animal protein for some tribes. In the cane fields they cause serious damage to the crop, stripping the cane of its outer bark to expose the soft central pith on which they feed.

Cane Rat *Thryonomys swinderianus*

RANGE Africa, south of the Sahara

HABITAT Grassy plains, sugarcane plantations

SIZE Body: 13¾–24 in (35–61 cm) Tail: 2¾–9¾ in (7–25 cm)

Cane rats do not normally live in burrows, preferring instead to construct a sleeping platform from chopped-up vegetation when needed. Occasionally, though, they do take over disused aardvark or porcupine burrows or seek refuge among a pile of boulders. In southern Africa, cane rats are known to mate from April to June and to give birth to litters of 2 to 4 young after a gestation period of 2 months. The young cane rats are well-developed at birth – their eyes are open and they are able to run around soon after they are born.

PETROMURIDAE: DASSIE RAT FAMILY

The single species in this family is an unusual rodent that looks more like a squirrel than a rat. Its common name links it in habit with the dassie, or rock hyrax, for both creatures share a love of the sun and spend much time basking on rocks, moving from place to place to catch the strongest rays. While the others bask, one member of the colony keeps a lookout for predators, such as mongooses, eagles or leopards, uttering a shrill warning call if danger threatens.

Dassie Rat *Petromus typicus*

RANGE Africa: Angola, Namibia, N.W. South Africa

HABITAT Rocky, arid hills

SIZE Body: 5½–7½ in (14–20 cm) Tail: 5¼–7 in (13–18 cm)

Dassie rats live in large colonies and are active in the daytime. They feed on fruit, seeds and berries. They mate in early summer (October) and give birth in late December to a litter of 1 or 2 young.

BATHYERGIDAE: MOLE-RAT FAMILY

There are 8 species of mole-rat, all found in Africa, south of the Sahara. They are highly specialized for a subterranean life, for they are virtually blind and have powerful incisor teeth and claws for digging. Their skulls also are heavy and strong, and they use their heads as battering rams. The underground storage organs of plants – tubers and bulbs – are their main food, and worms and insect larvae may be eaten occasionally. Most have thick velvety coats which resemble that of the mole, but the naked mole-rat is quite hairless.

Cape Dune Mole-rat *Bathyergus suillus*

RANGE South Africa to Cape of Good Hope

HABITAT Sand dunes, sandy plains

SIZE Body: 6¾–13 in (17.5–33 cm) Tail: 1½–2¾ in (4–7 cm)

This is the largest member of the mole-rat family. The Cape dune mole-rat may weigh up to 3 lb (1.5 kg). It has relatively huge incisor teeth (each one measuring ⅒ in (2 mm) across) and a fearsome bite.

It builds extensive burrow systems, usually close to the surface, which can be a serious menace to root crops. Between November and December females give birth to between 3 and 5 well-developed young.

Naked Mole-rat *Heterocephalus glaber*

RANGE Somalia, Ethiopia, N. Kenya

HABITAT Arid steppe, light sandy soil

SIZE Body: 3¼–3½ in (8–9 cm) Tail: 1½ in (3.5–4 cm)

This species, the smallest of its family, is one of the most curious mammals known, with a unique social structure more similar to some insects than to any other mammal. Each colony of naked mole-rats numbers about 100 individuals and is ruled by a single queen, who alone breeds. The queen is tended by a few non-workers of both sexes, which are fatter and more sluggish than the other colony members – the workers. It is the workers that dig the burrows and gather the roots and tubers for the whole colony to eat.

The queen appears to be able to inhibit the sexual maturation of all the other females in the colony, but how this is achieved is not known. The queen breeds throughout the year and may produce up to 20 young in each litter. If she dies or is removed, then one of the non-worker female becomes the new queen and begins to breed.

ELEPHANT SHREWS AND TENRECS

ORDER MACROSCELIDEA

MACROSCELIDIDAE:
ELEPHANT SHREW FAMILY

The 15 species of African elephant shrews have extraordinary trunklike noses. Although once assigned to the insectivores, elephant shrews are now classified in their own order.

Short-eared Elephant Shrew

Macroscelides proboscideus **VU**

RANGE Africa: Namibia, South Africa: Cape Province

HABITAT Plains, rocky outcrops

SIZE Body: 3¾–5 in (9.5–12.5 cm)
Tail: 3¾–5½ in (9.5–14 cm)

Elephant shrews are active day and night. They eat termites (sometimes burrowing into termite mounds), seeds, fruit and berries. The elephant shrews hop and jump from twig to branch on their powerful hind legs, using their tails as counterbalances.

A litter of 1 or 2 well-developed young is born during the rainy season. The young can walk and jump almost as soon as they are born and appear to suckle for only a few days.

ORDER INSECTIVORA

This order includes about 384 species found all over the world, except in Australia and the southern half of South America. Most are ground-dwelling or burrowing animals which feed on insects and invertebrates.

TENRECIDAE: TENREC FAMILY

This family includes the 24 species, all restricted to Madagascar and the Comoro Islands, and the 3 West African otter shrews. Tenrecs have adapted to a number of different lifestyles. *Tenrec* resembles the North American opossum. *Setifer* resembles hedgehogs. *Microgale* resembles shrews, and *Oryzorictes* has molelike characteristics.

All tenrecs retain some reptilian features, regarded as primitive in mammals, such as the cloaca, where the urogenital and anal canals open into a common pouch.

Tailless Tenrec *Tenrec ecaudatus*

RANGE Madagascar, Comoro Islands

HABITAT Brushland, dry forest clearings, highland plateaux

SIZE Body: 10½–15¼ in (27–39 cm)
Tail: ½–¾ in (10–16 mm)

The tailless tenrec bears a resemblance to a hedgehog with a sparse coat, set with stiff hairs and spines. It is active at night, searching for insects, worms and roots and fruit.

In the dry season, tailless tenrecs hibernate in deep burrows which they plug with soil. Before hibernation, the tenrec builds up its fat reserves to sustain it through its 6-month sleep. In early October, immediately after hibernating, tenrecs mate. Up to 25 young are born in November and about 16 survive.

Greater Hedgehog Tenrec *Setifer setosus*

RANGE Madagascar

HABITAT Dry forest, highland plateaux

SIZE Body: 6–7½ in (15–19 cm) Tail: ½–¾ in (10–16 mm)

The greater hedgehog tenrec has short, sharp spines, which cover its back like a dense, prickly mantle. If disturbed, it rolls itself into a ball and emits a series of squeaks and grunts. The female produces a litter of up to 6 young in January. The young have soft spines at birth, which harden in 2 weeks.

Streaked Tenrec

Hemicentetes semispinosus

RANGE	Madagascar
HABITAT	Scrub, forest edge
SIZE	Body: 6¼–7½ in (16–19 cm) Tail: vestigial

Although it is less densely spined than the hedgehog tenrec, the streaked species can still protect itself by partially curling up. When the creature is alarmed, a small patch of heavy spines in the middle of the back vibrate rapidly, making a clicking noise. The mother is believed to communicate with her young in this way.

Streaked tenrecs do not hibernate, but they do remain inactive during spells of cool weather. Like other tenrecs, they feed on insects and other invertebrates.

Females are sexually mature at 8 weeks, and produce a litter of 7 to 11 young between December and March after a gestation of at least 50 days.

Long-tailed Shrew Tenrec *Microgale longicaudata* **LR:lc**

RANGE	Madagascar
HABITAT	Forest: sea level to montane
SIZE	Body: 2–6 in (5–15 cm) Tail: 3–6½ in (7.5–17 cm)

The shrew tenrec, as its name implies, occupies the ecological niche filled by shrews in other parts of the world. The coat is short, but dense, and quite lacking in the spines that are so common in other members of this family.

Although it climbs well and the distal third of its tail is prehensile, the shrew tenrec seems to feed mostly on grubs, worms and insects on the forest floor.

This species is active at all hours of the day and night, but each individual maintains its own pattern of rest and activity. They do not appear to hibernate. Little is known of the breeding habits, but they are believed to produce litters of 2 to 4.

Rice Tenrec *Oryzorictes hova*

RANGE	Madagascar
HABITAT	Marshy areas
SIZE	Body: 3–5 in (8–13 cm) Tail: 1¼–2 in (3–5 cm)

Rice tenrecs, so called because they occupy the banks beside rice fields, spend most of their lives underground; their forelimbs are well adapted for digging. They feed on invertebrates, but there is some evidence that they also eat mollusks and crustaceans.

Although rice tenrecs are seen above ground only at night, they may be active underground at all hours. Nothing is known of their breeding habits, but they are sufficiently abundant to achieve pest status in the rice growing areas of Madagascar.

Giant Otter Shrew *Potomogale velox*

RANGE	W. and C. equatorial Africa
HABITAT	Streams: sea level to 6,000 ft (1,800 m)
SIZE	Body: 11½–14 in (29–35 cm) Tail: 9½–11½ in (24–29 cm)

Although they are geographically separated from the other tenrecs, the 3 otter shrews are believed to be a subfamily of the *Tenrecidae*. The giant otter shrew is, overall, the largest living insectivore and does bear a strong superficial resemblance to the otter, with its flattened head and heavy tail. Its coat is dense with a glossy overlayer of guardhairs.

Giant otter shrews live in burrows with entrances below water level. They emerge at dusk to hunt for crabs, fish and frogs, which they pursue through the water with great agility. They live solitary lives, but consort in pairs shortly before mating. Litters of 2 to 3 young are born throughout the year.

GOLDEN MOLES AND HEDGEHOGS

CHRYSOCHLORIDAE: GOLDEN MOLE FAMILY

The 18 species of golden moles bear a close resemblance to the true moles, but are, in fact, only distantly related. They have cylindrical bodies, short powerful limbs and no visible tail. Their fur is thick and dense and the metallic lustre it imparts gives the group its name. Golden moles are blind, their eyes being reduced to mere vestiges covered by fused hairy eyelids. The shovellike paws on their forelimbs are used for digging, and the enlarged flattened claws on the "index" and middle digits are employed as cutting edges.

Golden moles are found only in Africa, south of a line linking Cameroon with Tanzania. They occur in all habitats from rugged mountainous zones to sandy plains.

Cape Golden Mole *Chrysochloris asiatica*
RANGE South Africa: W. Cape Province
HABITAT Workable soil up to 9,000 ft (2,800 m)
SIZE Body: 3½–5½ in (9–14 cm)
Tail: absent

The Cape golden mole is a frequent visitor to gardens and farmland in much of southern Africa. It reveals its presence by raised tunnel tracks radiating out from a bush or shed. At night the moles may travel on the surface, and in damp weather they root about for beetles, worms and grubs.

Once a year, in the rainy season, females produce litters of 2 to 4 young. Shortly before the birth the mother makes a round grass-lined nest in a special breeding chamber. The young suckle for almost 3 months until their teeth erupt.

Hottentot Golden Mole *Amblysomus hottentotus*
RANGE South Africa
HABITAT Sand or peat plains
SIZE Body: 3¼–5 in (8.5–13 cm) Tail: absent

The Hottentot golden mole differs from other species in that it has only two claws on each forepaw. When these animals occur in orchards and young plantations, their burrowing may

seriously disturb roots and kill the trees, but generally they do more good than harm by eating insects, beetle larvae and other invertebrate pests.

Pairs breed between November and February when rainfall is high. They produce a litter of 2 young.

Giant Golden Mole *Chrysospalax trevelyani* **EN**
RANGE South Africa: E. Cape Province
HABITAT Forest
SIZE Body: 8–9½ in (20–24 cm) Tail: absent

As its name implies, the giant golden mole is the largest of its family and weighs up to 3 lb (1.5 kg). It is a rare species and is now on the brink of extinction.

Giant golden moles hunt above ground for beetles, small lizards, slugs and giant earthworms. When disturbed they dart unerringly toward their burrow entrance and safety, but how they are able to locate it is not known.

During the winter rainy season they are believed to produce a litter of 2 young.

ERINACEIDAE: HEDGEHOG FAMILY

This family contains 20 species of two superficially quite distinct types of animal: the hedgehogs, and the gymnures, or moonrats. Members of the hedgehog subfamily occur extensively across Europe and Asia to western China, and in Africa as far south as Angola. Moonrats live in Indo-China, Malaysia, Borneo, the Philippines and northern Burma. All feed on a varied diet of worms, insects and mollusks, as well as some berries, frogs, lizards and birds.

In the northern part of their range, hedgehogs hibernate during the winter months, but in warmer areas this is not necessary.

Western European Hedgehog *Erinaceus europaeus*

RANGE Britain, east to Scandinavia and Romania; introduced in New Zealand

HABITAT Scrub, forest, cultivated land

SIZE Body: 5½–10½ in (13.5–27 cm) Tail: ½–2 in (1–5 cm)

One of the most familiar small mammals in Europe, the hedgehog gets its name from its piglike habit of rooting around for its invertebrate prey in the hedgerows. It is quite vocal and makes a range of grunting, snuffling noises. The upper part of the head and the back are covered in short, banded spines. If threatened, the hedgehog rolls itself up, and a longitudinal muscle band, running around the edge of the prickly cloak, acts as a drawstring to enclose the creature within its spiked armor. The chest and belly are covered with coarse springy hairs.

Hedgehogs produce 1, sometimes 2, litters of about 5 young each year. The young are weaned at about 5 weeks. In the north of their range, hedgehogs hibernate throughout the winter.

Desert Hedgehog *Paraechinus aethiopicus*

RANGE N. Africa, Middle East to Iraq

HABITAT Arid scrub, desert

SIZE Body: 5½–9 in (14–23 cm) Tail: ½–1½ in (1–4 cm)

The desert hedgehog resembles its slightly larger European cousin, but its coloration is more variable. Generally the spines are sandy-buff with darker tips, but dark and white forms are not uncommon. Desert hedgehogs dig short, simple burrows in which they pass the day. At night, when the air is cool, they emerge to search for invertebrates and the eggs of ground-nesting birds. Scorpions are a preferred food; the hedgehogs nip

off the stings before eating them. In common with most desert mammals, these hedgehogs probably have highly adapted kidneys, enabling them to exist for long periods without water.

In July or August desert hedgehogs breed, producing a litter of about 5 young.

Moonrat *Echinosorex gymnurus*

RANGE Cambodia, east to Burma

HABITAT Forest, mangrove swamps

SIZE Body: 10–17¼ in (26–44 cm) Tail: 8–8¼ in (20–21 cm)

One of the largest insectivores, the moonrat has a long snout, an unkempt appearance and an almost naked, scaly tail. It can defend itself by producing a foul, fetid odor from a pair of anal glands, which repels all but the most persistent predators.

Moonrats live in crevices between tree roots, or in hollow logs. They emerge around dusk to forage for mollusks, insects and worms. Some fruit, and fish and crabs too, may be eaten. Little is known of the moonrats' breeding habits, but they seem to breed throughout the year, producing 2 young at a time.

Mindanao Moonrat *Podogymnura truei* **EN**

RANGE Philippines: Mindanao

HABITAT Upland forest and forest edge, from 5,250 to 7,500 ft (1,600–2,300 m)

SIZE Body: 5–6 in (13–15 cm) Tail: 1½–2¾ in (4–7 cm)

This curious creature is restricted to a small natural range and has never been common. Now, because of logging operations and slash-and-burn agriculture, much of its habitat is being destroyed and its survival is seriously threatened. It has long soft fur and a tail with more hairs than that of *Echinosorex*. It feeds on insects, worms and even carrion, which it finds in grasses and among stands of moss. Nothing is known of the breeding habits of the Mindanao moonrats.

SHREWS

SORICIDAE: SHREW FAMILY

There are more than 280 species of shrew, distributed throughout most of the world, except Australia and New Zealand, the West Indies and most of South America. Shrews are insectivores and most lead inoffensive lives among the debris of the forest floor or on pastureland, consuming many types of invertebrate. Water shrews are known to overpower frogs and small fish, which they kill with venomous bites – the saliva of many shrews contains strong toxins. Carrion may also be included in the shrew's diet.

Shrews are active creatures with high metabolisms. Their hearts may beat more than 1,200 times every minute and, relative to their body size, they have enormous appetites. Even in cold northern regions, they do not hibernate in winter; it would be impossible for them to build up sufficient fat reserves. Although shrews are heavily preyed upon by owls and hawks, acrid-smelling secretions from well-developed flank glands seem to deter most mammalian predators.

Some species of shrew are reported to eat their own feces and perhaps those of other creatures. By doing so, they boost their intake of vitamins B and K and some other nutrients. This habit may be related to the shrews' hyperactive life and enhanced metabolism. Shrews rely heavily on their senses of smell and hearing when hunting – their eyes are tiny and probably of little use.

Masked Shrew *Sorex cinereus*

RANGE	N. North America to New Mexico
HABITAT	Moist forest
SIZE	Body: 1¾–3¾ in (4.5–9.5 cm) Tail: 1–3 in (2.5–8 cm)

The masked shrew is a common species throughout North America, though less abundant in the arid regions to the south. It inhabits the surface layer of forest, living in and around burrows made by itself and other woodland animals. It is active day and night with about seven periods of feeding activity in each 24 hours. Earthworms and snails are preferred foods, but masked shrews eat a wide range of invertebrate prey.

Generally solitary animals, male and female pair only for mating. Several litters of up to 10 young are born during the late spring and summer. The young are weaned after about a month, but the family may remain together for another month – the only time during which these shrews are sociable.

Short-tailed Shrew *Blarina brevicauda*

RANGE	E. USA
HABITAT	Almost all terrestrial habitats
SIZE	Body: 3–4 in (7.5–10.5 cm) Tail: ½–1¼ in (1.5–3 cm)

This abundant and widespread species is unusual in two ways. First, it seems to be partly gregarious since in captivity it seeks out the company of other shrews. Second, it often climbs trees for food – most shrews climb only rarely. In much of the USA, the short-tailed shrew is an important controlling influence on larch sawflies and other destructive forest pests on which it feeds. It builds a grassy nest under a stump or log and produces three or four litters a year of up to 9 young each. The gestation period is 17 to 21 days.

Giant Mexican Shrew *Megasorex gigas*

RANGE	W. coastal strip of Mexico
HABITAT	Rocky or semidesert, dry forest
SIZE	Body: 3–3½ in (8–9 cm) Tail: 1½–2 in (4–5 cm)

The giant Mexican shrew has large prominent ears. In common with most desert mammals, it is active only at night, when it emerges from crevices between boulders or under rocks to search for insects and worms. Although it eats up to three-quarters of its own weight every 24 hours, it seems only to feed at night, unlike other shrews which feed throughout the day. Its breeding habits are not known.

Sri Lankan Long-tailed Shrew *Crocidura miya* EN

RANGE Sri Lanka

HABITAT Damp and dry forest, savanna

SIZE Body: 2–2½ in (5–6.5 cm) Tail: 1½–1¾ in (4–4.5 cm)

This shrew, with its long, lightly haired tail, spends much of its life among the debris of the forest floor where damp, cool conditions encourage a rich invertebrate population on which it feeds. It also eats small lizards and young birds on occasion. Strong-smelling scent glands seem to protect the shrew itself from much predation.

The breeding season of the long-tailed shrew lasts from March until November. The female produces about five litters in this time, each of about 6 young. After 8 days, the young leave the nest for the first time, each gripping the tail of the one in front in its mouth as the caravan, led by the mother, goes in search of food. This habit seems to be restricted to this particular genus of shrew.

Pygmy White-toothed Shrew *Suncus etruscus*

RANGE S. Europe, S. Asia, Africa

HABITAT Semiarid grassland, scrub, rocky hillsides

SIZE Body: 1¼–2 in (3.5–5 cm) Tail: 1–1¼ in (2.5–3 cm)

Usually regarded as the world's smallest terrestrial mammal, a fully grown pygmy shrew weighs about ¹⁄₁₄ oz (2 g). How such a tiny mammal can survive is not fully understood, but it must have a constant and reliable source of food, and that is one reason why it is restricted to the warmer parts of the Old World. Its coat is dense to prevent undue heat loss from its tiny body.

Pygmy shrews eat spiders and insects almost as large as themselves, including grasshoppers and cockroaches.

Nothing is known of the breeding habits of pygmy white-toothed shrews, but they remain quite abundant, and it may be that their small size protects them from heavy predation, since they share their habitat with larger, more tempting species.

Mouse Shrew *Myosorex varius*

RANGE South Africa, north to the Limpopo

HABITAT Moist areas, forest, scrub, river banks

SIZE Body: 2¼–4¼ in (6–11 cm) Tail: 1¼–2¼ in (3–5.5 cm)

The mouse shrew is perhaps the most primitive of existing shrews. It has two more teeth in its lower jaw than is normal among other members of the shrew family and thus resembles the extinct early mammals. In other respects, however, it is like most other shrews.

The mouse shrew does not appear to make or use burrows, but instead seeks out holes and hollows for daytime shelter. It makes small nests out of shredded grass for sleeping and for use as nurseries for its young.

Females produce up to 6 litters a year, each of 2 to 4 young.

Armored Shrew *Scutisorex somereni*

RANGE Africa: Uganda, near Kampala

HABITAT Forest

SIZE Body: 4¾–6 in (12–15 cm) Tail: 2¾–3¾ in (7–9.5 cm)

This is one of the most unusual members of the shrew family. The armored shrew has a spine which is fortified and strengthened by a mesh of interlocking bony flanges and rods. Despite this unique skeletal structure, the armored shrew moves much like other shrews, although its predatory behavior is characterized by rather ponderous and apparently well thought-out movements.

There are reports that an armored shrew is able to support the weight of a grown man without being crushed.

Armored shrews appear to eat plant food as well as invertebrates. They are believed to breed throughout the year.

SOLENODONS, MOLES AND FLYING LEMURS

SOLENODONTIDAE: SOLENODON FAMILY

There are 2 species only of solenodons alive today – *Solenodon cubanus* on Cuba and *Solenodon paradoxus* on the neighbouring islands of Haiti and the Dominican Republic. They are rather ungainly, uncoordinated creatures and, although they are about the size of rats, they look more like shrews with their probing snouts. Their eyes are small and rheumy and they are far more nocturnal than the wide-eyed rats.

Solenodons grow and breed slowly and this, combined with the predatory attacks of dogs and cats, means that their survival is now threatened. Conservation areas are being established for these animals, but their future is far from secure.

Cuban Solenodon *Solenodon cubanus* EN

RANGE Cuba

HABITAT Montane forest

SIZE Body: 11–12½ in (28–32 cm) Tail: 6½–10 in (17–25 cm)

Solenodons have a varied diet. At night they search the forest floor litter for insects and other invertebrates, fungi and roots. They climb well and feed on fruits, berries and buds, but have more predatory habits too. With venom from modified salivary glands in the lower jaw, the solenodon can kill lizards, frogs, small birds or even rodents. Solenodons seem not to be immune to the venom of their own kind, and there are records of cage mates dying after fights. They produce litters of 1 to 3 young.

TALPIDAE: MOLE FAMILY

The majority of the 29 species of mole lead an underground life, but 2 species of desman and the star-nosed mole are adapted for an aquatic life. Moles are widespread throughout

Europe and Asia, south to the Himalayas, and from southern Canada to northern Mexico. They need habitats with soft soil so that they are able to dig their extensive burrow systems.

All moles have highly modified hands and forearms, which act as pickax and shovel combined. Moles seldom come above ground and their eyes are tiny and covered with hairy skin. Their tactile sense is highly developed, however, and their facial bristles respond to the tiniest vibrations. Moles can move backwards or forwards with equal ease – when reversing, the stumpy tail is held erect and the sensory hairs on it provide warning of any approaching danger.

Pacific Mole *Scapanus orarius*

RANGE North America: British Columbia to Baja California

HABITAT Well-drained deciduous forest

SIZE Body: 4½–7¼ in (11–18.5 cm) Tail: ¾–2¼ in (2–5.5 cm)

The Pacific, or coast, mole and its close relatives, the broad-footed mole and Townsend's mole, all have nostrils which open upward. Their eyes are much more visible than those of other species, but this does not necessarily mean that their sight is better. Like other moles, they live underground and rarely venture up to the surface.

Coast moles feed on earthworms and soil-dwelling larvae and do much good by devouring the larvae of insect pests. Between 2 and 5 young are born in early spring after a 4-week gestation period.

European Mole *Talpa europaea*

RANGE Europe, E. Asia

HABITAT Pasture, forest, scrub

SIZE Body: 3½–6½ in (9–16.5 cm) Tail: 1¼–1½ in (3–4 cm)

The extensive burrow systems in which European moles live are excavated rapidly. A single individual can dig up to 66 ft (20 m) in one day. The moles feed primarily on earthworms, but also eat a wide range of other invertebrates, as well as snakes, lizards, mice and small birds.

In early summer the female produces a litter of up to 7 young, born in a leaf-lined underground nest and weaned at about 3 weeks. Occasionally there is a second litter.

Hairy-tailed Mole *Parascalops breweri*

RANGE S.E. Canada, N.E. USA

HABITAT Well-drained soil in forest or open land

SIZE Body: 4½–5½ in (11.5–14 cm) Tail: ¾–1½ in (2–3.5 cm)

As its name implies, this species is characterized by its almost bushy tail. Otherwise it is similar to other moles in habits and appearance. Hairy-tailed moles dig extensive tunnels at two levels: an upper level just beneath the surface, used in warm weather, and a lower tunnel, used as a winter retreat. The moles mate in early April and litters of 4 or 5 young are born in mid-May. The eastern mole, *Scalopus aquaticus* also a North American species, closely resembles the hairy-tailed, but has a nearly naked tail.

Star-nosed Mole *Condylura cristata*

RANGE S.E. Canada, N.E. USA

HABITAT Any area with damp soil

SIZE Body: 4–5 in (10–12.5 cm) Tail: 2¼–3¼ in (5.5–8 cm)

This species of mole has a fringe of 22 fingerlike tentacles, surrounding the nostrils, which it uses to search for food on the bottoms of ponds and streams. Although star-nosed moles dig and use tunnel systems, they seldom feed within them. They are excellent swimmers and divers and feed largely on aquatic crustaceans, small fish, water insects and other pond life. Their fur is heavy and quite waterproof. The female gives birth to a litter of 2 to 7 young in spring. The young are born with well-developed nostril tentacles.

Russian Desman *Desmana moschata* **VU**

RANGE E. Europe to C. W. Asia

HABITAT Pools and streams in densely vegetated areas

SIZE Body: 7–8½ in (18–21.5 cm) Tail: 6¾–8½ in (17–21.5 cm)

The largest member of the mole family, the desman has forsaken the underground for the aquatic life, although it does excavate short burrows as bank side residences. When swimming, the desman's flattened tail acts as a rudder and propellor. Its webbed feet, with their fringing hairs, make effective paddles. Desmans feed on a variety of aquatic life from fish and amphibians to insects, crustaceans and mollusks. Now much reduced in numbers, the desman is the subject of intensive conservation measures and there are projects to reintroduce the species in parts of its former range.

ORDER DERMOPTERA

CYNOCEPHALIDAE: FLYING LEMUR FAMILY

There are only 2 species of flying lemur or colugo. They were once classified as insectivores but are now given their own order.

Philippine Flying Lemur/Colugo *Cynocephalus volans* **VU**

RANGE Philippines

HABITAT Forest

SIZE Body: 15–16½ in (38–42 cm) Tail: 8¾–10½ in (22–27 cm)

This lemur "flies" with the aid of a gliding membrane (patagium) which stretches from the neck to the wrists and ankles and to the tip of the tail. It can glide through the trees for up to 450 ft (135 m). Almost helpless on the ground, it is an agile climber. It feeds on shoots, buds, fruit and flowers from a range of forest trees. Its main predator is the Philippine eagle. Flying lemurs mate in February, and after 2 months the female gives birth to a single young which she carries with her until it grows too heavy.

TREE SHREWS

ORDER SCANDENTIA

TUPAIIDAE TREE SHREW FAMILY

There is a single family in the order Scandentia, containing approximately 16 species of tree shrew, which live in the forests of eastern Asia, including Borneo and the Philippines. These biologically interesting, but visually undistinguished, mammals have affinities with the order Insectivora, because of their shrewlike appearance, and with the order Primates because of their complex, convoluted brains. They have been included in both of these orders. Most modern zoologists agree, however, that tree shrews should be placed in a distinct order so that their uniqueness is emphasized, rather than hidden in a large, diverse order. Until much more is known of their biology, tree shrews will remain an enigma.

Tree shrews resemble slim, long-nosed squirrels in general appearance, and their ears are squirrellike in shape and relative size. Their feet are modified for an arboreal existence, having naked soles equipped with knobbly pads, which provide tree shrews with a superb ability to cling to branches. This ability is enhanced by the presence of long flexible digits, with sharp, curved claws. The 16 species range from 4 to 8½ in (10 to 22 cm) in body length, with tails of 3½ to 8¾ in (9 to 22.5 cm). They run rapidly through the forest canopy, and most are active in the daytime, searching for insects and fruit to consume. They drink frequently and are also fond of bathing.

Despite the name, tree shrews are not exclusively arboreal, and many species spend a good deal of time on the ground. Their senses of smell, sight and hearing are good. Tree shrews usually live in pairs, and males, particularly, are aggressive toward one another. The borders of a pair's territory are marked with urine and glandular secretions.

There are between 1 and 4 young in a litter, but most usually only 1 or 2. The babies are born in a separate nest separate from the adults' normal sleeping quarters. The female visits her young only once a day or even every other day. The young are able to take sufficient milk in a short period to sustain them during her absences. Males and females look similar, but males are usually larger.

Tree shrews bear a close resemblance to fossils of the earliest mammals, so it may be assumed that the first true mammals looked, and possibly behaved, like these animals.

Common Tree Shrew *Tupaia glis*

RANGE S. and S.E. Asia: India to Vietnam and Malaysia, S. China, Indonesia

HABITAT Rain forest, woodland, bamboo scrub

SIZE Body: 5½–9 in (14–23 cm) Tail: 4¾–8¼ in (12–21 cm)

The common tree shrew is a squirrellike creature, with a long, bushy tail. It is active and lively and climbs with great agility in the trees, though it also spends a great proportion of its time on the ground feeding. Its diet is varied and includes insects (particularly ants), spiders, seeds, buds and probably also small birds and mice. This shrew normally lives alone or with a mate.

Breeding seems to occur at any time of year, and a rough nest is made in a hole in a fallen tree or among tree roots. In Malaysia, where breeding of this species has been most closely observed, females produce litters of 1 to 3 young after a gestation of 46 to 50 days. The newborn young are naked, with closed eyes, but are ready to leave the nest about 33 days after birth.

Mountain Tree Shrew *Tupaia montana* **VU**

RANGE Borneo

HABITAT Montane forest

SIZE Body: 4¼–6 in (11–15 cm) Tail: 4–6 in (10–15 cm)

The mountain tree shrew has a long, bushy tail and a slender, pointed snout. Although it is agile in trees, it spends much of its time on the ground, searching for food. Insects, fruit, seeds and leaves are all included in its diet, and it will sit back on its

haunches to eat, holding the food in both its forepaws. This species is thought to be slightly more social than other shrews and may live in small groups.

Breeding takes place at any time during the year. Litters, normally of 2 young, are born after a gestation period of between 49 and 51 days.

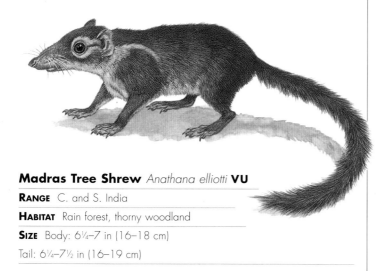

Madras Tree Shrew *Anathana elliotti* **VU**

RANGE C. and S. India

HABITAT Rain forest, thorny woodland

SIZE Body: 6¼–7 in (16–18 cm)
Tail: 6¼–7½ in (16–19 cm)

The Madras tree shrew is a squirrellike creature, which is similar in most aspects to the tree shrews of the *Tupaia* genus. It is identified, however, by its larger ears, heavier snout and the pale stripe on each shoulder.

The Madras tree shrew is active during the day, moving in trees and on the ground, searching for insects and probably fruit to eat. Little is known about its breeding habits, but they are probably similar to those of the *Tupaia* tree shrews.

Bornean Smooth–tailed Tree Shrew *Dendrogale melanura* **VU**

RANGE Borneo

HABITAT Montane forest above 3,000 ft (900 m)

SIZE Body: 4¼–6 in (11–15 cm)
Tail: 3½–5½ in (9–14 cm)

This species is the smallest of the tree shrews. It is distinguished by its smooth, short-haired tail, which ends in a point. Its body fur, too, is short and close with a dark reddish-brown on the back and lighter orange-buff on the underparts. More arboreal than the other members of its family, it finds much of its insect food on the lower branches of trees. Its breeding habits are not known.

Philippine Tree Shrew *Urogale everetti* **VU**

RANGE Philippines: Mindanao

HABITAT Rain forest, montane forest

SIZE Body: 6¾–7¾ in (17–20 cm) Tail: 4¼–6¾ in (11–17 cm)

A particularly elongate snout and a rounded, even-haired tail characterize the Philippine tree shrew. Its fur is brownish, but with orange or yellow underparts. This shrew is mainly active during the day. It climbs well and runs fast on the ground.

Its diet is varied and includes insects, lizards, young birds and birds' eggs and fruit.

In the wild Philippine tree shrews are thought to nest on the ground or on cliffs. Their breeding habits have been observed in captivity, where females have produced 1 or 2 young after a gestation period of 54 to 56 days.

Feather-tailed Tree Shrew *Ptilocercus lowi*

RANGE Malaysia, Sumatra, Borneo

HABITAT Rain forest

SIZE Body: 4¾–5½ in (12–14 cm) Tail: 6¼–7 in (16–18 cm)

This tree shrew is easily identified by its unusual tail, which is naked for much of its length, but has tufts of hair on each side of the terminal portion, making it resemble a feather. Its ears, which are large and membranous, stand away from the head. Its hands and feet are larger, relative to body size, than those of other tree shrews. The feather-tailed tree shrew is thought to be nocturnal. It spends much of its life in trees and is a good climber, using its tail for balance and support and spreading its toes and fingers wide for grip. Insects, fruit and some lizards are its main foods.

Feather-tailed tree shrews nest in holes in trees or branches, well off the ground, but their breeding habits are not known. They generally live in pairs.

MOUSE-LEMURS, LEMURS AND AYE-AYE

ORDER PRIMATES

There are about 233 species of primate divided into two main groups. The Strepsirhini includes more primitive primates, such as lemurs, the aye-aye, and lorises and tarsiers. The Haplorhini includes the tarsiers, monkeys, and apes.

CHEIROGALEIDAE: MOUSE-LEMUR FAMILY

The 7 species of mouse-lemur and dwarf-lemur occur in forest areas throughout the island of Madagascar and are among the smallest species of the primate order.

Russet Mouse-lemur *Microcebus rufus*

RANGE E. Madagascar

HABITAT Forest

SIZE Body: 5–6 in (12.5–15 cm) Tail: 5–6 in (12.5–15 cm)

Mainly nocturnal in its habits, this tiny primate moves swiftly and nimbly on fine branches amid dense foliage. It uses its long tail for balance and will leap across gaps between trees. It also comes down to the ground to forage in leaf litter for beetles. Insects and small vertebrates are its main foods, supplemented by fruit and buds. Though they normally move and hunt alone, russet mouse-lemurs often sleep in small groups in nests made in hollow trees or constructed from leaves.

LEMURIDAE: LEMUR FAMILY

There are about 10 species of lemur, all found in Madagascar and the nearby Comoro Islands. Most live in wooded areas and are agile tree-climbers.

Ring-tailed Lemur *Lemur catta* **VU**

RANGE S. Madagascar

HABITAT Dry, rocky country with some trees

SIZE Body: 17¾ in (45 cm) Tail: 21½ in (55 cm)

The ring-tailed lemur has a pointed muzzle, large eyes and triangular ears. Its fur is thick and soft, and its bushy, distinctively ringed tail accounts for more than half its total length. Both sexes have special scent glands on the lower forelimbs. Males have larger glands than females, with a horny spur near each and scent glands on the upper arms, under the chin and by the penis. Females have scent glands in the genital region. The lemurs use the secretions in these glands to mark territory boundaries, but will also mark when excited or disturbed. Troops of between 20 and 40 lemurs occupy a territory. Females and young form the core. Females are dominant. Males move between troops.

Ring-tailed lemurs are active during the day, sometimes climbing up trees, but also spending much time on the ground on all fours, with tail erect. They feed on fruit, leaves, bark, grass and resin, which they chisel from the trees with their lower incisors.

After a gestation of about 136 days females usually produce 1 young, though sometimes there are litters of 2 or 3. Babies are born well haired with open eyes and are independent at 6 months.

Ruffed Lemur

Varecia variegata **EN**

RANGE N.E. and E. Madagascar

HABITAT Rain forest

SIZE Body: 23½ in (60 cm) Tail: 23½ in (60 cm)

Distinguished by its long ruff, this lemur has white and black, brown or rufous fur. The ruffed lemur is a nimble climber. It is most active at dusk and during the first part of the night when it forages in the trees for fruit, leaves and bark. It rarely descends to the ground.

In November, after a gestation period of between 99 and 102 days the female ruffed lemur produces between 1 and 3 young. She gives birth in a nest in a hole in a tree or on a forked branch, which she lines with her own fur.

INDRIDAE: INDRI, AVAHI AND SIFAKA FAMILY

The 5 species in this family occur in the scrub country and forests of Madagascar. In all of these lemurs the snout is shortened and bare of fur giving them a resemblance to monkeys.

Verreaux's Sifaka
Propithecus verreauxi **VU**
RANGE W. and S. Madagascar
HABITAT Dry and rain forest
SIZE Body: 17¾ in (45 cm)
Tail: 21½ in (55 cm)

This large, long-limbed sifaka has a naked black face, large eyes, and ears that are nearly concealed by its fur. Coloration is highly variable, ranging from yellowish-white to black or a reddish-brown.

Troops of up to 10 animals occupy a well-defined territory, the boundaries of which are marked with urine or with secretions from the male's throat gland. They feed in the morning and afternoon on leaves, buds and fruit and are relaxed in their movements, spending much of the day resting and sun-bathing. Sifakas are primarily arboreal but sometimes come down to the ground.

Young are born from the end of June to August after a gestation of about 130 days. Females usually produce 1 young, which is suckled for about 6 months.

Woolly Lemur *Avahi laniger* **LR:lc**
RANGE E. and N.W. Madagascar
HABITAT Forest
SIZE Body: 11¾–17¾ in (30–45 cm)
Tail: 13–15¾ in (33–40 cm)

A nocturnal animal, the long-limbed woolly lemur sleeps up in the trees by day. It is active at night, when it searches for fruit, leaves and buds to eat. It is an agile climber and only occasionally descends to the ground, where it moves in an upright position.

The young are usually born in late August or September after a gestation period of about 150 days. The female normally produces a single young, which she suckles for about 6 months.

Indri *Indri indri* **EN**
RANGE N.E. Madagascar
HABITAT Forest up to 6,000 ft (1,800 m)
SIZE Body: 24–28 in (61–71 cm)
Tail: 1¼–2¼ in (3–6 cm)

The largest of the lemurs, the indri is easily identified by its stumpy tail. It has a longer muzzle than the sifakas and a naked black face. Indris live in family groups and are active during the day at all levels of the forest, looking for leaves, shoots and fruit.

Mating takes place in January or February, and the females give birth to 1 young after a gestation period of between 4½ and 5½ months.

DAUBENTONIIDAE: AYE-AYE FAMILY

The single species of aye-aye is a nocturnal, arboreal animal, found in the dense forests of Madagascar.

Aye-aye *Daubentonia madagascariensis* **EN**
RANGE Formerly N.E. Madagascar, now only in nature reserves
HABITAT Rain forest
SIZE Body: 14½–17½ in (36–44 cm) Tail: 19¾–23½ in (50–60 cm)

Well adapted for life in the trees, the extraordinary aye-aye has specialized ears, teeth and hands. It emerges from its nest at night to search for food, mainly insect larvae, plant shoots, fruit and eggs. All of its digits are long and slender, but the third is particularly elongate. The aye-aye uses this finger to tap on tree trunks to locate wood-boring insects. It listens for movement with its large, sensitive ears, and probes with its finger to winkle out the prey. Sometimes it tears open the wood with its powerful teeth. It also uses its teeth to open eggs or coconuts.

Every 2 or 3 years, females produce a single young, which is suckled for over a year.

LORISES, GALAGOS AND TARSIERS

LORIDAE: LORIS FAMILY

The 5 species in this primate family are found in Africa, India, Southeast Asia. It includes the lorises, potto and angwantibo, which have short tails or no tails at all and are slow and deliberate in their movements.

Slender Loris *Loris tardigradus* **VU**

RANGE Sri Lanka, S. India

HABITAT Rain forest, open woodland, swamp forest

SIZE Body 7–10¼ in (18–26 cm)
Tail: absent or vestigial

The slender loris spends most of its life in trees, where it moves slowly and deliberately on its long, thin limbs. It has a strong grip with its efficient grasping hands, and its thumbs and great toes are opposable. A nocturnal animal, it spends the day sleeping up in the trees, its body rolled up in a ball. Toward evening, it becomes active and hunts for insects – particularly grasshoppers – lizards, small birds and their eggs, as well as some shoots and leaves. It approaches prey stealthily, with its usual deliberate movements, and then quickly grabs it with both hands.

In India, the slender loris is known to breed twice a year, births occurring most often in May and December. Usually 1 young (but sometimes 2) is born, which makes its own way to the mother's teats, clinging to her fur.

Slow Loris *Nycticebus coucang*

RANGE S. and S.E. Asia E. India to Malaysia; Sumatra, Java, Borneo, Philippines

HABITAT Dense rain forest

SIZE Body: 10¼–15 in (26–38 cm) Tail: vestigial

A plumper, shorter-limbed animal than its relative the slender loris, the slow loris is, however, similar in its habits. It spends the day sleeping up in a tree, its body rolled into a tight ball. At night, it feeds in the trees on insects, birds' eggs, small birds and shoots and fruit. It seldom comes down to the ground. A slow but accomplished climber, its hands and feet are strong and capable of grasping so tightly that it can hang by its feet alone. The thumb and great toe are opposable to the digits.

Breeding takes place at any time of year, and 1 young (sometimes 2) is born after a gestation period of 193 days. Slow lorises are thought to live in family groups.

Potto *Perodicticus potto*

RANGE W., C. and E. Africa

HABITAT Forest, forest edge

SIZE Body: 11¾–15¾ in (30–40 cm)
Tail: 2–4 in (5–10 cm)

A thickset animal with dense fur, the potto has strong limbs and grasping feet and hands; the great toe and thumb are opposable. At the back of its neck are four horny spines, projections of the vertebrae that pierce the thin skin. The potto can quickly seize insect prey with its hands; snails, fruit and leaves are also eaten.

The female gives birth to 1 young a year, after a gestation of 6 to 6½ months. Although weaned at 2 or 3 months, the young may stay with its mother for up to a year.

Angwantibo

Arctocebus calabarensis **LR:nt**

RANGE W. Africa Nigeria, Cameroon, south to Congo River

HABITAT Dense rain forest

SIZE Body: 9¾–15¾ in (25–40 cm)
Tail: about ½ in (1.25 cm)

Also known as the golden potto because of the sheen to its fur, the arboreal angwantibo has strong hands and feet, adapted for grasping branches. Its first finger is a mere stump, and the second toe is much reduced. A skilled, but slow, climber, the angwantibo is active at night, when it feeds mostly on insects, especially caterpillars, and also on snails, lizards and fruit. Outside the breeding season, it is usually solitary.

Females give birth to 1 young after a gestation of 131 to 136 days. Offspring are weaned at 4 months and fully grown at 7.

GALAGONIDAE: GALAGO FAMILY.

The 9 species of galagos, or bushbabies are found only in Africa. All species are arboreal. They have long limbs and tails and are excellent leapers.

Greater Bushbaby

Otolemur crassicaudatus

RANGE Africa: Kenya, south to South Africa: Natal

HABITAT Forest, wooded savanna, bushveld, plantations

SIZE Body: 10½–18½ in (27–47 cm) Tail: 13–20½ in (33–52 cm)

The greater bushbaby is a strongly built animal, with a pointed muzzle and large eyes. Its hands and feet are adapted for grasping, with opposable thumbs and great toes. Much of the bushbaby's life is spent in the trees, where it is active at night and feeds on insects, reptiles, birds and birds' eggs and plant material. It makes a rapid pounce to seize prey and kills it with a bite. It has a call like the cry of a child (hence the name bushbaby) made most frequently in the breeding season.

The female is territorial. She gives birth to a litter of 1 to 3 young between May and October, after a gestation of 126 to 136 days. Males leave the mother's territory following puberty, but young females maintain their social relationship with the mother.

Lesser Bushbaby

Galago senegalensis

RANGE Africa: Senegal to Somalia and Tanzania

HABITAT Savanna, bush, woodland

SIZE Body: 5½–8¼ in (14–21 cm) Tail: 7¾–11¾ in (20–30 cm)

More active and lively than its relative the greater bushbaby, this species moves with great agility in the trees and hops and leaps with ease. Like all its family, it sleeps up in the trees during the day and hunts for food at night. Spiders, scorpions, insects, young birds, lizards, fruit, seeds and nectar are all included in its diet.

The lesser bushbaby lives in a family group, the members of which sleep together but disperse on waking.

Breeding habits vary slightly in different areas of the range. In regions where there are two rainy seasons, females have two litters a year, each usually of only 1 offspring. In areas where there is only one rainy season, females produce one litter, often, but not always, of twins. The gestation period varies between 128 and 146 days, and the young are fully developed at approximately 4 months.

TARSIIDAE: TARSIER FAMILY

The 4 species in this family occur in the Philippines and Indonesia. These little prosimian primates are primarily nocturnal and arboreal and climb and jump with great agility. They are better adapted to leaping than any other primates, with their elongate hind legs and feet (which are as long as the head and body combined) and grasping fingers. Their long tails are naked. The tarsiers' large, forward pointing eyes equip it well for night time hunting.

Western Tarsier

Tarsius bancanus

RANGE Sumatra, Borneo

HABITAT Secondary forest, scrub

SIZE Body: 3¼–6¼ in (8.5–16 cm) Tail: 5¼–10½ in (13.5–27 cm)

The western tarsier, like its two relatives, is identified by its long, naked tail and extremely large, round eyes. Its forelimbs are short and its hind limbs are long because of the adaptation of the tarsus, or ankle bones. This enables the tarsier to leap. The specialized tarsus is of course, the origin of both the common and scientific names.

A nocturnal, mainly arboreal animal, the tarsier sleeps during the day, clinging to a branch with its tail. At dusk, it wakes to prey on insects, its main food, which it catches by making a swift pounce and seizing the insect in its hands.

Courtship is highly active, involving much chasing and jumping in the trees. Breeding occurs at any time of year, and females give birth to 1 young after a gestation of about 6 months. The young tarsier is born well furred, with its eyes open, and is capable of climbing and hopping almost immediately. It becomes sexually mature at about 1 year. Pairs tend to occupy a territory with their one offspring and mark the boundary of their territory with urine.

MARMOSETS AND TAMARINS

CALLITRICHIDAE: MARMOSET AND TAMARIN FAMILY

Marmosets and tamarins make up 1 of the 2 families of primates that occur in the New World. Together with the monkeys, family Cebidae, they are known as the flat-nosed, or platyrrhine, monkeys. There are about 20 species of marmoset and tamarin, but more may sometimes be listed, depending on whether some variations are regarded as subspecies or species in their own right. Apart from the mouse-lemurs, marmosets are the smallest primates, varying from mouse-size to squirrel-size. Their fur is soft, often silky, and many have tufts or ruffs of fur on their heads. Their tails are furry and are not prehensile.

Active in the daytime, marmosets and tamarins are primarily tree-dwelling but do not have grasping hands or opposable thumbs like most primates. Neither do they swing from branch to branch, but they are rapid and agile in their movements and bound swiftly through the trees in a similar manner to squirrels. Their diet is varied, including both plant and animal material.

At night, marmosets sleep curled up in holes in trees. They are social animals and live in small family groups. The usual number of young is 2, and the male assists his mate by carrying one of the twins on his back. Often extremely vocal, marmosets make a variety of high-pitched cries.

Goeldi's Marmoset

Callimico goeldii **VU**

RANGE Upper Amazon basin

HABITAT Scrub, forest

SIZE Body: 7–8½ in (18–21.5 cm) Tail: 9¾–12½ in (25–32 cm)

Few Goeldi's marmosets have been seen or captured, and details of their habits are not well known. This marmoset is identified by the long mane around its head and shoulders and by the long hairs on its rump. It forages at all levels of the trees and bushes, searching for plant matter, such as berries, and for insects and small vertebrates. An agile animal, it walks and runs well and leaps expertly from branch to branch. It often goes down to the ground and will seek refuge on the ground when alarmed by a predator such as a bird of prey.

Strong, long-lasting pair bonds exist between males and females, and Goeldi's marmosets usually live in family groups of parents and offspring. The female bears a single young as a rule, after a gestation of 150 days. These marmosets are highly vocal and communicate with a variety of trills and whistles.

The exact state of the population of this species of marmoset is uncertain, but it is known to be rare and to have a patchy, localized distribution. In recent years it has suffered badly from the destruction of large areas of forest and from illegal trapping. More information is needed on these marmosets in order to set up suitable reserves and to ensure the survival of the species.

Pygmy Marmoset *Cebuella pygmaea*

RANGE Upper Amazon basin

HABITAT Tropical forest

SIZE Body: 5½–6¼ in (14–16 cm) Tail: 6–7¾ in (15–20 cm)

This is the smallest marmoset and one of the smallest primates. The pygmy marmoset is active in the daytime, but may rest at noon. It is particularly vulnerable to attack by large birds of prey because of its size, so it tries to keep out of sight and to avoid danger. It moves either extremely slowly or in short dashes, punctuated by moments of frozen immobility. Its cryptic coloration also helps it to hide from predators.

The pygmy marmoset is primarily a tree-dweller and sleeps in holes in trees. However, it does come down to the ground occasionally in order to feed or to move from one tree to another. It mainly eats fruit, insects, small birds and birds' eggs. It is also thought to feed on sap from trees, which it obtains by gnawing a hole in the bark.

Pygmy marmosets live in troops of 5 to 10 individuals in which the females are dominant.

Silvery Marmoset

Callithrix argentata

RANGE Brazil, Bolivia

HABITAT Forest, tall grass

SIZE Body: 6–11¾ in (15–30 cm)
Tail: 7–15¾ in (18–40 cm)

This marmoset can be recognized by its silky, silvery white body fur. It has no hair on its face and ears, which are reddish in color. There is often some gray on its back, and its tail is black.

With quick, jerky movements, the silvery marmoset runs and hops through the trees and bushes in its habitat, looking for food such as fruit, leaves, tree exudates, insects, spiders, small birds and birds' eggs. It usually moves in groups of 2 to 5.

Like most marmosets, it has a range of expressions, including facial grimaces and raising of the eyebrows, which are used to threaten rivals or enemies.

The female gives birth to 1 or 2 young, occasionally 3, after a gestation of 140 to 150 days. The male assists at the birth and is largely responsible for the care of the young.

Golden Lion Tamarin

Leontopithecus rosalia **CR**

RANGE S.E. Brazil

HABITAT Coastal forest

SIZE Body: 7½–8½ in (19–22 cm)
Tail: 10¼–13¼ in (26–34 cm)

A beautiful animal, this tamarin has a silky golden mane covering its head and shoulders and concealing its ears.

In common with the other members of its family, it leaps from branch to branch with great agility as it searches for fruit, insects, lizards, small birds and birds' eggs to eat. It lives in small groups and is highly vocal.

The female gives birth to 1 or 2 young, rarely 3, after a gestation of 132 to 134 days. The father assists in the care of the young, giving them to the mother at feeding time and by later preparing their first solid food by squashing and softening it in his fingers.

Habitat destruction has severely threatened this species.

Emperor Tamarin *Saguinus imperator*

RANGE W. Brazil, E. Peru, N. Bolivia

HABITAT Lowland forest

SIZE Body: 7–8¼ in (18–21 cm)
Tail: 9¾–12½ in (25–32 cm)

Easily identified by its flowing white mustache, the emperor tamarin is one of 12 species included in this genus. It is an active, agile animal, moving with quick, jerky movements in the shrubs and trees as it searches for fruit, tender vegetation insects, spiders, small vertebrate animals and birds' eggs. It lives in small groups and makes a great variety of shrill sounds.

The female produces twin offspring after a gestation of about 5 months. The father assists at the birth and cleans the newly born young. Like many other marmosets, he also helps at feeding time by handing the baby to the mother.

Black and Red Tamarin

Saguinus nigricollis

RANGE S. Colombia to adjacent areas of Ecuador and Brazil

HABITAT Primary and secondary forest

SIZE Body: 6–11 in (15–28 cm) Tail: 10½–16½ in (27–42 cm)

This tamarin is typical of its genus, with its unspecialized, short, broad hands, equipped with claws, and a small body. The hairs around its mouth are white, but the skin under the mustache is pigmented, as are the genitalia.

Family groups, consisting of a male, a female and 1 or 2 young, live in a defined territory – the female marks branches on the boundaries of the territory with secretions of her anal glands and urine. Insects, leaves and fruit are the main foods of these tamarins.

The female gives birth to 2 young after a gestation of 140 to 150 days.

NEW WORLD MONKEYS

CEBIDAE: NEW WORLD MONKEYS

Most of the New World monkeys of the family Cebidae are much larger in size than any of the marmosets and tamarins – the other group of flat-nosed (platyrrhine) American monkeys. There are about 43 species, including capuchins, howler monkeys, woolly monkeys, sakis and uakaris. Typically these monkeys have long, hairy tails, which in some species are prehensile and of great importance in arboreal locomotion.

With a few exceptions, cebid monkeys conform to the flat-nosed appearance so characteristic of New World monkeys. The nostrils are wide apart and open to the sides; they are a major distinguishing feature between New and Old World monkeys which have nostrils placed close together and opening forward. The long, thin fingers of the hands are useful manipulative organs and bear strong nails, but the thumbs are not opposable. The big toe, however, is large and can be opposed against the other toes for gripping branches. Thus equipped, cebid monkeys are excellent runners and leapers in wooded habitats in Central and South America, from Mexico in the north to Argentina in the south. They are gregarious and live in family-based groups with much vocal and visual communication. Diet is largely vegetarian.

Douroucouli/Night Monkey

Aotus trivirgatus

RANGE Panama to Paraguay (patchy distribution)

HABITAT Forest

SIZE Body: 9½–14½ in (24–37 cm) Tail: 12¼–15¾ in (31–40 cm)

The douroucouli has a heavily furred body and tail and is characterized by its large eyes and round head. It is usually grayish in colour, with dark markings on the head, and has an inflatable sac under the chin that amplifies its calls. A nocturnal monkey, it can see very well at night and moves with agility in the trees, leaping and jumping with ease. It rarely descends to the ground.

Fruit, leaves, insects and spiders are its main foods, but it also takes some small mammals and birds. Douroucoulis usually live in pairs, accompanied by their offspring. Several families may group together during the day to sleep in a hollow tree or in a nest among foliage. The female gives birth to a single young, which clings to its mother for the first few weeks of life before it starts to climb alone.

Monk Saki *Pithecia monachus*

RANGE Upper Amazon basin

HABITAT Forest

SIZE Body: 13¾–18¾ in (35–48 cm) Tail: 12¼–20 in (31–51 cm)

The monk saki has long, shaggy hair framing its face and on its neck, and a thick, bushy tail. A shy wary animal, it is totally arboreal, living high in the trees and sometimes descending to lower levels, but not to the ground. It generally moves on all fours, but may sometimes walk upright on a large branch and will leap across gaps. During the day, it moves in pairs or small family groups, feeding on fruit, berries, honey, some leaves, small mammals, such as mice and bats, and birds.

The female gives birth to 1 young.

Black-bearded Saki

Chiropotes satanas

RANGE N. South America to Brazil

HABITAT Forest

SIZE Body: 14¼–20½ in (36–52 cm) Tail: 14¼–19¾ in (36–50 cm)

The black-bearded saki is identified by its prominent beard and the long black hair on its head, the rest of the coat is reddish chestnut or blackish-brown. The tail is thick and heavily furred. Little is known of the habits of this monkey in the wild other than that it lives in large trees and feeds mainly on fruit. It requires many square kilometres of undisturbed habitat for successful breeding, however, and the widespread felling of primary forest poses a threat to its long-term survival.

White-fronted Capuchin *Cebus albifrons*

RANGE Parts of Colombia, Venezuela, upper Amazon area; Trinidad

HABITAT Forest

SIZE Body: 11¾–15 in (30–38 cm) Tail: 15–19¾ in (38–50 cm)

A lively, intelligent monkey like all the capuchins, this species is slender and long-limbed, with a partially prehensile tail. There is considerable variation in color over the range, but these capuchins are usually different shades of brown. Alert and fast-moving, they are inquiring by nature, have great manual dexterity and investigate all sorts of plants and fruit in the hope that they may be edible. Shoots, fruit, insects, young birds and birds' eggs are all part of their diet. Primarily arboreal, these capuchins do sometimes descend to the ground and may venture across open country. They are gregarious and live in territories in groups of 20 or 30. The female usually gives birth to 1 young, although twins have been known. The offspring is suckled for several months and is carried around by both parents.

Dusky Titi *Callicebus moloch*

RANGE Colombia to Bolivia

HABITAT Forest, thickets

SIZE Body: 11–15¼ in (28–39 cm) Tail: 13–19¼ in (33–49 cm)

An inhabitant of densely vegetated areas, the dusky titi often occurs in damp, waterlogged forest. It can move quite fast if necessary, but rarely does so. It generally stays within a fairly small area, feeding on fruit, insects, spiders, small birds and birds' eggs. Active in the daytime, it moves in pairs or family groups, which communicate by means of a wide repertoire of sounds. Dusky titis have rounded heads and thick, soft coats

and frequently adopt a characteristic posture, with the body hunched, limbs close together and tail hanging down.

The female gives birth to 1 young.

Squirrel Monkey *Saimiri sciureus*

RANGE Colombia to Amazon basin

HABITAT Forest, cultivated land

SIZE Body: 10¼–14¼ in (26–36 cm) Tail: 13¾–16½ in (35–42 cm)

The squirrel monkey is slender, with a long, mobile tail. It has a short, brightly coloured coat. It is highly active and lively, feeding during the day on fruit, nuts, insects, spiders, young birds and eggs, and it occasionally comes to the ground to feed. Squirrel monkeys sometimes raid fruit plantations. They are social and live in bands of 12 to 30 or more.

The female gives birth to 1 young after a gestation of 24 to 26 weeks. The newborn infant is able to climb soon after birth and receives little attention from its parents.

Bald Uakari *Cacajao calvus* **VU**

RANGE W. Brazil

HABITAT Forest

SIZE Body: 20–22½ in (51–57 cm) Tail: 6–6¼ in (15–16 cm)

The distinctive bald uakari has a naked face, long, shaggy hair and a beard. It is normally white but looks reddish in the sunlight. Its tail is fairly short – the 3 species of uakari are the only New World monkeys to have short tails. Extremely agile on all fours, this uakari rarely leaps, since it does not have a long, counterbalancing tail. It frequents the tree-tops, feeding largely on fruit, but also on leaves, insects, small mammals and birds. It seldom descends to the ground. Bald uakaris live in small troops of several adult males, females and young of different ages. They are active in the daytime.

NEW WORLD MONKEYS CONTINUED

Red Howler

Alouatta seniculus

RANGE Colombia to mouth of Amazon River, south to Bolivia

HABITAT Forest, mangroves

SIZE Body: 31½–35½ in (80–90 cm) Tail: 31½–35½ in (80–90 cm)

One of the largest New World monkeys, the red howler has reddish-brown fur and a sturdy body and legs. Its tail is prehensile, with an extremely sensitive naked area on the underside near the tip. All male howlers are renowned for the incredibly loud calls produced by their specialized larynxes, and this apparatus is most developed in the red howler. The chief adaptation of the larynx is the greatly expanded hyoid bone surrounding it that makes a resonating chamber for the sound. The jaw is expanded and deepened to accommodate the bulbous larynx and sports a thick beard. The male red howler occupies a territory and leads a troop of, usually, 6 to 8 animals. In order to defend his territory, he shouts for long periods at rival groups to signal his possession. Most shouting is done in the early morning and late afternoon, but red howlers may be heard at any time of day – from over 1¾ miles (3 km) away.

Red howlers live and move adeptly in the trees, although they frequent large branches because of their sturdy build. Their digits are adapted to facilitate grasping branches. The first two fingers are separated and opposable to the other

three. This arrangement does, however, make delicate manipulation of food items difficult. Red howlers leap well and use their prehensile tails for support. They sometimes go down to the ground and will even cross open land and they are good swimmers. Leaves and some fruit are the red howlers' staple diet. At night, these monkeys sleep in the trees on branches.

Breeding appears to occur at any time of year, and the female gives birth to 1 young after an average gestation of 20 weeks. The young howler clings to its mother's fur at first and later rides on her back. It is suckled for 18 months to 2 years.

Black Howler

Alouatta caraya

RANGE S. Brazil to N. Argentina

HABITAT Forest

SIZE Body: 31½–35½ in (80–90 cm) Tail: 31½–35½ in (80–90 cm)

Only male black howlers are black; females are brown. They live in troops, probably containing more than 1 male, and occupy territories, which they defend by their powerful shouts. The bulbous larynx, concealed under the beard, amplifies the shouts. Black howlers tend to be quieter and have smaller territories than red howlers.

This strongly built monkey has powerful limbs and a prehensile tail. It lives in the trees and eats leaves and fruit. The female gives birth to 1 young after a gestation of about 20 weeks. The offspring stays with her for up to 2 years.

Black Spider Monkey

Ateles paniscus **LR:lc**

RANGE N. South America to Brazil and Bolivia

HABITAT Forest

SIZE Body: 15¾–23½ in (40–60 cm) Tail: 23½–31½ in (60–80 cm)

Only surpassed by the gibbons for grace and agility in the trees, the black spider monkey, with its extremely long limbs and tail, is the most adept and acrobatic of all New World monkeys. This species is light in build, with a small head. The spider monkey has the most highly developed prehensile tail of all mammals and uses it as a fifth limb to grasp branches or food items as it moves through the trees. The monkey's whole weight can be supported by the tail, and when hanging by the tail with the long arms outstretched it has an amazing reach. Part of the underside of the tail nearest the tip is naked and patterned with fine grooves, resembling human fingerprint patterns. These increase friction and thus aid grip.

Spider monkeys frequently swing through the trees, using their hands like hooks to hang on to the branches. The hands are accordingly modified, with long, curved digits and only vestigial thumbs. While this structure makes the hands ideal for swinging in trees, it impedes delicate manipulation of food, but the monkey often uses its highly sensitive tail in order to gather food and to hold items, such as fruit, while it takes off the skin with its teeth.

Black spider monkeys rarely come to the ground. They feed in the trees, mainly on fruit and some nuts. They live in groups of 15 to 30 animals in a home range, but a group may split into smaller parties while foraging during the day. Most feeding is done in the early morning and the afternoon.

The female gives birth to 1 young after an average gestation of about 20 weeks. The young is dependent on its mother for 10 months or so.

Woolly Spider Monkey

Brachyteles arachnoides **EN**

RANGE	S.E. Brazil
HABITAT	Coastal forest
SIZE	Body: about 24 in (61 cm)
	Tail: about 26¼ in (67 cm)

The woolly spider monkey usually has a yellowish-gray to brown or reddish coat, and the naked facial skin is often red, especially when the animal becomes excited.

Its body is powerful and its limbs are long and slender. Like the spider monkeys, it has a highly efficient prehensile tail, which it uses as a fifth limb to help it move through the trees. The underside of the tail near the tip is naked and extremely sensitive. Woolly spider monkeys often move by swinging from branch to branch, although their thumbs are vestigial and of little use for such locomotion.

Wooly spider monkeys are active in the daytime when they feed in trees, mainly on fruit. They are gregarious animals, but little more is known of their social habits in the wild.

Common Woolly Monkey

Lagothrix lagotricha **LR:lc**

RANGE	Upper Amazon basin
HABITAT	Forest up to 6,600 ft (2,000 m)
SIZE	Body: 19¾–26¾ in (50–68 cm)
	Tail: 23½–28¼ in (60–72 cm)

Heavier in build than the spider monkeys, the common woolly monkey has short, thick hair. Its head is rounded, its body robust, and it has a prominent belly.

Fast and agile in the trees, it moves on all fours and by swinging hand over hand, but it is less graceful than the spider monkeys. Its thumbs and toes are well developed for grasping branches, and it has a strong, prehensile tail with a sensitive naked area near the tip.

Woolly monkeys are highly gregarious and live in troops of up to 50 animals. They forage in the daytime for plant material, mostly fruit, but are less active than many other New World monkeys. Primarily tree-dwelling, they do, nevertheless, often come down to the ground, where they walk upright, using their long tails as counterbalances.

The female gives birth to 1 offspring after a gestation period of 18 to 20 weeks. The young monkey holds on to the fur of its mother's belly or back at first and is carried around, but after a few weeks it is able to clamber about the branches unaided. The female suckles her young for 12 months or more. Common woolly monkeys become sexually mature at about 4 years old.

OLD WORLD MONKEYS

CERCOPITHECIDAE: OLD WORLD MONKEY FAMILY

The monkeys and apes of the Old World are usually grouped together as the catarrhine primates – those with closely spaced nostrils that face forward or downward. The Old World monkeys themselves are the largest group of catarrhines, with about 80 species known, in Africa, Asia and Indonesia. There are a few general differences between Old and New World monkeys. The Old World species are generally larger and often have bare buttock pads, which may be brightly colored, and their tails, although they are often long, are seldom, if ever, fully prehensile.

The family includes the macaques, baboons, mandrills, mangabeys, guenons, langurs, colobus and leaf monkeys and many other forms. Almost all are daytime-active animals, with excellent vision, hearing and sense of smell. Most are arboreal, but baboons are ground-feeding specialists, and the macaques are found both in the trees and on the ground. Generally Old World monkeys live in family or larger groups and communicate by a variety of visual and vocal signals. Males are often considerably larger than females.

Barbary Ape *Macaca sylvanus* **VU**

RANGE Gibraltar; Africa: Morocco, N. Algeria

HABITAT Rocky areas, forest clearings on mountains

SIZE Body: 21½–29½ in (55–75 cm) Tail: absent

The barbary ape is a robust, tailless monkey, with a rounded head and short muzzle. Males are larger than females and have longer hair on the crown. Formerly found elsewhere in southwest Europe, barbary apes now occur outside Africa only on Gibraltar, where the population is reinforced with animals from North Africa.

Barbary apes live in troops of 10 to 30 males, females and young in a defined territory. They sleep in trees or among rocks and feed in the early morning and afternoon, taking a rest at midday. They climb well and forage in trees and on the ground for grass, leaves, berries, fruit, roots, insects and spiders, and will plunder gardens and crops.

Females give birth to a single young, rarely twins, after a gestation of about 7 months. Births occur at any time of year, but peak from May to September. Males help females look after and carry young in the first few days. The offspring suckles for about 3 months and stays with the mother for up to 6 months.

Stump-tailed Macaque *Macaca arctoides* **VU**

RANGE Myanmar, S. China to Malaysia

HABITAT Forest, cultivated land

SIZE Body: 19¾–27½ in (50–70 cm) Tail: 1½–4 in (4–10 cm)

Distinguished by its pink-tinged face, shaggy hair and short tail, the stump-tailed macaque is an aggressive, fearless monkey that often invades gardens and cultivated fields. It spends much of its time on the ground but also climbs up into trees to sleep or to find food or a safe refuge, although it is not a particularly agile animal. Leaves, fruit, roots and crops, such as potatoes, are its main foods, and it usually picks up the items with its hands. Two cheek pouches are used for storing food, which is later removed and chewed at leisure. Stump-tailed macaques are active in the daytime and live in groups of 25 to 30, led by a dominant individual. Members of the group continually chatter and squeal to each other, and they also communicate by means of a wide range of facial expressions. Males are larger than females.

Little is known about reproduction in the wild, but females are thought to produce an infant every other year.

Japanese Macaque *Macaca fuscata* **EN**

RANGE Japan

HABITAT High-altitude forest

SIZE Body: 19¾–29½ in (50–75 cm) Tail: 9¾–11¾ in (25–30 cm)

The only monkey found in Japan, the Japanese macaque is the sole primate other than man able to withstand a cold, snowy winter and near-freezing temperatures. In some parts of its

range, it spends long periods immersed up to the neck in thermal pools. It is medium sized and well-built, with dense fur and long whiskers and beard. Active both on the ground and in trees, it feeds mainly on nuts, berries, buds, leaves and bark.

Social groups of up to 40 individuals live together, led by an older male. The relationship between females and their mothers is extremely important; as long as their mother lives, females remain in association with her, even when they have their own young, and such female groups are the core of a troop. Males stay with their mothers and kin until adolescence, when they may join a peripheral group of males that drifts between troops. After a period in such a group, or alone, the male joins a troop, usually not that of his birth.

Females give birth to 1 young after a gestation period of between 6 and 7 months.

Bonnet Macaque *Macaca radiata*

RANGE S. India

HABITAT Forest, scrub, cultivated and suburban areas

SIZE Body: 13¾–23½ in (35–60 cm) Tail: 18¾–25½ in (48–65 cm)

The common name of this macaque is derived from its unruly cap of dark hairs on its crown. Its face is normally pale pink, but the faces of lactating females are dark red. Males are much larger than females. The bonnet macaque is agile and active and spends most of its time in the trees. It moves easily on the ground and swims well. It feeds on leaves, fruit, nuts, seeds, insects, eggs and sometimes lizards.

The female gives birth to 1 young, sometimes twins, after a gestation period of about 150 days.

White-cheeked Mangabey *Cercocebus albigena*

RANGE Africa: Cameroon to Uganda, Kenya, Tanzania

HABITAT Forest

SIZE Body: 18–27½ in (45–70 cm) Tail: 27 in–3¼ ft (70 cm–1 m)

A slender, elegant monkey, the white cheeked mangabey is distinguished by its conspicuous eyebrow tufts and the mane of long hairs running down its neck and shoulders. Its semi-

prehensile tail is immensely long and mobile and covered with rather shaggy hairs. Males of the species are larger than females and have longer tails.

These mangabeys sleep and spend nearly all their time in trees; they feed during the day on fruit, nuts, leaves, bark and insects. Troops of 10 to 30 animals live together and are extremely noisy, constantly chattering and shrieking to one another across the tree tops.

The female gives birth to 1 young after a gestation of 174 to 180 days. The young is suckled for up to 10 months.

Agile Mangabey *Cercocebus galeritus* **LR:nt**

RANGE Africa: S.E. Nigeria, Zaire to E. Kenya

HABITAT Rain and swamp forest

SIZE Body: 17¾–25½ in (45–65 cm) Tail: 17¾–29½ in (45–75 cm)

This is a slender, but strongly built monkey. The agile mangabey has long legs and tail and a fringe of hairs on its forehead. There are several races, which vary slightly in coloration, one has no fringe on the forehead.

The details of this mangabey's daily habits are poorly known, but it is thought to be active on the ground and in trees and to feed on leaves, fruit, crops and insects.

It lives in troops of 12 to 20 animals, consisting of several old males, mature females and their young.

OLD WORLD MONKEYS CONTINUED

Olive Baboon
Papio anubis

RANGE Africa:
·Senegal, east to
N. Zaire, Ethiopia,
Kenya, Uganda,
N. Tanzania

HABITAT Savanna

SIZE Body: up to 3¼ ft
(1 m)
Tail: 17¾–29½ in
(45–75 cm)

The olive baboon is large and heavily built. It has a doglike muzzle and powerful teeth. Males have a mane around neck and shoulders and are larger than females. The tail has a tuft at its end, and the buttock area is naked, with broad callosities.

Olive baboons live in troops of 20 to 150 animals, organized in a strict hierarchy. They are mainly ground-living, but sleep at night in trees or rocks and travel to feeding grounds in the morning. Older juveniles lead, followed by females and young juveniles; then older males, mothers and infants. Young males bring up the rear. Baboons eat grass, seeds, roots, leaves, fruit, bark, insects, invertebrates, eggs, lizards and young mammals.

The female gives birth to 1 young, rarely 2, after a gestation of about 187 days. The baby clings to its mother's belly, but at 4 or 5 weeks rides on her back. It takes its first solid food at 5 or 6 months and is weaned and independent at 8 months. It is guarded by the mother until it is about 2 years old.

Hamadryas Baboon
Papio hamadryas
LR: nt

RANGE Africa: Ethiopia,
Somalia; S. Saudi Arabia

HABITAT Dry rocky country,
savanna, semidesert

SIZE Body: 19¾–37½ in
(50–95 cm)
Tail: 15¾–23½ in
(40–60 cm)·

The male hamadryas baboon is as much as twice the size of the female and has a heavy mane around its neck and shoulders. Females and younger males lack the mane and have brownish

hair. Like all baboons, this species has a doglike muzzle and a sloping back. Family troops of an old male and several females and their young live together, sleeping in trees or among rocks at night and wandering in search of food during the day. They eat almost any plants, insects and small animals.

The peak breeding season is May to July, and the female produces 1, rarely 2, young after a gestation period of between 170 and 175 days.

Chacma Baboon *Papio ursinus*

RANGE Africa: Angola, Zambia to South Africa

HABITAT Savanna, rocky areas

SIZE Body: up to 3¼ ft (1 m)
Tail: 15¾–29½ in (40–75 cm)

A large, yet slender baboon, with a prominent muzzle and a sloping back, the chacma baboon carries its tail in a characteristic posture as if "broken" near the base. It lives in troops of about 30 to 100 individuals, sleeping among rocks or in trees at night and searching for food during the day. These baboons feed early and late in the day and rest up at midday. Almost any plant and animal matter, such as leaves, fruit, insects, small invertebrates, lizards, birds and young mammals, is included in their varied diet, but they are predominantly vegetarian.

When on heat, the bare skin around the female's genital region swells, and at the peak of her fertile period only high-ranking males may mate with her. This is common to all savanna baboons.

The female gives birth to a single young, very rarely twins, after a gestation of 175 to 193 days, and suckles her offspring for about 8 months.

Drill *Mandrillus leucophaeus* **EN**

RANGE Africa: S.E. Nigeria, Cameroon

HABITAT Forest

SIZE Body: 17¾–35½ in (45–90 cm) Tail: 2¼–4¾ in (6–12 cm)

A powerfully built forest baboon, with a large head and a short, stumpy tail, the drill has a long muzzle, a ridged face and large nostrils. Males are much larger than females, sometimes twice the size, and have heavy manes on neck and shoulders. The skin of the buttock pads and the area around them is brightly colored, and the hue becomes more pronounced when the animal is excited. Although it climbs well and sleeps in low branches, the drill is essentially a ground-dwelling animal and moves about easily on all fours.

It lives in family troops of 20 or more individuals, which may join with other troops to form bands of as many as 200. The baboons communicate with each other using a variety of deep grunts and sharp cries, as well as with up and down movements of the head with mouth closed, to express threat, or side to side movements with teeth exposed, to express friendship. Old males dominate the troop and guard its safety; they are formidable animals, well equipped for fighting, with their sharp teeth and strong limbs.

Drills feed on plant matter, insects and small invertebrate and vertebrate animals.

Young are born at all times of year. The female produces 1 baby after a gestation of about 7 months.

Mandrill *Mandrillus sphinx* **LR:nt**

RANGE Africa: Cameroon, Gabon, Congo

HABITAT Forest

SIZE Body: 21½–37½ in (55–95 cm) Tail: 2¾–4 in (7–10 cm)

Male mandrills are large and heavily built with an long snout marked with deep, often colorful ridges. Adult females are much smaller and have less pronounced facial ridges and coloration. Mandrills sleep in trees, but live and feed on the ground in troops of about 20 to 50 animals, led by 1 or more old males. They eat fruit, nuts, leaves, insects and small invertebrates and vertebrates.

Births occur at any time of year, peaking from December to February. A single young is born after a gestation of about 7½ months.

Gelada *Theropithecus gelada* **LR:nt**

RANGE Africa: Ethiopia

HABITAT Mountains: rocky ravines, alpine meadows

SIZE Body: 19¾–29½ in (50–75 cm) Tail: 17¾–21½ in (45–55 cm)

The impressive gelada has a distinctive head, with a somewhat upturned muzzle marked with ridges, and the nostrils are located well back, not at the end of the muzzle as in other baboon species. The gelada's long sidewhiskers project backward and upward, and there is a heavy mane over the neck and shoulders, which can sometimes reach almost to the ground in the older males.

On the chest and throat there are three areas of bare red skin, which the male expands and brings into full view in his aggressive, threat posture. Females are about half the size of males and have much lighter manes.

The gelada is a ground-dweller and it even sleeps on rocky ledges and cliffs. It lives in family groups which comprise several females and their young, led by a large mature male. These family groups may sometimes gather into large troops of several hundred animals. Young and unattached males may form their own social units.

In the morning, the geladas leave the cliffs where they have slept and move off to alpine meadows, where they feed largely on plant material, such as grasses, seeds and fruit, and on insects and other small animals. They do not have a specific territory, and the male keeps his family together by means of a variety of calls and facial gestures. Geladas have excellent vision, hearing and sense of smell.

Most young are born between February and April. The female produces a single offspring, rarely twins, after a gestation period of between 147 and 192 days. The mother suckles the young gelada for up to 2 years and after giving birth, she will not have a period of heat for another 12 to 18 months.

OLD WORLD MONKEYS CONTINUED

Vervet Monkey *Cercopithecus aethiops*

RANGE Africa: Senegal to Somalia, south to South Africa

HABITAT Savanna, woodland edge

SIZE Body: 15¾–31½ in (40–80 cm) Tail: 19¾–27½ in (50–70 cm)

There are many races of this medium-to-large monkey, which vary in their facial markings and whiskers. Generally, however, they have black faces, white whiskers and grayish or yellowish-olive hair. Although they sleep and take refuge in trees, these adaptable monkeys forage in open country and will run some distance on the ground. They also climb, jump and swim well. Family troops of an old male and several females and young live together and may join with other troops during the day. Generally rather quiet monkeys, males utter a harsh cry, and others may scream when frightened. Mainly vegetarian animals, they feed on leaves, shoots, fruit, flowers, seeds and bark, but also eat some insects, spiders, lizards, birds' eggs and young birds.

Breeding occurs at any time of year. The female gives birth to a single young after a gestation of 175 to 203 days and suckles it for about 6 months. For the first few weeks, the baby clings to its mother's belly, but starts to leave her at 3 weeks and to climb at 4 weeks old. When males become sexually mature, their scrotums adopt a blue-green hue.

De Brazza's Monkey *Cercopithecus neglectus*

RANGE Africa: Cameroon, south to Angola, east to Uganda

HABITAT Rain and swamp forest, dry mountain forest near water

SIZE Body: 15¾–23½ in (40–60 cm)
Tail: 20¾–33½ in (53–85 cm)

The robust, heavily built De Brazza's monkey has a conspicuous reddish-brown band, bordered with black, on its forehead, and a well-developed white beard. Its back slopes upward to the tail so that the rump is higher than

the shoulders. Females look similar to males, but are smaller. Active during the day, this monkey is a good climber and swimmer and also moves with speed and agility on the ground, where it spends a good deal of its feeding time. Leaves, shoots, fruit, berries, insects and lizards are its main foods, and it will also raid crops. It lives in small family groups comprising an old male and several females with young. Sometimes there are larger troops of 30 or more animals.

The female gives birth to 1 young after a gestation of 177 to 187 days. After a week, the baby first starts to leave the safety of its mother body, and by 3 weeks, it is starting to climb and run.

Red-bellied Guenon *Cercopithecus erythrogaster* **VU**

RANGE Africa: Nigeria

HABITAT Forest

SIZE Body: about 18 in (45 cm) Tail: about 23½ in (60 cm)

This apparently rare monkey has a dark face with a pinkish muzzle, fringed with white side-whiskers. The breast and belly are usually reddish-brown, hence the common name, but can be gray in some individuals. Females look similar to males but have grayish underparts, arms and legs. Few specimens of this monkey have been found, and its habits are not known.

Diana Monkey *Cercopithecus diana* **VU**

RANGE Africa: Sierra Leone to Ghana

HABITAT Rain forest

SIZE Body: 15¾–22½ in (40–57 cm)
Tail: 19¾–29½ in (50–75 cm)

A slender, elegant monkey, the diana monkey has most striking coloration with its black and white face, white beard and chest and distinctive patches

of bright
chestnut on its back
and hind limbs. There are also conspicuous
white stripes on the otherwise dark hair of each thigh. Females
are smaller than males, but in other respects look similar.

An excellent climber, the diana monkey spends virtually all
its life in the middle and upper layers of the forest and is noisy
and inquisitive. Troops of up to 30 animals live together, led by
an old male. They are most active in the early morning and late
afternoon, when they feed on leaves, fruit, buds and other plant
matter, and also on some insects and birds' eggs and young.

The female bears a single young after a gestation period of
about 7 months and suckles it for 6 months.

Talapoin *Miopithecus talapoin*

RANGE Africa: Gabon to W. Angola

HABITAT Rain forest, mangroves, always
near water

SIZE Body: 9¾–15¾ in (25–40 cm)
Tail: 14¼–20½ in (36–52 cm)

One of the smallest African
monkeys, the talapoin has a slender body, a round
head, which is large relative to body size, and prominent
ears. Its legs are longer than its arms, and its tail exceeds
its head and body length.

Talapoins live in family troops of 12 to 20 or so
individuals, and each troop has its own territory,
although several troops may sometimes unite into a
larger group. These monkeys sleep in bushes and
mangroves and are active in the day time, particularly in
the early morning and late afternoon. Good climbers and
runners, they enter water readily and swim and dive well.
Leaves, seeds, fruit, water plants, insects, eggs and small animals
are all included in their diet, and they will raid plantation crops.

Most births occur between November and March. After a
gestation of about 6½ months, the female produces a single
young, which is born well haired and with its eyes open. The
young talapoin develops quickly and takes its first solid food at
3 weeks; it is largely independent at 3 months, although it
continues to suckle until it is 4 or 5 months old.

Patas Monkey *Erythrocebus patas*

RANGE Africa: Senegal, east to Ethiopia, south to Tanzania

HABITAT Grassland, dry savanna, forest edge, rocky plateaux

SIZE Body: 19¾–29½ in (50–75 cm) Tail: 19¾–29½ in (50–75 cm)

The slender,
long-legged
patas monkey is
among the fastest
moving of all primates on
the ground. It can attain
speeds of up to 31 mph
(50 km/h). The male may be as
much as twice the size of the female, and
the lower parts of his limbs are pure white; the limbs of females
are fawn or yellowish-white. Patas monkeys live in troops,
comprising an old male and up to 12 females and their young,
and occupy a large territory. They sleep in trees, usually at the
edge of forest, but spend virtually all of their day on the ground,
searching for fruit, seeds, leaves, roots, insects, lizards and birds'
eggs. While the troop feeds, the male leader keeps a look-out for
danger and warns his harem of the approach of any enemies.

Most births occur from December to February, and females
produce 1 young after a gestation of 170 days. The baby takes
its first solid food at about 3 months old.

Allen's Swamp Monkey *Allenopithecus nigroviridis* **LR:nt**

RANGE Africa: E. congo, Zaire

HABITAT Swampy forest

SIZE Body: 15¾–19½ in (40–50 cm) Tail: 17¾–21½ in (45–55 cm)

Allen's swamp monkey is sturdily built with relatively short
limbs and tail. Its head is rounded, with ruffs of whiskers from
the ears to the mouth. Males are slightly larger than females, but
otherwise look similar. Little is known about the habits of these
monkeys. They live in troops and feed on leaves, fruit and nuts
and also snails, crabs, fish and insects. They climb and jump
well and
enter water
readily.

The
female produces a
single young, which
clings to her belly and
suckles for 2 or
3 months.

OLD WORLD MONKEYS CONTINUED

Angolan Black and White Colobus *Colobus angolensis*

RANGE Africa: Angola to Kenya

HABITAT Forest

SIZE Body: 19¾–26¼ in (50–67 cm)
Tail: 24¾–35½ in (63–90 cm)

Colobus monkeys have long limbs and tails and robust bodies. They have only four fingers on each hand, their thumbs being vestigial or absent. The Angolan colobus is one of several black and white species and, with its sturdy body and rounded head, is typical of its genus. It is identified by the characteristic long white hairs on its shoulders, but the many races of this species differ slightly in the extent of the white on shoulders and tail.

These monkeys live in family troops of several females and their young, led and guarded by an old male. As young males mature, they either go off alone or found their own troops. Each troop has its own territory, with feeding areas and sleeping trees, but may sometimes join with other troops to form a group of 50 or so. The animals are active in the daytime, with a period of rest or grooming at midday. Much of their food, such as leaves, fruit, bark and insects, is found in the trees, where they run and leap with astonishing agility, so they rarely need to descend to the ground.

Breeding takes place all year round. The females give birth to 1 young after a gestation of 147 to 178 days. The baby starts to climb at 3 weeks, but suckles and stays with its mother for well over a year. Females will suckle young other than their own.

Red Colobus *Procolobus badius* **LR:nt**

RANGE Africa: Senegal to Ghana, Cameroon, Zaire, Uganda, Tanzania

HABITAT Rain, swamp and secondary forest, usually near water

SIZE Body: 18–27½ in (46–70 cm)
Tail: 16½–31½ in (42–80 cm)

There are many races of this slender, long-tailed colobus, with coloration ranging from orange-red to reddish-brown, often with black on the back and shoulders. The underparts are reddish-yellow to gray or white. Females are smaller than males, but otherwise look similar.

The red colobus lives in a troop of 50 to 100 animals made up of many small family groups, each comprising a male and several females and their young. The colobus troops are active during the day, when they feed among the branches on flowers, shoots, fruit and leaves, leaping acrobatically from tree to tree.

The female produces 1 young after a gestation period of between 4 and 5½ months. She nurses the infant until it is ready to be weaned at between 9 and 12 months.

Olive Colobus

Procolobus verus **LR:nt**

RANGE Africa: Sierra Leone to Ghana

HABITAT Rain, swamp and secondary forest

SIZE Body: 17–19¾ in (43–50 cm)
Tail: 22½–25¼ in (57–64 cm)

This species is the smallest of the colobus monkeys. The olive colobus has a little, rounded head, a short muzzle and rather subdued coloration. Male and female are about the same size, but the female lacks the crest of upright hairs that the male sports on his crown. This colobus lives in a family troop comprising an old male and several females and their young, usually 6 to 10 in all. Sometimes the group may be bigger, containing up to 20 individuals, with several adult males.

The monkeys sleep and take refuge in the middle layers of the forest, but feed on the lowest branches. These monkeys do not climb into the treetops and only rarely come down to the ground. Leaves and some flowers are their staple diet. They are rather quiet monkeys and make few sounds.

Reproductive details are not known for this species except that the mother carries her baby in her mouth for the first few weeks after birth – a habit shared only with other species of colobus.

Proboscis Monkey *Nasalis larvatus* **VU**

RANGE Borneo

HABITAT Mangroves, river banks

SIZE Body: 20¾–30 in (53–76 cm)

Tail: 21½–30 in (55–76 cm)

The sturdily built proboscis monkey lives in the tree-tops of mangrove swamp jungles, where the trees are strong and rigid and do not attain enormous heights. It is an agile animal and runs and leaps in the branches, using its long tail as a counterbalance; its long fingers and toes aid grip. The male is considerably larger than the female, perhaps twice her weight, and has an extraordinarily long, bulbous nose. When he makes his loud, honking call, the nose straightens out. The female has a much smaller nose and a quieter cry.

Proboscis monkeys live in small groups of 1 or 2 adult males and several females and their young. They are most active in the morning, when they feed on leaves and shoots of mangrove and pedada trees, as well as on the fruit and flowers of other trees. Much of the rest of the day is spent basking in the tree tops, where they also sleep at night.

Mating takes place at any time of year, and the female produces a single young after a gestation of about 166 days. These monkeys are difficult to keep in captivity and are becoming increasingly rare in the wild.

Snub-nosed Langur *Rhinopithecus roxellana*

RANGE S.W. and S. China, Tibet

HABITAT Mountain forest; winters in lower valleys

SIZE Body: 19¾–32½ in (50–83 cm) Tail: 20 in–3¼ ft (51 cm–1 m)

This large, long-tailed monkey has a distinctive upturned nose, hence its common name, and golden hairs on its forehead, throat and cheeks. Because

of their remote, mountainous range, few snub-nosed monkeys have yet been observed or caught. They are said to live in troops of 100 or more and to feed on fruit, buds, leaves and bamboo shoots.

Hanuman Langur *Semnopithecus entellus*

RANGE India, Sri Lanka

HABITAT Forest, scrub, arid rocky areas

SIZE Body: 20 in–3¼ ft (51 cm–1 m)

Tail: 28 in–3¼ ft (72 cm–1 m)

This large, long-limbed monkey has a black face and prominent eyebrows. It adapts well to many different habitats and will live near human habitation and raid shops and houses for food. In the Himalayas, the langur is believed to make regular migrations, moving up the mountains in summer and down again in winter.

Although it is an agile climber, the langur spends more than half of its time on the ground, where it finds much of its food. It is almost entirely vegetarian, feeding on leaves, shoots, buds, fruit and seeds. Very rarely it will eat insects.

Langurs live in groups of 1 or more adult males with females and juveniles, usually about 15 to 35 individuals in all, although in some areas groups of 80 or 90 have been observed. There are also, however, smaller all-male groups containing 4 to 15 animals. In groups with only one male, he is in sole charge of the movements and daily routine, and life is peaceful; in larger groups, the males contest and squabble, even though there is a dominant male.

Breeding takes place at any time of year except in areas with marked seasonal changes, where births are concentrated into the 2 or 3 most climatically favorable months. The female gives birth to 1, occasionally 2, young after a gestation period of between 6 and 7 months. Other females in the troop will often show a great interest in the newborn infant, and the mother allows them to touch it shortly after its birth. For the first few weeks of its life the baby clings tightly to its mother, but at 4 weeks it starts to move short distances independently and, at 3 months, it is allowed to play with other infants and to take some solid food. The infant continues to suckle for between 10 and 15 months, but nevertheless undergoes much stress during the weaning period.

GIBBONS

HYLOBATIDAE: GIBBON FAMILY

The 9 species of gibbons are found in Southeast Asia, Sumatra, Java and Borneo. Like the apes, gibbons lack an external tail and have a protruding jaw. The gibbons are agile, slender primates weighing between 11 and 28 lb (5 and 13 kg).

The gibbons are specialized arboreal forms very different externally from the great apes. They probably have the most remarkable adaptations of all mammals for rapid locomotion through trees. Gibbons use their extremely long hands to swing through the forest canopy and are spectacularly skilful climbers. All gibbons have long, slender hands, with the thumb deeply divided from the index finger. This gives additional flexibility. When standing upright the gibbon's long arms touch the ground, so they are often carried above the head. Gibbons are primarily vegetarian, but will also eat a diet of insects, young birds and eggs. The male and female of the gibbon species are generally similar in size.

Black Gibbon

Hylobates concolor **EN**

RANGE Indo-China, Hainan

HABITAT Rain forest

SIZE Body: 17¾–24¾ in (45–63 cm) Tail: absent

There are several subspecies of black, or crested, gibbons, occurring in various parts of Indo-China. The subspecies differ in details of fur coloration. The male black gibbon is slightly larger than the female and has a tuft of hair on the crown. The female is buff colored, sometimes with black patches.

Gibbons communicate with complex calls which help to maintain their pair bonds. The male has a throat sac, which acts as a resonating chamber to amplify his voice.

Black gibbons feed on a variety of foods, mostly ripe fruit, buds, leaves and insects, although occasionally small vertebrates may also be eaten.

Siamang

Hylobates syndactylus **LR:nt**

RANGE Malaysia, Sumatra

HABITAT Mountain forest

SIZE Body: 29½–35½ in (75–90 cm) Tail: absent

The largest of the gibbons, the siamang has entirely black fur. It is also distinguished by the web that unites the second and third toes of each foot. Siamangs are tree-dwelling and extremely agile, despite their size. They swing between branches and may walk upright on stronger tree boughs. At night, they sleep on high, strong branches. Fruit, especially figs, is a staple food, and they also eat flowers, leaves and shoots, some insects and even birds' eggs.

Adult siamang pairs live together in a territory with their offspring of different ages, but unmated adults live alone. Families communicate by short barks and a distinctive whooping call, which is amplified by the inflatable throat sac. The female siamang gives birth to a single young after a gestation of 230 to 235 days. The newborn baby is almost hairless and clings to its mother for safety and warmth.

Kloss's Gibbon *Hylobates klossii* **VU**

RANGE Mentawi Islands west of Sumatra

HABITAT Hill and lowland rain forest

SIZE Body: 25½–27½ in (65–70 cm) Tail: absent

Kloss's gibbon looks like a small version of the siamang and is very similar in its habits. It is the smallest of the gibbons. It is thought to represent the form and structure of ancestral gibbons. Strictly tree-dwelling, it leaps and swings in the trees with great dexterity and feeds on fruit, leaves, shoots and, perhaps, insects.

Family groups, each consisting of an adult pair and up to 3 offspring, occupy a territory and sleep and feed together. Females give birth to a single young.

Lar Gibbon

Hylobates lar **LR:nt**

RANGE S. Burma, Malaysia, Thailand, Kampuchea, Sumatra

HABITAT Rain forest, dry forest

SIZE Body: 16½–22½ in (42–58 cm)

Tail: absent

The lar gibbon may be black or pale buff, but the hands, feet, brow band and sides of the face are always pale. Like all gibbons, it is tree-dwelling and rarely descends to the ground. It moves in the trees by swinging from branch to branch by means of its long arms or by running upright along large branches.

Largely vegetarian, the lar gibbon feeds on fruit, leaves, shoots, buds and flowers and occasionally on insects.

Lar gibbons live in family groups of 2 to 6 individuals: an adult male and female and their young of different ages. The pair call to each other daily in a complex duet which is thought to reinforce their bond.

Females give birth to 1 young at intervals of between 2 and 4 years. The gestation period is between 7 and 7½ months. Young gibbons remain with their mothers for at least 2 years and are suckled by her throughout this period.

Pileated Gibbon *Hylobates pileatus* **VU**

RANGE S.E. Thailand

HABITAT Forest

SIZE Body: 17–23½ in (43–60 cm)

Tail: absent

The pileated, or capped, gibbons derive their common names from the black cap on the heads of both sexes. Like all gibbons, they are born white and the adult

pigmentation gradually spreads over the body down from the head. By the time they reach sexual maturity male pileated gibbons are completely black, while the females are buff colored with a black cap.

Pileated gibbons are strongly territorial and males scream and shout abuse to one another across their territory boundaries, although they seldom fight. The males give startling, loud solo calls at or before dawn.

This species feeds on a mixed diet of leaves, buds, tree resin and insects.

Hoolock Gibbon

Hylobates hoolock **DD**

RANGE Bangladesh, E. India, S. China, Myanmar

HABITAT Hill forest

SIZE Body: 18–24¾ in (46–63 cm)

Tail: absent

The hoolock has the long limbs and the shaggy fur that is characteristic of gibbons. Males and females are thought to be about the same size. The adult males are blackish-brown in color and the females are yellow-brown. Newborn hoolock gibbons are grayish-white and gradually darken as they age to become black at a few months old. The female's color fades at puberty, which occurs at about 6 or 7 years of age.

The hoolock gibbon is almost entirely tree-dwelling. It sleeps in the trees and in the daytime it swings itself quickly and easily from branch to branch and tree to tree, searching for food. Fruit, leaves and shoots make up the majority of its diet, but it will also sometimes supplement this with spiders, insects, larvae and birds' eggs.

Family groups, which comprise of a mated pair and their young, live together. Normally each family group feeds in its own territory, but several families may occasionally gather in the same feeding area.

The hoolock's loud calls are an important form of communication both within its own group and between groups. Mating occurs at the start of the rainy season, and females each bear a single young, some time between November and March.

APES

HOMINIDAE: APE FAMILY

The family Hominidae includes great apes – the orangutan, gorilla, and chimpanzees – and human beings. Great apeas are larger and more robust than their relatives the gibbons. An adult male gorilla can weigh as much as 595 lb (270 kg) while chimpanzees can weigh between 106 and 176 lb (48 and 80 kg).

All apes are able to walk on their hind legs, if briefly, although most – apart from humans – normally travel on all fours. Gorillas and chimpanzees are largely terrestrial, but the orangutan spends much of its time in the trees, where it swings from branch to branch with surprising agility. While gorillas are vegetarian animals, the chimpanzees and orangutans are more omnivorous in their eating habits.

Apes are generally gregarious and live in family-based groups which forage together during the day, and build sleeping nests at night. Male great apes are considerably larger than females and may have other special characteristics.

Orangutan

Pongo pygmaeus **VU**

RANGE Sumatra, Borneo

HABITAT Rain forest

SIZE Height: 4–5 ft (1.2–1.5 m) Tail: absent

The orangutan, with its reddish-brown, shaggy hair, has a strong, heavily built body and is the second-largest primate. The arms are long and powerful and reach to the ankles when the animal stands erect; there is a small thumb on each broad hand that is opposable to the first digit. The orangutan's legs are relatively short and are weaker than the arms. Males are much larger and heavier than the females and are also identified by the cheek flaps that surround the face of the mature adult. All adults have fatty throat pouches.

Orangutans live alone, in pairs or in small family groups and are active in the daytime at all levels of the trees. They walk along large branches on all fours or erect and sometimes swing by their hands from branch to branch. On the ground, they walk on all fours or stand erect. Fruit is their staple diet, but they also feed on leaves, seeds, young birds and eggs. The orangutan sleeps in the trees in a platform nest made of sticks. It may make a new nest every night.

After a gestation period of more than 9 months, the female gives birth to a single young. She cares for her offspring for some time (one captive young was suckled for 6 years) and the baby clings to the mother's fur as she moves around in the trees.

Gorilla *Gorilla gorilla* **EN**

RANGE Africa: S.E. Nigeria to W. Zaire; E. Zaire into adjacent countries

HABITAT Rain forest up to 3,000 m) 10,000 ft)

SIZE Male height: 5½–6 ft (1.7–1.8 m) Female height: 4½–5 ft (1.4–1.5 m) Tail: absent

The largest and most robust of the primates, the gorilla is also a gentle, intelligent and sociable animal, which lives a peaceful, quiet existence if undisturbed. Its body, covered with coarse black hair, is massive with a short broad trunk and wide chest and shoulders. The head is large, with a short muzzle, and the eyes and ears small; old males have high crowns. The muscular arms are longer than the short, thick legs, and the broad hands are equipped with short fingers and thumbs. Males are bigger and heavier than females, and those over 10 years old have silvery-gray hair on their backs – hence the name silverback, given to old males. There are two races: the lowland and the mountain gorilla, also referred to as eastern and western races.

On the ground, gorillas normally move in a stooped posture, with the knuckles of the hands resting on the ground, but they do stand erect on occasion. Females and juveniles climb trees, but males rarely do so because of their great bulk. Gorillas live in a closeknit group of a dominant male, 1 or 2 other males, several females and young; some groups may contain only the dominant male, 2 or 3 females and young. The group wanders in a home range of 4 to 15½ sq miles (10 to 40 km²), which is not defended or marked at the boundaries. There may be some conflict with neighboring groups, but encounters are generally avoided by communications such as drumming on the ground from a distance. Old males will threaten rivals by standing erect and beating the chest, while roaring and barking, and sometimes by tearing up and throwing plants. When the leader of a troop dies, younger males contest for dominance.

Gorillas are active in the daytime. The troop rises between 6 am and 8 am. It feeds for a while on plant material, such as leaves, buds, stalks, berries, bark and ferns, and then has a period of rest and relaxation. Gorillas do not appear to drink, but get the water they need from their juicy diet. They feed again in the afternoon and then retire for the night in nests made of twigs and leaves. Young gorillas under 3 years old sleep with their mothers, but all others have their own nests.

Breeding appears to take place at any time of year. The female gives birth to a single young after a gestation of more than 9 months. The young is completely dependent and clings to its mother's fur at first, but it is able to sit up at 3 months and to walk and climb at 5 months. It suckles for 12 to 18 months and remains with its mother for about 3 years.

Pygmy Chimpanzee/Bonobo *Pan paniscus* **EN**

RANGE Africa: Zaire

HABITAT Rain forest

SIZE Body: 21½–23½ in (55–60 cm) Height: up to 3¼ ft (1 m) Tail: absent

Similar to the chimpanzee, this species (sometimes regarded as only a sub-species), has longer, thinner legs, a more slender body and a narrow face. Its hair and facial skin are black. It moves in the trees and on the ground, feeding mainly on fruit, but also on leaves and shoots. A gregarious animal, the pygmy chimpanzee lives in a family group, and several families may gather in a good feeding area. Otherwise its habits are much the same as those of the chimpanzee.

The female bears 1 young, after a gestation of 227 to 232 days, which stays with her for up to 3 years.

Chimpanzee *Pan troglodytes* **EN**

RANGE Africa: Guinea to Zaire, Uganda and Tanzania

HABITAT Rain forest, savanna with woodland

SIZE Body: 26–37 in (68–94 cm) Height: 4–5 ft (1.2–1.7 m) Tail: absent;

The intelligent, social chimpanzee has a wide range of sounds and gestures for communication and is probably one of the most expressive of all animals. Thickset and robust, but more lightly built than the gorilla, the chimpanzee has a strong body and long limbs. The powerful arms are longer than the legs. Its hands and feet are narrow and long, with opposable thumbs on the hands. Males are slightly larger than females. There is great variability in the color of hair and facial skin, but the hair is generally blackish and the face light, darkening in older individuals. The rounded head bears broad, prominent ears, and the lips are mobile and protrusible.

Chimpanzees climb well but spend most of the time on the ground, where they generally walk on all fours, even though they stand erect on occasion, as when their hands are full of food.

Their social structure is more variable than that of the gorilla. Rain forest animals live in troops of males; of females with young; of males and females with young, or of adults of both sexes without young. The composition of the troop often changes. Savanna chimpanzees generally live in more stable troops of 1 or more males, several females and their young. They occupy a home range, the size of which depends on the size of the troop and on the food supply. Neighboring troops meet with much noise and communication, but there is usually little aggression involved.

Active in the daytime, chimpanzees rise at dawn and feed mainly on plant material, such as fruit, nuts, leaves, shoots and bark, and on eggs and insects. They will use stems or twigs as tools, to winkle termites or ants from their hiding places. Savanna chimpanzees will kill young animals for food by holding them by the hind limbs and striking their heads on the ground. At night, chimpanzees usually sleep in the trees, each making its own nest with interwoven, broken and bent branches. Young under 3 years old sleep with their mothers.

Females have regular periods of heat with swelling of the genital region, and may be mated by all the males in the troop. Usually 1 young is born, sometimes twins, after a gestation of 227 to 232 days. The young animal lives closely with its mother for 2 to 3 years.

FRUIT BATS

ORDER CHIROPTERA

One species in every four mammals is a bat, yet remarkably little is known of this order. Bats are the only mammals capable of sustained flight, as opposed to gliding, which they achieve by means of their well-designed wings. The four elongated fingers of each hand support the flight membrane, which is also attached to the ankles and sometimes also incorporates the tail.

PTEROPODIDAE: FRUIT BAT FAMILY

There are about 166 species of these large, fruit-eating bats, sometimes known as flying foxes, found in the tropical and subtropical regions of the Old World. Their eyes are large, their ears simple in structure like those of rodents, and they have a keen sense of smell. Males and females look alike.

On each hand there is a sturdy thumb, equipped with a robust claw. Some species have an extra claw at the tip of the second digit where it protrudes from the wing membrane.

Using their claws and their hind feet, fruit bats make their way along the branches of their feeding trees in search of fruit. Some also feed on pollen and nectar.

Greater Fruit Bat *Pteropus giganteus*

RANGE S. and S.E. Asia

HABITAT Forest, scrub

SIZE Body: 13¾–15¾ in (35–40 cm) Wingspan: 5 ft (1.5 m) Tail: absent

The wingspan of the greater fruit bat is the largest of any bat. It is a highly sociable creature and roosts by day in large trees in flocks of several thousand. At dusk the flocks take to the air and disperse in search of food.

The greater fruit bat crushes fruit between its peglike teeth to obtain the juice and spits out the seeds and flesh. Soft flesh, such as banana, is swallowed.

There is no general breeding season for this species, but in each part of its huge range births are more or less synchronized. One young is born after a gestation period of about 6 months and is carried about by its mother until it is 8 weeks old.

Hammerheaded Bat *Hypsignathus monstrosus*

RANGE Africa: Gambia to Uganda and Angola

HABITAT Mangrove and other swamps

SIZE Body: 10–12 in (25–30 cm) Wingspan: 27–37 in (70–95 cm) Tail: absent

The hammerheaded bat derives its name from a curious nasal swelling which develops in the male. The function of the male's strangely shaped nose remains a mystery, though it may be used to enhance the volume of his mating call. The hammerhead is one of the noisiest bats. Males gather in special trees and display to the females by chorusing for hours. The females visit this "lek" in order to pick out their mates.

Hammerheaded bats roost in small numbers. They feed on the juices of mangoes and soursops and may also have carnivorous tendencies. Females produce a single young after a gestation of 5½ months.

Egyptian Rousette Bat *Rousettus aegyptiacus*

RANGE Africa, east to India and Malaysia

HABITAT Forest; caves, tombs, temples

SIZE Body 4¼–5 in (11–13 cm) Wingspan: 12–18 in (30–45 cm) Tail: ½ in (1.5 cm)

Egyptian rousette bats roost deep in caves or tombs in large colonies, sometimes numbering millions of bats.

This species seems to rely on echolocation for flight navigation in the dark places that it inhabits. They are the only fruit bats to use this method of guidance, which is so important to the insectivorous bat species. The Egyptain rousette bat feeds on fruit juices, flower nectar and pollen and plays a useful ecological role as a pollinator. The bats must travel great distances each night in order to find enough food to survive.

The breeding season is from December to March. Females produce 1 young after a gestation of 15 weeks. The young bat clings to its mother and is transported everywhere until it can fly. It begins to feed on fruit at the age of 3 months.

Franquet's Fruit Bat
Epomops franqueti

RANGE Africa: Nigeria to Angola, east to Zimbabwe and Tanzania

HABITAT Forest, open country

SIZE Body: 5–7 (13.5–18 cm)
Wingspan: 9–10 in (23–25 cm)
Tail: absent

Franquet's fruit bat is also known as the epauleted bat on account of the distinct patches of white fur on each shoulder. Rather than crushing fruit to release the juice, this bat sucks it out. It encircles the fruit with its lips, pierces the flesh with its teeth and, while pushing the tongue up against the fruit, it sucks, using the action of its pharyngeal pump. Franquet's bats breed throughout the year, producing a single young at a time after a gestation of 3½ months.

Harpy Fruit Bat
Harpyionycteris whiteheadi

RANGE Philippines

HABITAT Forest, up to 5,575 ft (1,700 m)

SIZE Body: 5½–6 in (14–15 cm)
Wingspan: 9–12 in (23–30 cm) Tail: absent

The prominent incisor teeth of the harpy fruit bat appear to operate almost like the blades of a pair of scissors, and the bat seems to use them to snip off figs and other fruit from the trees.

Tube-nosed Fruit Bat
Nyctimene major

RANGE Sulawesi to Timor, New Guinea, N. Australia, Solomon Islands

HABITAT Forest

SIZE Body: 3–4¾ in (7–12 cm) Wingspan: 8–11 in (20–28 cm) Tail: ½–1 in (1.5–2.5 cm)

This bat has a pair of nasal scrolls which stand out on each side of the head like snorkel tubes. Their exact function is not clear, but they may help the bat to locate ripe fruit by bestowing a "stereo" effect on the nose. Guavas, figs and even the pulp of young coconuts make up the diet of the tube-nosed bat. Pieces of fruit are torn out with the teeth and then chewed and kneaded against the chest and belly. Only the juice is consumed, the rest is dropped to the ground.

Tube-nosed bats seem less social than other fruit bats and usually roost alone. They cling to the trunks of trees and are afforded some camouflage by their spotted wings. They breed in September and October and produce 1 young.

Long-tongued Fruit Bat
Macroglossus minimus

RANGE Myanmar, east to Malaysia and Bali

HABITAT Forest, plantations

SIZE Body: 2¼–2¾ in (6–7 cm)
Wingspan: 5½–6¾ in (14–17 cm) Tail: vestigial

The long-tongued fruit bat is one of the smallest fruit bats. It has adopted a solitary way of life, possibly in order to make itself less obvious to predators. By day it roosts in rolled-up banana or hemp leaves, emerging at dusk to feed on pollen and nectar from plants. It will also eat fruit, and is considered a plantation pest in some parts of its range.

These bats are quite vocal and make a shrieking noise at night. They breed between August and September, producing a single young after a gestation period of between 12 and 15 weeks.

Queensland Blossom Bat
Syconycteris australis

RANGE S. New Guinea, south to Australia: New South Wales

HABITAT Wet and dry forest

SIZE Body: 2–2½ in (5–6 cm)
Wingspan: 4¾–6 in (12–15 cm) Tail: vestigial

The Queensland blossom bat is the smallest fruit bat. It inhabits eucalyptus and acacia forests and seems to feed almost exclusively on the pollen and nectar of the many species of these trees. The bat feeds by inserting its long brushlike tongue deep into the long-necked blooms. As it travels from tree to tree it pollinates the flowers on which it feeds.

Females give birth to a tiny infant in the summer – in November or December.

MOUSE-TAILED BATS AND SHEATH-TAILED BATS

RHINOPOMATIDAE: MOUSE-TAILED BAT FAMILY

Mouse-tailed bats derive their name from their long, naked tails which equal the head and body in length. Their tails are not joined to the body with a membrane as they are in other families. There are 3 species, found from the Middle East through India to Thailand and Sumatra. These bats have occupied certain pyramids in Egypt for 3 millennia or more.

Greater Mouse-tailed Bat

Rhinopoma microphyllum

RANGE West Africa, North Africa, Middle East, India, Sumatra

HABITAT Treeless arid land

SIZE Body: 2¼–3 in (6–8 cm)

Wingspan: 6¾–10 in (17–25 cm)

Tail: 2¼–3 in (6–8 cm)

Colonies of thousands of mouse-tailed bats occupy roosts in large ruined buildings, often palaces and temples.

They feed exclusively on insects and, in those areas where a cool season temporarily depletes the food supply, the bats may enter a deep sleep resembling torpor. Before they enter this state they lay down thick layers of fat on their bodies, which may weigh as much as the bats themselves, and with this they can survive for many weeks with neither food nor water. As they sleep, the accumulated fat is used up and by the time the cold season is passed, nothing of it remains.

Mouse-tailed bats mate at the beginning of spring and the female produces a single offspring after a gestation period of about 4 months. The young bat is weaned at 8 weeks, but does not attain sexual maturity until its second year.

EMBALLONURIDAE: SHEATH-TAILED BAT FAMILY

There are 47 species of bat in this family and all have a characteristic membrane which spans the hind legs, the tail originates beneath the membrane and penetrates it through a small hole. The advantages of this arrangement are not clear, but the bat is able to adjust this versatile "tailplane" during flight by movements of its legs only, and it is possible that it may improve its aerial abilities.

Sheath-tailed bats range over tropical and subtropical regions of the world in a variety of habitats, but never far from trees. They are primarily insect-eaters, but may supplement their diet with additional fruit.

Scent-producing glandular sacs on the wings, in the crooks of the elbows, are another characteristic of these bats. The thick, pungent secretions of these glands are more profuse in males than females and may assist females in their search for mates.

Proboscis Bat *Rhynchonycteris naso*

RANGE S. Mexico to C. Brazil

HABITAT Forest, scrub; near water

SIZE Body: 1¼–1¾ in (3.5–4.5 cm) Wingspan: 4¾–6¼ in (12–16 cm)

Tail: ½–¾ in (1–2 cm)

Characteristic features of the proboscis bat are its long snout and the tufts of gray hair on its forearms.

Proboscis bats fly relatively slowly and are therefore ill-suited for hunting up in the tree-tops where they would make easy prey for birds. Instead they have developed the habit of feeding on insects, which they catch on the wing just above the surfaces of ponds, lakes and rivers.

Proboscis bats sometimes roost in rocky crevices, but often just cling to rocks or to concrete, where their color pattern gives them a resemblance to patches of lichen. Individuals roost a considerable distance from one another, perhaps to enhance the effect of the camouflage.

Between April and July, females each give birth to 1 young. Until the young bat is about 2 months old and able to fend for itself, its mother chooses a dark safe roost inside a log, or deep within a pile of stones, in which to leave it.

Two-lined Bat

Saccopteryx leptura

RANGE Mexico to Bolivia and Brazil

HABITAT Lowland forest

SIZE Body: 1½–2 in (4–5 cm) Wingspan: 7–8¾ in (18–22 cm)

Tail: ½ in (1 cm)

The two-lined bat is one of the most strikingly marked of all bats. Its common name is derived from the pair of wavy white lines running down its back from the nape of the neck to the rump. The lines serve to break up the body shape of the bat and may also provide some camouflage.

The male has a pair of well-developed saclike glands in the wing membrane, just above the crooks of the arms. The purpose of the sacs is not known, but it is thought that they may be used to attract females.

In Mexico, two-lined bats have been observed roosting under concrete bridges and on the walls of buildings. Each individual seems faithful to its roosting place, returning each morning to the precise spot that it left the evening before. Females give birth to young in the rainy season when their food supply – beetles and moths – is most plentiful. The young are weaned before they are 2 months old.

Old World Sheath-tailed Bat

Emballonura monticola

RANGE Thailand to Malaysia, Java, Sumatra, Borneo and Sulawesi

HABITAT Rain forest

SIZE Body: 1½–2¼ in (4–6 cm)

Wingspan: 6¼–7 in (16–18 cm)

Tail: ½ in (1 cm)

Old World sheath-tailed bats generally roost in rock fissures or caves in the forest in groups of a dozen or so. At dusk they depart simultaneously to feed and then return together at dawn. They appear to feed in the top layer of the tallest trees and to supplement their insect diet with fruit and occasionally flowers.

Although little is known of the breeding habits of the Old World sheath-tailed bats, they are likely to breed throughout the year, producing 1 young at a time.

Tomb Bat *Taphozous longimanus*

RANGE India, Sri Lanka to east to S. E. Asia

HABITAT Coconut groves, scrub, ruined tombs and palaces

SIZE Body: 2¾–3½ in (7–9 cm)

Wingspan: 9¾–13 in (25–33 cm)

Tail: ¾–1½ in (2–3.5 cm)

This bat's common name is derived from its habit of roosting inside manmade structures, such as tombs. Tomb bats appear in Chinese paintings of 2,000 years ago – almost the oldest recorded artistic impression of a bat. They are neat little creatures with short shiny coats.

Tomb bats leave their roosts in the evening and fly up as high as 330 ft (100 m) at dusk in search of their insect prey. As the night progresses, they gradually descend. While hunting, tomb bats emit loud cries which are easily heard by human ears.

White Bat *Diclidurus virgo*

RANGE S. Mexico, Central America

HABITAT Forest, open land

SIZE Body: 2–3¼ in (5–8 cm) Wingspan: 7–11¾ in (18–30 cm)

Tail: ½–1 in (1.5–2.5 cm)

The white bat, with its white fur and wing membrane, is a truly spectral creature. Since almost all other bats are dark, it is a mystery why this species should be white. However, it is just as successful at hunting insect prey as its dark relatives, which suggests that there is no evolutionary disadvantage in the light coloration. Another curious feature is the presence of saclike glands in the tail membrane. There are no wing glands.

It roosts in caves or crevices, usually alone, but occasionally in pairs. It appears to breed throughout the year.

HOG-NOSED BAT, SLIT-FACED BATS AND FALSE VAMPIRES

CRASEONYCTERIDAE: HOG-NOSED BAT FAMILY

The single species in this family was first discovered in 1973 in the karst region of western Thailand. It is the smallest bat yet recorded and may be the world's smallest mammal.

Hog-nosed Bat

Craseonycteris thonglongyai **EN**

RANGE Thailand

HABITAT Limestone caves, bamboo forests and teak plantations

SIZE Body: 1¼ in (3 cm)

Wingspan: 4¼–5 in (11–12.5 cm)

Tail: absent

A fully grown, adult hog-nosed bat weighs no more than ¹⁄₁₄ oz (2 g). It is the world's smallest bat. Its upperparts are brown to reddish or gray. The fur on the underside is slightly paler than that on the rest of the body, and the wings darker.

Its piglike nose is thought to be an adaptation for gleaning small insects and other invertebrates off the surface of leaves. At dusk, hog-nosed bats emerge from the caves, where they roost in small colonies, and forage around the tops of bamboo clumps and in the dense foliage of teak trees, which their tiny bodies can easily penetrate. Nothing is known of their breeding habits.

NYCTERIDAE: SLIT-FACED BAT FAMILY

There are 12 species in this family. All are distinguished by a distinctive pair of slits in the sides of the face which extend laterally from the nostrils to just above the eyes. Like most complex facial features in bats, these slits are thought to play a part in beaming ultrasonic signals, which the bat uses in conjunction with its well developed ears in order to find its way in the dark and to locate its prey. This family is generally insectivorous, though spiders and scorpions will also be eaten.

Another unusual feature of the slit-faced bat is the tail, which extends to the end of the tail membrane and then terminates in a "T" shaped bone, unique among mammals.

Female slit-faced bats give birth twice a year.

Egyptian Slit-faced Bat *Nycteris thebaica*

RANGE Middle East, Africa, south of the Sahara; Madagascar

HABITAT Dry plains, forest

SIZE Body: 1¾–3 in (4.5–7.5 cm) Wingspan: 6¼–11 in (16–28 cm) Tail: 1½–3 in (4–7.5 cm)

Egyptian slit-faced bats feed on a variety of invertebrate animals which they catch in trees or even on the ground. Scorpions seem to be a particularly favored food. The bats generally give birth to a single offspring in January or February and are thought to produce a second later in the year.

MEGADERMATIDAE: FALSE VAMPIRE FAMILY

In the struggle for survival among the many bat species, one family has evolved as specialist predators on other bats. The false vampire swoops silently down on a smaller bat and seems to chew it for a while before devouring the meat – a habit that led to the belief that these bats sucked blood. This is now known not to be the case and, in fact, not all false vampires are even carnivorous; those that are use their predatory skills only to supplement an insectivorous diet. There are 5 species of false vampire, all with long ears and fluted nose leaves.

Greater False Vampire

Megaderma lyra

RANGE India to Myanmar, S. China, Malaysia

HABITAT Forest, open land

SIZE Body: 22½–3¼ in (6.5–8.5 cm)

Wingspan: 9–11¾ in (23–30 cm) Tail: absent

The greater false vampire regularly supplements its diet of insects, spiders and other invertebrates with prey, such as bats, rodents, frogs and even fish. Groups of 3 to 50 false vampires roost together and are usually the sole inhabitants of their caves. Presumably their predatory tendencies deter other bats from sharing their abode.

False vampires mate in November, and 1 young is born after a gestation of 20 weeks. Shortly before females are due to give birth, males leave the roost and return 3 or 4 months later, to resume communal roosting.

Heart-nosed Bat *Cardioderma cor*

RANGE E. C. Africa: Ethiopia to Tanzania

HABITAT Forest, scrub

SIZE Body: 2¾–3½ in (7–9 cm) Wingspan: 10–13½ in (26–35 cm) Tail: absent

The heart-nosed bat closely resembles the greater false vampire in appearance and way of life, but has a wider, heartshaped nose leaf.

Like its relatives, it feeds on vertebrate animals as well as insects. Before the heat of the day has passed, the heart-nosed bat emerges from its roost and swoops to catch lizards – it will even enter houses in pursuit of rodents or wall lizards.

It is a strong flier and can take off from the ground carrying a load as big as itself. Heart-nosed bats attack smaller bats in flight, "boxing" them with their powerful wings to upset their directional stability.

Australian False Vampire bat *Macroderma gigas* **VU**

RANGE N. and W. tropical Australia

HABITAT Forest with rock caves

SIZE Body: 4½–5½ in (11.5–14 cm) Wingspan: 18–23½ in (46–60 cm) Tail: absent

On account of its pale coloration, the Australian false vampire is popularly known as the ghost bat. It is one of the most carnivorous of bats and feeds almost exclusively on mice, birds, geckos and other bats. Its method of attack is to flop down on the unsuspecting prey and enmesh it in its strong wings, then to deliver a single killing bite to the back of the prey's neck. It then takes off from the ground carrying a dead rodent and flies to a feeding perch in cave or tree.

Like all false vampires, this species has long ears which are joined by a membrane extending about halfway up their length.

Males forsake the communal roost in September or October, just before the young bats are due to be born. By January the young bats are as large as their mothers and accompany them on nighttime hunting trips. The males move back into the roosts by April.

This handsome species is now rare and active conservation measures are urgently required in order to ensure its survival.

Yellow-winged Bat

Lavia frons

RANGE Africa: Senegal to Kenya

HABITAT Swamps, lakes in forest and open country

SIZE Body: 2½–3 in (6.5–8 cm) Wingspan: 9½–11¾ in (24–30 cm) Tail: absent

The yellow-winged bat is a strikingly colored species. The body fur color is variable, ranging through blue-gray or brown to whitish. However, the ears and wings are always yellowish-red. This species has large ears and eyes. Its nose leaf – the fleshy growth around the nostrils and mouth, which is believed to be used to help with echolocation – is the most prominent feature of the false vampire family.

The yellow-winged bat roosts in trees and bushes, where only the flickering of its long ears gives away its presence. These bats often fly in the daytime, but seem to feed only during the night hours.

In contrast to the other false vampires, yellow-winged bats appear to restrict themselves to insect food. Their method of hunting is rather like that of the flycatcher birds. The bat hides on its favorite perch in a tree, quiet and still and obscured by the foliage. When an insect flies nearby the bat swoops down from the branch to snap it up, then returns to its hunting perch to lie in wait again.

Yellow-winged bats breed throughout the year; males do not leave the communal roost for the birth season.

HORSESHOE BATS

RHINOLOPHIDAE: HORSESHOE BAT FAMILY

The shape of the fleshy structure surrounding the nose distinguishes the horseshoe bat from other insectivorous bats. While most small bats emit their ultrasonic cries through open mouths, horseshoe bats "shout" through their nostrils. The nose leaf acts as an adjustable megaphone, enabling the bat to direct its "radar" beam wherever it wishes. Two other structures on the face, the lancet above the nostrils and the sella, which partially separates them, are immensely muscular and can vibrate at the same frequency as the sound pulse. Horseshoe bats wrap their wings around their bodies when roosting.

There are 132 species of horseshoe bat found in temperate and tropical parts of the Old World as far east as Japan and Australia. This order also includes about 63 species that were formerly classified in an order of their own – the Old World Leaf-nosed bats. Males and females generally look alike. Many of these bats are extremely numerous and of great benefit to man since they feed entirely on insects and destroy many insect pests.

Lesser Horseshoe Bat *Rhinolophus hipposideros* **VU**

RANGE	Europe, Asia, N. Africa
HABITAT	Open country with caves
SIZE	Body: 2¾–4 in (7–10 cm) Wingspan: 9–10 in (22.5–25 cm)
Tail: ½–1 in (1.5–2.5 cm)	

The lesser horseshoe bat is similar to the greater, and equally fluttering in flight, but it is more maneuvrable and hunts far more in the air. In summer it roosts in trees, hollow logs and houses, making incessant chattering noises. In winter the bats make short migrations to winter hibernation quarters in caves, which are frost-free but not necessarily dry.

Greater Horseshoe Bat *Rhinolophus ferrumequinum* **LR: cd**

RANGE	Europe, Asia, N. Africa
HABITAT	Forest; open and cultivated land
SIZE	Body: 4½–5 in (11–12.5 cm) Wingspan: 13–14 in (33–35 cm)
Tail: 1–1½ in (2.5–4 cm)	

The greater horseshoe bat is rather slow and fluttering in flight and not adept at catching insects in the air. It feeds largely on the ground, swooping down on beetles with unerring accuracy. These bats hibernate from October to March and often choose winter quarters deep within caves, crevices or potholes. Thousands hibernate together and make long migrations to reach these quarters. The female gives birth to 1 young in April and carries it about until it is 3 months old.

Philippine Horseshoe Bat *Rhinolophus philippinensis* **LR:nt**

RANGE	Philippine Islands
HABITAT	Primary forest, broken land
SIZE	Body: 2¾–3½ in (7–9 cm) Wingspan: 9–10¼ in (23–26 cm)
Tail: ½–1 in (1.5–2.5 cm)	

Within the rich bat fauna of its native islands, the Philippine horseshoe bat occupies its own special niche. It feeds on large slow-flying insects and on heavily armored ground beetles and using its sharp teeth, can slice through the thick wing cases and wings before devouring the insects.

Hibernation is not necessary in the Philippine climate and the bats remain active throughout the year. Breeding also occurs throughout the year. Young mature in their second year, and males are smaller than females.

Persian Trident Bat *Triaenops persicus*

RANGE Egypt, east to Iran, south to the Gulf of Eilat

HABITAT Arid land, semi-desert

SIZE Body: 1½–2¼ in (3.5–5.5 cm)

Wingspan: 6–7½ in (15–19 cm) Tail: ½ in (1.5 cm)

The Persian trident bat and the other 2 species in its genus are distinguished from the rest of their family by the structures above the nose disc. These bats roost in underground cracks and tunnels and emerge while it is still light to fly fast and low over the ground to their feeding areas where, high in the foliage, small insects are hunted down.

Trident bats breed between December and May. The births coincide with the rains. A single young is born and is left in the roost while its mother hunts.

Flower-faced Bat

Anthops ornatus **VU**

RANGE Solomon Islands

HABITAT Forest, mixed agricultural land

SIZE Body: 1¾–2 in (4.5–5 cm)

Wingspan: 55½–6½ in (14–16.5 cm)

Tail: ¼–½ in (0.5–1.5 cm)

The flower-faced bat is known only from a handful of specimens collected early this century. Its name comes from the flowerlike appearance of the nose disc which has several layers, superimposed one upon the other like the petals in a flower. Why such a bizarre device is required is not known.

Trident Leaf-nosed Bat *Asellia tridens*

RANGE N. Africa, east to India

HABITAT Arid scrub

SIZE Body: 2–2¼ in (5–6 cm)

Tail: ¾–1 in (2–2.5 cm)

The common name of this species comes from its three-pronged nasal lancet. Hundreds of these bats roost together in underground tunnels and cracks. They emerge in early evening to skim over the surface of the land toward palm groves where, in the shade and moisture, insects abound. Beetles and moths are favored foods.

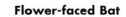

Large Malay Leaf-nosed Bat

Hipposideros diadema

RANGE S.E. Asia, New Guinea, Solomon Islands, N.E. Queensland

HABITAT Forest, often near human habitation

SIZE Body: 2¾–4 in (7–10 cm)

Wingspan: 9–10 in (22.5–25 cm)

Tail: 1–1¼ in (2.5–3 cm)

This sociable bat roosts in groups of many hundreds in caves or abandoned old buildings. At dusk the bats depart from their roost in order to hunt for food. They forage around flowers, snapping up insects, and occasionally they will tear open figs in order to dig out insect larvae hidden inside, at the same time consuming the fig pulp and seeds.

The single young bat is usually born some time between November and December.

Tail-less Leaf-nosed Bat *Coelops frithi*

RANGE Bangladesh through Indo-China to Java

HABITAT Forest

SIZE Body: 1–1¾ in (3–4.5 cm) Wingspan: 4¼–5¼ in (11–13 cm)

Tail: absent

The tailless leaf-nosed bat has a much less complex nose disc than its relatives. Its ears are shorter and more rounded than is usual in this family. Its broad wings make it extremely maneuverable in the air (although its poorly developed hind legs mean that it can not move easily on land) and it feeds on insects which it chases on the wing.

Small groups of a dozen or more tailless leaf nosed bats shelter together during the day in hollow trees or in human dwellings.

In Java, it has been observed that births occur towards the end of February.

FISHERMAN, MUSTACHED, NEW WORLD LEAF-NOSED AND FREE-TAILED BATS

NOCTILIONIDAE: Fisherman Bat Family

There are 2 species in this family, also known as Bulldog Bats, both found in Central America and northern South America. They inhabit swampy forests and mangroves and, as their name implies, feed on fish.

Fisherman Bat

Noctilio leporinus

RANGE Mexico, south to Argentina; Antilles, Trinidad

HABITAT Forest, mangrove swamps

SIZE Body: 4–5¼ in (10–13 cm) Wingspan: 11–12 in (28–30 cm) Tail: ½–1 in (1–2.5 cm)

With powerful, stiff-winged flight, the fisherman bat swoops to within an inch of the water, dipping briefly to impale a small fish with its long sharp claws and scoop it into its mouth. Fisherman bats also use their feet to catch insects, both in the water and the air, and these make up a substantial part of their diet in some regions. Just how they locate their prey is unknown, but, since they emit floods of ultrasound while hunting, it is thought that they can detect tiny ripples made by a surfacing fish.

In November or December fisherman bats mate, and a single young is born after a gestation of about 16 weeks.

MORMOOPIDAE: Mustached Bat Family

There are 8 species in this family, also known as Naked-backed bats which ranges from southern Arizona to Brazil. The bats derive their name from the fringe of hairs surrounding the mouth. Some species have wing membranes that meet and fuse in the middle of the back. These membranes give the back a naked appearance.

Mustached Bat

Pteronotus parnielli

RANGE N. Mexico to Brazil; West Indies

HABITAT Lowland tropical forest

SIZE Body: 1½–3 in (4–7.5 cm) Wingspan: 8–13 in (20–33 cm) Tail: ½–1¼ in (1.5–3 cm)

In addition to the fringe of hairs around its mouth, this bat has a platelike growth on its lower lip and small fleshy papillae projecting down from the upper lip. This structure helps the bat to collect its insect food.

Mustached bats are gregarious and roost in large groups in caves. They lie horizontally and do not hang in the usual manner of bats. Young are usually born in May when the bats' food supply is most abundant. Most females have just 1 young a year.

Leaf-chinned Bat *Mormoops megalophylla*

RANGE Arizona to N. South America; Trinidad

HABITAT Forest, scrub, near water

SIZE Body: 2–2½ in (6–6.5 cm) Wingspan: 10–11 in (25–28 cm) Tail: 1 in (2.5 cm)

A pair of fleshy flaps on the chin, and peglike projections on the lower jaw distinguish this species. Leaf-chinned bats shelter in caves, tunnels and rock fissures. They hunt somewhat later than most bats, emerging after dark to look for insects. They fly close to the ground and often feed near pools and swamps.

MOLOSSIDAE: Free-tailed Bat Family

The 80 species of free-tailed bat occur in the warmer parts of the Old and New World. The typical free-tailed bat has a rodentlike tail, which extends well beyond the free edge of the tail membrane, and rather narrow wings, which beat more rapidly than those of other insectivorous bats. Free-tailed bats feed entirely on insects, favoring hard-shelled species. They roost in vast hordes, and their droppings create guano which is used in the fertilizer industry.

Egyptian Free-tailed Bat *Tadarida aegyptiaca*

RANGE N. Africa, Middle East

HABITAT Arid scrub land

SIZE Body: 2¼–2¾ in
(5.5–7 cm) Wingspan: 6¾–7½ in (17–19 cm) Tail: 1¼–2 in (3–5 cm)

One of the most common mammals in the Middle East, the Egyptian free-tailed bat roosts in groups of many thousands. Almost any sizeable crevice suffices, even if it is already occupied by another animal. The bats mate in late winter and the female gives birth to a single young after a gestation of 77 to 84 days. A second pregnancy may follow immediately.

Velvety Free-tailed Bat

Molossus ater

RANGE S. Mexico, Central America, Trinidad

HABITAT Scrub, savanna, forest

SIZE Body: 2½–3½ in
(6–9 cm) Wingspan: 10–11 in
(26–28 cm) Tail: 1¼–1½ in (3–4 cm)

This species has dense, short, velvety fur. It hunts insects and catches several at a time, cramming them into its cheek pouches. On returning to its roost, the bat devours its catch. This behavior may have evolved to reduce the time the bats are out and at risk of predation. One or two litters are born in summer.

Mastiff Bat *Eumops perotis*

RANGE S.W. USA, Mexico, N. South America

HABITAT Forest, near human habitation

SIZE Body: 2¾–4 in (7–10 cm) Wingspan: 11–12 in (28–30 cm)
Tail: 1½–2¼ in (4–6 cm)

Mastiff bats emerge from their roost after dark and hunt small insects, usually ants, bees and wasps, wherever they may be found. In the mating season, the throat glands of males swell enormously and the odorous secretions of these glands may attract females. Young are born in late summer, and twins are not uncommon.

Wroughton's Free-tailed Bat

Otomops wroughtoni **CR**

RANGE S. India, Sri Lanka

HABITAT Open, partially forested land

SIZE Body: 3¾–4¼ in (9.5–11 cm)
Wingspan: 11–12 in (28–30 cm)
Tail: 1¼–2 in (3–5 cm)

This species roosts in small groups or alone; few specimens have been collected. Females give birth to a single young in December.

PHYLLOSTOMATIDAE:
NEW WORLD LEAF-NOSED BAT FAMILY

As night descends over the Central and South American jungles, leaf-nosed bats emerge from their roosts to feed on the pollen and nectar of flowers. About 140 species of leaf-nosed bat have evolved to exploit this particular way of life. Generally they are small, but the American false vampire has a wingspan which may exceed 3¼ ft (1 m), making it the largest New World bat.

Leaf-nosed bats may be tailless or have tiny tails in the tail membrane. Most members of the family have a nose leaf – a flap of tissue above the nostrils, but it is usually a simple flap of skin.

These abundant bats transfer pollen between flowers and a number of plants have become adapted to pollination by bats – flowering at night and producing heavy, musky odors.

This order includes the three species of vampire bat which are totally adapted to a diet of blood. These are the only mammals to qualify as parasites.

Short-tailed Leaf-nosed Bat

Carollia perspicillata

RANGE S. Mexico to S. Brazil

HABITAT Forest, plantations

SIZE Body: 2–2½ in (5–6.5 cm) Wingspan: 8¼–9¾ in (21–25 cm)
Tail: ¼–½ in (0.5–1.5 cm)

This bat feeds almost entirely on ripe fruit, such as bananas, figs, guavas and plantains, which it locates by smell. There is no defined breeding season for this species, and females produce their single youngster at any time of the year.

NEW WORLD LEAF-NOSED BATS

Long-tongued Bat

Glossophaga soricina

RANGE N. Mexico to Brazil, Paraguay and Argentina;
West Indies

HABITAT Woodland, often arid

SIZE Body: 2–2½ in (5–6.5 cm) Wingspan: 7¾–9½ in (20–24 cm)
Tail: ¼ in (0.5 cm)

The long-tongued bat is the mammalian equivalent of the
hummingbird. This bat hovers in front of flowers and scoops up
pollen and nectar from deep within them with the aid of its long
tongue. Tiny bristles on its surface help the pollen to stick fast.

Female bats form maternity colonies in summer, rejoining
their original roosts when the young are born. Twins do occur,
but a single young is more common.

American False Vampire

Vampyrum spectrum **LR:nt**

RANGE S. Mexico to Peru and Brazil; Trinidad

HABITAT Forest, often near human habitation

SIZE Body: 5–5¼ in (12.5–13.5 cm)
Wingspan: 31½ in–3¼ ft (80 cm–1 m) Tail: absent

This species, formerly believed to be a blood–sucker, is now
known to kill and eat rodents, birds and other bats. It is
surprisingly agile on all fours and stalks mice stealthily; it then
kills by an accurate pounce, which breaks the prey's neck or
shatters its skull.

The bats breed in June and the females are most solicitous
parents, licking their young incessantly and feeding them
pieces of chewed mouse flesh as they approach weaning.

Tent–building Bat *Uroderma bilobatum*

RANGE S. Mexico to Peru and Brazil; Trinidad

HABITAT Forest, plantations

SIZE Body: 2¼–3 in (5.5–7.5 cm)

Wingspan: 7¾–9½ in (20–24 cm) Tail: absent

The tent–building bat is
alert and active
by day and has
developed a simple
way of creating a
shady refuge.
Fan-shaped palm leaves are partially bitten through in a
semicircular line, a third of the way along a frond. The end of
the frond then collapses, making a tent–shaped refuge, from
which the bats fly out in search of ripe fruit. A colony of 20 or
30 bats may share a tent.

Pregnant females establish maternity tents and young are
born between February and April. The young remain in the
maternity tent until they are able to fly. Males live alone or in
small groups during the breeding season, returning to the
females when the young are weaned.

Spear-nosed Bat *Phyllostomus hastatus*

RANGE Belize to Peru, Bolivia and Brazil; Trinidad

HABITAT Forest, broken country

SIZE Body: 4–5¼ in (10–13 cm) Wingspan: 17¼–18½ in (44–47 cm)
Tail: 1 in (2.5 cm)

One of the larger American bats, the spear-nosed has virtually
abandoned an insectivorous diet in favor of a carnivorous one.
It feeds on mice, birds and small bats and occasionally also
on insects and fruit.

Huge flocks of these bats shelter in caves and
abandoned buildings and at dusk they depart
together for their feeding grounds.

Young are born between May and June in the
communal roost.

Yellow–shouldered Bat *Sturnira lilium*

RANGE N. Mexico to Paraguay and Argentina; Jamaica

HABITAT Lowland forest

SIZE Body: 2¼–2¾ in (6–7 cm) Wingspan: 9½–10½ in (24–27 cm)
Tail: absent

The yellow-shouldered bat feeds on ripe fruit and roosts alone or in small groups in old buildings, hollow trees or high up in the crowns of palm trees.

In the north of their range, these bats breed throughout the year, but in the south the young are born between May and July. Females generally produce 1 infant at a time.

Little Big–eared Bat *Micronycteris megalotis*

RANGE S.W. USA to Peru, Brazil; Trinidad, Tobago and Grenada

HABITAT Dry scrub to tropical rain forest

SIZE Body: 1½–2½ in (4–6.5 cm) Wingspan: 6¼–7¾ in (16–20 cm) Tail: ¼–½ in (0.5–1 cm)

Little big-eared bats roost in small groups in a great variety of shelter holes. They emerge as dusk is falling and swoop around fruit trees, chasing heavy, slow-flying insects, such as cockchafers, or plucking cockroaches from the ground. They appear to supplement this diet with the pulp of fruit, such as guava and bananas. Young are born between April and June, most females give birth to a single offspring.

Jamaican Fruit–eating Bat *Artibeus jamaicensis*

RANGE N. Mexico to Brazil and N. Argentina; West Indies

HABITAT Scrub, forest

SIZE Body: 3–3½ in (7.5–9 cm)
Wingspan: 9–10¼ in (23–26 cm)
Tail: absent

This bat is one of the most efficient mammalian food processors: it feeds on fruit, which passes

through its gut in as little as 15 minutes. There is no time for bacterial action to destroy material, so the bat is an important distributor of seeds.

The breeding season lasts from February to July, and females give birth to 1, sometimes 2, young.

Cuban Flower Bat *Phyllonycteris poeyi* **LR:nt**

RANGE Cuba

HABITAT Primary forest, cultivated land

SIZE Body: 3–3¼ in (7.5–8 cm) Wingspan: 8¼–9 in (21–23 cm)
Tail: ½ in (1–1.5 cm)

The Cuban flower bat has little or no nose leaf. It is a gregarious bat and roosts in thousands in caves and rock fissures. It uses its long, slender tongue to suck and lap up nectar and pollen from many types of flowers, and it also feeds on fruit.

These bats breed throughout the year; young are left in the roost until they are able to fly.

Vampire Bat *Desmodus rotundus*

RANGE N. Mexico to C. Chile, Argentina and Uruguay

HABITAT Forest

SIZE Body: 3–3½ in (7.5–9 cm)
Wingspan: 6¼–7 in (16–18 cm) Tail: absent

The vampire, like most bats, hunts at night. It has the most specialized diet of all bats, existing only on blood. It approaches its victim by alighting quietly on the ground a few feet away then walking over on all fours. With its four razor-sharp canine teeth, the vampire then makes a small, painless incision on a hairless or featherless part of the animal, such as the snout. The edges of the bat's long, protruded tongue are bent downward and form a tube, through which saliva is pumped out to prevent the blood from clotting while the bat sucks it in.

About half an hour's feeding each night is sufficient for a vampire bat, and although the host loses only a small amount of blood, the bite of the bat may transmit various diseases between animals through its saliva, including rabies.

EVENING BATS

VESPERTILIONIDAE: EVENING BAT FAMILY

There are some 318 species in this family, found around the world from the tropics to as far as about 68° North. Many species hibernate for 5 or 6 months to survive the winter in harsh northern latitudes.

Most have quite simple muzzles, though a few species have a nose-leaf and some have tubular nostrils. Ear sizes vary enormously and the color is generally quite dull.

Nearly all species are insectivorous, although one or two feed on fish which they scoop from the water. Insects are usually caught in the air, the bat tossing the insect into its tail membrane with its wing. All these bats make use of echolocation for finding prey and for plotting their flight course.

Evening bats are extremely numerous in the cool, northern parts of the world. Without their massive consumption of blackflies, midges and mosquitoes, life for humans during the short northern summers would be distinctly more uncomfortable.

Little Brown Bat *Myotis lucifugus*

RANGE N. America: from 62°N, south to Mexico

HABITAT Forest, built-up areas

SIZE Body: 1½ in (4 cm) Wingspan: 5½–7 in (14–18 cm)
Tail: 1 in (2.5 cm)

A common species in North America, the little brown bat adapts equally well to cold and hot climates. In the warmer parts of their range little brown bats do not hibernate, but northern populations may migrate hundreds of miles to hibernation sites. It feeds on whatever insects are abundant locally.

In summer, the females segregate themselves and roost in maternity sites. A single young, sometimes twins, is born in May or June after a gestation period of between 50 and 60 days. The young are mature at 1 year.

Fish-eating Bat *Pizonyx vivesi*

RANGE Coasts of Baja California and W. Mexico

HABITAT Caves, coastal rock piles

SIZE Body: 2¾–3¼ in (7–8.5 cm)
Wingspan: 9¾–12½ in (25–32 cm)
Tail: 2–2½ in (5–6.5cm)

This species is specialized for feeding on fish. It has feet with long rakelike toes, ending in razor-sharp claws. Late in the evening, the bat flies low over the sea and takes small fish and crustaceans from the surface by impaling them on its claws. It is not known how it locates its prey, but its "radar" system might be capable of noting irregularities in the water caused by a fish moving close to the surface.

The female bat bears a single young in May or June and carries her infant with her until it is half-grown. It is then left in a secure roost with other young, while the mother hunts.

Common Long-eared Bat *Plecotus auritus*

RANGE N. Europe, east to N.E. China and Japan

HABITAT Sheltered, lightly wooded areas

SIZE Body: 1½–2 in (4–5 cm) Wingspan: 9–11 in (23–28 cm)
Tail: 1¼–1¾ in (3–4.5 cm)

The distinguishing feature of the common long-eared bat is its large ears, which are three-quarters the length of its head and body combined. The ears are an essential part of the bat's hunting equipment. They are extremely sensitive and are used to listen for the movements and calls of insect prey as well as to pick up the echoes of the bat's echolocation pulses which bounce back off solid objects, such as obstacles in the bat's path or prey.

In summer these bats roost in buildings and trees and hunt primarily for the night-flying noctuid moths. They also feed on midges, mosquitoes and other flies, often picking them off vegetation in dive-bombing, swooping flights.

The female gives birth to a single young in June, and females and young form nursery roosts. Long-eared bats are mature at about a year old.

Common Pipistrelle *Pipistrellus pipistrellus*

RANGE Europe, east to Kashmir

HABITAT Open land

SIZE Body: 1¼–1¾ in (3–4.5 cm)
Wingspan: 7½–9¾ in (19–25 cm) Tail: 1–1¼ in (2.5–3 cm)

Perhaps the commonest European bats, pipistrelles roost in groups of up to a thousand or more in lofts, church spires, farm buildings and the like. In winter, these bats migrate to a suitable dry cave to hibernate in colonies of 100,000 or more. They feed on·insects, eating small prey in flight but taking larger catches to a perch to eat. Births occur in mid-June and twins have been recorded. The bats actually mate in September, prior to hibernation, and the sperm is stored in the female for 7 or 8 months before fertilization occurs and gestation starts.

Big Brown Bat *Eptesicus fuscus*

RANGE N. America: Alaska to Central America; West Indies

HABITAT Varied, often close to human habitation

SIZE Body: 2–3 in (5–7.5 cm)
Wingspan: 10¼–14½ in (26–37 cm)
Tail: 1¾–2¼ in (4.5–5.5 cm)

Big brown bats eat almost all insects except, it seems, moths, and also manage to catch water beetles. They have been recorded flying at a speed of 15½ mph (25 km/h). They will enter houses to hibernate, although huge numbers migrate to caves in Missouri and other southern states for this purpose. Young are born from April to July; a single young is the rule west of the Rockies, but twins are common in the east.

Red Bat *Lasiurus borealis*

RANGE N. America

HABITAT Forested land with open space

SIZE Body: 2¼–3¼ in (6–8 cm) Wingspan: 14¼–16½ in (36–42 cm) Tail: 1¾–2 in (4.5–5 cm)

The red bat's fur varies in shade from brick–red to rust, suffused with white. Males are more brightly colored than females. The species is unique among bats in the size of its litters, regularly giving birth to 3 or 4 young in June or early July. The female carries her young with her at first, even though their combined weights may exceed her own body weight. North American red bats migrate southward in autumn and north again in spring.

Noctule *Nyctalus noctula*

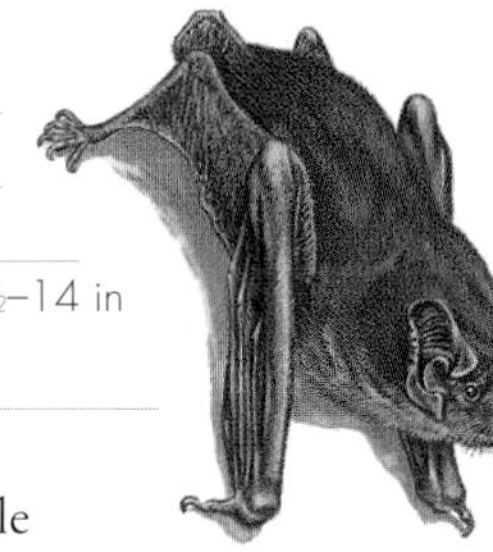

RANGE Europe, east to Japan

HABITAT Forest, open land

SIZE Body: 2¾–3¼ in (7–8 cm) Wingspan: 12½–14 in (32–35.5 cm) Tail: 1¼–2¼ in (3–5.5 cm)

One of the largest evening bats, the noctule feeds mainly on maybugs, crickets and dorbeetles, and there are reports of its killing house mice. In winter, noctules hibernate in trees or lofts, usually in small groups, but roosts of a few hundred do occur. They breed in June, producing 1, or sometimes 2 or even 3, young.

Barbastelle

Barbastella barbastellus **VU**

RANGE Europe, Morocco, Canary Islands

HABITAT Open land, often near water

SIZE Body: 1½–2 in (4–5 cm)
Wingspan: 9½–11 in (24.5–28 cm)
Tail: 1½–1¾ in (4–4.5 cm)

In early evening, often before sunset, barbastelles emerge to hunt for insects flying low over water or bushes. Males and females segregate for the summer and females form maternity colonies. From late September, barbastelles congregate in limestone regions to hibernate in deep, dry caves.

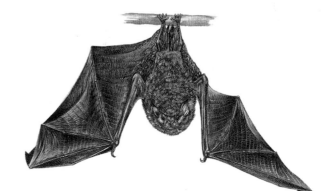

Painted Bat *Kerivoula argentata*

RANGE Africa: S. Kenya, Namibia, Natal

HABITAT Arid woodland

SIZE Body: 1¼–2¼ in (3–5.5 cm) Wingspan: 7–11¾ in (18–30 cm) Tail: 1¼–2¼ in (3–5.5 cm)

Small groups of painted bats are often found in the most unlikely roosts, such as in the suspended nests of weaver finches and sunbirds, or under the eaves of African huts. Doubtless the bright and broken coloration of these bats is a form of camouflage to protect them while they roost in vulnerable sites. Nothing is known of their breeding biology.

FUNNEL-EARED, SMOKY, DISC-WINGED, SUCKER-FOOTED AND SHORT-TAILED BATS

NATALIDAE: FUNNEL-EARED BAT FAMILY

The 5 species of funnel-eared bat occur in cavernous country in tropical South America. The family name comes from the large funnel-shaped ears, the outer surfaces of which bear glandular projections. Males and females look alike, except that on their muzzles males have thick glandular, or sensory projections, the function of which is not known.

Mexican Funnel-eared Bat *Natalus stramineus*

RANGE N. Mexico to Brazil; Lesser Antilles

HABITAT Tropical lowlands

SIZE Body: 1¼–2¼ in (3–5.5 cm) Wingspan: 7–9½ in (18–24 cm) Tail: 2–2¼ in (5–6 cm)

Funnel-eared bats roost in caves and mines, sometimes in huge numbers, but more often in groups of about a dozen. The bats emerge at dusk to search for slow-flying insects, and they themselves fly with fluttering, rather mothlike movements. Breeding takes place at any time of the year, and the sexes segregate just before the young are born.

FURIPTERIDAE: SMOKY BAT FAMILY

There are 2 species in this family, both characterized by their smoky coloration, by being thumbless and by having extremely long tail membranes. The family occurs in tropical South America and in Trinidad.

Smoky Bat *Furipterus horrens*

RANGE Costa Rica, northern South America: E. Peru, Guianas, Brazil; Trinidad

HABITAT Forest

SIZE Body: 1½–2¼ in (4–6 cm) Wingspan: 8½–11¾ in (22–30 cm) Tail: 1½–2¼ in (4–6 cm)

Unlike other bats, the smoky bat has no clawed thumbs, so that when it alights on the wall of its cave or tunnel roost, it must perform an aerial somersault in order to grasp the surface with its hind feet. Another curious feature of this bat and its fellow species is the high forehead – the snout and the brow join almost at right angles.

Practically nothing is known of the biology of either species of smoky bat. They certainly feed on insects, but how they avoid competing with the many other species of insect-eating bat within their range is not understood.

THYROPTERIDAE: DISC-WINGED BAT FAMILY

The 2 species in this family occur in Central America and in tropical South America, as far as Peru and southern Brazil. They derive their common name from suction pads at the base of each thumb and on the ankles. These discs are attached to the bat by short stalks and enable it to climb rapidly up smooth leaves and bare tree trunks. A curious characteristic of disc-winged bats is that they usually hang head upward when roosting – a feat made possible by the powerful suction discs.

Honduran Disc-winged Bat *Thyroptera discifera*

RANGE Belize, south to Ecuador and Peru

HABITAT Forest

SIZE Body: 1¼–2 in (3–5 cm) Wingspan: 7–9¾ in (18–25 cm)
Tail: 1–1¼ in (2.5–3 cm)

This small insect–eating bat has a similar high forehead to that of the smoky bat, but again the reasons for this are not known. It can climb up smooth surfaces, even glass, by means of its sucker discs, the suction pressure from a single disc is quite sufficient to support the entire weight of the bat. Suction is applied or released by specialized muscles in the forearms.

Disc–winged bats have unusual roosting habits: they roost in the young, curled leaves of plants such as bananas. These leaves, before they unfurl, form long tubes, and several bats may roost in a single leaf, anchored by their suckers to the smooth surface. The bats must find a new leaf practically every day as the previous roost unfurls.

Breeding takes place throughout the year, and the sexes do not appear to segregate before the females give birth. A single young is the normal litter and the mother carries it about with her until it weighs more than half her body weight. Her flying ability is not impaired by this extra load. Subsequently the young bat is left in the roost while she hunts.

MYZOPODIDAE: OLD WORLD SUCKER-FOOTED BAT FAMILY

The single species of sucker-footed bat is restricted to the island continent of Madagascar. The Myzopodidae is the only family of bats found solely on that island and represents a relict species, cut off from Africa when Madagascar broke free from that land mass.

Sucker–footed Bat
Myzopoda aurita **VU**

RANGE Madagascar

HABITAT Forest

SIZE Body: 2–2¼ in (5–6 cm)
Wingspan: 8½–11 in (22–28 cm) Tail: 1¾–2 in (4.5–5 cm)

Superficially the sucker-footed bat resembles the disc-winged

bats of the New World, for there are large suction discs at the base of each thumb and on each ankle. But the discs of this bat are quite immobile, in sharp contrast to those of the disc-winged bat, which are connected to the body by mobile stalks, and they appear to be less efficient.

The bat roosts inside curled leaves or hollow plant stems, and sometimes the smooth trunk of a tree may also serve it as a temporary nest.

Nothing is known of the breeding or feeding habits of these bats and they seem to be rather rare. Logging and the destruction of large areas of their forest habitat may be posing a threat to their survival.

MYSTACINIDAE: NEW ZEALAND SHORT-TAILED BAT FAMILY

The sole member of its family, the short–tailed bat is one of New Zealand's two native species of mammal (the other is a Vespertilionid bat called *Chalinolobus tuberculatus*).

New Zealand Short–tailed Bat *Mystacina tuberculata* **VU**

RANGE New Zealand

HABITAT Forest

SIZE Body: 2–2¼ in (5–6 cm) Wingspan: 8½–11 in (22–28 cm)
Tail: ½–¾ in (1.5–2 cm)

The short-tailed bat has a thick mustache fringing its small mouth. Each bristle of the mustache has a spoon-shaped tip. Its thumbs bear not only the usual heavy claws, but also have tiny secondary talons at their base and the hind feet have sharp claws.

Beetles and other ground-dwelling insects seem to form the bulk of the diet of the short-tailed bat. As an adaptation to hunting on the ground it is agile on all fours and can run rapidly, even up steeply sloping objects. The wing membranes are furled in such a way that the forearms can be used as walking limbs.

The short-tailed bat does not hibernate (the other New Zealand bat does). It roosts in small groups in hollow trees. A single young is born in October.

DOGS

ORDER CARNIVORA

There are 11 families in this order – dogs and foxes, bears, raccoons, mustelids, civets, mongooses, hyenas, cats, sea lions, walrus and true seals. Typically these animals are flesh-eating predators, but not all are totally carnivorous, and a specialized few feed only on plant matter. The last three families are adapted to life in water, their limbs have become flippers although they are still able to move, albeit awkwardly, on land, where they all spend part of their lives.

CANIDAE: DOG FAMILY

Dogs and their close relatives – the jackals, wolves, coyotes and foxes – represent one of the most familiar groups of carnivorous mammals. This familiarity is partly due to the fact that dogs were the first animals to be fully domesticated by man.

The family contains about 34 recognized species and is distributed almost worldwide. Domesticated versions aside, dogs are absent only from New Zealand, New Guinea, Madagascar and some other islands. The dingo was introduced into Australia by aboriginal man.

All dogs have the well-known, muscular, long-legged body, generally with a bushy tail. The ears are usually large, triangular in outline and erect, and the muzzle is long.

Canids are excellent runners, able to sustain a high speed for considerable distances, and long pursuits are an important part of the hunting technique of many species. Some canids hunt down large prey animals in packs, while others, such as foxes, are typically solitary hunters. Males and females generally look alike, although males are often slightly larger than females.

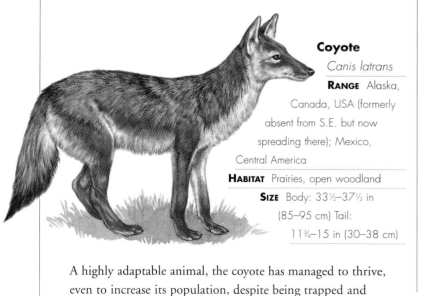

Coyote
Canis latrans

RANGE Alaska, Canada, USA (formerly absent from S.E. but now spreading there); Mexico, Central America

HABITAT Prairies, open woodland

SIZE Body: 33½–37½ in (85–95 cm) Tail: 11¾–15 in (30–38 cm)

A highly adaptable animal, the coyote has managed to thrive, even to increase its population, despite being trapped and poisoned for many years. Although the coyote probably does kill some sheep, young cattle and poultry, its diet consists mainly of rodents and rabbits and in this way it is of service to the farmer. It also eats snakes, insects, carrion, fruit, berries and grasses and will enter water to catch fish, frogs and crustaceans.

Coyote pairs mate in late winter, and a litter of 5 to 10 young is born after a gestation of 63 to 65 days. The male brings all the food for the female and young at first, but later both parents hunt for food. The young leave when about 6 or 7 months old to find their own home range.

The coyote is the North American equivalent of the jackals, which occur in Asia and Africa. Together with wolves, jackals are the ancestors of domestic dogs.

Gray Wolf *Canis lupus* **LR: lc**

RANGE E. Europe (isolated populations in Spain and Italy), east to India, Russia; Canada, USA: now only N. Michigan and Wisconsin; Mexico

HABITAT Tundra, steppe, open woodland and forest

SIZE Body: 3¼–4½ ft (1–1.4 m)

Tail: 11¾–18¾ in (30–48 cm)

One of the ancestors of the domestic dog, the gray wolf is a powerful muscular animal, with a thick, bushy tail. Wolves vary in color from almost white in the Arctic to yellowish-brown or nearly black farther south. Intelligent, social animals, wolves live in family groups or in packs that sometimes include more than one family or other individuals besides the family.

The pack members hunt together, cooperating to run down prey such as deer, caribou and wild horses, and they also eat small animals such as mice, fish and crabs. Social hierarchy in the pack is well-organized and is maintained by ritualized gestures and postures; the leading male signals his rank by carrying his tail higher than the others do. Pairs remain together for life.

The female gives birth to 3 to 8 pups after a gestation of about 63 days. Born blind and hairless, the pups venture outside the den at 3 weeks, and the whole pack then helps to care for and play with them.

Dingo *Canis dingo*

RANGE Australia

HABITAT Sandy desert to wet and dry sclerophyll forest

SIZE Body: about 5 ft (1.5 m)

Tail: about 14 in (35 cm)

The dingoes are descended from domesticated dogs which were introduced by the aboriginal human inhabitants of Australia many thousands of years ago. In anatomy and behavior dingoes are indistinguishable from domestic dogs, but the two have interbred for so long that there are now few pure dingoes. They live in family groups, but may gather into bigger packs to hunt large prey. Originally they fed on kangaroos, but when white settlers started to kill off the kangaroos, dingoes took to feeding on introduced sheep and rabbits.

A litter of 4 or 5 young is born in a burrow or rock crevice after a gestation period of about 9 weeks. The young are suckled by the mother for a period of 2 months and stay with their parents for at least a year.

Arctic Fox

Alopex lagopus

RANGE Arctic regions of Europe, Asia and N. America

HABITAT Tundra, open woodland

SIZE Body: 18–26¾ in (46–68 cm) Tail: up to 13¾ in (35 cm)

One of the few truly arctic mammals, the arctic fox has well-furred feet and small, rounded ears. It feeds on ground-dwelling birds, lemmings and other small rodents and also eats the leftovers from polar bear kills and carrion, such as stranded marine animals.

Burrows, usually in the side of a hill or cliff, provide shelter. Despite the harsh environment in which they live arctic foxes do not hibernate and are able to withstand temperatures as low as −58°F (−50°C).

Each pair produces a litter of 4 to 11 young between May and June after a gestation period of 51 to 57 days. The offspring are cared for by both parents.

Red Fox

Vulpes vulpes

RANGE Canada, USA (not Florida or Rockies); Europe (except Iceland); Asia to Japan and Indo-China; introduced in Australia

HABITAT Woodland, open country; recently increasing in urban areas

SIZE Body: 18–33¾ in (46–86 cm) Tail: 12–21¾ in (30.5–55.5 cm)

The versatile, intelligent red fox adapts well to different conditions and has excellent senses and powers of endurance. Although sometimes it moves about at all hours, it is most typically active at night, resting during the day in a burrow abandoned by another animal or dug by itself. It lives alone outside the breeding season and is a skilful hunter, preying largely on rodents but also on rabbits, hares, birds, insects and invertebrates. Fruit and berries are also eaten in autumn, and the red fox has also taken to scavenging on refuse in urban areas.

A litter of 4 young is born after a gestation of between 51 and 63 days. The male hunts for food for his family until the female is able to leave the cubs alone to hunt herself or else to take them out foraging.

Fennec Fox *Vulpes zerda*

RANGE N. Africa: Morocco to Egypt, south to N. Niger, Sudan; east to Sinai Peninsula and Kuwait

HABITAT Desert, semidesert

SIZE Body: 14½–16 in (37–41 cm) Tail: 7½–8¼ in (19–21 cm)

The smallest of the foxes, the fennec fox is identified by its relatively huge ears. It shelters in burrows, which it digs in the sand, and is generally active at night, when it preys on small rodents, birds, insects and lizards.

Fennec foxes are sociable animals which mate for life. Each pair or family has its own territory. A litter of 2 to 5 young is born in spring after a gestation period of 50 to 51 days.

DOGS CONTINUED

Dhole *Cuon alpinus* **VU**

RANGE C. and E. Asia, south to Sumatra and Java

HABITAT Forest, woodland; open country in north of range

SIZE Body: 30 in–3¼ ft (76 cm–1 m) Tail: 11–18¾ in (28–48 cm)

Dholes, or Asiatic wild dogs, are gregarious animals, which live in family groups or in packs of up to 30 that contain several families. Most of their hunting is done in the daytime, and although they are not particularly fast runners, dholes pursue their prey in a steady relentless chase, finally exhausting the victim. Both smell and sight are important to them when tracking their prey. Because they hunt in packs, dholes are able to kill animals much larger than themselves, such as deer, wild cattle sheep and pigs, water buffalo and the banteng.

A litter of 2 to 6 young is born after a gestation of about 9 weeks, in a sheltered spot among rocks or a hole in a bank. Several females may breed near each other. Dholes are now becoming rare after years of persecution by man, and they are also affected by the greatly reduced populations of many of their prey animals. They are protected in some parts of the range.

Bush Dog *Speothos venaticus* **VU**

RANGE Central and South America: Panama to Peru, Brazil and Paraguay

HABITAT Forest, savanna

SIZE Body: 22½–29½ in (57.5–75 cm) Tail: 5–6 in (12.5–15 cm)

Stocky and terrierlike, the bush dog has short legs and tail. It is now rare throughout its range, and little is known of its habits in the wild. A nocturnal dog, it is believed to hunt in packs, preying mainly on rodents, such as pacas and agoutis. Bush dogs swim well and readily pursue prey into water.

During the day, they take refuge in a hole or crevice, often the abandoned burrow of an armadillo. They mark the edges of

their territory with urine and secretions from anal glands.

Litter are thought to contain 4 or 5 young, which are tended by both parents.

Maned Wolf

Chrysocyon brachyurus

LR: nt

RANGE South America: Brazil, Bolivia, Paraguay, Uruguay, N. Argentina

HABITAT Grassland, swamp edge

SIZE Body: 4 ft (1.2 m) Tail: about 12 in (30 cm)

Similar to a red fox in appearance, with its long legs and muzzle, the maned wolf has a yellowish-red coat of fairly long hair, with an erectile mane on the neck and shoulders. The tail may be white or white-tipped. A wary, solitary animal, the maned wolf lives in remote areas and is active mainly at night. It runs fast with a loping gallop. It has less stamina than many canids and does not usually run down its prey. Large rodents, such as pacas and agoutis, birds, reptiles and frogs are all caught, and it also feeds on insects, snails and some fruit.

Up to 5 young are born after a gestation of about 2 months. At first, they have short legs and muzzles.

Crab-eating Fox *Cerdocyon thous*

RANGE South America: Colombia to N. Argentina

HABITAT Open woodland, grassland

SIZE Body: 23½–27½ in (60–70 cm) Tail: 11¾ in (30 cm)

The first specimen of this fox ever examined had a crab in its mouth hence the common name, but in fact crabs are only one item in a wide-ranging diet. This fox is also known as the common zorro. Mainly nocturnal and solitary, the crab-eating fox spends the day in a shelter, often a burrow abandoned by another animal.

It hunts small rodents, such as mice and rats, lizards, frogs and crabs and also feeds on insects and fruit, and digs for turtle eggs. Poultry also figures in the diet of the crab-eating fox.

The female gives birth to a litter of 2 to 6 young.

Raccoon-dog *Nyctereutes procyonoides*

RANGE E. Siberia, N.E. China, Japan, N. Indo-China; introduced in E. and C. Europe

HABITAT Forest and rocky banks near rivers and lakes

SIZE Body: 19¾–21½ in (50–55 cm) Tail: 5–7 in (13–18 cm)

Foxlike in build, but with shorter legs and tail, the raccoon-dog has a dark patch on each side of its face, reminiscent of the raccoon's black mask. It lives alone or in family groups of 5 or 6 and is primarily nocturnal. During the day, it shelters in a den among rocks or bushes, in a hollow tree or in a burrow abandoned by another animal. A raccoon-dog may sometimes dig its own burrow.

Usually found near water, the raccoon-dog is an excellent swimmer and frogs and fish are major food items. It also eats rodents, acorns, fruit and berries and scavenges on carrion and refuse around human habitation.

A litter of 6 to 8 young is born after a gestation of about 2 months. The pups are independent at about 6 months old.

Hunting Dog *Lycaon pictus* **EN**

RANGE Africa, south of the Sahara to South Africa: Transvaal; (not in rain forest areas of W. and C. Africa)

HABITAT Savanna, plains, semidesert, mountains up to 10,000 ft (3,000 m)

SIZE Body: 31½ in–3½ ft (80 cm–1.1 m) Tail: 11¾–15¾ in (30–40 cm)

Recognized by its dark-brown, black or yellowish coat, well mottled with light patches, the hunting dog has long legs and a short, extremely powerful muzzle. Hunting dogs live in packs of 6 to 30 or more, sometimes up to 90 individuals with a high degree of social cooperation and interaction between individuals in the pack. They communicate by means of gestures and body postures and a few calls. Nomadic animals, hunting dogs roam over a wide area looking for their prey and only remain in one place for more than a few days when the young are too small to travel.

During much of the day, the dogs rest and groom themselves in the shade. Most hunting is done in the early morning and evening or on bright, moonlit nights. After a mass greeting ceremony between pack members, the dogs move off to search for prey, such as gazelle, impala and zebra. Once the prey has been located by sight, the dogs follow it slowly for a while before starting the final chase. They may concentrate on one victim or follow several members of a herd before all switching to one particular animal. When close enough, the dogs start to bite the prey wherever they can, often seizing its legs and tail and causing it to fall. They disembowel it and immediately start tearing it to pieces and feeding. The pack shares the kill without aggression, allowing young animals to feed first and disgorging meat to latecomers. Some pack members return to the den and disgorge meat for the adults guarding the young. By expert cooperation, by taking turns in the chase and by combined attack, packs of hunting dogs can successfully bring down prey much bigger than themselves, even large wildebeest.

The female gives birth to 2 to 16 young (usually 7) after a gestation period of 69 to 72 days. The litter is born in a burrow, such as an abandoned aardvark or warthog hole, and more than one female may share the den. The young are blind at birth, but their eyes open at about 2 weeks, and they soon begin to venture out of the den. They are suckled for about 3 months and then fed on regurgitated food by pack members from the age of 2 weeks. The whole pack takes an interest in the young and will feed any motherless pups. At 6 months the young begin to learn to hunt and accompany the pack.

BEARS

URSIDAE: BEAR FAMILY

The 9 species of bear are an evolutionary offshoot of doglike ancestors. The family also includes the two species of panda which have previously been placed in their own family, or with the raccoon family.

Dogs and their relatives consume a certain amount of plant material in their largely carnivorous diet, and this omnivorous tendency is increased in the bears, which are adaptable consumers of a wide range of foods, including insects, small vertebrates, grass, leaves, fruit and nuts. Bears' teeth reflect their diet and they lack the shearing blades of cats and dogs which are necessary for tearing meat.

Bears are large, sturdily built animals, with big heads, short limbs and exceptionally short tails. They have flat, five toed feet with long, curving claws. Male and female look alike.

Only the polar bear inhabits Arctic regions; the others all occur in temperate and tropical areas of the northern hemisphere, and 1 species lives in northern South America. In cold, winter weather, many bears undergo a period of torpor. This winter sleep is not true hibernation, since temperature and respiration rate do not fall drastically, as they do in true hibernators.

Spectacled Bear

Tremarctos ornatus **VU**

RANGE South America: Venezuela, Colombia, Ecuador, Peru, W. Bolivia

HABITAT Forest, savanna, mountainous areas up to 10,000 ft (3,000 m)

SIZE Body: 5–6 ft (1.5–1.8 m) Tail: 2¾ in (7 cm)

The spectacled bear is the only South American bear species. It is generally black or dark brown in color, with white markings around the eyes, which are the origin of its common name, and sometimes on the neck. Mainly a forest dweller, although it also ranges into open country, this bear feeds largely on leaves, fruit and roots. It is also thought to prey on animals such as deer and vicuna. It is a good climber and sleeps in a tree in a large nest that it makes from sticks. The spectacled bear lives alone or in a family group. The female produces a litter of up to 3 young after a gestation period of 8 to 9 months.

Big Brown Bear/Grizzly Bear *Ursus arctos*

RANGE Europe: Scandinavia to Balkans, scattered populations in France, Italy and Spain; Russia; Asia, north of Himalayas; Alaska, W. Canada, mountainous areas of W. USA

HABITAT Forest, tundra

SIZE Body: 5–8¼ ft (1.5–2.5 m) Tail: absent

Many subspecies are covered by the scientific name *U. arctos*, including the Kodiak bear and the grizzly bears. At least 2 races of grizzly are rare or endangered. The races vary in color from pale yellowish-fawn to dark brown or nearly black. All are large, immensely strong bears, and they are among the biggest carnivores. The bears live alone or in family groups and are active night or day, although in areas where bears have been persecuted, they are nocturnal.

The diet varies greatly from area to area but may include plant material, such as fruit, nuts, roots and seaweed, as well as insects, fish, small vertebrates and carrion. Alaskan brown bears feed heavily on migrating salmon. Most individuals are too slow to catch wild, hoofed mammals, although they have been known to kill bison. Many are too heavy to climb trees. In late summer and autumn, the bears fatten up on vast quantities of fruit and berries in preparation for the winter sleep – a period of torpor, not true hibernation.

Females breed every 2 or 3 years and produce litters of 1 to 4 young after a gestation of 6 to 8 months. The new born young are blind and tiny, usually weighing only about 10½ to 25 oz (300 to 700 g). They remain with the mother for a year, sometimes longer.

American Black Bear

Ursus americanus

RANGE Alaska, Canada, USA: patchy distribution in New England, through Pennsylvania to Tennessee, Florida, S. Georgia, Mississippi, Louisiana, mountainous areas of the west; N. Mexico

HABITAT Wooded areas, swamps, national parks

SIZE Body: 5–6 ft (1.5–1.8 m) Tail: 4¾ in (12 cm)

American black bears vary in color from glossy black to dark brown reddish–brown or almost white. There is often a small white patch on the chest. This bear was once found throughout much of the USA, but it now lives only in the wilder, uninhabited areas and in national parks, where it is thriving. Black bears are usually active at night, when they roam for long distances in search of food, such as fruit, berries, nuts, roots and honey. They also eat insects, small mammals, fish and even carrion and refuse. Their sense of smell is good, but their hearing and eye sight are only fair. In autumn, black bears gorge on fruit to fatten themselves for their long winter sleep.

Except for females with cubs, black bears are usually solitary. A litter of 1 to 4 young is born in January or February after a gestation of about 7 months.

Asiatic Black Bear *Ursus thibetanus* **VU**

RANGE Afghanistan to China, Siberia, Japan, Korea, Taiwan, Hainan, S.E. Asia

HABITAT Forest and brush up to 11,800 ft (3,600 m)

SIZE Body: 4¼–5¼ ft (1.3–1.6 m) Tail: 2¾–4 in (7–10 cm)

Asiatic black bears are usually black, with some white markings on the snout and chest, some may be reddish or dark brown. They mainly eat plant matter and may raid crops or climb trees to obtain fruit and nuts. As well as eating insect larvae and ants, they can be aggressive predators and may kill cattle, sheep and goats. The female has a litter of 2 cubs, which are blind and extremely small at birth. The cubs stay with their mother until they are almost fully grown.

Polar Bear

Ursus maritimus **LR: cd**

RANGE Arctic Ocean to southern limits of ice floes

HABITAT Coasts, ice floes

SIZE Body: 7¼–8¼ ft (2.2–2.5 m) Tail: 3–5 in (7.5–12.5 cm)

A huge bear, with an unmistakable creamy-white coat, the polar bear is surprisingly fast and can easily outrun a caribou over a short distance. It wanders over a larger area than any other bear and, of course, swims well. Seals, fish, seabirds, arctic hares, caribou and musk-oxen are the polar bear's main prey, and in the summer it also eats berries and leaves of tundra plants.

Normally solitary animals outside the breeding season, polar bears mate in midsummer. A litter of 1 to 4 young is born after a gestation of about 9 months, and the young bears remain with their mother for about a year. Thus females breed only every other year.

Sun Bear *Helarctos malayanus* **DD**

RANGE S.E. Asia, Sumatra, Borneo

HABITAT Mountain and lowland forest

SIZE Body: 3½–4½ ft (1.1–1.4 m) Tail: absent

The sun bear is the smallest bear species. It nevertheless has a strong, stocky body and powerful paws, with long, curved claws that help it climb trees. It spends the day in a nest in a tree, sleeping and sunbathing, and searches for food at night.

Using its strong claws, the sun bear tears at tree bark in order to expose insects, larvae and the nests of bees and termites; it also preys on junglefowl and small rodents. Fruit and coconut palm, too, are part of its diet.

There are usually 2 young, born after a gestation period of about 96 days. The young are cared for by both parents.

RACCOONS AND PANDAS

Giant Panda *Ailuropoda melanoleuca* **EN**

RANGE Mountains of C. China

HABITAT Bamboo forest

SIZE Body: 4–5 ft (1.2–1.5 m) Tail: 5 in (12.5 cm)

One of the most popular, newsworthy mammals, the giant panda is a rare, elusive creature and surprisingly little is known of its life in the wild. It is large and heavily built, with a massive head, stout legs and a thick, woolly black and white coat, often with a brownish tinge to the black.

The panda's forepaw is specialized for grasping bamboo stems, its main food. It has an elongated wrist bone that effectively provides a sixth digit, against which the first and second digits can be flexed. The panda consumes huge amounts of bamboo in order to obtain sufficient nourishment and thus spends 50 to 75 per cent of its day feeding. It is also thought to eat some other plants and, occasionally, small animals.

Normally solitary, unless breeding or caring for young, pandas are primarily ground-dwelling, but regularly climb trees for shelter or refuge. The male leaves his territory to find a mate and courts her by uttering whines and barks. He will drive off any rival males before mating. The female gives birth to 1 blind, helpless young, which weighs only about 5 oz (140 g). It is tiny in comparison to its mother, which may weigh as much as 255 lb (115 kg). The cub grows rapidly, however, and by the time it reaches 8 weeks old it is more than 20 times its birth weight.

Lesser/Red Panda *Ailurus fulgens* **EN**

RANGE Nepal to Myanmar, S.W. China

HABITAT Bamboo forest

SIZE Body: 20–25 in (51–63.5 cm) Tail: 11–19 in (28–48.5 cm)

The lesser or red panda, with its beautiful rusty-red coat and long, bushy tail, resembles a raccoon more than it dos its giant relative. This creature is primarily nocturnal and spends the day sleeping, curled up on a branch with its tail over its head or its head tucked on to its chest. It feeds at night on the ground, on bamboo shoots, grass, roots, fruit and acorns and may also occasionally eat mice, birds and birds' eggs. The red panda is a quiet creature unless provoked, when it rears up on its hind legs and hisses.

It lives in pairs or family groups. In the spring the female gives birth to 1 to 4 young, usually only 1 or 2, after a gestation period of 90 to 150 days. The longer gestations recorded are thought to include a period of delayed implantation, during which the fertilized egg lies dormant in the womb, only starting to develop at the time that will ensure birth at the optimum season for the young's survival. The young stay with their mother for up to a year.

PROCYONIDAE: RACCOON FAMILY

There are about 18 species in this family, all of which inhabit temperate and tropical areas of the Americas. They are all long-bodied, active animals, thought to be closely linked to the dog-bear line of carnivore evolution. The raccoons are good climbers and spend much of their life in trees.

Males are usually longer and heavier than females, but otherwise the sexes look alike.

Raccoon
Procyon lotor

RANGE USA, south to Panama, S.Canada,

HABITAT Wooded areas, near water, swamps

SIZE Body: 16–23½ in (41–60 cm) Tail: 7¾–15¾ in (20–40 cm)

Raccoons have coped well with the twentieth century and today are even spotted in cities, scavenging for food. The raccoon is stocky but agile, with thick, grayish fur and a bushy tail ringed with black bands. Its pointed face has a characteristic "bandit" mask across the eyes. On the forepaws are long, sensitive digits, with which the raccoon dexterously handles food. Mainly active at night, the raccoon is a good climber and can swim if necessary. Its wide-ranging diet includes aquatic animals, such as frogs and fish, small land animals, birds, turtle eggs, nuts, seeds, fruit and corn.

A litter of 3 to 6 young is born in spring after a gestation period of about 65 days. The young raccoons' eyes are open at about 3 weeks. They young start to go out with their mother at about 2 months old, remaining with her until autumn.

Olingo *Bassaricyon gabbii* **LR:nt**

RANGE Central America, south to Venezuela, Colombia and Ecuador

HABITAT Forest

SIZE Body: 13¾–18¾ in (35–47.5 cm) Tail: 15¾–18¾ in (40–48 cm)

An expert climber, the olingo spends much of its life in trees and rarely descends to the ground. Using its long tail to help it balance, it leaps from tree to tree and runs along the branches. It is primarily nocturnal, and although it lives alone or in pairs, joins in groups with other olingos and with kinkajous to search for food. Fruit is its staple diet, but it also eats insects, small mammals and birds.

Breeding takes place at any time of year, and there is usually only 1 young in a litter, born after a gestation of 73 or 74 days. The female chases her mate away shortly before the birth and rears her offspring alone.

Coati *Nasua nasua*

RANGE Arizona south to Argentina

HABITAT Woodland, lowland forest

SIZE Body: 17–26¼ in (43–67 cm) Tail: 17–26¾ in (43–68 cm)

The coati is a muscular, short-legged animal, with a long, banded tail and a pointed, mobile snout. It lives in groups of up to 40 individuals, which hunt together day and night, resting in the heat of the day. With its mobile snout, the coati probes holes and cracks in the ground, rocks or trees, searching for the insects, spiders and other small ground-dwelling invertebrates that are its staple diet. Fruit and larger animals, such as lizards, are also eaten.

After mating, the group splits up and females go off alone to give birth. A litter of 2 to 7 young is born after a gestation of about 77 days, usually in a cave or a nest in a tree. Once the young are about 2 months old, the females and their offspring regroup with yearlings of both sexes. Males over 2 years old only accompany the group for the mating period. Even then they are subordinate to females.

Kinkajou *Potos flavus*

RANGE E. Mexico, through Central and South America to Brazil

HABITAT Forest

SIZE Body: 16–22½ in (41–57 cm) Tail: 15¾–22 in (40–56 cm)

The tree-dwelling kinkajou is an agile climber. It uses its prehensile tail as a fifth limb, leaving its hands free to pick food. During the day, the kinkajou rests, usually in a hole in a tree. It forages at night, mainly feeding on fruit and insects and sometimes small vertebrates. Its long tongue is used to extract soft flesh from fruit, such as mangoes, and for licking up nectar, insects and honey.

The female gives birth to 1 young, rarely 2, after a gestation of 112 to 118 days. The young kinkajou takes its first solid food at about 7 weeks and is independent at about 4 months old. It is able to hang by its prehensile tail after about 8 weeks.

MUSTELIDS, WEASELS AND MARTENS

MUSTELIDAE: MUSTELID FAMILY

The mustelid family of carnivores is a successful and diverse group of small to medium-sized mammals. There are about 65 species in 23 genera from all regions of the world except Australia and Madagascar and 2 species have been introduced into New Zealand to control rodents. Although there is a moderate range of physique, most mustelids conform to the pattern of long, supple body, short legs and long tails. Males are almost invariably larger than females.

Mustelids have adapted to various ecological niches. There are burrowers, climbers and swimmers. One species, the sea otter, is almost entirely marine.

Secretions from anal scent glands are used to mark territory boundaries. Some species, notably polecats and skunks, have particularly foul-smelling secretions which they spray in defence.

Stoat *Mustela erminea*

RANGE Europe, Asia, N. USA, Greenland; introduced in New Zealand

HABITAT Forest, tundra

SIZE Body: 9½–11½ in (24–29 cm) Tail: 3–4¾ in (8–12 cm)

The stoat is a highly skilled predator. It kills by delivering a powerful and accurate bite to the back of the prey's neck. Rodents and rabbits are the stoat's main diet, but it will also kill and eat other mammals – including some bigger than itself – as well as birds, eggs, fish and insects. At the beginning of winter, in the northern part of its range, the stoat loses its dark fur and grows a pure white coat, only the black tail-tip remaining. This white winter pelt is the ermine prized by the fur trade.

Stoats produce a litter of 3 to 7 young in April or May. The male assists in caring for and feeding the young, which are helpless at birth. Their eyes do not open until they are about 3 weeks old, but at 7 weeks old young males are already larger than their mother.

There are 15 species of *Mustela*, including the minks which are now farmed for their dense fur.

Black-footed Ferret *Mustela nigripes* **EW**

RANGE N. America: formerly Alberta to N. Texas

HABITAT Prairie

SIZE Body: 15–17¾ in (38–45 cm) Tail: 5–6 in (12.5–15 cm)

The black-footed ferret feeds mainly on prairie dogs, which are considered farm pests and large numbers are poisoned. The destruction of the ferret's prey has caused a drastic decline in their numbers and they are now protected by law. There is still a danger of extinction, however, and its survival depends on ongoing conservation. The black-footed ferret is generally nocturnal. In June the female produces a litter of 3 to 5 young.

Least Weasel *Mustela nivalis*

RANGE Europe, N. Africa, Asia, N. America; introduced in New Zealand

HABITAT Farmland, woodland

SIZE Body: 7–9 in (18–23 cm) Tail: 2–2¾ in (5–7 cm)

This weasel is the smallest carnivore. In the northern part of its range its coat changes color in winter. The least weasel preys mostly on mice which it pursues in their burrows. It is most active by night, but will hunt in the daytime. One or two litters a year, of 4 or 5 young are born.

Western Polecat *Mustela putorius*

RANGE Europe

HABITAT Forest

SIZE Body: 15–18 in (38–46 cm) Tail: 5–7½ in (13–19 cm)

This solitary and nocturnal animal hunts rodents, birds, reptiles and insects, mostly on the ground. The offensive secretions from the polecat's anal scent glands are used for defence and to mark territory. It breeds once or twice a year, bearing litters of 5 to 8 young.

American Marten *Martes americana*
RANGE Canada, N. USA
HABITAT Forest, woodland
SIZE Body: 14–17 in (35.5–43 cm) Tail: 7–9 in (18–23 cm)

The American marten is agile and acrobatic with a bushy tail. It spends much of its time in the trees, where it preys on squirrels. It also hunts on the ground and eats small animals and insects, fruit and nuts.

Martens make dens in hollow trees and produce yearly litters of 2 to 4 blind, helpless young, usually in April. Their eyes open at 6 weeks and they attain adult weight at about 3 months.

Sable *Martes zibellina*
RANGE Siberia; Japan: Hokkaido
HABITAT Forest
SIZE Body: 15–18 in (38–45 cm) Tail: 5–7½ in (12–19 cm)

The sable is one of 7 species of marten. It is a ground dweller and eats small mammals, as well as fish, insects, honey, nuts and berries. A yearly litter of 2 or 3 young is born in a burrow.

The sable has long been hunted for its fur. Conservation is now underway in Russia to save the decreasing wild population.

Grison *Galictis vittata*
RANGE S. Mexico to Peru and Brazil
HABITAT Forest, open land
SIZE Body: 18½–21½ in (47–55 cm) Tail: 6 in (16 cm)

The grison is an agile animal, good at climbing and swimming. It feeds on frogs and worms as well as other ground-living creatures. The abandoned burrow of another animal or a rock or tree-root crevice serves it as a den. A litter of 2 to 4 young is produced in the burrow in October.

There are 3 species of grison, all of which live in Central and South America. The local population uses grisons in the same way as ferrets, for flushing out chinchillas.

Tayra *Eira barbara*
RANGE S. Mexico to Argentina; Trinidad
HABITAT Forest
SIZE Body: 24–27 in (60–68 cm)
Tail: 15–18½ in (38–47 cm)

The single species of tayra runs, climbs and swims well. It preys on small mammals, such as tree squirrels and rodents, and also feeds on fruit and honey.

Tayras move in pairs or small family groups and are active at night and in the early morning. They are believed to produce a yearly litter of 2 to 4 young.

Zorilla *Ictonyx striatus*
RANGE Africa: Senegal and Nigeria to South Africa
HABITAT Savanna, open country
SIZE Body: 11–15 in (28.5–38.5 cm) Tail: 8–12 in (20.5–30 cm)

Also known as the striped polecat, the single species of zorilla ejects a nauseating secretion from its anal glands when alarmed. It is primarily nocturnal and feeds on rodents, reptiles, insects and birds' eggs. By day it rests in a burrow, or a crevice in rocks. There is a litter of 2 or 3 young.

MUSTELIDS CONTINUED

Wolverine *Gulo gulo* **VU**

RANGE Scandinavia, Siberia, Alaska, Canada, W. USA

HABITAT Coniferous forest, tundra

SIZE Body: 25½–34¼ in (65–87 cm) Tail: 6½–10 in (17–26 cm)

The single species of wolverine is a heavily built animal, immensely strong for its size and capable of killing animals larger than itself. Although they are largely carnivorous, wolverines also feed on berries. They are solitary animals and are mainly ground-dwelling, but they can climb trees.

Each male holds a large territory with 2 or 3 females, and mates in the summer. The female wolverine bears 2 or 3 young in the following spring, usually after a period of delayed implantation. Delayed implantation is an interesting phenomenon allowing animals to mate at the ideal time and bear young at the ideal time, even though the intervening period is longer than their actual gestation. The fertilized egg remains in a suspended state in the womb and development starts only after the required period of dormancy. The young suckle for about 2 months and remain with their mother for up to 2 years, at which time they are driven out of her territory. They become sexually mature at about 4 years of age.

Ratel *Mellivora capensis*

RANGE Africa; Middle East to N. India

HABITAT Steppe, savanna

SIZE Body: 23½–27½ in (60–70 cm) Tail: 7¾–11¾ in (20–30 cm)

The stocky ratel is also known as the honey badger because of its fondness for honey. In Africa a honey–eating association has developed between the ratel and a small bird, the honey guide. Calling and flying just ahead, the bird leads the ratel to a wild bees' nest. With its powerful foreclaws, the ratel then breaks open the nest, and both partners share the spoils. The unusually tough hide of the ratel protects it from bee stings and is also a good defence in another way: the skin is so loose on the body that the animal can twist about in its skin and even bite an attacker which has a hold on the back of its neck. In addition to honey and bee larvae, the ratel eats small animals, insects, roots, bulbs and fruit and will occasionally attack large animals such as sheep and antelope.

Although sometimes active in the daytime, ratels are generally nocturnal animals. They live singly or in pairs and produce a litter of 2 young in an underground burrow or a nest among rocks. The gestation period is between 6 and 7 months.

Eurasian Badger *Meles meles*

RANGE Europe to Japan and S. China

HABITAT Forest, grassland

SIZE Body: 22–32 in (56–81 cm) Tail: 4–7¾ in (11–20 cm)

The gregarious Eurasian badger lives in family groups in huge burrows with networks of underground passages and chambers and several entrances. A burrow system, or sett, may be used by successive generations of badgers, each making additions and alterations. Bedding material of grass, hay and leaves is gathered into the sleeping chambers and occasionally dragged out to air in the early morning. Around the sett are play areas, and the boundaries of the group's territory are marked by latrine holes.

Badgers are generally nocturnal and emerge from the sett around dusk. They are playful creatures, and at this time the young and adults will indulge in boisterous romping. Such play helps the badgers to strengthen their social bonds, crucial to group-living animals.

Badgers feed on large quantities of earthworms as well as on small animals, bulbs, fruit and nuts. They mate in the summer when social acitivity is at its height, but gestation of the fertilized eggs does not start until such a time as to ensure that the 2 to 4 young are not born until the following spring.

American Badger *Taxidea taxus*

RANGE S.W. Canada to C. Mexico

HABITAT Open grassland, arid land

SIZE Body: 16½–22 in (42–56 cm) Tail: 4–6 in (10–15 cm)

The single species of *Taxidea* is the only New World badger. It has a rather flattened body shape, but is otherwise similar to other badgers.

The American badger is a solitary creature. It is generally active at night, although it will come out of its burrow during the day. It is an excellent digger and burrows rapidly after disappearing rodents – its main food. Birds, eggs and reptiles make up the rest of its diet. It will sometimes bury a large food item for storage.

The badgers mate in late summer, but the 6-week gestation period does not begin until February, so the litter is born only the following spring. The 1 to 5 young, usually 2, are born on a grassy bed in the burrow and are covered with silky fur. Their eyes open at 6 weeks and they suckle for several months.

In northern parts of its range and at high altitudes, the American badger sleeps for much of the winter, surviving on its stored fat. However, it does not truly hibernate and becomes active in mild spells.

Hog Badger *Arctonyx collaris*

RANGE N. China, N.E. India, Sumatra

HABITAT Wooded regions in uplands and lowlands

SIZE Body: 21½–27½ in (55–70 cm) Tail: 5–6½ in (12–17 cm)

Similar in shape and size to the Eurasian badger, the hog badger is distinguished by its white throat and mostly white tail. The common name refers to the badger's mobile, piglike snout, used for rooting for plant and animal food. It is a nocturnal animal and spends its day in a rock crevice or deep burrow. Its habits are much the same

as those of the Eurasian badger. Like all badgers, the hog badger has anal scent glands with potent secretions, and its black and white markings constitute a warning to enemies that it is a formidable opponent.

The breeding habits of the hog badger are not well known, but in one observation a female gave birth to 4 young in April.

Stink Badger *Mydaus javanensis*

RANGE Sumatra, Java, Borneo

HABITAT Dense forest

SIZE Body: 15–20 in (37.5–51 cm)
Tail: 2–3 in (5–7.5 cm)

The 2 species of stink badger have particularly powerful anal gland secretions.

The stink badger's scent is said to be as evil-smelling as those of skunks. When threatened or alarmed, the stink badger raises its tail and ejects a stream of the fluid. However, like musk, although foul in concentration, the secretion can be sweet-smelling in dilution and was formerly used in the making of perfume. This nocturnal creature lives in a burrow and feeds on worms, insects and small animals. The second species, the Palawan badger, *M. marchei*, inhabits the Philippine and Calamian islands.

Chinese Ferret Badger *Melogale moschata*

RANGE N.E. India, S. China, IndoChina, Java, Borneo

HABITAT Grassland, open forest

SIZE Body: 13–17 in (33–43 cm)
Tail: 6–9 in (15–23 cm)

Distinctive masklike face markings distinguish the Chinese ferret badger from other oriental mustelids. This badger lives in burrows or crevices and is active at dusk and at night. It is a good climber and feeds on fruit, insects, small animals and worms. Ferret badgers are savage when alarmed and their anal secretions are foul-smelling.

The female gives birth to a litter of up to 3 young in May or June. There are 2 other species of ferret badger, both are found in Southeast Asia.

MUSTELIDS CONTINUED

Striped Skunk *Mephitis mephitis*

RANGE S. Canada to N. Mexico

HABITAT Semiopen country, woods, grassland

SIZE Body: 11–15 in (28–38 cm)
Tail: 7–10 in (18–25 cm)

Notorious for its pungent anal gland secretions, the striped skunk is one of the most familiar mustelids. It does not use its foul-smelling secretions against rival skunks, only against enemies. The fluid is an effective weapon because the smell temporarily stops the victim's breathing.

The striped skunk is a nocturnal animal, spending the day in a burrow or in a den beneath old buildings, wood or rock piles. It feeds on mice, eggs, insects, berries and carrion.

A litter of 5 or 6 young is born in early May in a den lined with vegetation. The hooded skunk, *M. macroura,* is a similar and closely related species; the black and white markings of both skunks are highly variable and constitute a warning display.

Hog-nosed Skunk *Conepatus mesoleucus*

RANGE S. USA to Nicaragua

HABITAT Wooded and open land

SIZE Body: 13¾–19 in (35–48 cm)   Tail: 6½–12 in (17–31 cm)

There are 7 species of hog-nosed skunk, all found in the southern USA and South America.

This nocturnal, solitary, slow-moving animal has the coarsest fur of all skunks. The common name derives from the animal's long piglike snout, which it uses to root in the soil for insects and grubs. It will also eat snakes, small mammals and fruit.

The hog-nosed skunk makes its dens in rocky places or abandoned burrows. The female produces a litter of 2 to 5 young each year.

Western Spotted Skunk *Spilogale gracialis*

RANGE W. USA to C. Mexico

HABITAT Wasteland, brush and wooded areas

SIZE Body: 9–13½ in (23–34.5 cm)
Tail: 4¼–8½ in (11–22 cm)

The white stripes and spots of the western spotted skunk are infinitely variable – no two animals have quite the same markings. A nocturnal, mainly terrestrial animal, this skunk usually makes its dens underground, but it is a good climber and sometimes shelters in trees. Rodents, birds, eggs, insects and fruit are the main items in its diet.

In the south of the spotted skunk's range, young are born at any time of year, but farther north the 4 or 5 young are produced in spring. The gestation period is about 4 months.

Eurasian Otter *Lutra lutra*

RANGE Europe, N. Africa, Asia

HABITAT Rivers, lakes, sheltered coasts

SIZE Body: 21½–31½ in (55–80 cm)
Tail: 12–19½ in (30–50 cm)

Although agile on land, otters have become well adapted for an aquatic life. The Eurasian otter has a slim body, but its tail is thick, fleshy and muscular to propel it in water. Its feet are webbed and its nostrils and ears can be closed when it is in water. Its fur is short and dense and keeps the skin dry by trapping a layer of air around the body. It eats fish, frogs, water birds, voles and other water creatures.

Otters are solitary, elusive creatures, now rare in much of their range. They den in a river bank in a burrow called a holt and are most active at night. Even adult otters are playful. A litter of 2 or 3 young is born in the spring – or at any time of year in the south of the otter's range. There are 8 species of *Lutra,* all with more or less similar habits and adaptations.

Giant Otter

Pteronura brasiliensis **VU**

RANGE Venezuela to Argentina

HABITAT Rivers, slow streams

SIZE Body: 1¼–5 ft (1–1.5 m) Tail: 27½ in (70 cm)

The giant otter is similar in appearance to *Lutra* species, but is larger and has a flattened tail with crests on each edge. It generally travels in a group and is active during the day.

Giant otters feed on fish eggs, aquatic mammals and birds. They den in holes in a river bank or under tree roots and produce yearly litters of 1 or 2 young.

Now endangered, the giant otter is protected in some countries, but enforcement of the law in the vast, remote areas of its range is difficult and numbers are still decreasing.

African Clawless Otter *Aonyx capensis*

RANGE Africa: Senegal, Ethiopia, South Africa

HABITAT Slow streams and pools; coastal waters, estuaries

SIZE Body: 37–39 in (95–100 cm) Tail: 21½ in (55 cm)

The African clawless otter swims and dives as well as other otters, although its feet have only small connecting webs. As its name suggests, this otter has no claws other than tiny nails on the third and fourth toes of the hind feet. It has less dense fur than most otters so has not been hunted as extensively.

Crabs are the most important item of the clawless otter's diet, and it is equipped with large, strong cheek teeth for crushing the hard shells, it also feeds on mollusks, fish, reptiles, frogs, birds and small mammals. Like most otters, it comes ashore to eat and feeds from its hands. Clawless otters seem to be particularly skilful with their hands.

Clawless otters do not dig burrows, but live in crevices or under rocks in family groups, in pairs or alone. The litter of 2 to 5 young stays with the parents for at least a year.

Sea Otter *Enhydra lutra*

RANGE Bering Sea; USA: California coast

HABITAT Rocky coasts

SIZE Body: 1¼–4 ft (1–1.2 m) Tail: 10–14½ in (25–37 cm)

This species is the most highly adapted of all of the otter family for an aquatic existence. The sea otter spends almost all of its life at sea, always in water less than 66 ft (20 m) deep. Its body is streamlined and its legs and tail are short. The hind feet are webbed and flipperlike, and the forefeet are small.

Unlike most other marine mammals, the sea otter does not have an insulating layer of fat under its skin, but instead relies on a layer of air trapped in its dense fur for protection against the cold water. This otter spends a lot of time and effort on grooming its dense, glossy fur because the fur's insulating and waterproof qualities are lessened if it becomes unkempt.

Sea otters feed on clams, sea urchins, mussels, abalone and other mollusks which they collect from the sea bed and eat while lying in the water. In order to cope with the hard shells of much of its food, the sea otter has discovered how to use rocks as tools. When diving for food, the sea otter also brings up a rock from the sea bed. Placing the stone on its chest as it lies on its back in the water, the otter bangs the prey against the stone until the shell breaks, revealing the soft animal inside.

At dusk, the sea otter swims into the huge kelp beds which are found in its range and entangles itself in the weed so that it does not drift during the night while it sleeps.

Sea otters breed every two years or so and give birth to 1 pup after a gestation period of between 8 and 9 months. The pup is born in an unusually well-developed state, with its eyes open and a full set of milk teeth. The mother carries and nurses the pup on her chest as she swims on her back.

At one time sea otters were hunted for their beautiful fur and became rare, but they have been protected by law for some years.

CIVETS

VIVERRIDAE: CIVET FAMILY

The 34 or so species in this family include civets, palm civets, and Malagasy civets. They are found in south-west Europe, Africa, Madagascar, and Asia.

The civet family closely resembles the ancestors of the carnivores and they are believed to have remained more or less unchanged for millions of years, although between species within the family there is great variation in build. Most have large, pointed ears on the top of the head, five toes with claws and at least partial webbing. The coat is usually spotted or striped in some way.

Most civets are nocturnal, solitary tree-dwellers and they are generally omnivorous, though the palm civet will eat only fruit.

Many species emit a strong-smelling oily secretion from anal scent glands (civet glands) which is used to advertise the presence of the animal in a territory and probably to attract a mate. The active ingredient of these secretions – musk – has been used by man in the manufacture of perfume for several centuries and for some African and oriental countries it remains an important export, despite the introduction of synthetic musk.

Banded Linsang
Prionodon linsang

RANGE Thailand, Malaysia, Sumatra, Borneo

HABITAT Forest

SIZE Body: 14¾–17 in (37.5–43 cm)
Tail: 12–14 in (30.5–35.5 cm)

The slender, graceful banded linsang varies from whitish-gray to brownish-gray in color, with four or five dark bands across its back and dark spots on its sides and legs. It is nocturnal and spends much of its life in trees, where it climbs and jumps skilfully, but it is just as agile on the ground. Birds, small mammals, insects, lizards and frogs are all preyed on, and this linsang also eats birds' eggs.

The breeding habits of this species are not well known, but it is believed to bear two litters a year of 2 or 3 young each. Young are born in a nest in a hollow tree or in a burrow.

Masked Palm Civet *Paguma larvata*

RANGE Himalayas to China, Hainan, Taiwan, S.E. Asia, Sumatra, Borneo

HABITAT Forest, brush

SIZE Body: 19¾–30 in (50–76 cm) Tail: 20–25¼ in (51–64 cm)

The masked palm civet has a plain gray or brownish-red body, with no stripes or spots, but with distinctive, white masklike markings on the face. It is nocturnal and hunts in the trees and on the ground for rodents and other small animals, as well as for insects, fruit and plant roots. The secretions of its anal glands are extremely strong-smelling and can be sprayed considerable distances to discourage any attacker.

A litter of 3 or 4 young is born in a hole in a tree. The young are grayer than adults and do not have conspicuous face masks at first, but gradually develop them with age.

African Linsang *Poiana richardsoni*

RANGE Africa: Sierra Leone to Zaire

HABITAT Forest

SIZE Body: 13 in (33 cm) Tail: 15 in (38 cm)

A nocturnal animal, the African linsang is a good climber and spends more time in the trees than on the ground. During the day it sleeps in a nest, built of green vegetation in a tree, and then emerges at night to hunt for insects and young birds. It also feeds on fruit, nuts and plant material. Elongate and slender, this linsang is brownish-yellow to gray, with dark spots on the body and dark bands ringing the long tail.

Little is known of the African linsang's breeding habits. It is thought that each female has 2 or 3 young once or twice a year.

African Palm Civet *Nandinia binotata*

RANGE Africa: Guinea, east to S. Sudan, south to Mozambique

HABITAT Forest, savanna, woodland

SIZE Body: 17¼–23½ in (44–60 cm) Tail: 18¾–24½ in (48–62 cm)

Active at night, the African palm civet is a skilful climber and spends much of its life in trees. Its diet is varied, ranging from insects, lizards, small mammals and birds to many kinds of fruit (which may sometimes be its sole food), leaves, grass and some carrion. It is a solitary animal and it spends the day resting in the shelter of the trees.

The male tends to be larger and heavier than the female and both have short legs and long, thick tails. The short muzzle is adorned with long whiskers. Usually grayish-brown to dark reddish-brown in color, this civet has a pale, creamy spot on each shoulder. This is the origin of its other common name – the two-spotted palm civet.

The male occupies a home range and he uses his scent gland to mark its boundaries. Mating takes place in June and the female gives birth to a litter of 2 or 3 young after a gestation period of about 64 days.

African Civet *Viverra civetta* **CR**

RANGE Africa, south of the Sahara to South Africa: Transvaal

HABITAT Forest, savanna, plains, cultivated areas

SIZE Body: 31½–37½ in (80–95 cm) Tail: 15¾–20¾ in (40–53 cm)

Large and doglike, the African civet has a broad head, strong neck and long legs. The hind legs are longer than the forelegs.

Its coat is generally gray, with darker legs, chin and throat, and the back and flanks are patterned with dark stripes and patches. The size and spacing of these dark markings is highly variable.

By day, the African civet sleeps in a burrow or in cover of vegetation or rocks. It rarely climbs trees except to escape from an enemy, but it swims well. It emerges from its sleeping place at night to forage on the ground in its territory, which it marks with heaps of dung and by leaving marks from its scent gland on trees, shrubs, rocks and grass. Mammals (up to the size of young antelope), birds (including poultry and their eggs), reptiles, frogs, toads and insects are all hunted, and this civet will also take some carrion, as well as eating fruit and berries.

The female becomes sexually mature at about 1 year old and gives birth to l to 4 young in each litter, usually 2, after a gestation period of between 63 and 68 days. The young take their first solid food at about 3 weeks, and often kill insects for themselves at an early age. They are weaned at about 3 months. The mother calls her young to her when she wants to share food with them with a distinctive chuckling call. The female may produce as many as three litters a year.

Congo Water Civet *Osbornictis piscivora*

RANGE Africa: N.E. Zaire

HABITAT Rain forest near streams

SIZE Body: 17¾–19¾ in (45–50 cm)
Tail: 13¾–16½ in (35–42 cm)

The Congo water civet, which is also known as the aquatic genet and the fishing genet, is an elusive animal that has been seen only rarely. It is thought to be nocturnal and to lead a semi-aquatic life. It is believed to feed largely on fish, and possibly also on crustaceans and other aquatic creatures, which it probably finds by touch with its naked palms under rocks, then grabbing with its semi-retractile claws and delivering a quick, sharp killing bite.

The Congo water civet has a slender body and a small head with a pointed snout. It has short legs and the hind legs are longer than the forelegs. The tail is long, thick and bushy. The civet's coat is reddish, chestnut-brown, with darker hair on the backs of the ears and the middle of the back and tail, and a white chin and throat.

CIVETS CONTINUED

Small-spotted
Genet *Genetta genetta*
RANGE S.W. Europe: S.W. France, Spain and Portugal; Africa, Middle East

HABITAT Semidesert, scrub, savanna

SIZE Body: 19¾–23½ in (50–60 cm)
Tail: 15¾–18¾ in (40–48 cm)

The small-spotted genet is a slender, short-legged animal. It is marked with dark spots, which may form lines down its whitish to brownish-gray body. Its head is small and its muzzle is pointed. The genet's long, impressive tail is encircled down its length with black bands.

An agile, graceful animal, the small-spotted genet moves on land with its tail held straight out behind and climbs well in trees and bushes.

It spends the day sleeping in an abandoned burrow of another animal, in a rock crevice or on the branch of a tree and starts to hunt at dusk.

Sight, hearing and sense of smell are good, and the genet stalks its prey, crouching almost flat before pouncing. Most prey, such as rodents, reptiles and insects, is taken on the ground, but the genet will climb trees to take roosting or nesting birds; it also kills poultry.

The small-spotted genet normally lives alone or in pairs. A litter of 2 or 3 young is born in a hole in the ground, in a tree, or among rocks after a gestation period of between 68 and 77 days. The young genets are born blind, and their eyes open after between 5 and 12 days. They are suckled for up to 3 months and become fully independent by about 9 months.

Binturong *Arctictis binturong*
RANGE S.E. Asia, Palawan, Sumatra, Java, Borneo

HABITAT Forest

SIZE Body: 24–38 in (61–96.5 cm) Tail: 22–35 in (56–89 cm)

A large viverrid with long, coarse fur, the binturong has distinctive ear tufts and a prehensile tail, which it uses as a fifth limb when climbing. It is the only carnivore other than the kinkajou, a member of the raccoon family, to possess such a tail.

During the day, it sleeps up in the trees and emerges at night to climb slowly, but skilfully, among the branches, searching for fruit and other plant matter, as well as insects, small vertebrates and carrion.

After a gestation of 90 to 92 days, the female produces a litter of 1 or 2 young. Both parents care for the young, which are born blind and helpless.

Fanalouc *Eupleres goudotii* **EN**
RANGE N. Madagascar

HABITAT Rain forest, swamps

SIZE Body: 18–19¾ in (46–50 cm) Tail: 8½–9½ in (22–24 cm)

The fanalouc, also known as the small toothed mongoose, with its long, slender body, pointed muzzle and short legs, does resemble a mongoose. The hind legs are longer than the forelegs. The tail is thick and bushy. Active at dusk and during the night, the fanalouc does not climb or jump well, but slowly hops along the ground, searching for earthworms (its main food), insects, water snails, frogs and sometimes even small mammals and birds. It readily wades into water in pursuit of prey. When food is abundant, the fanalouc stores fat near the base of its tail and lives on it during the dry season.

Fanaloucs pair for life. Each pair lives in a territory, the boundaries of which are marked with secretions from the scent glands. The female bears 1 young, after a gestation of about 12 weeks, which is born with a full covering of hair and with its eyes open; it is weaned at 9 weeks.

These civets are becoming rare outside nature reserves due to the destruction of forests, competition from introduced civets, and overhunting.

Otter-civet *Cynogale bennettii* **EN**

RANGE Indo-China, Malaysia, Borneo, Sumatra

HABITAT Swamps, near rivers

SIZE Body: 22½–26¼ in (57–67 cm) Tail: 5–7¾ in (13–20 cm)

The otter-civet spends much of its life in water and has several adaptations for its aquatic habits. Like many aquatic mammals, it has short, dense underfur, which is waterproof, covered by a layer of longer, coarse guard hairs. Its nostrils open upward and can be closed off by flaps, and the ears can also be closed. The otter-civet's feet are supple and have broad webs; these webs are only partial and do not extend to the tips of the digits, so the animal is able to move as well on land as in water.

With only the tip of its nose above the water, the otter-civet is almost invisible as it swims and so is able to ambush creatures that come to the water's edge to drink, as well as taking prey in water. Fish, small mammals, birds and crustaceans are all included in the otter-civet's diet, and it also eats fruit. It has long, sharp teeth for seizing prey and broad, flat molars, which it uses to crush hard-shelled items such as crustaceans. On land, it climbs well and may take refuge in a tree if attacked, rather than making for water.

A litter of 2 or 3 young is born in a burrow or hollow tree. They become independent at about 6 months old.

Fossa *Cryptoprocta ferox* **VU**

RANGE Madagascar

HABITAT Forest

SIZE Body: 23½–29½ in (60–75 cm) Tail: 21½–27½ in (55–70 cm)

The largest Madagascan carnivore, the fossa resembles a cat as much as a viverrid and has a rounded, catlike head, but with a longer muzzle. Its body is slender and elongate and its hind legs are longer than its forelegs, which raises the animal's rear. The tail is long and the coat reddish-brown. Its catlike physique in fact resulted in it once being classified as part of the felid order.

The fossa is mainly active at dusk and at night. It is an excellent climber and is equally agile in trees and on the ground. It lives alone and hunts for mammals up to the size of lemurs, as well as for birds, lizards, snakes and insects. It will also kill domestic poultry.

Fossas mate between September and October and the female bears 2 or 3 young in a burrow, a hole in a tree or a den among rocks after a gestation period of about 3 months. She cares for them alone. The young are born with their eyes closed and they open at between 16 and 25 days. They are weaned at 4 months and are fully grown and independent at 2 years, although they do not reach sexual maturity for another 2 years.

Banded Palm Civet *Hemigalus derbyanus*

RANGE Malaysia, Sumatra, Borneo

HABITAT Forest

SIZE Body: 16–20 in (41–51 cm) Tail: 9¾–15 in (25–38 cm)

The banded palm civet has a slender, elongate body and a tapering, pointed snout. It is usually whitish to orange buff in color, with broad, dark stripes on the head and neck, behind the shoulders and at the base of the tail.

The banded palm civet is a nocturnal animal and rests during the day in holes in tree trunks. It is an excellent climber, with strong feet well adapted to life in the trees, and it forages for its prey in trees, on the forest floor and beside streams. Worms and locusts are its main foods, but it also eats rats, lizards, ants, spiders, crustaceans, land and aquatic snails and frogs. Little is known of its breeding habits, though between 1 and 3 young are born in each litter and the offspring begin to eat solid food at about 10 weeks old.

MONGOOSES

HERPESTIDAE MONGOOSE FAMILY

The 37 species of mongooses are found in Africa, Madagascar, and Asia. They are small, fast-moving, ground-dwellers with long, cylindrical bodies well-adapted to chasing prey, such as insects, scorpions, and small vertebrates, down burrows.

Bushy-tailed Mongoose *Bdeogale crassicauda*

RANGE E. Africa: Kenya to Zimbabwe and Mozambique

HABITAT Coastal forest, savanna

SIZE Body: 15¾–19¾ in (40–50 cm) Tail: 7¾–11¾ in (20–30 cm)

This robust mongoose has a broad muzzle, sturdy legs and a broad, heavily furred tail. It is an elusive, nocturnal animal, which rests by day in a burrow, often one taken over from another animal, or in a hole in a tree. At night it hunts for insects and lizards, snakes, rodents and other small creatures.

Indian Mongoose

Herpestes auropunctatus

RANGE Iraq to India, south to Malaysia; introduced in West Indies, Hawaii and Fiji

HABITAT Desert, open scrub, thin forest, dense forest

SIZE Body: 13¾ in (35 cm) Tail: 9¾ in (25 cm)

This widespread mongoose varies in appearance according to its environment, though generally the soft, silky fur is olive-brown and the tail is shorter than the head and body length.

At night, the Indian mongoose rests in a burrow, which it digs itself. During the day it hunts for food, treading the same paths repeatedly under the cover of vegetation. It eats almost anything it can catch, such as rats, mice, snakes, scorpions, wasps and other insects. It is useful to man because it keeps pest species, such as rats, at bay and it has been introduced into areas outside its native range for this purpose.

Females may produce two litters of 2 to 4 young a year, after a gestation of about 7 weeks. The newborn are blind and hairless, and their mother carries them in her mouth.

Marsh Mongoose *Atilax paludinosus*

RANGE Africa, south of the Sahara

HABITAT Marshland, tidal estuaries, swamps

SIZE Body: 17¾–23½ in (45–60 cm) Tail: 11¾–15¾ in (30–40 cm)

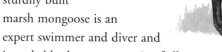

The large, sturdily built marsh mongoose is an expert swimmer and diver and is probably the most aquatic of all mongooses. Its feet are not webbed, but have short, strong claws. This nocturnal mongoose swims or roams stream banks or marshes in search of crabs, insects, fish, frogs and snakes. It crushes hard-shelled animals, such as crabs, by dashing them against a rock or tree.

This species has complex scent marking behavior – standing on its forepaws, with its tail over its back, to mark the underside of branches with scent from its anal glands.

Marsh mongooses live alone or in pairs or small family groups. The female gives birth to 1 to 3 young in a burrow or in a nest amid a pile of vegetation.

Banded Mongoose *Mungos mungo*

RANGE Africa, south of the Sahara

HABITAT Savanna, often near water

SIZE Body: 11¾–17¾ in (30–45 cm) Tail: 7¾–11¾ in (20–30 cm)

The banded mongoose has a stout body and a rather short snout and tail. Its color varies from olive-brown to reddish-gray, and light and dark bands alternate across its back from shoulders to tail. It is active in the day – in hot weather in the morning and evening only – and also sometimes emerges on moonlit nights. It is a good climber and swimmer. The banded mongoose often digs and forages in the ground and in leaf litter for food such as insects, spiders, scorpions, lizards, snakes, small mammals and birds. It also eats fruit, plant shoots and eggs.

Family troops of up to 30 animals live together, sheltering in hollow trees, rock crevices or burrows. If attacked, they defend themselves vigorously.

A litter of 2 to 6 young is born in a burrow after a gestation of about 8 weeks. The infants' eyes open at 10 days.

Cusimanse *Crossarchus obscurus*

RANGE Africa: Sierra Leone to Ghana

HABITAT Rain forest

SIZE Body: 11¾–15¾ in (30–40 cm) Tail: 6–9¾ in (15–25 cm)

The cusimanse has a long, narrow head and snout. The nose protrudes beyond the lower lip. It lives in family groups of up to 12 animals, which keep in touch with chattering calls as they search for food. They dig for worms, woodlice, spiders, snails and insects and also eat crabs, frogs, reptiles, small mammals and birds and their eggs. To break eggs and hard-shelled prey, cusimanse throw them against a tree or stone. At night, they sleep in burrows, which they often dig in old termite mounds. They only climb to escape enemies.

The female bears several litters a year, each of 2 to 4 young. The gestation period is about 70 days.

White-tailed Mongoose *Ichneumia albicauda*

RANGE Africa, south of the Sahara

HABITAT Savanna, dense bush, forest edge, often near water

SIZE Body: 18½–27 in (47–69 cm) Tail: 14¼–19¾ in (36–50 cm)

This mongoose has a bushy tail, which is usually gray at its base, becoming white or off-white at the tip. It lives alone or in pairs and is normally nocturnal, though in secluded areas it may emerge in late afternoon. It is a poor climber and can swim, though it rarely does so. It hunts mainly on the ground and eats insects, frogs, reptiles, rodents, ground-living birds, snails, crabs, eggs, berries and fruit.

The female gives birth to a litter of 2 or 3 young.

Meerkat *Suricata suricatta*

RANGE Africa: Angola to South Africa

HABITAT Open country, savanna, bush

SIZE Body: 9¾–12¼ in (25–31 cm) Tail: 7½–9½ in (19–24 cm)

The meerkat, also known as the suricate, has the long body and short legs typical of many mongooses. Its coat is mainly grayish-brown to light gray in color, marked with dark bands across the body, but it has dark ears and nose and a light-colored head and throat. The belly fur is thin and helps the meerkat to regulate its body temperature. It sits up sunning itself or lies on warm ground to increase its temperature and reduces it by lying belly-down in a cool, dark burrow.

Meerkats are gregarious and live in family units. Sometimes several families live together in a group of 30 or so. The colony occupies a home range, which contains shelters, such as burrows or rock crevices, and feeding sites. The animals move to a different area several times a year when food supplies dwindle. Meerkats are good diggers. They make burrows with several tunnels and chambers.

Active in the daytime, they forage in pairs or small groups, often sitting up on their hindlegs to watch for prey or danger. They eat insects, spiders, scorpions, centipedes, small mammals, lizards, snakes, birds and their eggs, snails, roots, fruit and other plant material. Meerkats have good hearing and sense of smell and excellent eyesight. They are constantly alert for birds of prey, their main enemies, and dive for cover if alarmed. They cover short distances quickly, but do not climb or jump well.

Breeding takes place mainly between October and April. The female gives birth to 2 to 5 young, usually 2 or 3, in a grass-lined underground chamber after a gestation of about 77 days. The young are born blind, but their eyes open 12 to 14 days after birth, and they take their first solid food at 3 or 4 weeks.

Salano *Salanoia concolor* VU

RANGE N.E. Madagascar

HABITAT Rain forest

SIZE Body: 13¾–15 in (35–38 cm) Tail: 7–7¾ in (18–20 cm)

Salanos are gregarious. They pair for life and live in family groups in a territory, marking the boundaries with secretions from their anal glands. At night, salanos rest in a burrow that they dig or take over from other animals, or in hollow trees. During the day, they search for insects (their main food), reptiles, amphibians, and occasionally small mammals and birds. It eats eggs, which it cracks by hurling them against a stone or tree with its hind legs.

The female gives birth to 1 young.

HYENAS

HYAENIDAE: HYENA FAMILY

The hyenas of Africa and southwest Asia and the aardwolf of southern Africa together constitute a small family of land-dwelling carnivores that is related to viverrids and cats, although all hyenas have an extremely doglike body form.

The 3 species of hyena, particularly, resemble dogs, but are more heavily built in the forequarters than their hindquarters. They have massive heads. Indeed the jaws of the spotted hyena, the largest member of the group, are the most powerful of any mammal. All hyenas are able to crush the biggest bones of their prey in order to extract the marrow.

Hyenas specialize in feeding on carrion, often the kills of lions and other large carnivores in their range, and are able to drive smaller predators, such as cheetah, away from their own kills. They are, however, also predators in their own right, particularly spotted hyenas. By hunting in packs they can kill animals as large as zebras. Near villages and towns, hyenas are useful scavengers and feed on any refuse that is left out at night.

The aardwolf is a highly adapted offshoot of the hyena stock. It is more lightly built, has a narrow, pointed head, large ears and tiny teeth. It feeds mostly on termites.

Males and females look alike in all members of the family, but males may be larger.

Aardwolf *Proteles cristatus*

RANGE Africa: Sudan, south to South Africa, Angola

HABITAT Open dry plains, savanna

SIZE Body: 25½–31½ in (65–80 cm) Tail: 7¾–11¾ in (20–30 cm)

A smaller and more lightly built version of the hyena, the aardwolf has a pointed muzzle, slender legs and an erectile mane on the neck and along the back. There are dark stripes on its yellowish to reddish-brown body and legs. Unless in a family group with young, the aardwolf lives alone in a territory centred on a den, which may be the abandoned burrow of an aardvark or a hole it digs itself. The boundaries of the territory are marked by anal gland secretions. Active at night, the aardwolf has extremely acute hearing and can detect the movements of termites, its main food. These are lapped from the ground or grass by means of the aardwolf's long tongue, which is covered with sticky saliva, making the task easier. It also eats other insects, birds' eggs, small mammals and reptiles.

A litter of 2 to 4 young is born in a burrow. After weaning, both parents feed the young on regurgitated termites.

Striped Hyena *Hyaena hyaena*

RANGE Africa: Senegal to Tanzania; Middle East to India

HABITAT Dry savanna, bush country, semidesert, desert

SIZE Body: 3¼–4 ft (1–1.2 m) Tail: 9¾–13¾ in (25–35 cm)

The striped hyena is identified by the dark stripes on its gray or yellowish-gray body and by the erectile mane around its neck and shoulders that extends down the middle of its back. Males are usually larger than females and both have the heavy head and sloping back typical of the hyenas.

Although they live in pairs in the breeding season, striped hyenas are generally solitary animals. Each has a home range, which must contain some thick cover. The territorial boundaries are marked by anal-gland secretions rubbed on to grass stems.

The striped hyena is active at night. It feeds on carrion, such as the remains of the kills of big cats, and preys on young sheep and goats, small mammals, birds, lizards, snakes and insects; it will also eat fruit. Striped hyenas stay well away from the larger spotted hyenas.

After a gestation of about 3 months, a litter of 2 to 4 young is born in a hole in the ground or among rocks. Both parents help to care for the young, which are blind at birth and are suckled for up to a year.

Brown Hyena *Hyaena brunnea* **LR:lc**

RANGE Africa: Angola to Mozambique, south to N. South Africa

HABITAT Dry savanna, plains, semidesert

SIZE Body: 3½–4 ft (1.1–1.2 m) Tail: 9¾–11¾ in (25–30 cm)

This hyena has an appearance that is typical of its family, with a bulky head and a back which slopes toward the rear. The brown hyena has long, rough hair over much of its body, with a mane of even longer hair on the neck and shoulders. Its coat is usually dark brown to brownish-black in color, with a lighter brown mane and legs.

Unless in a family group, the brown hyena tends to be a solitary animal, although it does sometimes gather with others at a big carcass or to form a hunting pack. It lives in a large territory, which it marks with secretions from its anal scent glands and with piles of dung.

During the day the brown hyena sleeps in a burrow, often one which has been abandoned by another animal, such as an aardvark. Alternatively it will rest among rocks or tall grass. It emerges at night and may travel long distances in search of carrion or to hunt prey, such as rodents, birds (including domestic poultry), reptiles or wounded large animals. It is primarily a scavenger and the bulk of its diet consists of insects, small vertebrates as well as eggs and fruit and vegetables. Near the coast, brown hyenas will also feed on dead fish, mussels and the stranded corpses of seals and whales on the shore. When this species discovers a large source of food it will remove and hide parts of its find in small caches and return to them later.

The mother gives birth to a litter of 2 to 4 blind, helpless young in the safety of a burrow after a gestation period of between 92 and 98 days. The young are suckled by the mother for about 3 months, but remain with their parents for up to 18 months, during which time the male supplies them with solid food in the den.

Although this species is protected in game reserves, brown hyenas are considered as pests by local people because of their habit of attacking livestock. As a consequence large numbers have been killed by farmers.

Spotted Hyena *Crocuta crocuta* **LR:cd**

RANGE Africa, south of the Sahara

HABITAT Semidesert to moist savanna

SIZE Body: 4–6 ft (1.2–1.8 m) Tail: 9¾–11¾ in (25–30 cm)

The spotted hyena is the largest member of the hyena family. It has a big, powerful head, slender legs and a sloping back. Its tail is short and bushy, and a short mane covers its neck and shoulders. The head and feet are always a lighter brown than the rest of the body, and irregular dark spots are scattered over the whole body. The spots vary greatly in their color and arrangement between individuals.

The spotted hyena is an inhabitant of open country and does not enter forest. It lives in packs of 10 to 30 or so animals (sometimes as many as 100), each pack occupying its own territory. The boundaries of the territory are marked with urine, droppings and anal-gland secretions and are carefully guarded to keep out rival packs. Males are dominant in the pack.

Hyenas sleep in burrows, which they dig themselves. Alternatively, they rest among tall grass or rocks. They emerge at dusk and are normally active at night only, although they may hunt during the day in some areas. As well as feeding on carrion, spotted hyenas cooperate to hunt large mammals, such as antelope, zebra and domestic livestock. The victim is often brought down by a bite in the leg and then torn to pieces by the pack while it is still alive. Spotted hyenas are extremely noisy animals, making a variety of howling screams when getting ready for the hunt, as well as eerie sounds like laughter when they kill and when mating.

When courting, spotted hyenas eject strong-smelling anal-gland secretions, and the male prances around the female and rolls her on the ground. The gestation period is between 99 and 130 days, and the 1 or 2 young are born in a burrow. Their eyes are open and some teeth are already through at birth. The young are suckled for between a year and 18 months, by which time they are able to join the hunting pack.

CATS

FELIDAE Cat Family

There are approximately 36 species in the cat family as classified here, but numbers differ according to source, and there is considerable disagreement as to the organization of the family. Of all predators, cats are probably the most efficient killers. Coloring, size and fur patterning vary within the family, but all species from the smallest to the largest are basically similar in appearance and proportions to the domestic cat – an ideal predatory body form.

Cat bodies are muscular and flexible, and the head is typically shortened and rounded, with large forward-directed eyes. Limbs can be proportionately short or long, but in all species except the cheetah, there are long, sharp, completely retractile claws on the feet for the grasping of prey. The overpowering of prey animals, however, practically always involves a bite from the powerful jaws, which are armed with well-developed, daggerlike canines. Shearing cheek teeth, carnassials, are used for slicing through flesh.

This successful family is distributed almost worldwide, being absent only from Antarctica, Australasia, the West Indies and some other islands, and from Madagascar, which is inhabited by the catlike viverrids, the fossas. Male and female look alike in most species, but males are often slightly larger.

Sadly, the fine fur of the cats has long been coveted by man, and many species have been hunted until they are rare and in danger of extinction.

African Golden Cat *Profelis aurata* **LR:lc**

RANGE	Africa: Senegal to Zaire (not Nigeria), Kenya
HABITAT	Forest, forest edge
SIZE	Body: 28¼–36½ in (72–93 cm) Tail: 13¾–17¾ in (35–45 cm)

A robust, medium-sized cat, the golden cat has rather short, sturdy legs and small, rounded ears. Coloration varies enormously from brownish-red to slate-gray on the upper parts; some golden cats have distinct spots all over the body, some only on the underside.

An inhabitant of dense forest, this cat spends much of its life in trees

and is mainly active at night. During the day it sleeps up in a tree. It is a solitary, elusive creature and little is known of its habits. It preys on mammals up to the size of small antelope and on birds up to the size of guineafowl.

Leopard Cat *Prionailurus bengalensis*

RANGE	S.E. Asia, Sumatra, Borneo, Java, Philippines
HABITAT	Forest
SIZE	Body: about 23½ in (60 cm) Tail: about 14 in (35 cm)

A nocturnal, rarely seen creature, the leopard cat rests during the day in a hole in a tree. It is an agile climber and preys on small birds and on mammals up to the size of squirrels and hares; it may occasionally kill a small deer. The coloration and pattern of the leopard cat are variable, but it is usually yellowish, gray or reddish-brown on the upper parts of the body, with a whitish belly, and is dotted overall with dark spots. These spots are in regular lines and may merge to form bands.

The breeding habits of this cat are not well known, but the female is thought to produce litters of 3 or 4 young in a cave or a den under fallen rocks.

Pampas Cat *Oncifelis colocolo* **LR:lc**

RANGE	South America: Ecuador, Peru, Brazil to S. Argentina
HABITAT	Open grassland, forest
SIZE	Body: 23½–27½ in (60–70 cm) Tail: 11½–12½ in (29–32 cm)

A small, but sturdily built animal, the pampas cat has a small head and thick, bushy tail. Its long fur is variable in color, ranging from yellowish-white to brown or silvery-gray. In the north of its range, it lives in forest and, although primarily ground-dwelling, will take refuge in trees. Farther south, it inhabits the vast grasslands, where it takes cover among the tall pampas grass. Active at

night, it hunts small mammals, such as cavies, and ground-dwelling birds, such as tinamous.

The female gives birth to litters of 1 to 3 young after a gestation thought to be about 10 weeks.

Caracal *Caracal caracal*

RANGE Africa (except rain forest belt); Middle East to N.W. India

HABITAT Savanna, open plains, semidesert, sand desert

SIZE Body: 25½–35½ in (65–90 cm) Tail: 7¾–11¾ in (20–30 cm)

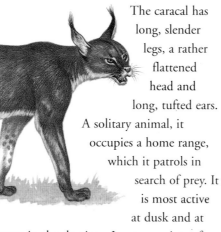

The caracal has long, slender legs, a rather flattened head and long, tufted ears. A solitary animal, it occupies a home range, which it patrols in search of prey. It is most active at dusk and at night, but may also emerge in the daytime. It eats a variety of mammals, from mice to reedbuck, and it also feeds on birds, reptiles, and domestic sheep, goats and poultry.

The male caracal courts his mate with yowls similar to those of the domestic cat. In a well-concealed den in a rock crevice, tree hole or abandoned burrow, the female bears a litter of 2 or 3 young after a gestation of 69 or 70 days. The young suckle for 6 months and are not independent until 9 to 12 months old.

Mountain Lion *Puma concolor*

RANGE S.W. Canada, W. USA, Mexico, Central and South America

HABITAT Mountainsides, forest, swamps, grassland

SIZE Body: 3¼–5¼ ft (1–1.6 m) Tail: 23½–33½ in (60–85 cm)

The widespread mountain lion, also known as the cougar or puma, is now becoming increasingly rare and some subspecies are in danger of extinction.

It varies greatly in color and size over its range, but tawny and grayish-brown are predominant. A solitary creature, the mountain lion occupies a defined territory. A male's home range may overlap with the territories of one or more females, but not with the territory of another male.

Normally active in the early morning and evening, the mountain lion may emerge at any time. Its main prey are mule deer and other deer, but it also eats rodents, hares and occasionally, domestic cattle. Having stalked its prey, the mountain lion pounces and kills with a swift bite to the nape of the neck.

Young are born in the summer in the temperate north and south of the range, or at any time of year in the tropics. Male and female pair for the season, maybe longer, and during his mate's period of sexual receptivity, or heat, the male fights off any rivals. The litter of 2 to 4 young is born after a gestation of 92 to 96 days in a den, among rocks or in thick vegetation, which the female may use for some years. At 6 or 7 weeks old the young start to take solid food, brought to them by their mother, and remain with her for 1 or even 2 years.

Lynx *Lynx lynx*

RANGE Europe: Scandinavia, east through Asia to Siberia

HABITAT Coniferous forest, scrub

SIZE Body: 31½ in–4¼ ft (80 cm–1.3 m) Tail: 1½–3 in (4–8 cm)

The lynx is recognized by its short tail and its tufted ears and cheeks. Its coat varies in coloration over its wide range, particularly in the degree of spotting, which may be either faint or conspicuous. Although strictly protected in most countries, lynx are becoming scarce, and some races are in danger of extinction. A solitary, nocturnal animal, the lynx stalks its prey on the ground or lies in wait for it in low vegetation. Hares, rodents, young deer and ground-living birds, such as grouse, are its main prey.

Breeding normally starts in the spring, and a litter of 2 or 3 young is born in a den among rocks or in a hollow tree, after a gestation of about 63 days. The cubs remain with their mother throughout their first winter.

CATS CONTINUED

Ocelot *Leopardus pardalis*

RANGE USA: Arizona, Texas; Mexico, Central and South America to N. Argentina

HABITAT Humid forest, thick bush, marshy areas

SIZE Body: 37½ in–4¼ ft (95 cm–1.3 m)
Tail: 10½–15¾ in (27–40 cm)

The characteristic dark markings that pattern the ocelot's coat are so variable that no two animals are quite alike. Generally nocturnal, the ocelot sleeps on a branch or in cover of vegetation during the day and emerges at night to hunt for small mammals, such as young deer and peccaries, agoutis, pacas and other rodents, as well as birds and snakes. It is an extremely secretive animal and rarely shows itself in open country. Males and females live in pairs in a territory, but do not hunt together.

Ocelots mate at night, and courting males make loud, screeching calls, similar to those of domestic cats. A litter of 2 young, sometimes 4, is born after a gestation of about 70 days, in a safe den in a hollow tree or in thick vegetation.

These beautiful cats have become rare, both because of the destruction of their forest habitat and because they have long been hunted for their fur. It is now illegal in many countries to trade ocelot skins, but such laws are hard to enforce, when the demand continues, and the black market price is high.

Bobcat *Lynx rufus*

RANGE S. Canada, USA (mostly western states), Mexico

HABITAT Chaparral, brush, swamp, forest

SIZE Body: 25½ in–3¼ ft (65 cm–1 m) Tail: 4¼–7½ in (11–19 cm)

The bobcat is short-tailed, like the lynx, but is generally smaller than the latter and has less conspicuous ear tufts. It varies considerably in size, the largest individuals occurring in the north of the range, and the smallest in Mexico. Adaptable to a variety of habitats, the bobcat is ground-dwelling, but does climb trees and will take refuge in a tree when chased. It is solitary and nocturnal for the most part, but may hunt in the daytime in winter. Small mammals, such as rabbits, mice, rats and squirrels, are its main prey, and it also catches ground-dwelling birds such as grouse. It hunts by stealth, slowly stalking its victim until near enough to pounce.

The female bobcat gives birth to a litter of 1 to 6 young, usually 3, after a gestation of about 50 days. The young first leave the den at about 5 weeks and start to accompany their mother on hunting trips at between 3 and 5 months old.

Pallas's Cat *Otocolobus manul* **LR:lc**

RANGE C. Asia: Iran to W. China

HABITAT Steppe, desert, rocky mountainsides

SIZE Body: 19¾–25½ in (50–65 cm) Tail: 8¼–12¼ in (21–31 cm)

Pallas's cat has a robust body and short, stout legs. Its head is broad, and its ears low and wide apart, protruding only slightly from the fur. The fur varies in color from pale gray to yellowish-buff or reddish-brown and is longer and more dense than that of any other wild cat. An elusive, solitary creature, this cat lives in a cave or rock crevice or a burrow taken over from another mammal, such as a marmot, usually emerging only at night to hunt. It preys on small mammals, such as mice and hares, and on birds.

Mating occurs in spring, and females give birth to litters of 5 or 6 young in summer.

Serval *Leptailaurus serval*

RANGE Africa, south of the Sahara to South Africa: S. Transvaal

HABITAT Savanna, open plains, woodland

SIZE Body: 25½–35½ in (65–90 cm) Tail: 9¾–15 in (25–35 cm)

A slender, long-legged cat, with a small head and broad ears, the serval has a graceful, sprightly air. Coloration varies from yellowish-brown to dark olive-brown; lighter-colored animals tend to have rows of large black spots on their fur, while darker individuals are dotted with many fine spots. Servals have excellent sight and hearing. It is usually active in the daytime and lives in a small territory, the boundaries of which are

marked with urine. It is generally solitary, but a female may enter a male's territory. Mammals, from the size of rodents up to small antelope, are its main prey. It also eats birds, poultry, lizards, insects and fruit. A litter of 1 to 4, usually 2 or 3, young is born in a safe den among rocks or vegetation or in a burrow taken over from another mammal. The gestation period is 67 to 77 days.

Wild Cat *Felis silvestris*

RANGE Scotland, S. Europe; Africa (not Sahara), Middle East to India

HABITAT Forest, scrub, savanna, open plains, semidesert

SIZE Body: 19¾–25½ in (50–65 cm) Tail: 9¾–15 in (25–38 cm)

One of the ancestors of the domestic cat, the wild cat is similar in form but slightly larger, and has a shorter, thicker tail, which is encircled with black rings. Coloration varies according to habitat, cats in dry sandy areas being lighter than forest-dwelling cats. Largely solitary and nocturnal, the wild cat lives in a well-defined territory. Although it is an agile climber, it stalks most of its prey on the ground, catching small rodents and ground-dwelling birds.

Rival courting males howl and screech as they vie for the attention of a female, and it is she who eventually makes the selection. She bears 2 or 3 young after a gestation of 63 to 69 days. The young first emerge from the den, in a cave, hollow tree or fox hole, when they are 4 or 5 weeks old and leave their mother after about 5 months.

Cheetah *Acinonyx jubatus* **VU**

RANGE Africa, east to Asia: E. Iran

HABITAT Open country: desert, savanna

SIZE Body: 3½–4½ ft (1.1–1.4 m) Tail: 25½–31½ in (65–80 cm)

The cheetah is the fastest of the big cats, able to attain speeds of 69½ mph (112 km/h). Its body is long and supple, with high muscular shoulders, and its legs are long and slender. The tail aids balance during the cheetah's high-speed sprints.

Cheetahs live in territories in open country, alone, in pairs or in family groups. They are active in the daytime, and sight is the most important sense in hunting. Having selected its prey when in hiding, the cheetah stalks its victim and then attacks with a short, rapid chase, knocking over the prey and killing it with a bite to the throat. Hares, jackals, small antelope, the young of larger antelope, and birds, such as guineafowl, francolins, bustards and young ostriches, are the cheetah's main prey. Several adults may, however, cooperate to chase and exhaust larger animals such as zebra.

Rival males compete in bloodless struggles for the attention of a female. She bears a litter of 2 to 4 young after a gestation of 91 to 95 days and brings them up alone. The young stay with the mother for up to 2 years.

Clouded Leopard *Neofilis nebulosa* **VU**

RANGE Nepal to S. China, Taiwan, Sumatra, Borneo

HABITAT Forest

SIZE Body: 24½–41¾ in (62–106 cm) Tail: 24–35¾ in (61–91 cm)

The rare, elusive clouded leopard has a long, powerful body, relatively short legs and a long tail. It is a good climber and hunts by pouncing from trees, as well as by stalking prey on the ground. Birds, pigs, small deer and cattle are the clouded leopard's main victims, and it kills with a single bite from its exceptionally long canine teeth.

A litter of 1 to 5 cubs is born after a gestation period of between 86 and 92 days.

CATS CONTINUED

Lion *Panthera leo* **VU**

RANGE Africa, south of the Sahara; N.W. India;
formerly more widespread in Asia

HABITAT Open savanna

SIZE Body: 4½–6½ ft (1.4–2 m)
Tail: 26¼ in–3¼ ft (67 cm–1 m)

The lion is powerfully built with a broad head, thick, strong legs and a long tail, tipped with a tuft of hair that conceals a claw-like spine. The male is larger than the female and has a heavy mane on the neck and shoulders which may be light yellow to black. Body color varies from tawny-yellow to reddish-brown.

Lions spend 20 or more hours a day resting and normally hunt during the day, but in areas where they are persecuted they are active only at night. They live in groups (prides) consisting of up to 3 adult males and up to 15 females and their young, in a territory that is defended against intruders. A small group of young males may live together.

Lions prey on mammals, such as gazelle, antelope and zebra, and may cooperate to kill larger animals, such as buffalo. Smaller animals and birds, even crocodiles, may also be eaten. Lionesses do most of the hunting, often in groups. Lions stalk their prey and approach it as closely as possible then make a short, rapid chase and pounce. They kill with a bite to the neck or throat.

Breeding occurs at any time of year. A litter of 1 to 6 young, usually 2 or 3, is born after a gestation of 102 to 113 days. The cubs are suckled for about 6 months, but from 3 months an increasing proportion of their food is meat. The cubs are left behind with one or two adults while the rest of the pride goes off to hunt, but if a kill is made, a lioness will return and lead them to it. Once they are over 4 months old, the cubs accompany their mothers everywhere. They become sexually mature at about 18 months old; young males are driven from the pride at about this age, but females remain with their family.

Jaguar *Panthera onca* **LR:nt**

RANGE S.W. USA, N. Mexico, Central and
South America to N. Argentina

HABITAT Forest, savanna

SIZE Body: 5–6 ft (1.5–1.8 m) Tail: 27½–35¾ in (70–91 cm)

The jaguar is the largest South American cat. This powerful creature has a deep chest and massive, strong limbs. Its coloration varies from light yellow to reddish-brown, with characteristic dark spots on the coat.

Although not quite as graceful and agile as the leopard, the jaguar climbs trees, often to lie in wait for prey. It is also an excellent swimmer. Like lions, jaguars cannot sustain high speeds and depend on getting close to prey in order to make successful kills. Peccaries and capybaras are often prey, and jaguars also kill mountain sheep, deer, otters, rodents, ground-living birds, turtles, caimans and fish.

Normally solitary animals, male and female jaguars stay together for a few weeks when breeding. A litter of 1 to 4 young is born, after a gestation period of between 93 and 105 days, in a secure den in vegetation, among rocks or in a hole in a river bank. The female is aggressive in her protection of the young from any intruder, including even the father.

Leopard *Panthera pardus*

RANGE Asia: Siberia to Korea, Sri Lanka and Java; Middle East; Africa

HABITAT Desert to forest, lowland plains to mountains

SIZE Body: 4¼–6¼ ft (1.3–1.9 m) Tail: 3½–4½ ft (1.1–1.4 m)

Although it was formerly widespread, the leopard is now patchily distributed and many of its sub-species have become extinct or endangered. A strong, but elegant, cat, it has a long body and relatively short legs. Most leopards are buff or tawny, with characteristic rosette-shaped black spots, but some are entirely black and are known as panthers. Panthers and leopards are otherwise identical.

Leopards are solitary and normally hunt day or night, but in areas where they are persecuted, they are nocturnal. They swim and climb well and often lie basking in the sun on a branch. Their sight and sense of smell are good, and their hearing is exceptionally acute.

Prey includes mammals such as large antelope, young apes (particularly baboons and monkeys), birds, snakes, fish and domestic livestock. Large items may be dragged up into a tree for safety while the leopard feeds; it will also feed on carrion.

Females have regular fertile periods, and males may fight over sexually receptive females. The litter of 1 to 6, but usually 2 or 3, young is born in a den in a rock crevice or hole in a tree after a gestation period of about 90 to 112 days. The young are suckled for 3 months and become independent at between 18 months and 2 years. The mother hunts alone and if she makes a kill, she hides it while she goes to fetch her cubs to share her food. Older cubs may catch some small prey, such as insects for themselves.

Tiger *Panthera tigris* **EN**

RANGE Siberia to Java and Bali

HABITAT Forest

SIZE Body: 6–9¼ ft (1.8–2.8 m) Tail: about 3ft (91 cm)

The largest of the big cats, the tiger has a massive, muscular body and powerful limbs. Males and females look similar, but males have longer, more prominent, cheek whiskers. Coloration varies from reddish-orange to reddish-ochre, and the pattern of the tiger's distinctive dark, vertical stripes is extremely variable between individuals. Tigers of the northern subspecies tend to be larger and paler than tropical subspecies.

Tigers are generally shy, nocturnal creatures and usually live alone, although they are not unsociable and are on amicable

terms with their neighbors. They climb well, move gracefully on land, and are capable of galloping at speed when chasing prey. Wild pigs, deer, and cattle, such as gaur and buffalo, are the tiger's main prey, and it also kills other mammals, such as the sloth bear.

Male and female associate for only a few days in order to mate. The female gives birth to a litter of, usually 2 or 3 young after a gestation period of 103 to 105 days. The young may stay with their mother for several years.

Most races of these magnificent animals are now rare and the Bali and Java tigers are now extinct because of indiscriminate killing earlier this century and the destruction of forest habitats.

Snow Leopard *Uncia uncia* **EN**

RANGE Pakistan, Afghanistan, Himalayas, east to China

HABITAT Mountain slopes, forest

SIZE Body: 4–5 ft (1.2–1.5 m) Tail: about 3ft (91 cm)

In summer, the snow leopard, which is also know as the ounce in some areas has a soft gray coat, shading to white on the belly with solid dark brown blotches and a black streak along the back. It inhabits the alpine meadows above the tree-line in mountain areas, amid snow and glaciers. In the winter months it follows the migrations of its prey animals down to the level of forest and scrub at about 6,600 ft (2,000 m).

This powerful, agile animal is capable of making huge leaps over ravines. The snow leopard stalks its prey, such as ibex, markhor, wild sheep and goats, boar and ground-dwelling birds, such as pheasants, partridges and snowcocks. In winter this leopard will also sometimes take domestic livestock.

Females may sometimes be accompanied by young, but otherwise snow leopards are solitary animals, constantly roaming around their enormous territories. They are active mainly in the early morning and late afternoon. The female gives birth to 2 or 3 cubs (but there may occasionally be 4 or 5), after a gestation period of between 98 and 103 days. The young start to accompany their mother on hunting trips when they are about 2 months old.

FUR SEALS, SEA LIONS AND WALRUS

OTARIIDAE: SEA LION FAMILY

There are approximately 14 species of fur seal and sea lion. The main features that distinguish these animals from the seals, family Phocidae, are the presence of external ears and their ability to tuck the hind flippers forward to facilitate locomotion on land. Sea lions occur in the southern Atlantic and Indian oceans and in the North and South Pacific, and come to land, or haul out, on coasts and islands.

Generally gregarious, these animals haul out in large numbers at traditional breeding sites, called rookeries, where males compete for the best territories. Males are considerably larger than females, and have big, bulbous heads.

Females give birth to the young conceived the previous year and mate again some days later. Mating and giving birth are synchronized in this convenient manner as a result of the phenomenon of delayed implantation. The embryo lies dormant for a period before development starts, thus ensuring the correct timing of the birth without producing young of undue size.

South American Fur Seal

Arctocephalus australis

RANGE South Pacific and Atlantic Oceans, from Brazil around to Peru

HABITAT Breeds on coasts and islands

SIZE 4½–6 ft (1.4–1.8 m)

The South American fur seal usually has deep reddish-brown underfur, the male has a coarse mane. It feeds on marine invertebrates, fish, squid and penguins and prefers to haul out on rocky coasts.

These fur seals are extremely territorial in the breeding season. Males take up their territories in November, competing for the prime spots and rigorously enforcing boundaries, since those with the best and largest sites mate with the most females. Males are joined 2 weeks later by the females, who give birth to their young within a few days. The female remains with her pup for up to 12 days, during which period she mates with the male whose territory she is in, then goes to sea to feed, returning at intervals to suckle the pup. The males rarely leave their territories until all the mating is over.

Northern Fur Seal *Callorhinus ursinus* **VU**

RANGE Bering Sea, Okhotsk Sea

HABITAT Breeds on islands in range such as Aleutian and Pribilof Islands

SIZE 5–6 ft (1.5–1.8 m)

Northern fur seals have larger rear flippers than other otariids, and both male and female have a pale patch on the neck. The male may be four times the female's weight. Usually alone or in pairs at sea, these fur seals feed on fish and squid and rarely come to land outside the breeding season.

Males establish territories on the breeding beaches before females arrive to give birth to their young. The female stays with her single offspring for 7 days before going off on brief feeding trips, returning to suckle it at intervals.

California Sea Lion *Zalophus californianus*

RANGE Pacific coasts: British Columbia to Mexico; Galápagos Islands

HABITAT Breeds on coasts and islands in south of range

SIZE 5½–7¼ ft (1.7–2.2 m)

This attractive sea lion takes well to training and is the most commonly seen species in circuses and marine shows. Females and juveniles are tan-colored when dry, while the larger males are brown; males are also distinguished by the horny crest on their heads. Social animals, these sea lions occur in groups and often come on to land outside the breeding season. They feed mainly on fish, octopus and squid.

Males gather at a breeding site, but only establish territories when the females arrive and start to give birth; territories are ill-defined and somewhat unstable. The female produces 1 young, and mates again a few days later.

Australian Sea Lion *Neophoca cinerea* **LR:lc**

RANGE Off S. and S.W. Australia

HABITAT Coasts and islands

SIZE Up to 7¾ ft (2.4 m)

A nonmigratory species, this sea lion does not travel far from the beach where it was born and often comes out on to land throughout the year. It moves quite easily on land despite its bulk and may travel several kilometers. Fish, squid and penguins are its main foods.

This is a gregarious species, and is usually found in small groups. The males establish well-defined territories, which they defend vigorously, and usually manage to prevent females on their sites from leaving. The female produces 1 young and remains with it for 14 days, during which time she mates. She then goes to sea, returning at 2-day intervals in order to suckle the pup, which she feeds for up to 2 years.

Steller Sea Lion *Eumetopias jubatus* **EN**

RANGE N. Pacific Ocean

HABITAT Breeds on Pribilof and Aleutian Islands, Kurile Islands, islands in Okhotsk Sea, coasts of N. America to San Miguel Island off S. California

SIZE 7¾–9¼ ft (2.4–2.8 m)

The largest otariid, the steller sea lion overlaps in its range with the California sea lion, but is distinguished by its size and lighter color. It feeds on fish, squid and octopus. Examination of stomach contents have revealed that the steller sea lion dives to 600 ft (180 m) or more to find food. Males establish well-defined territories at breeding grounds and maintain the boundaries with

ritual threat displays. They remain there throughout the breeding period, mating with the females in their area, and do not feed for about 2 months. Shortly after arriving, the female gives birth to 1 young. She remains with the pup constantly for the first 5 to 13 days before going briefly to sea to feed, leaving her pup in the company of other young.

ODOBENIDAE: WALRUS FAMILY

The single species of walrus resembles the sea lions in that its hind flippers can be brought forward in order to help it move on land. However, it cannot move as fast or adeptly as sea lions, and will often just drag itself forward.

Walrus *Odobenus rosmarus*

RANGE Arctic Ocean; occasionally N. Atlantic Ocean

HABITAT Pack ice, rocky islands

SIZE Male: 8¾–11½ ft (2.7–3.5 m) Female: 7¼–9½ ft (2.2–2.9 m)

The largest, heaviest pinniped, the male walrus is a huge animal. The male has large, heavy tusks, which have evolved from the upper canine teeth, which extend downward. Females also have tusks, but they are shorter and thinner. Walruses have thick skin, which acts as a protection against injury. The adult males tend to have less hair than females and young males.

Walruses swim quite slowly and use mainly their hind quarters for propulsion. They are good divers and feed on bottom living invertebrates, particularly mollusks, of which they consume only the soft muscular foot or siphon. How they extract these is still a mystery, but it is thought to be through some form of suction. They also feed on crustaceans, starfish, fish and even mammals.

Walruses are gregarious throughout the year. During the mating season, they congregate in traditional areas, where males compete for space near potential mates and display. After mating implantation is delayed by 4 or 5 months. Gestation is 11 months, so females can breed every other year at most. Usually 1 young is born (rarely 2) and the calf may be suckled for up to 2 years.

SEALS

PHOCIDAE: SEAL FAMILY

Often known as earless seals because they lack external ears, the 19 species in this family have made the most complete transition from terrestrial to aquatic way of life of all the pinnipeds. Their hind flippers cannot be turned forward like those of other pinnipeds. They move on land by dragging themselves forward with the foreflippers. They are skilful swimmers and divers, moving with undulatory movements of the hind portion of the body and the hind flippers. Seals have sophisticated mechanisms to enable them to dive deeply for food and to stay underwater for long periods. During a dive, the heart rate may drop from 120 to about 4 beats a minute, but without any drop in blood pressure. This is achieved by the restriction of the blood supply to the muscles of the heart and to the brain, thus reserving the blood oxygen for only the most vital organs.

The body of a seal is typically torpedo shaped, thick layers of fatty blubber under the skin accounting for much of its weight. The flippers as well as the body are furred, and the seals undergo an annual molt.

In some species, males are much bigger and heavier than females, but in others, females are the larger sex. Some are monogamous, but others, such as the elephant seals, are gregarious and polygamous. In most species there is a delay between fertilization and the actual start of gestation – delayed implantation. This ensures that birth and mating can be accomplished within the short period while the seals are on land.

Gray Seal *Halichoerus grypus*
RANGE N. Atlantic Ocean
HABITAT Breeds on rocky coasts of Scandinavia and Britain; Iceland and Faroe Islands; Labrador, Gulf of St. Lawrence, Newfoundland
SIZE 5¼–7½ ft (1.6–2.3 m)

The largest of the seals, excepting the elephant seals, a male gray seal may weigh up to 660 lb (300 kg) and be more than twice as heavy as a female. The male is also identified by his massive shoulders, covered with thick skin which forms heavy folds and wrinkles and by the elongated snout, rounded forehead and wide, heavy muzzle. The female has a flatter profile and a daintier, more slender muzzle.

Gray seals travel far from breeding sites, but stay mostly in coastal waters, feeding on fish and also on some crustaceans, squid and octopus.

The timing of breeding differs in the three areas of the gray seal's range, but females always arrive at breeding grounds first and give birth before the males appear. The males take up positions on the beach. The older, experienced individuals get the best places, but there is little fighting, and males may move sites from day to day. Having suckled her pup for about 3 weeks, the female mates and then leaves the area.

Harp Seal *Pagophilus groenlandica*
RANGE N. Atlantic and Arctic Oceans: N. Russia to Scandinavia and Greenland; Labrador, Newfoundland
HABITAT Subarctic and arctic waters
SIZE 5¼–6¼ ft (1.6–1.9 m)

The harp seal is identified by its black head and the dark band along its flanks and over its back; the rest of the body is usually pale gray, but this is highly variable. It is an expert, fast swimmer, and spends much of the year at sea making regular north-south migrations. It can also move fast over ice if necessary. Fish and crustaceans are the harp seal's main foods, and it is renowned for its ability to dive deeply and stay underwater for long periods in search of food.

It is generally a gregarious species, and only old males live alone. Females form whelping groups on the ice and give birth to their young in late February and early March. The pups are suckled for 2 to 4 weeks, growing rapidly on the nourishing milk, which is rich in fat. They are then left by the mothers, who go off to feed for a few weeks before migrating north to summer feeding grounds. Courting males fight rivals with their teeth and flippers and probably mate with females 2 or 3 weeks after they have given birth.

Common Seal/Harbor Seal *Phoca vitulina*

RANGE N. Atlantic and N. Pacific Oceans

HABITAT Temperate and subarctic coastal waters

SIZE 4½–6 ft (1.4–1.8 m)

The common seal has a proportionately large head and short body and flippers. Although often gray with dark blotches, these seals vary considerably in coloration and spots may be light gray to dark brown or black. Males are larger than females.

Generally non-migratory, the common seal often hauls out on protected tidal rocks and even travels up rivers and into lakes. It feeds mostly during the day on fish, squid and crustaceans and has been known to make dives lasting 30 minutes, although they normally last only 4 or 5 minutes.

Courtship and mating take place underwater. The single pup is closely guarded by its mother and suckles for 2 to 6 weeks. Born in an advanced state of development, the pup can swim from birth and dive for 2 minutes when 2 or 3 days old. After weaning, the pup is left, and the mother mates again.

Crabeater Seal *Lobodon carcinophagus*

RANGE Antarctic

HABITAT Edge of pack ice

SIZE 6½–7¾ ft (2–2.4 m)

Crabeater seals may well be the most abundant of all pinnipeds, and in their remote habitat they have few enemies other than killer whales. Capable of rapid movement over the ice, the crabeater seal thrusts with alternate forelimbs and the pelvis, and it is thought to achieve speeds of as much as 15½ mph (25 km/h). Krill, small shrimplike crustaceans, are its main food, which are strained from the water by means of the seal's trident-shaped teeth.

Births and mating probably occur from October to the end of December. The pup is well developed at birth and suckles for about 5 weeks.

Bearded Seal *Erignathus barbatus*

RANGE Arctic Ocean

HABITAT Shallow waters; breeds on ice floes

SIZE 6¾–7¾ ft (2.1–2.4 m)

Numerous long bristles on the snout are the identifying feature of the bearded seal and the source of its common name. It is a robust, heavily built species, in which females are slightly longer than males. Bottom-dwelling invertebrates, such as crustaceans and mollusks, and fish are its main foods.

During the breeding season the males call underwater. The female gives birth to 1 pup each year from the age of about 6 years. The pup, which can swim immediately, suckles for between 12 and 18 days, during which time the female usually mates again.

SEALS CONTINUED

Leopard Seal *Hydrurga leptonyx*

RANGE Southern Ocean

HABITAT Pack ice, coasts, islands

SIZE 9¾–11½ ft (3–3.5 m)

An unusually slender seal, the leopard seal is built for speed and has a large mouth, well suited to grasping the penguins, and sometimes other seals, that are its main prey. It catches penguins under water or as they move off the ice and, using its teeth, tears away the skin with great efficiency before eating them. Squid, fish and crustaceans are also caught.

Mating is thought to take place from January until March, but there is little information available.

Northern Elephant Seal *Mirounga angustirostris*

RANGE Pacific coast of N. America: Vancouver Island to C. Baja California

HABITAT Breeds on offshore islands

SIZE Male: up to 19¾ ft (6 m) Female: up to 9¾ ft (3 m)

The largest seal in the northern hemisphere, the male elephant seal may weigh a massive 6,000 lb (2,700 kg), much of it accounted for by the thick layer of blubber. Females rarely weigh more than 2,000 lb (900 kg). Because of its size, this species was a major target for commercial sealers, and by the end of the nineteenth century the population was dangerously low. Only one of the breeding islands appeared to be used, and that by only a hundred or so seals. With strict protection, numbers have increased since then, and between 1957 and 1976, the population tripled to over 47,000 – a remarkable recovery.

Northern elephant seals feed on fish and squid and make long, deep dives. Adult males haul out for breeding in late November and fight for dominance in the social hierarchy – high-ranking males mate with most females. With the aid of the greatly enlarged nasal chamber, which creates the elephantine snout, males utter loud, vocal threats against rivals. Females arrive a couple of weeks after males and each gives birth to a single pup, which is suckled for about a month. The bond between mother and young is close, and the female defends the pup from other adults and rarely leaves the breeding colony, existing on her blubber until the pup is weaned. She then mates again and leaves the breeding ground. Weaned pups gather in a group on the beach, where they remain for another month, living on fat reserves built up while suckling.

longest duration 73 minutes. Dives to 1,000 and 1,300 ft (300 and 400 m) are common, and antarctic cod, which are abundant at these depths, are one of the Weddell seal's main food species. This seal is able to reach such depths because, when diving, its heart rate slows down to 25 per cent of the predive rate.

Weddell seals are normally solitary outside the breeding season, but young animals may form groups. In the breeding season, males seem to set up underwater territories, which females can enter freely. The female gives birth on land to 1 pup, with which she stays constantly for about 12 days. She then spends about half of her time in water until the pup is weaned at about 6 weeks. When only 7 weeks old, the pup is able to dive to 295 ft (90 m). Females mate once their pups are weaned.

Mediterranean Monk Seal *Monachus monachus* **CR**

RANGE W. Atlantic Ocean: Canary Islands to Mediterranean Sea; Turkish coast of Black Sea

HABITAT Breeds on rocky islets and cliffs

SIZE 7½–8¾ ft (2.3 m–2.7 m)

The Mediterranean monk seal is becoming rare now that its previously remote hauling-out spots on islets and cliffs are becoming more accessible to humans with motor boats and scuba diving equipment. These seals often become entangled in fishing nets. They are extremely upset by any disturbance, and mothers and pregnant females in particular are nervous of any approach, and when the females are in danger or under stress pregnancies may be spontaneously aborted.

Births occur between May and November, with a peak in September and October. The pups are suckled for about the first 6 weeks of their lives.

Weddell Seal *Leptonychotes weddelli*

RANGE Antarctic

HABITAT Edge of pack ice

SIZE Up to 9½ ft (2.9 m)

The Weddell seal is one of the larger seals in the family. It has a small head in proportion to its body and an appealing, short-muzzled face. The female is longer than the male.

It makes deeper, longer dives than any other seal, the maximum recorded depth being 2,000 ft (600 m), and the

Hooded Seal *Cystophora cristata*

RANGE N. Atlantic Ocean: arctic and subarctic waters

HABITAT Edge of pack ice

SIZE 6½–8½ ft (2–2.6 m)

Hooded seals spend much of their lives in open seas, diving deeply in search of fish and squid, which are their main food source.

Hooded seals make regular migrations to areas of pack ice in the Denmark Strait and east of Greenland. On the pack ice the adults gather to haul out and molt. After molting, the seals disperse again to reassemble at breeding grounds in different areas the following spring.

Pups are born in March on ice floes and are suckled for between 7 and 12 days. During this period, the female is courted by a male, who stays in the water near to her and her pup, chasing away any rivals. If necessary, the male hauls out and displays or fights, making threat calls that are amplified by his enormous inflatable nasal sac. The female then mates with her successful suitor about 2 weeks after giving birth.

AARDVARK AND PIGS

ORDER TUBULIDENTATA

ORYCTEROPODIDAE AARDVARK FAMILY

There is one family in this order, containing a single species that lives in Africa. Its relationship to other mammal groups is obscure. The aardvark's teeth are unique: they have no enamel and consist of dentine columns, interspersed with tubes of pulp.

Aardvark *Orycteropus afer*

RANGE Africa, south of the Sahara

HABITAT All regions with termites, from rain forest to dry savanna

SIZE Body: 3¼–5¼ ft (1–1.6 m) Tail: 17½–23½ in (44.5–60 cm)

The aardvark is a solitary, nocturnal, insect-eating animal. Its sight is poor, but its other senses are excellent, it has large ears, which are normally held upright but can be folded and closed, and highly specialized nostrils for sniffing out its prey. Dense hair surrounds the nostrils and seals them off when the aardvark digs. It uses its powerful forelimbs to excavate burrows for shelter and to smash the nests of the ants and termites that are its main food. It sweeps up the prey with its long, sticky tongue.

The female gives birth to a single young after a gestation of 7 months. The offspring is suckled for 4 months.

ORDER ARTIODACTYLA

This, the largest and most diverse order of hoofed herbivorous mammals. Artiodactyls have an even number of toes. Weight is carried on digits 3 and 4, which are typically encased in hoofs. The first digit is absent, and digits 2 and 5 are reduced. Artiodactyls can run rapidly and have specialized teeth for eating vegetation, which is digested in a four-chambered stomach with the aid of enzymes and symbiotic micro-organisms.

SUIDAE: PIG FAMILY

Pigs are more omnivorous than other artiodactyls. There are about 9 species, found in Europe, Asia and Africa, usually in forested or brush areas. Pigs are stocky, with long heads and mobile, flattened snouts used to root for food. The upper canine teeth usually form tusks. Each foot has four toes, but only the third and fourth reach the ground and form hooves.

Bush Pig *Potamochoerus porcus*

RANGE Africa, south of the Sahara; Madagascar

HABITAT Forest, bush, swamps, thickets in savanna

SIZE Body: 3¼–5 ft (1–1.5 m) Tail: 11¾–17¾ in (30–45 cm)

This pig has an elongate snout and long, tufted ears. Its bristly coat varies from reddish to grayish-brown, with a white dorsal mane and whiskers. Bush pigs live in groups of up to 12 or so, led by an old male. They eat almost anything, including grass, roots, fruit, small mammals, birds and carrion. Normally active in the day, they are nocturnal in areas where they are hunted.

Breeding occurs throughout the year, particularly when food is abundant. The female gives birth to 3 to 6 young after a gestation of 120 to 130 days.

Warthog *Phacochoerus aethiopicus*

RANGE Africa: Ghana to Somalia, south to South Africa: Natal

HABITAT Savanna, treeless open plains

SIZE Body: 3½–4½ ft (1.1–1.4 m) Tail: 13¾–19¾ in (35–50 cm)

The warthog has long legs, a large head and a broad muzzle with tusks. The big head bears two wartlike protuberances (the origin of the common name). Its bristly coat is sparse and a mane of bristles runs to the middle of the back. There are whiskers on the lower jaw. The female is smaller than the male.

Warthogs live in family groups in a territory that may be

shared by several families. They prefer to have water for drinking and wallowing in their range and shelter, such as holes among rocks, where they rest. Warthogs eat short grass, fruit, bulbs, tubers, roots and occasionally small mammals and carrion.

The breeding season tends to be associated with local rainy seasons. The female gives birth to 2 to 4 young after a gestation of 170 to 175 days. The young suckle for up to 4 months, but after a week, leave the burrow to feed on grass.

Wild Boar *Sus scrofa*

RANGE S. and C. Europe, N.W. Africa; Asia to Siberia, south to Sri Lanka, Taiwan and S.E. Asia

HABITAT Forest, woodland

SIZE Body: 3½–4¼ ft (1.1–1.3 m) Tail: 6–7¾ in (15–20 cm)

This ancestor of the domestic pig has a heavy body covered with dense, bristly hair, thin legs and a long snout. The male has prominent tusk. Wild boars live alone or in small groups of up to 20. Males stay separate from, but close to, the females. Active at night and in the morning, they forage over a wide area, digging for bulbs and tubers and also eating nuts and other plant material, as well as insect larvae and, occasionally, carrion. This agile, fast-moving animal, is aggressive if alarmed.

Breeding seasons vary with regional climate. In Europe, wild boars mate in winter and give birth to up to 10 young in spring or early summer, after a gestation of about 115 days.

Bearded Pig *Sus barbatus*

RANGE Malaysia, Sumatra, Borneo

HABITAT Rain forest, scrub, mangroves

SIZE Body: 5¼–6 ft (1.6–1.8 m) Tail: 7¾–11¾ in (20–30 cm)

The bearded pig has an elongate head, a narrow body, abundant whiskers on its chin and a bristly wartlike protuberance beneath each eye. These warts are more conspicuous in males than in females. Fallen fruit, roots, shoots and insect larvae are this pig's staple foods.

After a gestation of about 4 months, the female gives birth to 2 or 3 young.

Giant Forest Hog *Hylochoerus meinertzhageni*

RANGE Africa: Liberia, Cameroon, east to S. Ethiopia, Tanzania, Kenya

HABITAT Forest, thickets

SIZE Body: 5–6 ft (1.5–1.8 m) Tail: 9¾–13¾ in (25–35 cm)

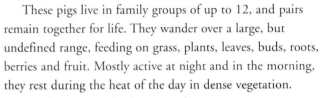

The largest of the African pigs, the giant forest hog has a huge elongate head, a heavy body and rather long legs for its family. Its muzzle is broad, and there are glandular swellings in the skin under its eyes and across its cheeks. Males are bigger and heavier than females.

These pigs live in family groups of up to 12, and pairs remain together for life. They wander over a large, but undefined range, feeding on grass, plants, leaves, buds, roots, berries and fruit. Mostly active at night and in the morning, they rest during the heat of the day in dense vegetation.

The female gives birth to 1 to 4 young, sometimes up to 8, after a gestation period of 4 to 4½ months.

Babirusa *Babyrousa babyrussa* **VU**

RANGE Sulawesi, Sula Islands

HABITAT Moist forest, lake shores and river banks

SIZE Body: 34¼–42 in (87–107 cm) Tail: 10½–12½ in (27–32 cm)

The babirusa has unusual upper tusks, which grow upward through the muzzle and curve back toward the eyes. Only males have prominent lower tusks, and these are thought to be a sexual characteristic used to attract females. Elusive animals, babirusas prefer to forage in dense cover near water. They are fast runners and good swimmers, even in the sea. They move in small groups, the male doing most of the rooting and unearthing of food, while females and young trail behind, feeding on items such as roots, berries, tubers and leaves.

The female gives birth to 2 young after a gestation period of between 125 and 150 days.

PECCARIES AND HIPPOPOTAMUSES

TAYASSUIDAE: PECCARY FAMILY

The 3 species of peccary occur only in the New World, from the southwestern USA to central Argentina. The New World equivalent of pigs in their habits, peccaries resemble pigs, but are smaller and differ from them in a number of ways. First, they have only three toes on each hind foot (pigs have four); second, peccaries have a prominent musk gland on the back about 74 in (20 cm) in front of the tail; and third, their tusks are directed downward, not upward like those of pigs.

Chaco Peccary *Catagonus wagneri* **EN**

RANGE	Bolivia, Argentina, Paraguay
HABITAT	Semiarid thorn scrub, grassland
SIZE	Body: about 3¼ ft (1 m) Tail: 34¼ in (87 cm)

Once thought to be extinct, the chaco peccary is now believed to be reasonably abundant in areas where it is left undisturbed, although the species as a whole is vulnerable. The animals have suffered from excessive hunting and from the loss of much of their thorn scrub habitat, which has been cleared for cattle ranching.

A long tailed, long-legged animal, this species is active during the day and has better vision than other peccaries. It moves in small groups of up to 6 animals, among which there are strong social bonds, and feeds largely on cacti and the seeds of leguminous plants.

White-lipped Peccary *Tayassu pecari*

RANGE	Mexico, Central and South America to Paraguay
HABITAT	Forest
SIZE	Body: 37½ in–3¼ ft (95 cm–1 m) Tail: 1–2¼ in (2.5–5.5 cm)

The white-lipped peccary has a heavy body, slender legs and a long, mobile snout. A gregarious animal, it gathers in groups of 50 to 100 individuals of both sexes and all ages. Active in the

cooler hours of the day, these peccaries are fast, agile runners, even over rugged ground. Using their sensitive snouts, they dig on the forest floor searching for plant material, such as bulbs and roots, and for small animals. Although their sight is poor and hearing only fair, these peccaries have an acute sense of smell and can find bulbs underground by scent alone.

The female gives birth to a litter of 2 young after a gestation period of about 158 days.

Collared Peccary *Tayassu tajacu*

RANGE	S.W. USA; Mexico, Central and South America to Patagonia
HABITAT	Semidesert, arid woodland, forest
SIZE	Body: 29½–35½ in (75–90 cm) Tail: ½–1¼ in (1.5–3 cm)

Collared peccaries are robust, active animals, able to run fast and swim well. They live in groups of 5 to 15 individuals, and the musky secretions of the gland on each animal's back seem to play a part in maintaining the social bonds of the herd, as well as being used for marking territory. With their sensitive snouts, collared peccaries search the ground for roots, herbs, grass and fruit; they also eat insect larvae, worms and small vertebrates. In summer, they feed only in the morning and evening, but in winter they are active all day, treading well-worn, regular paths through their home range. Hearing is the most acute of this peccary's senses.

Several males in a herd may mate with a female on heat, and there is rarely fighting or rivalry. After a gestation of 142 to 149 days, the female leaves the herd and gives birth to 2 or 3 young. The young are soon active and the family rejoins the herd after a couple of days.

HIPPOPOTAMIDAE: HIPPOPOTAMUS FAMILY

There are 2 species of hippopotamus both found only in Africa, although fossil evidence shows that the family was once more widely distributed in the southern parts of the Old World. Both species are amphibious, spending much of their lives in water, and they have various adaptations for this mode of life, including nostrils that can be closed and specialized skin glands that secrete an oily, pink substance, which protects their virtually hairless bodies from external damage.

Hippopotamus *Hippopotamus amphibius*

RANGE Africa, south of the Sahara to Namibia
and South Africa: Transvaal

HABITAT Rivers or lakes in grassland

SIZE Body: Male 10½–13¾ ft (3.2–4.2 m) Female 9¼–12 ft (2.8–3.7 m)
Tail: 13¾–19¾ in (35–50 cm)

One of the giants of Africa, the hippopotamus has a bulky body and a massive head and mouth equipped with an impressive set of teeth; the canine teeth form tusks. Its legs are short and thick, and there are four webbed toes on each foot.

When the hippopotamus is in water, it lies with much of its vast body submerged; often only the bulging eyes, ears and nostrils are visible. It swims and dives well and can walk along the river or lake bottom. Daytime hours are spent mainly resting in water or on the shore, then, in the evening, the hippopotamus emerges to graze on land, taking short grass and other plants and fallen fruit.

Hippopotamuses play a vital role in the ecology of inland waters, both by keeping down bankside vegetation and by excreting tons of fertilizing manure into the water, which encourages the growth of plankton and invertebrates and thus sustains the whole ecosystem.

Hippopotamuses are gregarious animals and live in groups of up to 15 or so, sometimes more, led by an old male. Males are aggressive and will fight for prime positions on the river bank or for dominance of the group. To threaten or challenge a rival, the male opens his mouth in a huge, yawning gape and bellows. All adults are fierce in defence of their young.

Mating takes place in water at any time of year, but is generally timed so that births coincide with the rains and thus, the luxuriant growth of grass. A single young is born on land or in shallow water after a gestation period of 233 to 240 days. The young is suckled for about a year, and females usually give birth every 18 months to 2 years.

Pygmy Hippopotamus
Hexaprotodon liberiensis **VU**

RANGE Guinea to Nigeria

HABITAT Rain forest,
swamps and thickets
near water

SIZE Body: 5½–6¼ ft
(1.7–1.9 m)
Tail: 6–8¼ in
(15–21 cm)

The pygmy hippopotamus is much less aquatic than its giant relative and has a proportionately smaller head and longer legs; only the front toes are webbed. It lives near water, but stays on land for much of the time, feeding at night on leaves, swamp vegetation and fallen fruit and also on roots and tubers which it digs up. Usually alone, except for breeding pairs or females with young, it occupies a territory, which it defends against rivals. When alarmed, the pigmy hippopotamus seeks refuge in dense cover or in water.

The female gives birth to a single young after a gestation of 180 to 210 days. The young stays with its mother for up to 3 years. Rare over almost all its range, the pygmy hippopotamus may have become extinct in some places. The population has suffered from excessive hunting, combined with the destruction of large areas of its forest habitat.

CAMELS

CAMELIDAE: CAMEL FAMILY

The 4 surviving species in this formerly more diverse family are the most primitive of the ruminants, or cud-chewing animals. Of the 4, dromedaries and most of the bactrian camels are wholly domesticated. There are still wild bactrians in the Gobi Desert, and guanacos and vicuñas maintain wild populations in parts of South America.

Camels and their relatives have highly specialized feet. They have evolved to the point of having only two toes on each foot, but the foot bones are expanded sideways to produce the support for two broad, flat pads on each foot, with a nail on the upper surface of each toe. This foot structure is particularly well developed in the camel species and it enables them to walk on soft, sandy soil, where conventional hoofs would sink in deeply.

The head of a camelid is relatively small, with an elongate snout terminating in a cleft upper lip. Vegetation is cropped by using long, forward-pointing lower incisors that work against tough upper gums. Camelids have complex three-chambered stomachs and ruminate, or chew the cud.

The humps of the 2 species of camel are fat stores, which provide food reserves – vital in the unpredictable conditions of the camel's desert habitat.

Guanaco
Lama guanicoe

RANGE South America: Peru to Patagonia

HABITAT Semidesert to about 16,500 ft (5,000 m)

SIZE Body: 4–5½ ft (1.2–1.7 m) Tail: 9¾ in (25 cm)

The guanaco is a slender, long-limbed animal, which is capable of fast movement over rugged terrain and is able to leap nimbly up mountain trails. It is adaptable to heat or cold and lives in open country and feeds on grass.

Males are polygamous and lead harems of 4 to 10 females with their young, which they defend, fighting off any rivals or intruders that try to steal one of their females. Young males and males without harems also form herds.

The female gives birth every other year, producing a single young after a gestation period of between 10 and 11 months. The young guanaco is active soon after birth and is able to run with speed and grace.

Llamas and alpacas are domesticated forms of the guanaco and they are bred as draft animals and fleece producers respectively. They interbreed readily with one another and with wild guanacos.

Vicuña *Vicugna vicugna* **LR:cd**

RANGE South America: Peru to N. Chile

HABITAT Semi-arid grassland at altitudes over 13,000 ft (4,000 m)

SIZE Body: 4½–5¼ ft (1.4–1.6 m) Tail: 6 in (15 cm)

The vicuña's tawny-brown coat is thick and woolly and longest on the sides. It enables the animal to tolerate the cold, snow and ice of its mountain habitat. Gregarious animals, vicuñas live in groups of up to 15 females led by a male, or in all-male herds. The harem band lives in a territory which is fiercely guarded by the adult male; at the first sign of any danger he alerts the females so that they can escape. Male troops consist mainly of young animals and do not have a specific territory but wander nomadically. Since most of the best grazing is appropriated by the territorial family males, these nomads are continually trespassing and being driven away. Rival males have a characteristic habit of spitting at each other as they fight.

Vicuñas are fast, graceful animals, capable of maintaining speeds of 29 mph (47 km/h) over long distances, even at high altitudes. They feed on grass and small plants. Eyesight is their most acute sense while hearing is fair and smell poor.

The female gives birth to 1 young after a gestation period of between 10 and 11 months. The young can stand and walk soon after birth and suckles for about 10 months. Vicuñas have long been hunted by man for their fine wool and meat, but despite this, a few years ago the vulnerable population was said to be on the increase again.

slow-moving animal used as a beast of burden, and a light graceful, fast-running racer, used for riding. Both have short, coarse hair, longest on the crown, neck, throat and hump.

Dromedaries feed on grass and any other plants and can survive in areas of sparse, tough vegetation Certain adaptations fit the dromedary for life in hot, dry climates; the most significant is its ability to go for long periods without drinking, linked with its ability to conserve water in the body. Its hump is an important specialization. It gives protection from the sun by absorbing heat and carries fat stores, which are metabolized to provide energy and water. The camel does not store water in the hump, but can do so in the stomach lining. The kidneys are able to concentrate urine to avoid water loss, and moisture can be absorbed from fecal material. The body temperature of the camel drops at night and rises so slowly during the day that the animal does not need to sweat to cool itself for a long time. During an extended period without water, the camel is able to lose up to 27 per cent of its body weight without detrimental effect. This loss can be recovered in 10 minutes by drinking. In one experiment, a thirsty camel drank 104 litres (27 gal) in a few minutes.

Females breed every other year. After a gestation of 365 to 440 days, the female moves away from the herd to give birth to a single calf. When it is able to walk, after a day or so, they rejoin the herd. The calf is suckled for almost a year, but starts to nibble plants as soon as it is born, and by 2 months old is regularly eating vegetation.

Bactrian Camel *Camelus bactrianus* **EN**

RANGE C. Asia: China, Mongolia

HABITAT Desert, steppe

SIZE Body: about 9¾ ft (3 m) Tail: about 21 in (53 cm)

The bactrian (two-humped) camel has been domesticated, but has not spread outside its native range to the same extent as the dromedary. Only a small number of bactrian camels live wild in the Gobi Desert, and even these may be part domestic stock. It is thought that Mongolian stocks may be slowly increasing.

Apart from its two humps, the main characteristic of the bactrian camel is its long, shaggy hair, which keeps it warm in winter, but is shed in summer, leaving the body almost naked. Docile, slow moving animals, these camels move with a rolling gait which is the result of their ability to raise both legs on one side at the same time. They feed on virtually any vegetation, such as grass, the foliage of trees and bushes, and small plants.

After a gestation of 370 to 440 days, the female gives birth to 1 young, which is active within only 24 hours. It is suckled for about a year and fully grown when about 5 years old.

Dromedary *Camelus dromedarius*

RANGE N. Africa, Middle East; introduced in Australia

HABITAT Semiarid and arid grassland, desert, plains

SIZE Body: 7¼–11 ft (2.2–3.4 m) Tail: 19¾ in (50 cm)

The dromedary, or one-humped camel now exists only as a domesticated animal, which it has been, so it is thought, since 4000 B.C. Before then it probably lived in North Africa and Arabia. Today there are two main types: a heavily built,

CHEVROTAINS, MUSK DEER AND DEER

TRAGULIDAE: CHEVROTAIN FAMILY

There are 4 species of chevrotain, or mouse deer, found in tropical forest and mangrove swamps in Africa and Asia. They are tiny, delicate creatures, which look like minute deer with mouselike heads, but are probably related to camels and pigs. They stand only 7¾ to 13¾ in (20 to 35 cm) high at the shoulder and weigh only 5 to 10¼ lb (2.3 to 4.6 kg). Active at night, they feed largely on plants and fruit.

Water Chevrotain *Hyemoschus aquaticus* **LR:nt**

RANGE Africa: Guinea to cameroon, Zaire, Gabon, Central African Republic

HABITAT Forest, near water

SIZE Body: 29½–33½ in (75–85 cm) Tail: 4–6 in (10–15 cm)

About the size of a hare, with a hunched back, small head and short, slender legs, the water chevrotain has a variable pattern of white spots on its back and up to three white stripes along its flanks. It rests during the day in thick undergrowth or in a hole in a river bank and emerges at night to forage for grass, leaves and fruit, as well as some insects, crabs, fish, worms and small mammals. Water chevrotains are solitary except in the breeding season, each individual occupying its own territory. Chevrotains always live near water and are good swimmers; if danger threatens, they often escape by diving deeply.

At breeding time, the male simply finds the female by scent, and they mate without aggression. The female gives birth to a single young after a gestation period of about 4 months. The young is suckled for 8 months but begins to take some solid food at 2 weeks old.

Lesser Malay Chevrotain

Tragulus javanicus

RANGE S.E. Asia, Indonesia

HABITAT Lowland forest, usually near water

SIZE Body: 15¾–18½ in (40–47 cm)

Tail: 2–3¼ in (5–8 cm)

The tiny, deerlike Malay chevrotain has a robust body on extremely slender legs. It has no horns, but in males, the canine teeth in the upper jaw are enlarged into tusks. A nocturnal creature, it lives in the dense undergrowth, making little tunnel-like trails; it feeds on grass, leaves, fallen fruit and berries. It lives alone except when breeding. The female gives birth to 1 young after a gestation of about 5 months.

MOSCHIDAE: MUSK DEER FAMILY

The 4 species of musk deer, all in the genus *Moschus*, occur in central and northeastern Asia. Sometimes classified with the chevrotains or with the true deer, musk deer are in several respects intermediate between these two groups. They stand about 19¾ to 23½ in (50 to 60 cm) high at the shoulder and have no horns, but they do possess large tusks, formed from the upper canine teeth. The name musk deer comes from the waxy secretions produced by a gland on the abdomen of the male.

Forest Musk Deer

Moschus chrysogaster **LR:nt**

RANGE Himalayas to C. China

HABITAT Forest, brushland at 8,500–11,800 ft (2,600–3,600 m)

SIZE Body: about 3¼ ft (1 m)

Tail: 1½–2 in (4–5 cm)

Long, thick, bristly hairs cover the body of the forest musk deer and help to protect the animal from the often harsh weather conditions of its habitat. Male and female look more or less alike, but the male has larger tusks, developed from the upper canine teeth, and a gland on the abdomen, which secretes musk during the breeding season. Only mature males have these glands.

Usually solitary, musk deer may occasionally gather in groups of up to 3. They are active in the morning and evening, feeding on grass, moss and shoots in summer and lichens, twigs and buds in winter.

At the onset of the breeding season, males fight to establish dominance and access to the females. They wrestle with their necks, trying to push one another to the ground, and may inflict deep wounds with their tusks. The female gives birth to 1 young after a gestation of about 160 days.

CERVIDAE: DEER FAMILY

There are about 40 species of true deer, distributed over North and South America, Europe, northwest Africa and Asia. Found in habitats ranging from the Arctic to the tropics, deer are slim long-legged, elegant herbivores. Their most obvious characteristic is the pair of antlers, possessed by males of all species except the Chinese water deer. Most deer shed and regrow their antlers in an annual cycle, shedding them in late winter or early spring and growing them in summer, before the autumn rutting contests for dominance.

Chinese Water Deer *Hydropotes inermis* **LR:nt**

RANGE China, Korea; introduced in England

HABITAT River banks with reedbeds and rushes, grassland, fields

SIZE Body: 30½ in–3¼ ft (77.5 cm–1 m) Tail: 2¼–3 in (6–7.5 cm)

The only true deer to lack antlers, the Chinese water deer has tusks, formed from enlarged upper canine teeth; these are larger in males than in females. Both male and female have small scent glands on each side of the groin and are the only deer to possess such glands. A nocturnal animal, this deer usually lives alone or in pairs and rarely gathers in herds. It feeds on reeds, coarse grass and other vegetation.

Males contest in fierce fights for dominance in the rutting season before breeding. After a gestation period of about 6 months, the female gives birth to 4 young – this is the largest litter produced by any deer.

Chinese Muntjac *Muntiacus reevesi*

RANGE S.E. China, Taiwan; introduced in England and France

HABITAT Dense vegetation, hillsides; parkland in introduced range

SIZE Body: 31½ in–3¼ ft (80 cm–1 m) Tail: 4¼–7 in (11–18 cm)

The antlers of the male Chinese muntjac are small, rarely exceeding 6 in (15 cm) in length, but this deer also has tusks, formed from the upper canine teeth; females have smaller tusks than males. The Chinese muntjac lives in a territory, which it rarely leaves, and it prefers to stay hidden in the cover of vegetation. It lives alone or in pairs and seldom forms herds. Primarily nocturnal, it may be active in the morning in quiet, undisturbed areas. It feeds on grass, low-growing leaves and shoots.

In dominance contests during the rutting season, males fight with their tusks, rather than their antlers, and make doglike barking noises. The female usually gives birth to 1 young after a gestation period of about 6 months.

Tufted Deer *Elaphodus cephalophus* **DD**

RANGE S. China, N. Myanmar

HABITAT Dense undergrowth, near water

SIZE Body: about 5¼ ft (1.6 m) Tail: 2¾–4¾ in (7–12 cm)

The male tufted deer is characterized by the tuft of hair on the forehead at the base of the antlers. The antlers them-selves are short and are often almost hidden by the tuft. This species is a nocturnal, normally solitary deer. It feeds on grass and other plant material.

The female gives birth to a single young after a gestation of about 6 months.

DEER CONTINUED

Père David's Deer

Elaphurus davidianus

RANGE Originally China; now in wildlife parks and reintroduced in China

HABITAT Wildlife parks

SIZE Body: 6½ ft (2 m) Tail: 14 in (35 cm)

This interesting deer became extinct in the wild in the late 19th century. However, at the beginning of this century, some of the few remaining specimens left in China were brought to England to live in the grounds of Woburn Abbey, in Bedfordshire, where they have thrived. Populations of Père David's deer can now be found in zoos and parks around the world and they have been reintroduced in China.

Père David's deer has a mane of thick hair around its neck and throat and a longer tail than most deer. One tine of each antler usually points backward, while the other points upward and forks. Although they feed mainly on grass, the deer supplement their diet with water plants. For most of the year they live in herds led by a dominant male, but the male lives alone for 2 months before and 2 months after the rutting season.

In the rutting season, the males fight to gain dominance over a harem. Females give birth to 1 or 2 young after a gestation of about 288 days.

White-tailed deer

Odocoileus virginianus

RANGE S. Canada, USA, Central and South America to Peru and Brazil

HABITAT Forest, swamps, open brushland

SIZE Body: 5–6½ ft (1.5–2 m) Tail: up to 11 in (28 cm)

One of the most adaptable animals in the world, the white-tailed deer is found from near-Arctic regions to the tropics. Its adaptability is reflected in its feeding habits: it browses and grazes on many kinds of grasses, weeds, shrubs, twigs, fungi, nuts and lichens. A slender, sprightly creature, the white-tailed deer has a long tail, white on its underside a white band across its nose and a white patch on the throat.

White-tailed deer are shy, elusive animals and they do not usually congregate in large herds. In severe winter weather, however, they may congregate in a group in a sheltered spot, out of the cold wind.

It is not certain whether or not males are polygamous, but in the breeding season, they engage in savage battles over mates. The gestation period is between 6½ and 7 months. Young females usually produce only a single offspring, but older females may produce litters of 2 or even 3. The infants are able to walk and run right away and stay close to their mother. They are suckled for about 4 months.

Moose *Alces alces*

RANGE N. Europe and Asia: Scandinavia to Siberia; Alaska, Canada, N. USA; introduced in New Zealand

HABITAT Coniferous forest, often near lakes and rivers

SIZE Body: 8¼–9¼ ft (2.5–3 m) Tail: 2–4¾ in (5–12 cm)

The largest of the deer, the moose is identified by its size, its broad, overhanging muzzle and the flap of skin, known as the bell, hanging from its throat. The massive antlers of the male are flattened and palmate, with numerous small branches.

The moose is less gregarious than other deer and is usually alone outside the breeding season. In winter, it feeds on woody plants, but in summer water plants are also eaten. It wades into water to feed and swims well.

Bellowing males display to attract females, and they engage in fierce contests with rivals. Following an 8-month gestation, the female gives birth to a single calf, occasionally to twins. The calf is suckled for about 6 months, but stays with its mother for about 12 months.

Caribou/Reindeer *Rangifer tarandus*

RANGE N. Europe and Asia: Scandinavia to Siberia; Alaska, Canada, Greenland

HABITAT Tundra

SIZE Body: 4–7½ ft (1.2–2.2 m) Tail: 4¾ in (10–21 cm)

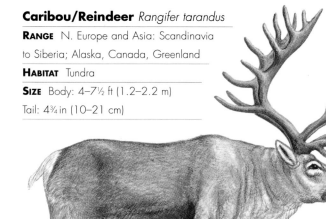

Once divided into several species, all caribou and reindeer, including the domesticated reindeer, are now considered races of a single species. The races vary in coloration from almost black to brown, gray and almost white. The caribou is the only deer in which both sexes have antlers. The antlers are unique in that the lowest, forward pointing tine is itself branched.

Females are gregarious and gather in herds with their young, but adult males are often solitary. Some populations migrate hundreds of miles between their breeding grounds on the tundra and winter feeding grounds farther south. Grass and other tundra plants are their main food in summer, but in winter caribou feed mainly on lichens, scraping away the snow with their hooves to expose the plants.

In autumn, males fight for harems. The female produces 1 (occasionally 2) young after a gestation of about 240 days. Calves can run with the herd within a few hours of birth.

Wapiti/Red Deer *Cervus elaphus*

(conspecific with *C. canadensis*)

RANGE W. Europe, N.W. Africa, Asia to W. China, N.W. America; introduced in New Zealand

HABITAT Open deciduous woodland, mountains, plains, moorland

SIZE Body: 5¼–8¼ ft (1.6–2.5 m) Tail: 4¾–10 in (12–25 cm)

Known as the wapiti, or elk, in North America and the red deer in Britain, this deer is reddish-brown in summer but grayish-brown in winter. Most older males have antlers with two forward-pointing tines near the base, while young males usually have one tine. In autumn and winter, the male has a mane of longer hair on the neck.

A gregarious species, red deer live in herds and are active in the morning and late afternoon or evening, feeding on grass, heather, leaves and buds.

In the autumn, males take part in fierce, antler-clashing fights in order to obtain territories and to gather harems of females to mate with. The males defend their females throughout the breeding season and then return to all male herds in the winter. Females give birth to 1 calf, rarely 2, after a gestation period of about 8 months. The young deer is able to walk a few minutes after birth.

Roe Deer *Capreolus capreolus*

RANGE Europe and Asia: Britain to S.E. Siberia, S. China

HABITAT Woodland

SIZE Body: 37½ in–4½ ft (95 cm–1.3 m) Tail: ¼–1½ in (2–4 cm)

The smallest of the native European deer, the roe deer is unique in having almost no tail. It has a pale rump, and the rest of its coat is reddish-brown in summer and grayish-brown in winter. Fawns have a spotted coat. The antlers of the male never have more than three points apiece.

These shy, graceful deer are generally solitary, except during the breeding season, but they may gather in small groups in the winter. The roe deer are active at night and they browse on shrubs and broadleafed trees.

In the breeding season, the male takes a territory and marks its boundaries by rubbing the trunks of trees with his antlers until the bark is frayed and the wood exposed. He has only 1 mate and defends her and his territory against rivals.

The period between mating and birth is 9 or 10 months, which is much longer than that of most deer and includes a period of delayed implantation. Once the egg is fertilized, it lies dormant in the uterus for about 4 months before it implants in the womb and true gestation begins. This mechanism ensures that both mating and birth can take place at the optimum time of year.

Before giving birth to her 1 or 2 young, the female roe deer chases away her offspring from the previous year.

DEER, GIRAFFES AND PRONGHORNS

Pampas Deer *Ozotoceros bezoartieus* **LR:nt**

RANGE South America: Brazil, Paraguay, Uruguay, N. Argentina

HABITAT Grassland, open plains

SIZE Body: 3½–4¼ ft (1.1–1.3 m) Tail: 4–6 in (10–15 cm)

Pampas deer once lived only in pampas grass, but now much of this land is used for agriculture and the deer may frequent woodland. The male has antlers and glands in the feet which give off a garlicky smell, noticeable over ½ mile (1 km) away. In winter, the deer live alone or in pairs. In spring they may form larger groups. They rest in cover during the day and emerge in the evening to feed on grass. Some races are now rare, due to hunting and loss of habitat. The male stays with the female after her 1 offspring is born and helps her to guard it.

Northern Pudu *Pudu mephistophiles* **LR:nt**

RANGE South America: Colombia to N. Peru

HABITAT Forest, swampy savanna at 6,600–13,000 ft (2,000–4,000 m)

SIZE Body: 25½ in (65 cm) Tail: 1–1¼ in (2.5–3.5 cm)

The smallest New World deer, the northern pudu has a rounded back and small, simple antlers. Its dark-brown hair is thick and dense. Little is known of its habits, but it is thought to live in small groups or alone and to eat leaves, shoots and fruit. Females produce a single young, sometimes twins, usually between November and January.

GIRAFFIDAE: GIRAFFE FAMILY

The giraffe family is a specialized offshoot of the deer family. It probably originated in the Old World and is now reduced to only 2 species: the giraffe and the okapi, both found in Africa. Both animals have unique, skin-covered, blunt horns, which are not shed. The giraffe is the tallest terrestrial animal.

Giraffe *Giraffa camelopardalis* **LR:cd**

RANGE Africa, south of the Sahara

HABITAT Savanna

SIZE Body: 9¾–13 ft (3–4 m) Tail: 3–3½ ft (90 cm–1.1 m)

The giraffe, with its long legs and its amazingly long neck, when erect stands up to 11 ft (3.3 m) at the shoulder and nearly 19½ ft (6 m) at the crown. Its characteristic coloration of a light body and irregular dark spots is very variable, both geographically and between individuals, some animals may be almost white or black, or even unspotted. Both male and female have skin-covered horns, one pair on the forehead and sometimes a smaller pair farther back, on the crown and some animals have another small horn, or bump, in between. The tail ends in a tuft of long hairs.

Gregarious animals, giraffes usually live in troops of up to 6, sometimes 12, and may occasionally gather in larger herds. A troop consists of females and their offspring, led by a male. Males fight over females, wrestling with their heads and necks. The troop ambles around its territory, feeding mostly in the early morning and afternoon on the foliage, buds and fruits on the top of acacia and thorn trees. They may also eat grass, plants and grain crops. At midday, giraffes rest in shade and at night lie down for a couple of hours or rest standing.

Females give birth to a single offspring, rarely twins, after a gestation of between 400 and 468 days. Births invariably occur at first light. The young is suckled for 6 to 12 months and continues to grow for 10 years.

Okapi *Okapia johnstoni* **LR:nt**

RANGE Zaire

HABITAT Rain forest

SIZE Body: 4–6½ ft (1.2–2 m) Tail: 11¾–16½ in (30–42 cm)

An inhabitant of dense forest, the okapi, though long hunted by the local pygmy tribes, was only made known to the outside world in 1901, when it was discovered by the then Governor of Uganda. He thought it was related to the zebra because of its stripes, but, in fact, it bears a remarkable resemblance to primitive ancestors of the giraffe. The okapi has a compact body, which slopes down toward the hindquarters, and stripes on its legs. Only males possess short, skin-covered horns, similar to those of the giraffe. The tongue is so long that the okapi can use it to clean its own eyes and eyelids.

Okapis live alone, each in its own home range, and meet only in the breeding season.

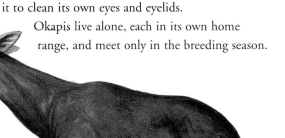

They eat leaves, buds and shoots of trees (which they reach with their long tongues), grass, ferns, fruit, fungi and manioc.

Pairing usually takes place between May and June or November and December, but may occur at any time. The female gives birth to 1 young after a gestation of 421 to 457 days. The young okapi suckles for up to 10 months and is not fully developed until 4 or 5 years of age.

ANTILOCAPRIDAE: PRONGHORN FAMILY

The North American pronghorn, found in Canada, USA and northern Mexico is the sole living representative of a New World group of antelopelike ruminants. There is also, however, a body of opinion that suggests this animal should be included in the cattle family Bovidae, but it is kept apart on account of its curious horn structure.

Pronghorn

Antilocapra
americana

RANGE C. Canada,
W. USA, Mexico

HABITAT Open prairie, desert

SIZE Body: 3¼–5 ft (1–1.5 m)
Tail: 3–4 in (7.5–10 cm)

Male and female pronghorns have true, bony horns, although those of females are small. The horns are covered with sheaths of specialized, fused hairs, which are shed annually. The small, forward-pointing branch on each horn, is part of the sheath.

One of the fastest mammals in North America, the pronghorn can achieve speeds of up to 40 mph (65 km/h). It is also a good swimmer. In summer, it moves in small, scattered groups but congregates in larger herds of up to 100 animals in winter. Pronghorns are active during the day, feeding mostly in the morning and evening on grasses, weeds and shrubs. White hairs on the pronghorn's rump become erect if the animal is alarmed and act as a warning signal.

Some males collect harems, fighting rivals. The female gives birth to her young after a gestation of 230 to 240 days. There is usually only 1 in a female's first litter, older females produce 2 or 3 young. Only 4 days after birth, pronghorns can run.

Pronghorns are now rare, due to overhunting, competition from domestic livestock and the destruction of their habitat.

BOVIDS

BOVIDAE: BOVID FAMILY

This biologically and economically important family of herbivorous ungulates contains about 137 species, of which domesticated cattle, sheep and goats must be the best known members. The family probably originated in Eurasia and moved only recently to North America; it is absent from South America and most diverse in Africa.

Over their wide range, bovids utilize almost all types of habitat, from grassland, desert and tundra to dense forest. Coupled with this diversity of habitat is great diversity of body form and size, and bovids range between buffaloes and tiny antelope. There are, however, common features within the group. Fore and hind toes are reduced to split, or artiodactyl (even-toed), hoofs, based on digits 3 and 4. There is a complex four-chambered stomach in which vegetable food is degraded by microorganism symbiosis. Linked with this digestive system, bovids chew the cud, bringing up food from the first stomach and re-chewing it. Normally both male and female have defensive hollow horns, which are larger in the male.

Greater Kudu *Tragelaphus strepsiceros* **LR:cd**

RANGE Africa: Lake Chad to Eritrea, Tanzania; Zambia to Angola and South Africa; introduced in N. Mexico

HABITAT Thick acacia bush; rocky, hilly country; dry river beds, near water.

SIZE Body: 6–8 ft (1.8–2.45 m) Tail: 13¾–21½ in (35–55 cm)

The large, slender male kudu has long horns, which spread widely in two to three open spirals; the female occasionally has small horns. When running, the bull lays his horns flat along his back.

Over the kudu's wide range, there are variations in coloration and the number of stripes on the sides. Kudu are browsers feeding early and late on leaves, shoots and seeds and, in dry areas, wild melons. They also make night raids on cultivated fields and can jump over a 6½ ft (2 m) fence. Their senses of hearing and smell are good, although their sight seems poor.

Kudu live mostly in herds of 6 to 12 females with young, sometimes with 1 or 2 older bulls. Otherwise males are solitary or form bachelor herds. After a gestation of about 7 months, the female produces 1 calf, which suckles for about 6 months.

Eland *Ttagelaphus oryx* **LR:cd**

RANGE Africa: Ethiopia, E. Africa to Angola and South Africa; mostly in game parks in Namibia, N. Cape Province, Natal, Mozambique

HABITAT Open plains, savanna, mopane bush, montane forest to 14,750 ft (4,500 m), semidesert

SIZE Body: 6¾–11½ ft (2.1–3.5 m) Tail: 19¾–35½ in (50–90 cm)

The eland is the largest of the antelopes. A fully grown bull may weigh 2,000 lb (900 kg). Cows are smaller and more slight, with lighter horns and no mat of hair on the forehead. Eland live in troops of 6 to 24 animals and are always on the move, looking for food and water. In times of drought, they wander widely and form large herds. Old solitary bulls are common; young bulls form male troops. Eland are browsers, feeding in the morning, at dusk, and even on moonlit nights, on leaves, shoots, melons, tubers, and bulbs. They have a good sense of smell and sight.

There is usually 1 calf, born after a gestation of 8½ to 9 months; it lies hidden for a week, then follows the female, who suckles it for about 6 months.

Bongo
Tragelaphus eurycerus **LR:nt**

RANGE Africa: Sierra Leone to Sudan (not Nigeria), Kenya, Tanzania

HABITAT Forest, bush, bamboo jungle

SIZE Body: 5½–8¼ ft (1.7–2.5 m) Tail: 17¾–25½ in (45–65 cm)

The adult male bongo is the largest of the forest-dwelling antelopes and may weigh up to 500 lb (227 kg); the chestnut coloured coat darkens with age in the male. Both sexes have narrow, lyre-shaped horns, which they lay along their slightly humped backs when running, to prevent them catching branches. Shy animals, bongos rest in dense cover during the day, browsing at dawn and dusk on leaves, shoots, bark, rotten wood and fruit, they also dig for roots with their horns. At night they venture into clearings and plantations to feed on grass.

They live in pairs or small groups of females and young with a single male. Old males are solitary. One young is born after a gestation of 9½ months.

Nyala *Tragelaphus angasii* **LR:cd**

RANGE Africa: Malawi to South Africa: Natal

HABITAT Dense lowland forest, thickets in savanna, near water

SIZE Body: 4½–6½ ft (1.35–2 m) Tail: 15¾–21½ in (40–55 cm)

Nyala live in dense cover, emerging only at dusk and dawn. Males are large and slender, with big ears and shaggy coats. Females and juveniles are reddish-brown and lack the long fringe of hair underneath the body, horns and the white facial chevron that distinguish the males. Females are much smaller than males. Nyala live in groups of 8 to 16 cows and young, sometimes with one or more bulls. Solitary bulls and herds of bulls also occur. Near the end of the dry season, herds of up to 50 animals may form. They browse on leaves, shoots, bark and fruit, (standing on their hind legs to reach the leaves) and new grass. A single young is born after a gestation of 8½ months, females mate a week after the birth.

Nilgai *Boselaphus tragocamelus* **LR:cd**

RANGE Peninsular India (not Sri Lanka)

HABITAT Forest, low jungle

SIZE Body: 6½–6¾ ft (2–2.1 m) Tail: 18–21¼ in (46–54 cm)

The nilgai is the only member of its genus and is the largest antelope native to India. It has slightly longer front legs than hind ones and a long, pointed head. The male has short horns and a tuft of hair on the throat; both sexes have short, wiry coats, reddish-brown in the male and lighter in the female. Females and calves live in herds. Males are usually solitary or form small parties. Nilgai are browsers but also like fruit and sugarcane and can do considerable damage to the crop.

Females commonly produce 2 calves after a gestation of about 9 months. Bulls fight each other on their knees for available females, which mate again immediately after calving.

Four-horned Antelope *Tetracerus quadricornis* **VU**

RANGE Peninsular India (not Sri Lanka)

HABITAT Open forest

SIZE Body: 30 ft (1 m) Tail: 5 in (12.5 cm)

This little antelope is the only one in its genus. The male is unique among Bovidae in having two pairs of short, unringed, conical horns: the back pair 3¼ to 4 in (8 to 10 cm) long, the front pair 1 to 1½ in (2.5 to 4 cm) long; these maybe merely black, hairless skin. These are not gregarious antelope – normally only two are found together, or a female with her young. They graze on grasses and plants and drink often, running for cover at the least hint of danger with a peculiar, jerky motion.

Four-horned antelope mate during the rainy season and usually produce between 1 and 3 young after a gestation period of about 6 months.

BOVIDS

Gaur *Bos frontalis* VU

RANGE India, S.E. Asia

HABITAT Hill forest

SIZE Body: 6½–8¼ ft (2–2.5 m)
Tail: 23½–31½ in (60–80 cm)

Once common in hilly, forested areas throughout their range, gaur now only occur in scattered herds in remote areas and in parks and reserves. Gaur are legally protected, but this is hard to enforce except in reserves, and the population is still threatened.

The gaur is a strong, heavily built animal, with a massive head, thick horns and a prominent muscular ridge on its shoulders that slopes down to the middle of its back. Females are smaller than males and have shorter, lighter horns. Gaur range in colour from reddish to dark brown or almost black, with white hair on the lower half of the legs. In small herds of up to 12 animals, they take shelter in the shade and seclusion of forest in the heat of the day and at night, but they venture out into the open to feed in the early morning and late afternoon, when they graze and also sometimes browse on the leaves and bark of available trees.

During the breeding season, the timing of which varies from area to area, bulls roam through the forest searching for females on heat. When a male finds a mate, he defends her from other males. The female moves slightly away from the herd to give birth to her offspring in a safe, secluded spot; they rejoin the herd a few days later.

Banteng *Bos javanicus* EN

RANGE Bali, Myanmar to Java, Borneo

HABITAT Forested, hilly country to 6,600 ft (2,000 m)

SIZE Body: 6½ ft (2 m) Tail: 33½ in (85 cm)

The banteng is blue-black, with white stockings and rump, and is quite cowlike in its appearance; females and young are a bright reddish-brown. Bulls may reach 5 ft (1.5 m) at the shoulder, and they have a hairless shield on the crown between the horns. Wary and shy, bantengs are found in thickly forested areas, where there are glades and clearings in which they can graze during the night. In the monsoon season, they move up the mountains and browse on bamboo shoots.

Gregarious animals, bantengs live in herds of 10 to 30 animals, although occasionally large bulls may become solitary. They mate during the dry season, and females produce 1 or 2 calves after a gestation of 9½ to 10 months. Small populations of two subspecies are found: *B. j. biarmicus* in Burma, Thailand and parts of Indo-China; *B. j. lowi* in Borneo.

Asian Water Buffalo *Bubalus arnee* EN

RANGE India, S.E. Asia; introduced in Europe, Africa, Philippines, Japan, Hawaii, Central and South America, Australia

HABITAT Dense growth, reed grass in wet areas

SIZE Body: 8¼–9¾ ft (2.5–3 m)
Tail: 23½ in–3¼ ft (60 cm–1 m)

A large, thickset, clumsy creature, with huge splayed hoofs, the water buffalo stands 5 to 6 ft (1.5 to 1.8 m) at the shoulder. It has a long, narrow face, and the span of its flattened, crescent-shaped horns is the largest of all bovids – they can measure as much as 4 ft (1.2 m) along the outer edge. Its bulky body is sparsely covered in quite long, coarse, blackish hair, and there is a tuft of coarse hair in the middle of the forehead. Water buffaloes feed early and late in the day and at night on the lush grass and vegetation that grows near and in lakes and rivers. When not feeding, they spend much of their time submerged, with only their muzzles showing above water, or wallowing in mud, which, when dried and caked, gives them some protection from the insects that plague them. Water buffaloes are gregarious and live in herds of various sizes. In the breeding season, males detach a few cows from the main herd and form their own harems. Each cow produces 1 or 2 calves after a gestation of 10 months, which it suckles for almost a year. Water buffaloes live for about 18 years.

Tame and docile, these animals have been domesticated and used as beasts of burden in India and Southeast Asia since about 3000 B.C. They also yield milk of good quality and their hides make excellent leather. It is estimated that the domestic population in India and Southeast Asia alone is now at least 75 million and water buffaloes have been widely introduced in countries where conditions are suitable. Some of these introduced populations have become feral, as in Australia. Truly wild stocks number no more than 2,000.

Lowland Anoa *Bubalus depressicornis* **EN**

RANGE Sulawesi

HABITAT Lowland forest

SIZE Body: 5¼–5½ ft (1.6–1.7 m) Tail: 7–12½ in (18–31 cm)

The anoa is the smallest of the buffaloes, an adult male standing only 27 to 42 in (69 to 106 cm) at the shoulder. However, it is stockily built, with a thick neck and short, heavy horns, which are at most 15 in (38 cm) long. Although wary, the anoa is aggressive when cornered. Juveniles have thick, woolly, yellow-brown hair, which becomes dark brown or blackish, blotched with white, in adults; old animals may have almost bare skins. Perhaps because of this, anoas appear to enjoy bathing and wallowing in mud. They feed alone during the morning, mainly on water plants and young cane shoots, then spend the rest of the day lying in the shade, generally in pairs. They only form herds just before the females are due to calve. Usually 1 young is born after a gestation of 9½ to 10 months.

When unmolested, anoas have a life span of 20 to 25 years, but destruction of their normal habitat has driven them into inaccessible, swampy forest, and their survival is further threatened by unrelenting hunting for their horns, meat and thick hides.

Wild Yak *Bos grunniens* **VU**

RANGE W. China, Tibetan plateau, N. India, Kashmir

HABITAT Desolate mountain country to 20,000 ft (6,100 m)

SIZE Body: Male up to 10½ ft (3.25 m) Tail: 19¾–31½ in (50–80 cm)

Originally these massive animals were found throughout their range, but centuries of hunting and persecution have forced them to retreat into remote and inaccessible areas of mountain tundra and ice desert, and now they cannot live in warm, lowland areas. Sturdy and sure-footed and covered in long, blackish-brown hairs which form a fringe reaching almost to the ground, they are, however, well equipped to cope with the rigours of the rough terrain and extremely harsh climate within their habitat.

Male Yaks may stand up to 6½ ft (2 m) at the shoulder, females are smaller and weigh only about one-third as much as males. Both males and females have heavy, forward-curving horns, which they use for defence. When a group is threatened, they form a phalanx, facing outward with horns lowered, with the calves encircled for protection.

Yaks feed morning and evening on whatever vegetation they can find, spending the rest of the time relaxing and chewing the cud. They are usually found in large groups consisting of females and young with a single bull; bachelor bulls roam in groups of 2 or 3. The female produces 1 calf in the autumn, after a gestation period of between 9½ and 10 months.

Although wild yaks are an endangered species, they have been domesticated for centuries in Tibet, where, as well as being used as pack animals and to pull carts, they also provide milk, meat, hides and hair and wool, which the local population weave into warm cloth. Domestic yaks are usually about half the size of wild ones and are often without horns. The coat of the domestic yak is redder than that of the wild yak, mottled with brown, black and sometimes white.

BOVIDS

American Bison *Bison bison*
LR:cd

RANGE N. America

HABITAT Prairie, open woodland

SIZE Body: 6¾–11½ ft (2.1–3.5 m) Tail: 19¾–23½ in (50–60 cm)

Although there were once millions of bison roaming the North American grasslands, wholesale slaughter by the early European settlers brought this species almost to extinction by the beginning of the twentieth century. Since then, due to a great extent to the efforts of the American Bison Society, herds have steadily been built up in reserves, where they exist in a semiwild state, and it is estimated that there are now about 20,000 American bison.

The male may be as much as 9½ ft (2.9 m) at the shoulders, which are humped and covered in the shaggy, brownish-black fur that also grows thickly on the head, neck and forelegs. The female looks similar to the male but is smaller; young are more reddish brown. Both sexes have short, sharp horns.

Primarily grazers, bison live in herds that vary from a family group to several thousand; huge numbers formerly made seasonal migrations in search of better pasture. They feed morning and evening, and during the day rest up, chewing the cud or wallowing in mud or dust baths in order to rid themselves of parasites.

During the mating season, bulls fight amongst themselves for cows. The cows give birth to a single calf, away from the herd, after a gestation period of 9 months. Within an hour or two of the birth both the mother and calf rejoin the herd. The calf is suckled for about 12 months and it remains with its mother until it reaches sexual maturity at about 3 years old.

European Bison *Bison bonasus* **EN**

RANGE E. Europe

HABITAT Open woodland, forest

SIZE Body: 6¾–11½ ft (2.1–3.5 m) Tail: 19¾–23½ in (50–60 cm)

Like its American counterpart, the European bison, which was formerly found throughout Europe, has been reduced to semiwild herds in reserves: three in Poland and eleven in what was the USSR, with the largest in the Bialowieza Forest on the border between them. The drop in numbers has been caused by the almost total eradication of forests, for these bison are browsers, living mainly on leaves, ferns, twigs, bark and, in autumn, almost exclusively on acorns.

The European bison closely resembles the American, but is less heavily built, with longer hind legs. It has more scanty, shorter hair on the front of the body and head, and the horns, too, are lighter and much longer, reaching as much as 20 in (51 cm) in the male. The female produces a single calf after a gestation period of 9 months and it remains with her for 2 to 3 years.

African Buffalo *Synceros caffer* **LR:cd**

RANGE Africa, south of the Sahara

HABITAT Varied, always near water

SIZE Body: 6¾–9¾ ft (2.1–3 m) Tail: 29½ in–3½ ft (75 cm–1.1 m)

The powerfully built African buffalo is the only member of its genus, although 2 types exist, the smaller, reddish forest-dwelling buffalo, *S. c. nanus*, and *S. c. caffer*, described here, which lives in savanna and open country. It has a huge head with a broad, moist muzzle, large drooping ears and heavy horns, the bases of which may meet across the forehead. An aggressive animal and a formidable fighter, it is extremely dangerous to hunt, since it may charge without provocation or, if wounded, wait in thick bush and attack a pursuing hunter. Apart from man, its enemies are the lion and occasionally the crocodile, both of which usually succeed in killing only young or sick animals.

African buffaloes have adapted to live in a variety of conditions, from forest to semidesert, wherever there is adequate grazing and plenty of water, for they drink morning and evening and enjoy lying in water and wallowing in mud. They feed mainly at night, on grass, bushes and leaves, resting up in dense cover during the day. Although their eyesight and hearing are poor, they have a strongly developed sense of smell.

Buffaloes are gregarious, living in herds which range from a dozen or so to several hundred animals, often led by an old female, but dominated by a mature bull. Old bulls are ousted from the herd and live alone in groups of 2 to 5.

Although normally silent, buffaloes bellow and grunt during the mating season which varies throughout the range and appears to be related to climate. A single calf is born after a gestation period of 11 months; it is covered in long, blackish-brown hair, most of which is lost as it matures. African buffaloes live for about 16 years.

Bay Duiker *Cephalophus dorsalis* **LR:nt**

RANGE Africa: Sierra Leone to E. Zaire and N. Angola

HABITAT Thick forest and jungle

SIZE Body: 27½ in–3¼ ft (70 cm–1 m) Tail: 3–6 in (8–15 cm)

The subfamily Cephalophinae contains two groups: the forest duikers, of which the bay duiker is one, and the bush duikers. The bay duiker is typical of its group, with rather slender legs, a slightly hunched back and a smooth, glossy coat. Both male and female have small backward-pointing horns, which are sometimes obscured by the crest of hairs on the forehead. Duikers are timid and when disturbed dash for thick cover – the name duiker means "diving" buck. They are mainly active at night when they feed on grass, leaves and fruit, even scrambling up into bushes or on logs to reach them.

Bay duikers live singly or in pairs and produce 1 young after a gestation period of 7 to 8 months. The young is independent at about 3 months old.

Yellow Duiker

Cephalophus silvicultor **LR:nt**

RANGE Africa: Senegal to Kenya, Zambia, N. Angola

HABITAT Moist highland forest

SIZE Body: 3¾–4¾ ft (1.15–1.45 m)
Tail: 4¼–8 in (11–20.5 cm)

Another forest duiker and the largest of its subfamily, the yellow duiker is remarkable for the well-developed crest of hairs on its forehead and for the yellowish-orange patch of coarse, erectile hairs that grow in a wedge shape on its back. Both sexes have long, thin sharp-pointed horns. The young loses its dark coloration at about 8 months.

Yellow duikers live in pairs or alone, keeping to thick cover. They are active at night. Their varied diet includes leaves, grass, herbs, berries, termites, snakes, eggs and carrion. They are hunted by man for meat and have many other enemies, including leopards, jackals, pythons and large birds of prey.

Common/Gray Duiker *Sylvicapra grimmia*

RANGE Africa, south of the Sahara

HABITAT All types except desert and rain forest, up to 15,000 ft (4,600 m)

SIZE Body: 31½ in–3¾ ft (80 cm–1.15 m) Tail: 4–8½ in (10–22 cm)

The common bush duiker has a straighter back and thicker, grizzled coat than the forest duiker. The crest is quite well developed. The male has sharp horns, which the female does not always have. Common duikers can survive in almost any habitat from scrub country to open grassland. The male establishes a fiercely defended territory. At night they browse on leaves and twigs, (standing on their hind legs to reach them) and also eat fruit, berries, termites, snakes, eggs and guineafowl chicks.

Usually found alone or in pairs, they may form small groups in the breeding season, which varies throughout the range and appears to be linked to the rains. The female produces 1 young after a gestation of 4 to 4½ months; normally 2 young are born each year.

BOVIDS

Lechwe
Kobus leche **LR:cd**

RANGE Africa: Zaire, Zambia, Angola, Botswana, South Africa

HABITAT Flood plains, swamps, lakes

SIZE Body: 4¼–5½ ft (1.3–1.7 m) Tail: 11¾–17¾ in (30–45 cm)

There are 3 races of lechwe, whose coloration varies from bright chestnut to grayish-brown. In all races, the male has thin, lyre-shaped horns, up to 3 ft (91 cm) long, which form a double curve; they are particularly fine in *K. l. kafuensis*. With their long, pointed, widespreading hoofs, lechwe are perfectly adapted to an aquatic way of life and cannot move quickly on dry ground. They come out of the water only to rest and calve, spending most of their time wading in water up to about 20 in (50 cm) deep, where they feed on grasses and water plants. They swim well and will even submerge, with only the nostrils showing, if threatened. Apart from man, they are preyed on mainly by lion, cheetah, hyena and hunting dogs.

Lechwe are sociable and form herds of several hundred during the breeding season, when males fight fiercely, even though they are not territorial. At other times, young males form large, single-sex herds. After a gestation period of 7 to 8 months, the female produces a single calf, which she suckles for 3 to 4 months.

Uganda Kob
Kobus kob thomasi **LR:cd**

RANGE Africa: Uganda to south of Lake Victoria

HABITAT Open grassy plains, lightly wooded savanna, near permanent water

SIZE Body: 4–6 ft (1.2–1.8 m) Tail: 7–15¾ in (18–40 cm)

A graceful, sturdily built, medium-sized antelope, the Uganda kob is a subspecies of the nominate race, which it closely resembles except that the white on the face completely encircles the eyes. Male and female look alike, but only the male has horns, which are lyre shaped, with an S-curve when seen from the side. Kob usually live in single sex herds of 20 to 40, sometimes up to 100. They are grazers, feeding usually in the morning and at dusk, although during the day they will go into the water and eat water plants. They are preyed on mainly by lion, leopard, spotted hyena and hunting dogs. These solitary animals often lie flat and hide when threatened.

In the breeding season, each rutting male has an area 30 to 50 ft (9 to 15 m) in diameter, which he defends against other males. Females move freely through these rutting areas, mating with several males. One young is born after a gestation period of 8½ to 9 months, and, since the female mates again almost at once, two births are possible in a year.

Common/Defassa Waterbuck
Kobus ellipsiprymnus **LR:cd**

RANGE Africa, south of the Sahara to the Zambezi, east to Ethiopia

HABITAT Savanna, woodland, stony hills, near water

SIZE Body: 6–7¼ ft (1.8–2.2 m) Tail: 8¼–17¾ in (22–45 cm)

The many races of this waterbuck vary in coloration from yellowish-brown or reddish-brown to gray and grayish-black; some have a white ring or patch on the rump. It has large, hairy ears, which are white inside and tipped with black, and the male has heavy, much-ringed horns, which sweep back in a crescent shape. A large animal, standing 4 to 4½ ft (1.2 to 1.4 m) at the shoulder, it weighs 350 to 500 lb (159 to 227 kg). Glands in the skin exude a musky-smelling oily secretion, and the meat is easily tainted when the animal is skinned, so it is not much hunted. The chief predators are lion, leopard and hunting dogs. True to their name, waterbuck spend much time near water and drink often, they take refuge in reedbeds when threatened. They are grazers feeding on tender young grass shoots.

Common waterbuck move in small herds of up to 25, usually females and young with a master bull; young bulls form bachelor herds. The female produces 1 young after a gestation of about 9 months.

Southern Reedbuck
Redunca arundinum **LR:cd**

RANGE Africa: Zaire, Tanzania, south to South Africa

HABITAT Open plains, hilly country with light cover, near water

SIZE Body: 4–4½ ft (1.2–1.4 m) Tail: 7–11¾ in (18–30 cm)

A medium-sized antelope, about 3 ft (91 cm) at the shoulder, the common reedbuck is a graceful animal, with distinctive movements. It runs with a rocking motion, flicking its thick, hairy tail, and the male marks and defends his territory by displaying his white throat patch and making bouncing leaps with his head raised. Reedbuck also make a characteristic clicking sound when running and whistle through their noses when alarmed. The female resembles the male but is smaller and lacks his ridged, curved horns; juveniles are a grayish-brown. Reedbuck are always found near water, although not in it, and they spend much time lying up in reedbeds or tall grass. They graze on grass and shoots and will raid crops.

Reedbuck are usually found alone, in pairs or in small family groups. A single young is born after a gestation period of 7¾ months and reaches maturity, acquiring adult coloration, at about a year old.

Roan Antelope *Hippotragus equinus* **LR:cd**

RANGE Africa, south of the Sahara

HABITAT Open woodland, dry bush, savanna, near water

SIZE Body: 8–8½ ft (2.4–2.6 m) Tail: 23½–27½ in (60–70 cm)

There are approximately 6 races of roan antelope, which vary in coloration from gray to reddish-brown. The roan is a large antelope, the largest in Africa after the eland and kudu, and as the name suggests, it superficially resembles a horse, with its long face and stiff, well-developed mane. The male's backward-curving horns are short but strong; the female's are lighter. Roan antelope usually live in herds of up to 20 females and young, led by a master bull, often alongside oryx, impala, wildebeest, buffalo, zebra and ostriches. Young males form bachelor herds. The roan antelope is preyed on mainly by lion, leopard, hunting dogs and hyena. At least 90 per cent of the roan's food intake is grass, and they rarely eat leaves or fruit, so they need to drink often.

Roan antelope are aggressive, and males will fight on their knees with vicious, backward sweeps of their horns. In the breeding season, the bull detaches a cow from the herd and they live alone for a while. The female produces 1 calf after a gestation of 8½ to 9 months; it attains sexual maturity at 2½ to 3 years old.

Rhebok *Pelea capreolus* **LR:cd**

RANGE South Africa

HABITAT Grassy hills and plateaux with low bush and scattered trees

SIZE Body: 3–3¼ ft (1–1.2 m) Tail: 4–7¾ in (10–20 cm)

A small, graceful antelope, weighing 50 lb (22.5 kg) at most, the rhebok is covered in soft, woolly hair. The male has upright, almost straight horns, 6 to 10½ in (15 to 27 cm) long. Rhebok feed on grass and the leaves of shrubs and are very wary, bouncing off the moment they are disturbed, with a run that jerks up their hindquarters. They are found in family parties, consisting of a master ram with a dozen or more females and young; immature males are normally solitary. The male is highly territorial and marks out his fairly extensive range by tongue clicking, display and urination. Despite his small size, the ram is extremely pugnacious and is known to attack and even kill sheep, goats and mountain reedbuck; he will also attack smaller predators.

In the breeding season, males stage fierce mock battles without actually doing any harm, and they will also chase each other. One, sometimes 2, young are born after a 9½-month gestation.

BOVIDS

Arabian Oryx

Oryx leucoryx **EN**

RANGE S.E. Saudi Arabia: Rub' al Khali area

HABITAT Desert

SIZE Body: 5¼ ft (1.6 m) Tail: 17¾ in (45 cm)

This is the smallest and rarest of the oryx and the only one found outside Africa. It lives in extreme desert conditions, feeding on grass and shrubs and travelling widely in order to find food. It is well adapted to its arid habitat, for it can live without drinking, obtaining the moisture it needs from its food, it also uses its hoofs and horns to scrape out a hollow under a bush or alongside a dune in which to shelter from the sun.

Although generally sociable, male oryx fight among themselves in the breeding season, and if cornered, will attack. One young is born after an 8-month gestation.

The present endangered status of the Arabian oryx is the result of overhunting, for its slender horns, its hide and meat are all prized. This led to its extinction in the wild although captive breeding programs have now resulted in its re-introduction.

Blue Wildebeest *Connochaetes taurinus* **LR:cd**

RANGE Africa: S. Kenya to N. South Africa

HABITAT Open grassland, bush savanna

SIZE Body 5½–8 ft (1.7–2.4 m) Tail: 23½ in–3¼ ft (60 cm–1 m)

The clumsy appearance of the blue wildebeest, the lugubrious expression given by its black face and tufty beard, its rocking-horse gait and its constant snorts and grunts have earned it a reputation as a "clown". Nevertheless, it is a most successful species.

Wildebeest are extremely gregarious, and herds numbering tens of thousands may be seen in East Africa during the dry season, when they make migrations of as much as 1,000 miles (1,600 km) in search of water and grazing. Breeding herds usually consist of up to 150 females and young, with l to 3 males. The bulls patrol the outside of their herd, keeping it closely grouped and defending a zone around it, even when migrating. Wildebeest feed almost exclusively on grass and need to drink often. They are frequently seen in association with zebra and ostrich; perhaps the wariness of the former offers them some protection against their common predators: lion, cheetah, hunting dog and hyena.

The female looks like the male but is smaller. After a gestation period of 8½ months, she produces 1 calf, which can stand within 3 to 5 minutes of birth.

Addax *Addax nasomaculatus* **EN**

RANGE Africa: E. Mauritania, W. Mali; patchy distribution in Algeria, Chad, Niger and Sudan

HABITAT Sandy and stony desert

SIZE Body 4¼ ft (1.3 m) Tail: 9¾–13¾ in (25–35 cm)

With its heavy head and shoulders and slender hindquarters, the addax is a clumsy-looking animal. Coloration varies widely between individuals, but there is always a mat of dark-brown hair on the forehead, and both sexes have thin, spiral horns.

Addax are typical desert dwellers, with their large, widespreading hoofs, which are well-adapted to walking on soft sand. They never drink, instead obtaining all the moisture they need from their food, which includes succulents. Their nomadic habits are closely linked to the sporadic rains, for addax appear to have a special ability to find the patches of desert vegetation that suddenly sprout after a downpour. They are normally found in herds of between 20 and 200.

The female produces 1 young after a gestation period of 8½ months.

Haartebeest *Alcelaphus buselaphus* **LR:cd**

RANGE Africa, south of the Sahara

HABITAT Grassy plains

SIZE Body: 5½–8 ft (1.7–2.4 m) Tail: 17¾–27½ in (45–70 cm)

The nominate race, the bubal haartebeest, is extinct, but there are 12 subspecies, a further 2 of which (*A. b. swayne* and *A. b. tora*) are endangered, due to disease, hunting and destruction of their natural habitat.

Haartebeest are strange-looking animals, with backs that slope down slightly from high shoulders and long heads, with a pedicle on top from which spring the horns. Both male and female have horns, which show great intraspecific variation in both size and shape. Coloration also varies from deep chocolate to sandy fawn; females are paler than males.

These sociable antelope are found in herds of from 4 to 30, consisting of females and young with a master bull. He watches over his herd, often from a vantage point, usually on top of a termite mound.

Although haartebeest can go for long periods without water, they drink when they can and enjoy wallowing; they also use salt licks with avidity. They are partial to the young grass that grows after burning and often graze with zebra, wildebeest and gazelle and, like these, are preyed on largely by lion.

A single calf is born after a gestation period of 8 months. It remains with its mother for about 3 years, at which time young males form a troop of their own.

Bontebok *Damaliscus dorcas* **LR:cd**

RANGE South Africa: W. Cape Province

HABITAT Open grassland

SIZE Body: 4½–5¼ ft (1.4–1.6 m) Tail: 11¾–17¾ in (30–45 cm)

The strikingly marked bontebok was at one time almost extinct but is now fully protected and out of danger, and the population in game reserves numbers several thousand. The very similar blesbok,

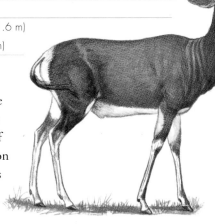

D. d. phillipsi (= *albifrons*), was also endangered, but it too is now flourishing, since it has been established in many reserves.

The sexes look alike, but females and juveniles are paler. Bontebok are grazers, active morning and evening. When disturbed, they move off swiftly upwind in single file. They are remarkably agile and can scale fences or wriggle under or through them.

The female produces a single calf after a 7½-month gestation period, and young remain with their mothers until they are about 2 years old, when young males form bachelor herds. Outside the breeding season, bontebok live in mixed herds of from 20 to 500 animals.

Sassaby/Tsessebi *Damaliscus lunatus* **LR:cd**

RANGE Africa, south of the Sahara, east to Ethiopia, Somalia

HABITAT Open plains, flood plains, grassland with scattered bush

SIZE Body: 5–6½ ft (1.5–2 m) Tail: 15¾–23½ in (40–60 cm)

The nominate race of sassaby is found from Zambia to northern South Africa. It is probably conspecific with *D. korrigum*, known as the tiang or topi, which is found elsewhere in its range. Together, sassabys and topis are the most numerous of all antelope in Africa. In shape they are similar to the true haartebeests, but neither the slope of the back nor the length of the head are so exaggerated. Coloration and horns vary from race to race and between sexes. Females are usually paler than males. Sassabys are active early and late in the day, when they feed on grass and herbage and also drink. They are able, however, to go without water for as long as 30 days.

Sassabys are not as gregarious as the haartebeests and generally move in small parties of 8 to 10 individuals, which may join up to form herds of up to 200 animals in the dry season. The mature male is highly territorial and marks his central stamping ground with dung and with scent, by rubbing his face and neck on bushes, grass stems and the ground. He watches over his territory and his harem and defends them from rivals and predators.

The female produces a single calf after a gestation period of 7½ to 8 months.

BOVIDS

Klipspringer *Oreotragus oreotragus* **LR:cd**

RANGE Africa: N. Nigeria, east to Somalia, south to South Africa

HABITAT Rocky outcrops, hills, mountains to 13,000 ft (4,000 m)

SIZE Body: 29½ in–3¾ ft (75 cm–1.15 m)
Tail: 2¾–9 in (7–23 cm)

The klipspringer occurs where there are rocky outcrops interspersed with grassy patches and clumps of bush. It is fairly small, with strong legs and blunt-tipped hoofs the consistency of hard rubber. It fills a niche similar to that of the chamois. As it leaps about among the rocks, it is cushioned from bumps by its long thick, bristly coat. The female is slightly heavier than the male and except in 1 race, *O. o. schilllngsi,* does not have horns.

Klipspringers are sometimes found in small parties, more often in pairs, in a territory marked out by glandular secretions and defended against interlopers. They feed morning and evening and on moonlit nights, and will stand on their hind legs to reach the leaves, flowers and fruit that form the bulk of their diet. They also eat succulents, moss and some grass and drink when water is available.

Klipspringers probably mate for life. The female produces 1 young after a gestation of about 7 months, and there may be 2 young born in a year.

Beira Antelope
Dorcatragus megalotis **VU**

RANGE Africa: Somalia

HABITAT Dry, bush-clad mountains, stony hills

SIZE Body: 31½–35½ in (80–90 cm)
Tail: 2¼–3 in (6–7.5 cm)

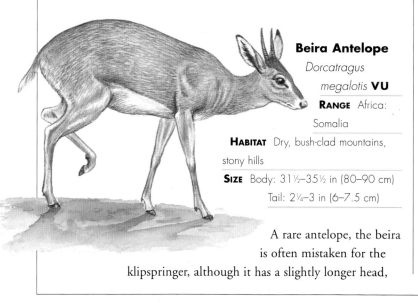

A rare antelope, the beira is often mistaken for the klipspringer, although it has a slightly longer head, much bigger ears and longer, slimmer legs. The hind legs, especially, are long, with the result that the rump is higher than the shoulders. There is no crest, and only the male has horns; the female is larger than the male.

Beiras live in pairs or small family parties on extremely stony hillsides close to a grassy plain. Their highly specialized hoofs have elastic pads underneath which give a good grip on the stones. Beiras feed in the early morning and late afternoon on leaves of bushes, particularly mimosa, grass and herbage and do not need to drink.

Little is known of their habits or biology, for not only are they rare but their coloration blends so well with the background that they are impossible to spot unless they move. The female gives birth to a single young.

Oribi *Ourebia ourebi* **LR:cd**

RANGE Africa: Sierra Leone to Ethiopia, Tanzania, Zambia, South Africa

HABITAT Wide, grassy plains with low bush, near water

SIZE Body: 3–3½ ft (92 cm–1.1 m) Tail: 2¼–4¼ in (6–10.5 cm)

The oribi is small and graceful, with a long neck and slender legs, longer behind than in front. The silky coat has a sleek, rippled look, and the black-tipped tail is conspicuous when the animal runs. Below each large, oval ear there is a patch of bare skin that appears as a black spot. The female has no horns and is larger than the male.

Pairs or small parties of up to 5 animals live together in a territory, which the dominant male marks out by rubbing glandular secretions on twigs and grass stems. Here the oribis have regular runs, resting and defecating places.

They are active early and later in the day and on moonlit nights, when they feed on grass, plants and leaves. During the day and when danger threatens, they lie quietly in long grass or by a bush or rock.

The female gives birth to 1 young after a gestation period of between 6½ and 7 months.

Royal Antelope
Neotragus pygmaeus
LR:nt
RANGE Africa: Sierra Leone, Liberia, Côte d'Ivoire, Ghana, Guinea
HABITAT Forest, forest clearings
SIZE Body: 13¾–16 in (35–41 cm) Tail: 2–2¼ in (5–6 cm)

This dainty, compact little animal, the smallest African antelope, weighs 7 to 10 lb (3 to 4.5 kg) – not much more than a rabbit. Indeed, it is called "king of the hares" by local tribespeople and so "royal" antelope by Europeans. It has a rounded back and a short tail, which it holds tightly against its rump. The male has tiny, sharp horns, which the female lacks; young are darker in colour than adults.

Royal antelopes live in pairs or alone in a small territory, which they usually mark out with dung heaps. They are timid and secretive and are mainly active at night, when quite large numbers may feed together on leaves, buds, shoots, fungi, fallen fruit, grass and weeds. They sometimes venture into vegetable plots and cocoa and peanut plantations. Although they are preyed on by a wide range of mammals, birds and even large snakes, their small size often enables them to slip away unseen from danger, with their bellies almost on the ground. Their vulnerability is also compensated for by their astounding ability to leap, like springboks, as much as 10 ft (3 m) up into the air.

Royal antelopes probably pair for life. The female produces a single young at a time.

Kirk's Dik-dik *Madoqua kirki*
RANGE Africa: Somalia to Tanzania; S.W. Angola, Namibia
HABITAT Bush country with thick undergrowth and scattered trees
SIZE Body: 21½–22½ in (55–57 cm) Tail: 1½–2¼ in (4–6 cm)

There are 7 races of this small, dainty antelope, which occur in two widely separated regions.

Coloration of the soft coat varies from pale gray-brown in dry habitats to a much darker shade in wet habitats. The nose is slightly elongated and the legs long and thin, with the hind legs always bent, so the hindquarters slope downward. Males have tiny horns, with a crest of long hair between them. The slightly larger female does not have horns.

Dik-diks are found alone or in pairs often with their 2 most recent young. Males scent-mark and fiercely defend the boundaries of a clearly defined territory, within which there are regularly used paths and places for resting and defecating. Shy, secretive animals, dik-diks browse at sunset and at night on leaves, shoots, buds and flowers, especially those of the Acacia. They also eat fallen fruit, and dig up roots and tubers with their horns and hoofs and frequent salt licks. They do not need to drink. Their many enemies include leopard, caracal, serval, wild cats, eagles and man.

Dik-diks pair for life and produce 1 young after a gestation period of 6 months; there are two litters a year.

Cape Grysbok
Raphicerus melanotis
LR:cd
RANGE Africa: South Africa
HABITAT Grassy plains, bush savanna at the foot of hills
SIZE Body: 23½–29½ in (60–75 cm) Tail: 2–3 in (5–8 cm)

This rough-coated, stocky little antelope has relatively short legs, slightly longer behind, which give it a sloping back. Males have short, sharply pointed horns and generally darker coloration than females. The grysbok is solitary outside the breeding season, and each establishes a fairly small territory, which is marked out by means of scent and dropping sites. This antelope feeds in the morning and late in the afternoon on the foliage of trees and bushes and it is particularly fond of grapevine leaves.

During the day, the grysbok rests up in the shade of a bush or rock or in areas of long grass. Its main predators are leopards, caracals and crowned eagles, and when threatened, the antelope lies flat, darting away with a zigzag gallop when the enemy approaches, only to dive suddenly for cover and disappear again.

The breeding biology of the grysbok is not very well known, but it is believed to be similar to that of the steenbok, which produces a single young after a gestation period of about 5½ months.

BOVIDS

Impala *Aepyceros melampus* **LR:cd**

RANGE Africa: Kenya, Uganda, south to N. South Africa

HABITAT Light mopane woodland, acacia savanna

SIZE Body: 4–5¼ ft (1.2–1.6 m) Tail: 11¾–17¾ in (30–45 cm)

A graceful, medium-sized antelope, with a glossy coat, the impala is identified by the unique bushy tuft of dark hairs above the hind "heels", the vertical dark stripes on white on the back of the thighs and tail and, in the male, the long, elegant, lyre-shaped horns. The impala is remarkable also for its fleetness and for the amazing leaps it makes – as far as 33 ft (10 m) and as high as 10 ft (3 m) – seemingly for enjoyment, as well as to escape from predators.

Impalas are extremely gregarious, and in the dry season troops may join to form herds of 200 or so. They are active day and night and eat quantities of grass and leaves, flowers and fruit. In the breeding season, the ram establishes a territory and a harem of 15 to 20 females which he defends fiercely; immature males form separate troops. After a gestation period of 6½ to 7 months, the female produces 1 young, which is born at midday, when many predators are somnolent, and remains hidden until it is strong enough to join the herd.

Blackbuck

Antilope cervicapra **VU**

RANGE India, Nepal, Pakistan

HABITAT Open grassy plains

SIZE Body: 4 ft (1.2 m) Tail: 7 in (18 cm)

The only species in its genus, the blackbuck is one of the few antelope in which the coloration of male and female is dissimilar. The dominant male in the herd is dark, almost black on back and sides and has long, spirally twisted horns; the

female is yellowish-fawn and lacks horns. Subordinate males have smaller horns and retain female coloration. They only darken and develop large horns if they assume the dominant position in a herd, following the death of the leading male.

Blackbucks feed largely on grass and are active morning and evening, resting in the heat of the day. The female is unusually alert, and it is she who first gives warning of danger. When alarmed blackbucks flee with leaps and bounds that soon settle into a swift gallop.

Blackbucks are normally found in herds of 15 to 50 – smaller groups consisting of a dominant male with females and young; as males mature, they are driven out and form their own small parties. The breeding male sets up a territory and defends it and his harem against rivals. One young, sometimes 2, is born after a gestation period of 6 months.

Springbok

Antidorcas marsupialis

LR:cd

RANGE Africa: Angola, South Africa, Botswana (Kalahari Desert)

HABITAT Treeless grassland (veld)

SIZE Body: 4–4½ ft (1.2–1.4 m) Tail: 7½–10½ in (19–27 cm)

The brightly coloured, strikingly marked springbok has a most unusual glandular pouch in its skin that stretches from the middle of the back to the base of the tail. When the animal is excited or alarmed, the pouch opens and reveals a crest of long, stiff, white hairs. Male and female look alike, both with ridged strong horns. The springbok's name is derived from its ability to bound as high as 11½ ft (3.5 m) into the air, half a dozen times in succession, either in alarm or play, with back curved, legs stiff and crest displayed.

Springboks eat the leaves of shrubs and bushes and grass and are independent of water. They were once exceedingly numerous, and in times of drought, herds of up to a million would make long migrations in search of fresh grazing, devastating the pasture and farmland that lay in their path. As a result, thousands were slaughtered, but they have now been reintroduced throughout their range and are again thriving. In the breeding season, the male may establish a territory and a harem of 10 to 30, but large mixed herds are the norm. The female produces 1 young after a gestation period of about 6 months.

Dibatag
Ammodorcas clarkei **VU**

Range Africa: Somalia, E. Ethiopia

Habitat Sandy or grassy plains with scattered bushes

Size Body: 5–5¼ ft (1.5–1.6 m)
Tail: 11¾–14¼ in (30–36 cm)

Although superficially it resembles the gerenuk, the dibatag is much grayer, and the male has shorter and quite different horns. The long, thin, black-tufted tail is generally held upright when the animal is running and gives it its name, which derives from the Somali words dabu (tail) and tag (erect). These animals live in pairs or family parties, consisting of an adult male and 3 to 5 females with young, in a seasonal territory, moving with the rains wherever food supplies are plentiful. They are active morning and evening, browsing on leaves and young shoots of bushes, which, like the gerenuk, they stand on their hind legs to reach. They also eat flowers, berries and new grass; they do not need to drink.

As a rule, 1 calf is born in the rainy season after a gestation of 6 to 7 months but it is possible for a female to produce 2 young in a year.

Gerenuk *Litocranius walleri* **LR:cd**
Range Africa: Somalia, Ethiopia to Kenya, Tanzania
Habitat Dry thornbush country, desert
Size Body 4½–5¼ ft (1.4–1.6 m)
Tail: 9–13¾ in (23–35 cm)

This large, graceful-looking gazelle is remarkable chiefly for its long neck (gerenuk means giraffe-necked in Somali) and for its long legs. It has a small, narrow head, large eyes and mobile lips, there are tufts of hair on the knees, and the short, almost naked tail is held close against the body except in flight, when it is curled up over the animal's back. The male has horns and is larger than the female.

Gerenuks are usually found in pairs or family parties consisting of a male and 2 to 5 females with young. They are browsers, living almost entirely on leaves and young shoots of thorny bushes and trees, which they reach by standing against the trunk on their hind legs, using a foreleg to pull down the branches, and stretching their necks. They feed morning and evening, standing still in the shade at midday. They are quite independent of water. Their main predators are cheetah, leopard, lion, hyena and hunting dog.

A single young is born, usually in the rainy season, after a gestation of about 6½ months.

Thomson's Gazelle
Gazella thomsonii **LR:cd**

Range Africa: Sudan, Kenya, N. Tanzania

Habitat Open plains with short grass

Size Body: 31½ in–3½ ft (80 cm–1.1 m)
Tail: 7½–10½ in (19–27 cm)

This graceful, small gazelle has a distinctive broad, dark stripe along its sides in marked contrast to the white underparts. The male is larger than the female and has much stronger horns. There are about 15 races of Thompson's gazelle which show only minor variations of colouring or horn size. They feed morning and evening, mainly on short grass and a small amount of foliage. They need to drink only when grazing is dry. Their chief predators are cheetah, lion, leopard, hyena and hunting dog.

These gazelles live in loosely structured groups, which may vary between 1 old ram with 5 to 65 females; herds of 5 to 500 young males; and groups of pregnant and recently calved females. When grazing is good, mature male may establish a territory which he marks by urination and droppings and by scraping and smearing of ground and bushes with horns and glandular secretions. Females calve at any time of year after a 6-month gestation and may produce 2 calves a year.

BOVIDS

Saiga *Saiga tatarica* VU

RANGE River Volga to C. Asia

HABITAT Treeless plains

SIZE Body: 4–5½ ft (1.2–1.7 m)
Tail: 3–4 in (7.5–10 cm)

The saiga is migratory and well-adapted to its cold, windswept habitat. It has a heavy fawnish-cinnamon coat, with a fringe of long hairs from chin to chest. In the winter it changes to a uniformly creamy-white and becomes thick and woolly. It is thought that the saiga's enlarged nose, with downward-pointing nostrils, may be an adaptation for warming and moisturizing air. The nasal passages are lined with hairs, glands and mucous tracts. In each nostril there is a sac, lined with mucous membranes that appears in no other mammal but the whale. The male's horns are thought to have medicinal value by the Chinese; this led to overhunting. Saigas have been protected since 1920, and there are now over a million of them.

Saigas feed on low-growing shrubs and grass, and in autumn large herds gather and move off southward to warmer, lusher pastures. When spring comes, groups of 2 to 6 males begin to return northward, followed by the females. In May, after a gestation of about 5 months, the female gives birth to 1 to 3 young, which are suckled until the autumn.

Serow *Capricornis sumatraensis* VU

RANGE N. India to central and S. China;
S.E. Asia to Sumatra

HABITAT Bush and forest at
2,000–9,000 ft (600–2,700 m)

SIZE Body: 4½–5 ft (1.4–1.5 m)
Tail: 3–8¼ in (8–21 cm)

The slow, but sure-footed serow, with its short, solid hoofs, is found on rocky slopes and ridges of thickly vegetated mountains. It is active early and late in the day, feeding on grass and leaves; it lies up in the shelter of an overhanging rock for the rest of the time. The hairs on its back and sides are light at the base and black at the tip, giving the coat an overall dark appearance, there is a completely black stripe along the center of the back, and the mane varies from white to black on different individuals. Both male and female have horns, which they use to defend themselves, particularly against the dogs with which they are hunted by the Chinese, who believe that different parts of the serow have great healing properties.

Little is known of their breeding habits but 1, or more often 2, young are born after a gestation of about 8 months.

Common Goral *Nemorhaedus goral* LR:nt

RANGE Bhutan, India, Nepal, Pakistan

HABITAT Mountains at 3,300–6,600 ft (1,000–2,000 m)

SIZE Body: 3–4¼ ft (90 cm–1.3 m)
Tail: 3–7¾ in (7.5–20 cm)

These animals are mountain-dwellers, found where there are grassy hills and rocky outcrops near forests. They have long, sturdy legs and their long coats, of guardhairs overlaying a short, woolly undercoat, give them a shaggy appearance. Male and female look alike, both possessing horns. The male has a short, semi-erect mane.

Apart from old bucks, which live alone for most of the year, gorals normally live in family groups of 4 to 8. They feed on grass in the early morning and late afternoon, resting on a rocky ledge in the middle of the day. The female gives birth to 1, rarely 2, young after a gestation of about 6 months.

Mountain Goat *Oreamnos americanus*

RANGE N. America: Rocky Mountains from Alaska to
Montana, Idaho, Oregon; introduced in South Dakota

HABITAT Rocky mountains above the tree line

SIZE Body: 4¼–5¼ ft (1.3–1.6 m)
Tail: 6–7¾ in (15–20 cm)

This splendid-looking animal is not a true goat, but a goat-antelope, and is the only one in its genus. It is found among boulders and rocky screes above the tree line and is well adapted to its cold, harsh habitat. It has thick, woolly underfur and a long, hairy, white coat, which is particularly thick and stiff on the neck and shoulders, forming a ridge, or hump. The hooves have a hard, sharp rim, enclosing a soft, spongy inner pad, which gives the mountain goat a good grip for clambering on on rocks and ice. Both sexes have beards and black, conical horns.

Mountain goats are slow-moving, but sure-footed, climbing to great heights and seemingly inaccessible ledges in their search for grass, sedges and lichens to eat. They also browse on the leaves and shoots of trees and will travel considerable distances to search out salt licks. In winter they come down to areas where the snow is not too deep. In really severe weather, they may take refuge under overhanging rocks or in caves.

These goats are probably monogamous, and the female produces 1 or 2 kids in the spring after a gestation of about 7 months. The young kids are remarkably active and within half an hour of birth are able to jump about among the rocks.

Chamois *Rupicapra rupicapra*

RANGE Europe to Middle East

HABITAT Mountains

SIZE Body: 35½ in–4¼ ft (90 cm–1.3 m) Tail: 1¼–1½ in (3–4 cm)

For nimbleness, audacity and endurance, the chamois is unparalleled among mountaindwellers. It thrives in wild and inhospitable surroundings, where weather conditions may be

savage, and has been known to survive as long as 2 weeks without food. It is the only species in its genus. It is slimly built, with distinctive horns that rise almost vertically, then sweep sharply backward to form a hook. The legs are sturdy, and the hoofs have a resilient, spongy pad underneath, which gives the chamois a good grip. The coat is stiff and coarse, with a thick, woolly underfleece.

Chamois graze on the tops of mountains in summer, on herbs and flowers; in winter, they come farther down the slopes and browse on young pine shoots, lichens and mosses. They are wary animals and a sentinel is always posted to warn of danger. Females and young live together in herds of 15 to 30. Old males are solitary except in the rutting season in the autumn. Fighting is common among males, with older rams locking horns. The female usually has 1 kid, but 2 or 3 are fairly common.

Ibex *Capra ibex*

RANGE European Alps, Middle East

HABITAT Alps to 10,000 ft (3,000 m)

SIZE Body: 5 ft (1.5 m) Tail: 4¾–6 in (12–15 cm)

From Roman times, different parts of these animals have been regarded as possessing healing powers, and ibex were hunted to the point of extinction. Today, however, a few small, protected herds survive in reserves. The male ibex has long, backward-sweeping horns; the female has shorter horns. The coat is a brownish-gray. Longer hair on the back of the neck forms a mane in old males. The male has a small beard.

The ibex live above the tree line, only descending to the upper limits of forest in the harshest winter conditions. In summer, they climb up into alpine meadows, where they graze on grass and flowers. At this time, females are found with young and subadults, and males form their own groups, within which token fights often take place to establish an order of rank. Only in the winter rutting season do males rejoin female herds. The female gives birth to 1 young after a gestation period of between 5 and 6 months.

BOVIDS

Musk Ox *Ovibos moschatus*

RANGE N. Canada, Greenland

HABITAT Tundra

SIZE Body: 6¼–7½ ft (1.9–2.3 m) Tail: 3½–4 in (9–10 cm)

In prehistoric times, the musk ox occurred throughout northern Europe, Siberia and North America. It was largely exterminated, surviving only in northern Canada and Greenland; however, it has now been successfully reintroduced in Norway and Alaska. It is the only species in its genus.

The musk ox is superbly equipped for life in harsh, arctic conditions, for it has a dense undercoat, which neither cold nor water can penetrate and an outer coat of long, coarse hair that reaches almost to the ground and protects it from snow and rain. The broad hooves prevent it from sinking in soft snow. Both sexes have heavy horns that almost meet at the base, forming a broad, tough frontal plate. Facial scent glands in the bull emit a strong, musky odour in the rutting season, hence the animal's name.

Musk oxen are gregarious, living in herds of as many as 100. In the mating season, young bulls are driven out by old master bulls and form small bachelor groups or remain solitary. The female produces 1 young after a gestation period of 8 months.

When threatened, musk oxen form a circle, facing outward with horns lowered, with the young in the middle; this is an effective defence against wolves, their natural enemies, but not against men with guns. Musk oxen feed mainly on grass, but they also eat mosses, lichens and leaves and will dig through the snow in order to find food.

Himalayan Tahr *Hemitragus jemlahicus* **VU**

RANGE India: Kashmir (Pir Pamjal Mountains), Punjab; Nepal, Sikkim

HABITAT Tree-covered mountain slopes

SIZE Body: 3½ ft (1.1 m) Tail: 3½ in (9 cm)

Although the tahr appears much like a goat, with its heavy, shaggy coat that forms a mane around the shoulders, it differs from true goats in having a naked muzzle and no beard. The horns are long and not twisted, and there are glands on the feet.

Tahrs are goatlike in their habits – they live on precipitous mountainsides, where they climb and leap with supreme ease. They are gregarious, living in herds of 30 to 40 on almost any vegetation they can reach. Wary animals, they always post a sentinel to watch for danger.

The breeding season peaks in the winter, when the female gives birth to 1 or 2 young after a 6 to 8-month gestation.

Takin *Budorcas taxicolor* **VU**

RANGE Asia: Myanmar; China: Szechuan and Shensi Provinces

HABITAT Dense thickets in mountain forest, 7,900–14,000 ft (2,400–4,250 m)

SIZE Body: 4 ft (1.2 m) Tail: 4 in (10 cm)

The takin lives in dense bamboo and rhododendron thickets near the upper limits of the tree line in some of the most rugged country in the world. It is a clumsy-looking, solidly built animal, with thick legs and large hoofs with dew claws. The coat ranges from yellowish-white to blackish-brown, always with a dark stripe along the back. Both males and females have horns.

Old bulls are generally solitary, but in summer they join large herds. They graze in the evening on grass and herbage near the tops of mountains; in winter takin move down to the valleys, where they live in smaller groups, eating grass, bamboo and willow shoots. They are shy, and spend most of their time under cover following regularly used paths through the thickets to their grazing grounds and salt licks.

The female produces 1 young after a gestation of about 8 months; it is able to follow its mother after about 3 days.

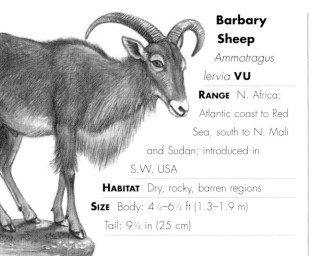

Barbary Sheep

Ammotragus lervia **VU**

RANGE N. Africa: Atlantic coast to Red Sea, south to N. Mali and Sudan; introduced in S.W. USA

HABITAT Dry, rocky, barren regions

SIZE Body: 4¼–6¼ ft (1.3–1.9 m) Tail: 9¾ in (25 cm)

The barbary sheep is the only sheep indigenous to Africa, and the only species in the genus. The mane of long, soft, thick hairs on its throat, chest and upper forelegs differentiates it from other wild sheep, but, like them, both sexes have horns, those of the female being almost as heavy as the male's.

Small family parties, consisting of a breeding pair and their offspring of various litters, wander about in search of food: grass, herbaceous plants, and leaves and twigs of low-growing bushes. They obtain all the water they need from this diet and by licking up dew. Barbary sheep, having no cover in which to hide when danger threatens, rely on the camouflage effect of their sandy coloured coats and remain perfectly still. They are killed by man for their flesh, hides, hair and sinews.

In captivity, barbary sheep produce one litter a year of 1 or 2 young. They have been successfully crossed with domestic goats, and the offspring with chamois.

American Bighorn *Ovis canadensis* **LR:cd**

RANGE N.W. America

HABITAT Upland and mountainous areas

SIZE Body: 4–6 ft (1.2–1.8 m) Tail: 6 in (15 cm)

The American bighorn is found on high mountain pastures in summer, when groups of males or females with young graze independently on grass and herbage. In winter, they form mixed herds and move to lower pastures.

The high-ranking male bighorn sheep is a most impressive animal, with massive spiral horns up to 3¾ ft (1.15 m) long. Horn size is of great significance in establishing rank order among males; smaller-horned

and, therefore, lower-ranking males are treated as females by dominant males, which perhaps prevents them being driven out of the herd. In the rutting season, high-ranking males of comparable horn size have fierce battles rushing at each other and crashing their horns together. The fighting may proceed for hours, and occasionally an animal is killed. Females have exceptionally short horns.

Ewes produce 1 or 2 lambs, born after a gestation period of about 6 months, and are assiduous in care of the young.

Mouflon *Ovis orientalis* **VU**

RANGE Sardinia, Corsica; C. and S. Asia, introduced in Germany, Hungary, Austria and Czechoslovakia

HABITAT Rugged mountains

SIZE Body: 4 ft (1.2 m) Tail: 2¾ in (7 cm)

The mouflon, the wild sheep of Europe, is now found only in reserves in Sardinia and Corsica, but even there is inadequately protected. The male has long, spiral horns, often with the tips curving inward; those of the female are short. It has a woolly underfleece, covered in winter by a coarse, blackish-brown top coat, with a distinctive white saddle patch in the male. In the summer this patch disappears. The female and young are gray or darker brown, with no patch.

Mouflon are active early and late in the day and do not wander far, even when food is scarce. They appear to be able to eat every type of vegetation – grass, flowers, buds and shoots of bushes and trees, even poisonous plants such as deadly nightshade, and so manage to survive.

They live in separate groups composed of females with young or males on their own in the summer. In the rutting season, a mature ram will detach a female from the herd and mate with her. Fierce fighting may take place if an old ram is challenged, but there are seldom casualties.

The ewe produces 1 lamb after a gestation period of 5 months.

RIVER DOLPHIN AND PORPOISES

ORDER CETACEA

There are 77 species of whale, dolphin and porpoise. They are the only aquatic mammals to spend their entire lives in water. All are streamlined animals with strong, horizontally set tail flukes. Their front limbs are modified into flippers and there are no visible hind limbs. As a general rule, whales produce only one young at a time, although twins are known.

There are two groups within the order. First, the toothed whales, with 67 species of small whale, dolphin and porpoise, all of which prey on fish and squid. To help locate their prey, they use a form of ultrasonic sonar: they emit high-frequency clicking sounds which bounce off objects, the echoes informing the whale with astonishing accuracy of the size, distance and speed of travel of the object. All of these whales have teeth, some a pair, some as many as 200.

In the second group are the 10 largest whales, known as the baleen whales. These marine giants feed on tiny planktonic animals, which they extract from the sea by filtering water through plates of fringed horny material hanging from their upper jaws. These baleen plates, as they are called, act as sieves to trap the plankton. There are 3 families of baleen whale: rorquals, gray and right whales.

PLATANISTIDAE: RIVER DOLPHIN FAMILY

The 5 species in this family all inhabit rivers in South America and Asia. They look alike and are grouped as a family, but the resemblance may be more to do with evolutionary pressures of similar habitat than close relationship. All the river dolphins are small for cetaceans, with long slender beaks and prominent rounded foreheads. The rivers these dolphins inhabit are muddy and full of sediment, and visibility is poor; as a result they rely heavily on echolocation to find food and avoid obstacles, and their eyes have become much reduced.

Boutu *Inia geoffrensis* VU

RANGE	Amazon basin
HABITAT	Rivers, streams
SIZE	6–9 ft (1.8–2.7 m)

The boutu has a strong beak, studded with short bristles, and a mobile, flexible head and neck. Most boutus have a total of 100 or more teeth. Their eyes, although small, seem to be more

functional than those of other river dolphins. Boutus feed mainly on small fish and some crustaceans, using echolocation clicks to find their prey. Boutus live in pairs and seem to produce young between July and September.

Ganges Dolphin *Platanista gangetica* EN

RANGE	India: Ganges and Brahmaputra river systems
HABITAT	Rivers, streams
SIZE	5–8 ft (1.5–2.4 m)

The Ganges dolphin has a beak, which can be as long as 18 in (46 cm), and has up to 120 teeth. Its forehead curves up steeply from the beak. An agile animal, it generally swims on its side and returns to the normal upright position to breathe. It can dive for a maximum of 3 minutes at a time, but usually remains underwater for about 45 seconds.

The Ganges dolphin is blind – its eyes have no lenses – but it finds its food by skilful use of echolocation signals. It feeds mainly on fish and some shrimps and hunts in the evening and at night. The dolphins are usually seen in pairs and may gather in groups of 6 or so to feed. They mate in autumn, and the calves are born the following summer after a gestation period of about 9 months.

Whitefin Dolphin/Baiji *Lipotes vexillifer* CR

RANGE	China: Yangzte River; formerly Lake Tungting
HABITAT	Muddy-bottomed rivers
SIZE	6½–8 ft (2–2.4 m)

Since 1975 this species has been protected by law in China, but although the total numbers are not known, population still seems to be low. The whitefin dolphin has a slender beak, which

turns up slightly at the tip, and a total
of 130 to 140 teeth. With little or no
vision, it relies on sonar for hunting prey, mainly fish, but may
also probe in the mud with its beak for shrimps.

Groups of 2 to 6 dolphins move together, sometimes
gathering into larger groups for feeding. In the rainy summer
season, they migrate up small swollen streams to breed, but no
further details are known of their reproductive behavior.

PHOCOENIDAE: PORPOISE FAMILY

Although the name porpoise is sometimes erroneously applied to
members of other families, strictly speaking, only the 6 members
of this family are porpoises. They are small, beakless whales,
rarely exceeding 7 ft (2.1 m) in length, and usually with
prominent dorsal fins. They have 60 to 80 spatular teeth and
feed mainly on fish and squid.

Porpoises live in coastal waters throughout the northern
hemisphere, often ascending the estuaries of large rivers. One
species, the spectacled porpoise, *Phocoena dioptrica*, occurs off
the coasts of South America.

Common Porpoise/Harbor Porpoise

Phocoena phocoena **VU**

RANGE N. Atlantic, N. Pacific Oceans; Black and Mediterranean Seas

HABITAT Shallow water, estuaries

SIZE 4½–6 ft (1.4–1.8 m)

Gregarious, highly vocal animals,
porpoises live in small groups of up to 15 individuals. There is
much communication within the group, and porpoises will
always come to the aid of a group member in distress. Porpoises
feed on fish, such as herring and mackerel, and can dive for up
to 6 minutes to pursue prey, which are pin-pointed by the use
of echolocation clicks.

Breeding pairs mate in July and August and perform
prolonged courtship rituals, caressing one another as they
swim side by side. The gestation period is between 10 and 11

months, and calves are suckled for about 8 months.
While her calf feeds the mother lies on her side at the
surface so that it can breathe easily.

Dall's Porpoise *Phocoenides dalli* **LR:cd**

RANGE Temperate N. Pacific Ocean

HABITAT Inshore and oceanic deeper waters

SIZE 6–7½ ft (1.8–2.3 m)

Dall's porpoise is larger and heavier than most porpoises. Its
head is small, and the lower jaw projects slightly beyond the
upper. It lives in groups of up to 15, which may gather in
schools of 100 or more to migrate north in summer and south
in winter. It feeds on squid and fish, such as hake, and most
probably uses echolocation when hunting.

Pairs mate at any time of the year, and the young are suckled
for as long as 2 years.

Finless Porpoise *Neophocaena phocaenoides*

RANGE E. and S.E. Asia: Pakistan to Borneo and Korea; Yangtze River,
E. China Sea

HABITAT Coasts, estuaries, rivers

SIZE 4½–6 ft (1.4–1.8 m)

The finless porpoise is different from other porpoises in that it
has a prominent rounded forehead, which gives the appearance
of a slight beak, and a ridge of small rounded projections just
behind where the dorsal fin should be. Finless porpoises dive for
less than a minute in search of prey and are quick and agile in
the water. They feed largely on crustaceans, squid and fish and
are skilful echolocators. Although finless porpoises generally
move in pairs, groups of up to 10 are sometimes seen. Little is
known of their breeding behavior, but young calves travel
clinging to the projections on their mothers' backs.

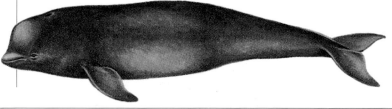

DOLPHINS

DELPHINIDAE: DOLPHIN FAMILY

There are 32 species in this, the largest, most diverse cetacean family, which is found in all oceans and some tropical rivers. Most have beaked snouts and slender streamlined bodies and they are among the smallest whales. Typically, the dolphin has a bulging forehead, housing the melon, a lens-shaped pad of fat thought to help focus the sonar beams. A few species, notably the killer whale, are much larger and do not have beaks. Male dolphins are usually larger than females, and in some species the sexes differ in the shape of their flippers and dorsal fins. Dolphins swim fast and feed by making shallow dives and surfacing several times a minute. They are extremely gregarious and establish hierarchies within their social groups.

Indo-Pacific Humpbacked Dolphin *Sousa chinensis* **DD**

RANGE Indian Ocean, S.W. Pacific Ocean, Yangtze River

HABITAT Coasts, estuaries, swamps

SIZE 6½–10 ft (2–3 m)

The young of this species all have the normal streamlined body shape, but adults have humps of fatty tissue on the back. The beak is long, and there is a total of at least 120 teeth. These dolphins feed in shallow water on fish, mollusks and crustaceans and use echolocation when searching for prey. They are gregarious creatures, living in groups of up to 20 individuals.

Striped Dolphin *Stenella coeruleoalba* **LR:cd**

RANGE Atlantic and Pacific Oceans, temperate and tropical areas

HABITAT Deep offshore waters

SIZE 8–10 ft (2.4–3 m)

Color is variable in this species, but there is always a dark stripe running along the side and usually a dark band curving from the dorsal

fin toward the eye. Striped dolphins have between 90 and 100 teeth and feed on small fish, squid and shrimps. They move in large schools of several hundred, even several thousand individuals, which are organized into age-segregated groups. Females breed about every 3 years. The gestation period is 12 months, and calves are nursed for between 9 and 18 months.

Common Dolphin *Delphinus delphis* **LR:lc**

RANGE Worldwide, temperate and tropical oceans

HABITAT Coastal and oceanic waters

SIZE 7–8½ ft (2.1–2.6 m)

The classic dolphin depicted by artists for centuries, the common dolphin is a beautifully marked animal with a long beak and pointed flippers. The markings are the most complex of any whale and are extremely variable. There are a number of geographically recognizable forms of this widespread species.

Dolphins live in hierarchical groups of 20 to 100 or more; groups sometimes join together, forming huge schools. There are many reports of these highly intelligent social animals coming to the aid of injured companions. Active animals, they roll and leap in the water and often swim at the bows of ships. Although they normally breathe several times a minute, they can dive for as long as 5 minutes to depths of 920 ft (280 m) to feed on fish and squid and certainly make good use of echolocation when hunting. Young are born in the summer, after a gestation period of 10 or 11 months.

Bottle-nose Dolphin *Tursiops truncatus* **DD**

TRUNCATUS RANGE Worldwide, temperate and tropical oceans

HABITAT Coastal waters

SIZE 10–14 ft (3–4.2 m)

Now the familiar performing dolphin in zoos and on screen, this dolphin is a highly intelligent animal which is, tragically, still hunted and killed by man in some areas. It is a sturdy creature with a broad, high fin and a short, wide beak. Its lower jaw projects beyond the upper and this, combined with the curving line of the mouth, gives it its characteristic smiling expression.

Bottle-nose dolphins live in groups of up to 15 individuals, sometimes gathering into larger schools, and there is much cooperation and communication between the group members. They feed mainly on bottom-dwelling fish in inshore waters, but also take crustaceans and large surface-swimming fish. They are highly skilful echolocators, producing a range of click sounds in different frequencies to analyze any object at a distance with great precision. Up to 1,000 clicks a second are emitted.

Breeding pairs perform gentle courtship movements, caressing one another before copulation. Gestation lasts 12 months, and two adult females assist the mother at the birth and take the calf, which is normally born tail first, to the surface for its first breath. The mother feeds her calf for about a year, so there must be at least a 2-year interval between calves. Like all whales, the bottle-nose dolphin produces extremely rich milk with a fat content of over 40 per cent to satisfy the high energy demands of her fast-growing youngster.

Killer Whale *Orcinus orca* **LR:cd**

RANGE	Worldwide, particularly cooler seas
HABITAT	Coastal waters
SIZE	23–32 ft (7–9.7 m)

The largest of the dolphin family, the killer whale is a robust yet streamlined animal, with a rounded head and no beak. The characteristic dorsal fin of an adult male is almost 6½ ft (2 m) high; and while the fins of females and juveniles are much smaller and curved, they are still larger than those of most other cetaceans. Adults have a total of 40 to 50 teeth.

Killer whales are avid predators and feed on fish, squid, sea lions, birds and even other whales. Their echolocation sounds are unlike those of other dolphins and are probably used to find food in turbid water.

Extended family groups of killer whales live together and cooperate in hunting. They have no regular migratory habits, but do travel in search of food.

Long-finned Pilot Whale *Globicephala melaena* **LR:lc**

RANGE	N. Atlantic Ocean; temperate southern oceans
HABITAT	Coastal waters
SIZE	16–28 ft (4.8–8.5 m)

The long-finned pilot whale has an unusual square-shaped head and long, rather narrow flippers. Pilot whales have a vast repertoire of sounds, some of which are used for echolocation purposes. Squid is their main food, but they also feed on fish, such as cod and turbot. Social groups are made up of 6 or more whales and they have particularly strong bonds. Groups may join into larger schools. Gestation lasts about 16 months and the mother feeds her young for well over a year.

The range of this species is unusual in that it occurs in two widely separated areas.

Risso's Dolphin *Grampus griseus* **DD**

RANGE	Worldwide, temperate and tropical oceans
HABITAT	Deep water
SIZE	10–13 ft (3–4 m)

Most adult Risso's dolphins are badly marked with scars, apparently caused by members of their own species, since the marks correspond to their own tooth pattern. The body of this dolphin is broad in front of the fin and tapers off behind it. It has no beak, but there is a characteristic crease down the centre of the forehead to the lip. There are no teeth in the upper jaw and only three or four in each side in the lower jaw. Squid seems to be its main food.

SPERMWHALES AND WHITE WHALES

PHYSETERIDAE: SPERM WHALE FAMILY

There are 3 species of sperm whale, 1 of which is the largest of all toothed whales, while the other 2 are among the smallest whales. Their characteristic feature is the spermaceti organ, located in the space above the toothless upper jaw; this contains a liquid, waxy substance which may be involved in controlling buoyancy when the whale makes deep dives. All sperm whales have underslung lower jaws but have little else in common.

Pygmy Sperm Whale *Kogia breviceps* **LR:lc**

RANGE All oceans

HABITAT Tropical, warm temperate seas

SIZE 10–11 ft (3–3.4 m)

Its underslung lower jaw gives the pygmy sperm whale an almost sharklike appearance, belied by its blunt, square head. The pygmy sperm whale's head accounts for only about 15 per cent of its total length. There are 12 or more pairs of teeth in the lower jaw. Short, broad flippers are located far forward, near the head. The body tapers off markedly behind the small dorsal fin.

Pygmy sperm whales are thought to be shy, slow-moving animals. They feed on squid, fish and crabs from deep and shallow water. These whales have often been sighted alone, but they are thought to form social units of 3 to 5 individuals.

Little is known of the reproductive habits of pygmy sperm whales. Gestation is believed to last about 9 months; calves are born in the spring and fed by the mother for about a year.

Dwarf Sperm Whale *Kogia simus* **LR:lc**

RANGE All oceans

HABITAT Tropical and subtropical seas

SIZE 8–9 ft (2.4–2.7 m)

Superficially similar to the pygmy sperm whale, the dwarf sperm whale tends to have a more rounded head than its relative, though there is considerable individual variation in shape. The whale's lower jaw is set back, and it contains up to 11 pairs of teeth.

Little is known of the biology and habits of this whale, but fish and squid are believed to be its main items of diet. Species found in the stomachs of dwarf sperm whales are all known to live at depths of more than 250 m) 800 ft), so there seems little doubt that these whales make prolonged dives for food.

Sperm Whale *Physeter catodon* **VU**

RANGE All oceans

HABITAT Temperate and tropical waters

SIZE 36–66 ft (11–20 m)

The largest of the toothed whales, the sperm whale has a huge head, as great as one-third of its total body length, and a disproportionately small lower jaw, set well back from the snout. On its back is a fleshy hump and behind this are several smaller humps. Its flippers are short, but the tail is large and powerful and useful for acceleration. Surrounding the nasal passages in the huge snout is a mass of the waxy substance known as

spermaceti. When the whale dives, it allows these passages to fill with water and by controlling the amount and temperature of the water taken in at different depths, it can alter the density of the wax and thus the buoyancy of its whole body. This enables the whale to make its deep dives and to remain at neutral buoyancy, while searching for prey. Sperm whales are known to dive to 3,300 ft (1,000 m) and may dive to more than twice this depth. They feed mainly on large, deepwater squid, as well as on some fish, lobsters and other marine creatures. Their sonar system is vital for finding prey in the black depths of the ocean.

All sperm whales migrate toward the poles in spring and back to the Equator in autumn, but females and young do not stray farther than temperate waters. Adult males, however, travel right to the ice caps in high latitudes. They return to the tropics in winter and contest with each other in order to gather harem groups consisting of 20 to 30 breeding females and young. Males under about 25 years old do not generally hold harems, but gather in bachelor groups.

The gestation period for sperm whales is about 14 to 16 months. When a female gives birth, she is surrounded by attendant adult females, waiting to assist her and to help the newborn to take its first breath at the surface. As with most whales, usually only 1 young is produced at a time, but twins have been known. Mothers suckle their young for up to 2 years.

MONODONTIDAE: WHITE WHALE FAMILY

There are 2 species in this family, both of which live in Arctic waters. They are distinctive whales with many features in common. Both have more flexible necks than is usual for whales, and their tails, too, are highly maneuvrable. They do not have dorsal fins. In both species males are larger than females.

White Whale *Delphinapterus leucas* VU

RANGE Arctic Ocean and subarctic waters

HABITAT Shallow seas, estuaries, rivers

SIZE 13–20 ft (4–6.1 m)

The white whale is often known as the beluga. It has a rounded, plump body and just a hint of a beak. There is a short raised ridge along its back where the dorsal fin would normally be. At birth, these whales are a dark brownish-red colour, but they then turn a deep blue-gray and gradually become paler until, at about 6 years of age, they are a creamy-white colour. They have about 32 teeth.

White whales feed on the bottom in shallow water, mainly on crustaceans and some fish. They actually swim underneath pack ice and can break their way up through the ice floes in order to breathe.

Sexual maturity is attained when the whales are between 5 and 8 years old. The whales mate in spring and calves are born in the summer after a gestation period of about 14 months. Since the young are suckled for at least a year, white whales are able to breed only every 3 years or so.

All white whales are highly vocal and make a variety of sounds for communication, as well as clicks used for echolocation. Their intricate songs caused them to be known as sea canaries by the nineteenth century whalers. White whales congregate in herds of hundreds of individuals in order to migrate south in winter and then return to rich northern feeding grounds in summer.

Narwhal *Monodon monoceros* DD

RANGE High Arctic Ocean (patchy distribution)

HABITAT Open sea

SIZE 13–20 ft (4–6.1 m)

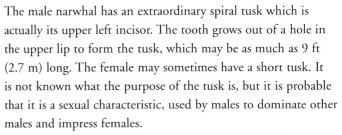

The male narwhal has an extraordinary spiral tusk which is actually its upper left incisor. The tooth grows out of a hole in the upper lip to form the tusk, which may be as much as 9 ft (2.7 m) long. The female may sometimes have a short tusk. It is not known what the purpose of the tusk is, but it is probable that it is a sexual characteristic, used by males to dominate other males and impress females.

Narwhals feed on squid, crabs, shrimps and fish. Groups of 6 to 10 whales form social units and may gather into larger herds when migrating. They do make click sounds, as well as other vocal communications, but it is not certain whether or not these are used for echolocation.

Narwhals mate in early spring, and gestation lasts 15 months. Mothers feed their calves for up to 2 years. At birth, calves are a dark blue-gray but as they mature this changes to the mottled brown of adults.

BEAKED WHALES

ZIPHIIDAE: BEAKED WHALE FAMILY

There are 18 species of beaked whale, found in all oceans. Most are medium-sized whales with slender bodies and long narrow snouts, some species have bulging, rounded foreheads. A particular characteristic of the family is the pair of grooves on the throat. Although Shepherd's beaked whale has more than 50 teeth, all other beaked whales have only one or two pairs, and the arrangement and shape of these are a useful means of defining identification.

Beaked whales feed largely on squid. They are deep divers and are believed to dive deeper and to remain submerged for longer periods than any other marine mammals. They generally move in small groups, but adult males are often solitary.

Although the second-largest family of whales (the dolphin family is the largest with 32 species), beaked whales are a little-known group. Some species are known to exist only from a few skulls and bones. The 12 species in the genus *Mesoplodon* are particularly unresearched but interesting. Only males have functional teeth, with a single pair protruding from the lower jaw. The shape and length of these differ from species to species, culminating in *M. Iayardi*, in which the backward-pointing teeth grow upward out of the mouth like tusks.

Northern Bottle-nose Whale *Hyperoodon ampullatus* **LR:cd**

RANGE	Arctic, N. Atlantic Oceans
HABITAT	Deep offshore waters
SIZE	24–33 ft (7.3–10 m)

A sturdy, round-bodied whale, the northern bottle-nose has a prominent bulbous forehead that is particularly pronounced in older males. Males are generally larger than females. The adult male has only two teeth, which are in the lower jaw, but these are often so deeply embedded in the gums that they cannot be seen. Adult females also have only two teeth, and these are always embedded in the gum. Some individuals have further vestigial, unusable teeth in the gums.

Squid, some fish, such as herring and sometimes starfish, make up the main diet of the northern bottle-nose whale. A member of a deep-diving family, the bottle-nose is believed to dive to greater depths than any other whale and certainly remains under water for longer.

These are gregarious whales, and they collect in social units of 4 to 10 individuals, a group usually consisting of a male and several females with young. Pairs mate in spring and summer, and gestation lasts about 12 months. The whales are sexually mature at between 9 and 12 years of age.

Since commercial whaling of this species began in 1887, populations have been seriously depleted.

Cuvier's Beaked Whale *Ziphius cavirostris* **DD**

RANGE	All oceans, temperate and tropical areas
HABITAT	Deep waters
SIZE	21–23 ft (6.4–7 m)

Cuvier's beaked whale has the typical tapering body of its family and a distinct beak. Adult males are easily distinguished by the two teeth which protrude from the lower jaw. In females, however, these teeth remain embedded in the gums. The colouring of this species is highly variable – Indo-Pacific whales are generally various shades of brown, many individuals have darker backs or almost white heads, while in the Atlantic, Cuvier's whales tend to be a gray or gray-blue colour. All races of beaked whales, however, are marked with scars and with discolored oval patches that are caused by the feeding action of parasitic lampreys.

Squid and deep-water fish are the main food of Cuvier's whales, and they make deep dives, lasting up to 30 minutes, in order to find their prey.

There is no definite breeding season, and calves are born at any time of the year. Groups of up to 15 individuals live and travel together.

Sowerby's Beaked Whale

Mesoplodon bidens **DD**

RANGE N. Atlantic Ocean

HABITAT Deep, cool coastal waters

SIZE 16½–20 ft (5–6 m)

There are 12 closely related species of beaked whale in the genus *Mesoplodon.* Most species tend to live in deep water, staying clear of ships, so they are rarely seen and their habits are little known or documented.

All have fairly well-rounded bodies, with small flippers in proportion to body size. Males are larger than females. Mature whales are generally marked with many scars; some of these are caused by parasites and others are, perhaps the result of fights between individuals of the same species.

Sowerby's beaked whale was the first beaked whale to be recognized officially and described as a species, in 1804. The male has a pointed tooth at each side of the lower jaw. Females have smaller teeth in this position or no visible teeth at all. Squid and small fish are the main food of Sowerby's whale.

Its breeding habits are not known, but it is thought to migrate south in winter and to give birth in its wintering area.

Shepherd's Beaked Whale *Tasmacetus shepherdi* **DD**

RANGE New Zealand seas; off coasts of Argentina and Chile

HABITAT Coasts, open ocean

SIZE 20–22 ft (6–6.6 m)

Shepherd's beaked whale was not discovered until 1933, and very few individuals have since been found or sighted. Until recently, the species was believed to occur only around New Zealand, but in the 1970s identical specimens were found off Argentina and Chile. This species is unique in its family for its tooth pattern. Shepherd's beaked whale has a pair of large teeth at the tip of its lower jaw, with 12 or more pairs behind them, and about 10 pairs in the upper jaw. It resembles the rest of the family in habits and appearance. Squid and fish are believed to be its main food.

Baird's Beaked Whale *Berardius bairdi* **LR:cd**

RANGE Temperate N. Pacific Ocean

HABITAT Deep water over 3,300 ft (1,000 m)

SIZE 33–39 ft (10–12 m)

The largest of the beaked whales, Baird's beaked whale has a distinctive beak, with the lower jaw extending beyond the upper. A pair of large teeth protrudes at the tip of the lower jaw, and behind these is a pair of smaller teeth.

Female Baird's whales are generally larger than males and lighter in color, but they have smaller teeth. Adult males are usually marked with scars, caused by their own species, suggesting that there is much rivalry and competition for leadership of groups of breeding females.

The normal social unit is a group of 6 to 30, led by a dominant male. The whales mate in midsummer and gestation lasts for 10 months, sometimes longer.

The migration pattern of this species is the exact opposite of the normal migration habits of whales. They spend the summer in warm waters to the south of their range off California and Japan, then move northwards in winter to the cooler waters of the Bering Sea and similar areas. These movements are most probably connected with the local abundance of food supplies. Baird's whales are deep divers and feed on squid, fish, octopus, lobster, crabs and other marine invertebrates.

Arnoux's beaked whale, *B. arnouxii*, which occurs in the temperate South Pacific and South Atlantic, is the closely related southern counterpart of Baird's whale. Although rarely seen, it is believed to be similar in both appearance and habits.

GRAY WHALE, RORQUALS AND RIGHT WHALES

ESCHRICHTIIDAE: GRAY WHALE FAMILY

There is a single species in this family, which is in some ways intermediate between the rorqual and right whales, the other 2 baleen whale families. The gray whale differs from both of these in that it has two or sometimes four throat grooves instead of the 100 or more in the other baleen whales.

Gray Whale *Eschrichtius robustus* **LR:cd**

RANGE	N.E. and N.W. Pacific Ocean
HABITAT	Coastal waters
SIZE	40–50 ft (12.2–15.3 m)

The gray whale has no dorsal fin, but there is a line of bumps along the middle of its lower back. Its jaw is only slightly arched and the snout is pointed. Males are larger than females. Like all baleen whales, it feeds on small planktonic animals by filtering water through rows of fringed horny plates, suspended from the upper jaw. Any creatures in the water are caught on the baleen plates and the water is expelled at the sides of the mouth. Using its tongue, the whale takes the food from the baleen to the back of its mouth to be swallowed. The gray whale feeds at the bottom of the sea, unlike other baleen whales, stirring up the sediment with its pointed snout then sieving the turbulent water.

Gray whales perform migrations of some 12,500 miles (20,000 km) between feeding grounds in the north and breeding grounds in the south. They spend the summer months in the food-rich waters of the Arctic, when they do most of their feeding for the year. At the breeding grounds, they gather to perform courtship rituals, and breeding animals pair off with an extra male in attendance. They lie in shallow water and, as the pair mate, the second male lies behind the female, apparently supporting her. The gestation period is 12 months, so the calf is born at the breeding grounds a year after mating has taken place and travels north with its mother when it is about 2 months old.

BALAENOPTERIDAE: RORQUAL FAMILY

There are 6 species of rorqual whale. All except the humpback whale are similar in appearance, but they differ in size and color. Most have about 300 baleen plates on each side of the jaws and there are a large number of grooves on the throat.

Minke Whale, *Balaenoptera acutorostrata* **LR:nt**

RANGE	All oceans, temperate and polar areas
HABITAT	Shallow water, estuaries, rivers, inland seas
SIZE	26–33 ft (8–10 m)

The smallest of the rorqual family, the minke whale has a distinctive, narrow pointed snout and 60 to 70 throat grooves. In polar areas, minke whales feed largely on planktonic crustaceans, but temperate populations eat fish and squid more often than any other baleen whale. Out of the breeding season, these whales tend to occur alone or in pairs, but they may congregate in rich feeding areas. Gestation lasts 10 or 11 months and calves are suckled for 6 months.

Sei Whale *Balaenoptera borealis* **EN**

RANGE	All oceans (not polar regions)
HABITAT	Open ocean
SIZE	49–65½ ft (15–20 m)

The sei whale is streamlined and flat-headed and can achieve speeds of 26 mph (50 km/h). It eats almost any kind of plankton, as well as fish and squid, usually feeding near the surface. Family groups of 5 or 6 whales occur and pair bonds are strong and may last for years. The gestation period is 12 months, and the calf is fed by its mother for 6 months.

Blue Whale *Balaenoptera musculus* **EN**

RANGE All oceans

HABITAT Open ocean

SIZE 82–105 ft (25–32 m)

The largest mammal that has ever existed, the blue whale may weigh more than 161 US t (146 te). Its body is streamlined and, despite its enormous bulk, it is graceful in the water. It has 64 to 94 grooves on its throat. These gigantic whales feed entirely on small planktonic crustaceans and, unlike many baleen whales, are highly selective, taking only a few species. They feed during the summer months, which they spend in nutrient-rich polar waters, and over this period take up to 4.4 US t (4.1 te) of small shrimps apiece each day.

In autumn, when ice starts to cover their feeding grounds, the blue whales migrate toward the Equator but eat virtually nothing while in the warmer water. They mate during this period and, after a gestation of 11 or 12 months, the calves are born in warm waters the following year.

Even though blue whales have been protected since 1967, populations of this extraordinary animal are still low, and it is in danger of extinction.

Humpback Whale

Megaptera novaeangliae **VU**

RANGE All oceans

HABITAT Oceanic, coastal waters

SIZE 48–62 ft (14.6–19 m)

The humpback has a distinctly curved lower jaw and an average of 22 throat grooves. Its most characteristic features are the many knobs on the body and the flippers, which are about 16 ft (5 m) long and scalloped at the front edges. Humpback whales are more gregarious than blue whales and are usually seen in family groups of 3 or 4, although they may communicate with many other groups.

In the southern hemisphere, humpbacks feed on planktonic crustaceans, but in the northern hemisphere they eat small fish. Populations in both hemispheres feed in polar regions in summer and then migrate to tropical breeding areas for the winter. The gestation period is 11 or 12 months, and a mother feeds her calf for almost a year.

Humpbacks perform the most extraordinary, complex songs of any animal. The songs may be repeated for hours on end and are specific to populations and areas. They may change from year to year.

BALAENIDAE: RIGHT WHALE FAMILY

It is in the 3 species of right whale that the baleen apparatus is most extremely developed. Right whales have enormous heads, measuring more than a third of their total body length, and highly arched upper jaws to carry the long baleen plates. They have no throat grooves.

Regarded by whalers as the "right" whales to exploit, they have been killed in such numbers by commercial whalers over the last century that they are rare today.

Bowhead Whale/Greenland Right Whale

Balaena mysticetus **LR:cd**

RANGE Arctic Ocean

HABITAT Coastal waters

SIZE 49–65½ ft (15–20 m)

The bowhead has a massive head and a body that tapers sharply toward the tail. Its jaws are strongly curved to accommodate the 15 ft (4.5 m) long baleen plates, the longest of any of the filter-feeding whales.

Bowheads feed on the smallest planktonic crustaceans, which they catch on the fine fringes of their baleen. They mate in early spring, the gestation period is 10 to 12 months, and the calf is fed for almost a year. Occasionally twins are produced.

HORSES AND TAPIRS

ORDER PERISSODACTYLA

There are only 3 surviving families of perissodactyl – or odd-toed, hoofed mammals: horses, tapirs and rhinoceroses. Nine other families, now extinct, are known from fossils.

EQUIDAE: HORSE FAMILY

Horses, asses and zebras make up a family of about 8 species of hoofed mammals, highly adapted for fast, graceful running. In this group the foot has evolved to a single hoof on an elongate third digit. The family has a natural distribution in Asia and Africa, but the domesticated horse has spread to other areas.

In the wild, all equids live in herds, migrate regularly and feed mainly on grass. Their teeth are adapted for grass-cropping and grinding, with chisel-shaped incisors and large premolars and molars, with convoluted surfaces. The skull is elongate to accommodate the large cheek teeth.

Common Zebra *Equus burchelli*

RANGE E. and S. Africa

HABITAT Grassy plains, lightly wooded savanna, hills

SIZE Body: 6¼–7¾ ft (1.9–2.4 m) Tail: 17–22½ in (43–57 cm)

Great variation in pattern occurs in these zebras, both between individuals and the subspecies. Toward the south of the range, stripes on the hind parts of the body generally become lighter. The body is rounded, and the legs slender. A small erect mane runs down the back of the neck. The body varies from white to yellowish with light to dark brown or black stripes.

Common zebras leave their resting place at dawn and move to grazing grounds to feed on grass and sometimes leaves and bark. They must drink regularly.

Zebras live in families of up to 6 females and their young, each family led by an old male. When the male is 16 to 18 years old, he is peacefully replaced by a younger male of 6 to 8 years and then lives alone. Several families may form large herds, but they can still recognize each other by sight, sound and scent.

The female gives birth to a single young, rarely twins, after a gestation of about a

year. Until the foal learns to recognize its mother – in 3 or 4 days – she drives other animals away. It suckles for about 6 months and is independent at about a year.

Grevy's Zebra

Equus grevyi **EN**

RANGE E. Africa: Kenya, Ethiopia

HABITAT Savanna, semidesert

SIZE Body: 8½ ft (2.6 m) Tail: 27½–29½ in (70–75 cm)

Grevy's zebra has a long head, broad, rounded ears and a relatively short, strong neck. An erect mane runs from its crown down the back of its neck. Its body is white with black stripes, both narrower and more numerous than those of the common zebra. Grevy's zebra grazes during the day, and rests in shade in the noon heat. It likes to drink daily. Mature males live alone, each in his own territory. Males without a territory form troops. Females and young live in separate troops of a dozen or more. In the dry season, male and female troops migrate. Lone males stay on unless there is a severe drought.

The female gives birth to a single young after a gestation of about a year. A foal can recognize its mother after a few days. It suckles for 6 months and stays with its mother for up to 2 years.

African Ass *Equus africanus* **CR**

RANGE N.E. Africa

HABITAT Open grassy plains, rugged rocky country, semidesert, mountains

SIZE Shoulder height: 4 ft (1.2 m)

This ancestor of the domestic ass is rare in the wild due to hunting and competition from domestic stock. The remaining animals are probably cross-bred with domestic stock. Of the 4 subspecies, 1 is extinct and 2 nearly so.

The African ass has a

large head with long, narrow ears, and short, smooth hair, which varies from yellowish-brown to bluish-gray in color. It is a good climber and is adept at moving over rugged country. It feeds on grass, herbage and sometimes foliage, and needs to drink regularly. Most active at dusk and night-time and in the early morning, it spends much of the day resting in shade. Females live in loose-knit troops with their young or in mixed troops of young animals. Older males live alone or in male troops.

The female gives birth to 1 young after a gestation period of between 330 and 365 days.

Przewalski's Wild Horse *Equus przewalskii* **EW**

RANGE Mongolia, W. China

HABITAT Plains, semidesert

SIZE Body: 6–6½ ft (1.8–2 m) Tail: 35½ in (90 cm)

This ancestor of the domestic horse has an erect mane and no forelock. Populations have declined drastically because of hunting, cold winters and competition and interbreeding with domestic animals. True wild horses are now extinct, but they are bred in captivity as part of a breeding program including many zoos. They live in small herds, each led by a dominant male. Young are born in April or May.

Onager/Asiatic wild ass *Equus hemionus* **VU**

RANGE Iran, Afghanistan, Russia

HABITAT Steppe, gorges, river margins

SIZE Body: about 6½ ft (2 m) Tail: 16¼ in (42.5 cm)

The onager has declined due to human settlement, competition for grazing from domestic livestock, and hunting. In summer, the onager lives in high grassland areas, feeding on many types of grass. It needs a good supply of fresh water to survive. Onagers live in troops of up to 12 females and their young, each led by a dominant male. Females give birth to a single young after a gestation period of about a year.

TAPIRIDAE: TAPIR FAMILY

The 4 living species of tapir are thought to resemble the ancestors of the perissodactyls. These stocky, short-legged animals, have four toes on the forefeet and three on the hind feet. Short, bristly hair covers the body giving it a smooth appearance. The snout and upper lip are elongated into a short, mobile trunk. Tapirs are mainly nocturnal forest-dwellers and feed on vegetation. Of the 4 species, 3 occur in Central and South America and l in Southeast Asia.

Malayan Tapir

Tapirus indicus **VU**

RANGE S.E. Asia: Myanmar to Malaysia, Sumatra

HABITAT Humid, swampy forest

SIZE Body: 8¼ ft (2.5 m) Tail: 2–4 in (5–10 cm)

The Malayan tapir has a unique grayish-black and white coloration. Its trunk is longer and stronger than those of the tapirs from South America. A shy, solitary animal, it is active only at night. It eats aquatic vegetation and the leaves, buds and fruit of some land plants. It swims well and, if alarmed, heads for water.

The female gives birth to a single young after a gestation of about 395 days. The young tapir is camouflaged with stripes and spots, which disappear at about 6 to 8 months. Malayan tapirs have been badly affected by the destruction of large areas of forest and are now extremely rare.

Brazilian Tapir *Tapirus terrestris* **LR:nt**

RANGE South America: Colombia, Venezuela, south to Brazil and Paraguay

HABITAT Rain forest, near water or swamps

SIZE Body: 6½ ft (2 m) Tail: 2–3 in (5–8 cm)

The Brazilian tapir is nearly always found near water. It moves quickly even over rugged land and is a good swimmer. It is dark brown and its low erect mane runs from the crown to the back of the neck. Its mobile snout is used to feed on leaves, buds, shoots, small branches, fruit, grass, and water plants.

The female gives birth to a single spotted and striped young after a

RHINOCEROSES AND HYRAXES

RHINOCEROTIDAE: RHINOCEROS FAMILY

There are 5 species of rhinoceros, found in Africa and Southeast Asia, and all have huge heads with one or two horns and a prehensile upper lip, which helps them to browse on tough plant material. The legs are short and thick, with three hoofed toes on each foot, and the skin is extremely tough, with only a few hairs. Male and female look similar. Females have smaller horns.

Indian Rhinoceros

Rhinoceros unicornis **EN**

RANGE Nepal, N.E. India

HABITAT Grassland in swampy areas

SIZE Body: 13¾ ft (4.2 m) Tail: 29½ in (75 cm)

The Indian rhinoceros is the largest of the Asian species. It has a thick, dark-gray hide, studded with many small protuberances. The skin falls into deep folds at the joints.

Both sexes have a single horn on the head, but the female's horn is smaller. Generally a solitary animal, the Indian rhinoceros feeds in the morning and evening on grass, weeds and twigs and rests during the rest of the day.

Females give birth to 1 young after a gestation of about 16 months. Calves suckle for about 2 years.

Sumatran Rhinoceros *Dicerorhinus sumatrensis* **CR**

RANGE Indonesia, Malaysia, Myanmar, Thailand, Vietnam

HABITAT Dense forest, near streams

SIZE 8¼–9¼ ft (2.5–2.8 m) Tail: about 23½ in (60 cm)

The smallest member of its family, the Sumatran rhinoceros has two horns; those of the female are smaller than the

male's. Bristlelike hairs are scattered over the thick skin and fringe the edges of the ears. Sumatran rhinoceroses are usually solitary, although a male and female pair may live together. They feed mostly in the early morning and evening on leaves, twigs, fruit and bamboo shoots and may trample small trees in order to browse on their foliage. Like other rhinoceroses, this species has good hearing and sense of smell, but its sight is poor.

The female bears a single young after a gestation period of between 7 and 8 months.

Square-lipped/White Rhinoceros

Ceratotherium simum **LR:cd**

RANGE Africa: N.W. Uganda and adjacent regions; Zimbabwe to N. South Africa

HABITAT Savanna

SIZE Body: 11¾–16½ ft (3.6–5 m) Tail: 3–3¼ ft (90 cm–1 m)

The largest living land animal after the elephant, the square-lipped rhinoceros has a hump on its neck and a long head, which it carries low. Its muzzle is broad, with a squared upper lip. This rhinoceros is generally grayish in color but takes on the color of the mud in which it has been wallowing.

The square-lipped rhinoceros is a placid animal and tends to flee from trouble rather than attack. Each old male occupies his own territory, which may be shared by younger males, but the female is sociable and is usually accompanied by her own young and another female with young. They feed only on grass, grazing and resting from time to time throughout the day and night.

The female gives birth to 1 calf after a gestation of about 16 months. The calf suckles for at least a year and stays with its mother for 2 or 3 years, leaving only when the next calf is born.

Black Rhinoceros *Diceros bicornis* **CR**

RANGE   Africa: S. Chad and Sudan to South Africa

HABITAT   Bush country, grassland, woodland

SIZE   Body: 9¾–11¾ ft (3–3.6 m) Tail: 23½–27½ in (60–70 cm)

The black rhinoceros is actually gray, but its color varies depending on the mud in which it wallows. It has a large head which bears two and sometimes three horns, but no hump. The upper lip is pointed and mobile and helps it to browse on the leaves, buds and shoots of small trees and bushes. Black rhinoceroses live alone, except for mothers and young. Adults live in overlapping ranges, with boundaries marked by dung heaps. Male and female remain together for only a few days when mating. The female gives birth to 1 calf after a gestation of about 15 months. The calf suckles for about a year and stays with its mother for 2 or 3 years, until her next calf is born.

ORDER HYRACOIDEA

PROCAVIIDAE: HYRAX FAMILY

Small herbivores found in Africa and the Middle East, the hyraxes, conies or dassies generally look like rabbits with short, rounded ears. There are about 6 species, and the family is the only one in its order. Some hyraxes are agile climbers in trees, while others inhabit rocky koppies, or small hills. The feet have flattened nails, resembling hoofs, and a central moist cup that works as an adhesive pad when the hyrax climbs.

Tree Hyrax *Dendrohyrax arboreus*

RANGE   Africa: Kenya to South Africa: Cape Province

HABITAT   Forest

SIZE   Body: 15¾–23½ in (40–60 cm)
Tail: absent

The tree hyrax is an excellent climber and lives in a tree hole or rock crevice where it rests during the day. It emerges in the

afternoon or evening to feed in the trees and on the ground on leaves, grass, ferns, fruit and other plant material. Insects, lizards and birds' eggs are also eaten on occasion.

Tree hyraxes normally live in pairs and are extremely noisy animals, uttering a wide range of loud screams, squeals and grunts. A litter of 1 or 2 young is born after a gestation period of about 8 months.

Small–toothed Rock Hyrax *Heterohyrax brucei*

RANGE   Africa: Egypt to South Africa: Transvaal;
Botswana and Angola

HABITAT   Open country, plains to mountains,
forest, savanna

SIZE   Body: 15¾–22½ in (40–57 cm)
Tail: absent

Despite its name, this hyrax lives among trees as well as rocks. Depending on its habitat, it finds shelter in crevices or holes. Rock hyraxes are sociable animals and they form colonies of up to 30 animals, each colony generally consists of several old males, many breeding females and their young. The rock hyraxes feed during the day, mainly on leaves of trees, but also on small plants and grass.

The female gives birth to 1 or 2 young, rarely 3, after a gestation period of between 7½ and 8 months.

Large-toothed Rock Hyrax *Procavia capensis*

RANGE   Arabian Peninsula; Africa: N.E. Senegal to
Somalia and N. Tanzania,
S. Malawi, S. Angola to South
Africa: Cape Province

HABITAT   Rocky hillsides,
rock piles

SIZE   Body: 17–18½ in (43–47 cm)
Tail: absent

This hyrax lives among rocky outcrops and it is an agile climber. It feeds mostly on the ground on leaves, grass, small plants and berries, but readily climbs to feed on fruits, such as figs. In winter bark is eaten. The hyraxes spend much of the rest of the day lying in the sun or shade in order to maintain their body temperature, and at night they huddle together in order to minimize loss of body heat. These hyraxes are sociable and live in colonies of 50 or more individuals.

Males are aggressive at mating time and reassert their dominance over rivals and younger males. The female gives birth to 1 to 6 young, usually 2 or 3, after a gestation period of between 7 and 8 months.

ELEPHANTS, DUGONG AND MANATEES

ORDER PROBOSCIDEA

The elephants are the only surviving representatives of this once diverse and widespread group, which formerly contained many species of huge herbivorous mammal.

ELEPHANTIDAE: ELEPHANT FAMILY

The two species of elephant are by far the largest terrestrial mammals; they may stand up to 13 ft (4 m) at the shoulder and weigh as much as 13,000 lb (5,900 kg). One species lives in Africa, the other in India and Southeast Asia. Elephants have thick, pillarlike legs, and their feet are flattened, expanded pads. On the head are huge ears, which are fanned to and fro to help dissipate excess body heat. The elephant's most remarkable of adaptations, the trunk, is an elongated nose and upper lip, which is extremely flexible and has a manipulative tip. This sensitive organ is used for gathering food, drinking, smelling and fighting.

Both species of elephant have suffered badly from destruction of forest and vegetation in their range, and large numbers have been killed for their ivory tusks. Although hunting is now strictly controlled, poaching continues.

African Elephant *Loxodonta africana* **EN**

RANGE Africa, south of the Sahara

HABITAT Forest, savanna

SIZE Body: 19¾–24½ ft (6–7.5 m) Tail: 3¾–4¼ ft (1–1.3 m)

The African elephant has larger ears and tusks than the Asian species and two finger-like extensions at the end of its trunk. Females are smaller than males and have shorter tusks. Elephants rest in the midday heat and have one or two periods of rest at night, but are otherwise active at any time, roaming in search of food. Depending on its size, an elephant may consume up to 440 lb (200 kg) of plant material a day, all of which is grasped with the trunk and placed in the mouth. The diet includes leaves, shoots, twigs, roots and fruit from many plants, as well as cultivated crops on occasion.

Elephants are social animals, particularly females. A troop centers around several females and their young of various ages. As they mature, young males form separate all-male troops. Old males may be shunned by the herd when they are displaced by younger males.

Breeding occurs at any time of year, and a female on heat may mate with more than one male. The gestation period is about 22 months, and usually only 1 young is born. The female clears a secluded spot for the birth and is assisted by other females. The calf is suckled for at least 2 years and remains with its mother even longer. She may have several calves of different ages under her protection and gives birth every 2 to 4 years.

Asian Elephant *Elephas maximus* **EN**

RANGE India, Sri Lanka, S.E. Asia, Sumatra

HABITAT Forest, grassy plains

SIZE Body: 18–21¼ ft (5.5–6.5 m) Tail: 4–5 ft (1.2–1.5 m)

Although an equally impressive animal, the Asian elephant has smaller ears than its African counterpart, a more humped back and only one fingerlike extension at the end of its mobile trunk. The female is smaller than the male and has only rudimentary tusks.

The main social unit is a herd led by an old female and including several females, their young and an old male, usually all related. Other males may live alone but near to a herd, and will sometimes feed or mate with members of the herd. The herd rests in the heat of the day, but spends much of the rest of the time feeding on grass, leaves, shoots, and fruit, all of which identified by its tail, which has a crescent-shaped, horizontal fluke. Its head is heavy, with a fleshy, partially divided snout. The male has two tusks formed from the incisor teeth, but these are usually barely visible under the fleshy lips. Its nostrils are placed on the upper surface of the muzzle, so the dugong can breathe, while remaining almost submerged. Seaweed and sea grass are its main food.

The dugong is a shy, solitary animal, and it leads a quiet, sedentary life, lying on the sea bed for much of the time and only rising to the surface every couple of minutes in order to breathe.

Little is known of the dugong's reproductive habits, but the gestation period is thought to be about a year. The single young is born in the water and is helped to the surface by its mother.

TRICHECHIDAE: MANATEE FAMILY

There are 3 species of manatee; 2 of which live in fresh water in West Africa and the Amazon, and the third in coastal waters of the tropical Atlantic Ocean.

American Manatee

Trichecus manatus **VU**

RANGE Atlantic Ocean: Florida to Guyana

HABITAT Coastal waters

SIZE Up to 9 ¾ ft (3 m)

The manatee has a heavier body than the dugong and is also distinguished by its oval, horizontal tail fluke. There are three nails in each of its flippers, which the manatee uses to gather food. It feeds at night, foraging by touch and smell. Its diet is quite varied, since it will eat any sort of vegetation and also often also takes in small invertebrate animals with the plants.

For much of the day, the manatee lies on the sea bed, rising every couple of minutes in order to breathe at the surface.

Manatees are social animals and live in family groups, which sometimes gather together in larger herds.

The gestation period is about a year. One young is born in water and is helped by its mother to the surface to breathe.

they search out and grasp with their trunks. Their hearing and sense of smell are excellent, and eyesight poor.

The male's heat period, called musth, may be accompanied by a secretion from a gland on the side of the head, and animals can become excited and unpredictable. The female usually gives birth to a single young after a gestation of about 21 months.

ORDER SIRENIA

Sirenians are the only completely aquatic herbivorous mammals. The 2 families – dugongs and manatees – contain 4 species. All have streamlined bodies and flipperlike forelimbs. The hind limbs have been lost in the formation of a tail.

DUGONGIDAE: DUGONG FAMILY

There is now only l species in this family, the other member, Steller's sea cow, having been exterminated in the 18th century by excessive hunting, only 25 years after its discovery.

Dugong *Dugong dugon* **VU**

RANGE Coast of E. Africa, Indian Ocean, Red Sea to N. Australia

HABITAT Coastal waters

SIZE Up to 9 ¾ ft (3 m)

The dugong is a large, but streamlined, animal,

GLOSSARY

Abdomen
The part of an animal's body that lies between the **thorax** and pelvis in vertebrates. In mammals, the abdomen is separated from the thorax by the diaphragm.

Adaptation
Part of the process of evolutionary change that animals undergo to occupy a **niche**. Changes can concern the structure, physiology, development or behavior of animals, and are driven by **natural selection**.

Adult
A fully developed and mature individual, capable of breeding.

Air sac
Non-respiratory air bags connected to the lungs of a bird.

Albino
An animal lacking coloring, or pigment, and therefore having pale or white skin or fur, and pink eyes. This characteristic is passed down in the **genes**.

Alimentary canal
The passage that extends from the mouth to the anus, for the digestion and absorption of food and elimination of waste matter.

Algae
Primitive marine and aquatic plants that lack a system of roots, stems, and leaves.

Amphibian
Cold-blooded animals belonging to the class Amphibia, such as frogs, which live on land but breed in water.

Anadromous
Fish, such as salmon and certain species of herring, which migrate from the sea to freshwater to spawn.

Anal fin
Fin that lies along the underside of the body, behind the anus in fishes. The anal fin works in conjunction with other fins for swimming and turning.

Alpine
Of the Alps in Europe; or any mountainous region having an altitude of over 4,500 ft (1,500m)

Anatomy
The study of the internal structure of plants and animals. Also the physical structure of an animal or plant, or any of its parts.

Antarctic
Pertaining to the south polar region.

Aquatic
Living mainly or wholly in water.

Arboreal
Living mainly in or among trees.

Archipelago
A large group of islands.

Arctic
Pertaining to the north polar region.

Asexual reproduction
Reproductive process that is not **sexual**; the parent organism splits into two or more organisms, or produces buds.

Avian
Pertaining to birds.

Baleen
Horny slats that hang vertically from the roof of a whale's mouth, with fringed inner edges for filtering food.

Barbel
A fleshy, thin, antenna-like protuberance found around the mouth of many species of fish

Basking
A form of temperature regulation whereby some animals, especially reptiles, expose themselves to sun to raise their body temperature.

Bill
The beak of a bird or the jaws of a fish.

Bioluminescence
The production of light by some organisms, such as the hatchetfish, by biochemical means.

Biome
A community of plants and animals occupying a large geographical area. For example, **rain forest**, **desert**, or **tundra**.

Bipedal
Walking on two legs. Some primates may travel bipedally for short distances; only humans exhibit habitual bipedalism.

Bipolar
Occurring in both polar regions.

Bird
A class of animals called Aves, consisting of feathered, warm-blooded **tetrapods** with forelimbs adapted for flying. Examples include eagles, ostriches, and parrots.

Bisexual
Pertaining to animals and plants that have both male and female reproductive organs. Also known as **hermaphrodite**.

Blubber
A layer of fatty insulating tissue found directly beneath the outer layer of skin (**epidermis**) in marine mammals.

Brackish
Water that is a mixture of seawater and freshwater. May be found in river estuaries where seawater enters the river mouth.

Brood
The eggs or offspring of a single female from one mating; any group of young animals being cared for by an adult.

Browser
A **herbivore** that feeds on the leaves and shoots of shrubs and trees, as opposed to grasses.

Buccal cavity
The cheek or mouth cavity leading to the pharanx, and (in vertebrates) the esophagus.

Calf
A young cow or bull, buffalo, seal or whale.

Camouflage
When an animal conceals itself by adopting the color and texture of its surroundings, either physically or by concealing itself in a suitable place.

Canine teeth
In **carnivorous** mammals, the two long and pointed teeth in the upper and lower jaws, behind the **incisors** that are used for seizing and holding prey. In Pinnipedia, a suborder that includes sea lions and walruses, they can take the form of tusks.

Canopy
In forests, an almost continuous layer of foliage at the level of the tree tops, produced by the intermingling of vegetation. The crowns of some trees may project above the canopy layer and are known as emergents.

Carapace
A skeletal shield of bone or chitin (tough fibrous material) covering the bodies of reptiles such as tortoises or terrapins.

Carcass
The dead or rotting flesh of an animal, which is a source of food for scavengers.

Carnassial teeth
An opposing pair of teeth adapted especially to shear with a scissor-like, cutting edge.

Carnivore
A flesh-eating animal (but not necessarily a member of the order Carnivora).

Cartilage
Strong elastic connective tissue between bones; also called gristle.

Cementum
Hard material coating the roots of teeth in mammals. In some **species** it is laid down in layers annually, and the number of layers can be used to help determine an animal's age.

Cell
The basic structural unit of all living organisms.

Chromosome
An assembly of **genes** (units of **DNA**), which determine hereditary characteristics.

Cladogram
A diagram used to show how groups of organisms have evolved from a common ancestor.

Class
A **taxonomic** rank superior to **order**, but subordinate to **phylum**.

Clutch
The number of eggs laid, and simultaneously incubated, by a female.

Cock
A male bird, crab, lobster or salmon.

Cold-blooded
An animal with no internal temperature mechanism, such as a **reptile** or an

amphibian, whose body temperature is determined by external temperatures.

Colony
A **population** of animals living and breeding together in one place.

Communal
Cooperative behavior between animals, such as can be found in the nest building of some birds.

Coniferous forest
Forest comprising largely evergreen conifers, such as pines, spruces, and firs. Usually found in northern latitudes.

Conservation
Preservation of the environment and natural resources.

Continental shelf
An area of relatively shallow water adjacent to a continental land mass and rarely deeper than 600 ft (200m).

Coral reef
An organic marine reef composed of solid coral and coral sand.

Courtship
Communication between individual animals of opposite sexes of a species to facilitate breeding.

Crepuscular
Mainly active during the twilight hours around dawn and dusk.

Crest
A prominent tuft of feathers on the heads of some species of bird.

Cue
A signal produced by an animal to elicit a response in another individual, for example, in **courtship**.

Deciduous forest
Temperate and tropical forest with moderate rainfall and marked seasons. Trees normally shed their leaves during cold or dry periods.

Dentition
The arrangement of the animal's teeth, which varies according to the species.

Desert
An area with low average rainfall, with sparse scrub, or grassland vegetation, or no vegetation at all.

Detritus
Dead organic or inorganic material.

Digit
A finger or a toe.

Dispersal
Movement of animals away from their home range as they reach maturity. Distinct from dispersion, where animals or food sites are distributed or scattered.

Display
Conspicuous behaviour to convey specific information to others, usually to other members of a species. May be visual or vocal, and used as a threat to **predators** or in **courtship**.

Distal
Farthest point away from center of the body, for example, the tip of an animal's tail.

DNA
Deoxyribonucleic acid, a long molecule resembling a chain made up of four kinds of link, the sequence of which codes hereditary information. **Genes** are units of DNA. The DNA molecule consists of two strands joined in a spiral, an arrangement known as a double helix.

Dormancy
A period of inactivity. For example, many bears are dormant for a period during winter. This is not true **hibernation** as the animal's pulse rate and body temperature do not drop significantly.

Dorsal
The upper surface or plane of an animal's body.

Dorsal fin
In fishes, the **fin** that lies along the spine on the upper side of the body. The dorsal fin works in conjunction with the other fins in swimming, turning and balancing.

Eardrum
A thin membrane in the middle ear which vibrates in response to airborne sounds.

Echolocation
A process used by Cetaceans (whales, dolphins), bats and some species of birds to detect distant or invisible objects (in darkness), by means of sound waves that are reflected back to the emitter from the object.

Eclipse plumage
Dull plumage of birds, which is superseded by more striking plumage in the breeding season.

Ecology
The study of plants and animals in relation to their natural environmental setting.

Ecosystem
A part of the environment in which both living and non-living elements exist and interact.

Eft
A lizard or newt.

Egg tooth
A specially modified tooth that a new-hatched reptile or bird uses to break free of the egg on hatching.

Elongate
Relatively long. For example, canine teeth are elongate compared to adjacent teeth.

Embryo
The developing egg until it hatches. Or the early stages of a developing mammal. Once the mammalian embryo begins to resemble an adult animal, it is known as a **fetus**.

Emigration
The departure of an animal, or animals, from its group or from its place of birth, often on reaching maturity. Also known as **dispersal**.

Enamel
A hard substance that forms the outer layer of a vertebrate tooth.

Environment
External surroundings; the physical, biological, and chemical influences that act on an individual organism.

Enzyme
An organic substance produced by living cells that catalyses biochemical changes.

Epidermis
The outermost layer of cells comprising the outer layer of skin of a mammal, or the outer tissue of stems or leaves in plants.

Equator
A theoretical line around the Earth's surface midway between the north and south poles. Equatorial regions are those areas located at, or lying close to, the equator.

Estrus
When female mammals are receptive to mating and are attracted to males. Also when ovulation occurs and mature eggs are released from the ovaries.

Estuary
The mouth of a river where the tide enters, the resulting body of water is a mixture of **freshwater** and seawater.

Eutherian
Pertaining to mammals whose **embryos** receive nourishment from the placenta.

Evolution
The act or process of gradual change where the characteristics of a **species** or **population** alter over many generations.

Excretion
The elimination of waste products from the body.

Extant
Living, still in existence, and therefore not **extinct**.

Extinct
According to available evidence, no longer in existence, having died out.

Family
A **taxonomic** rank superior to **genus**, but subordinate to **order**.

Fang
In carnivorous mammals, a **canine** tooth. In snakes, a modified tooth carrying poison.

Fauna
All of the animal life of a region, geological period, or special environment.

Feces
The remains of indigestible food excreted from an animal's bowels.

Feral
A wild or undomesticated animal, descended from domestic animals.

Fertilization
The process of union of two sex cells (**gametes**) to form a new animal. In mammals, reptiles, and birds, fertilization takes place within the female's body, whereas in most species of fish and amphibians, fertilization takes place externally.

Fetus
An **embryo** of a mammal in the later stages of development, when it shows the features of the fully developed animal.

Filter feeders
Animals, such as certain whale species, that obtain their food from straining or filtering water to sift out small organic particles.

Fin
A flat, projecting organ, used by fishes and other aquatic animals, such as whales and seals, to swim, turn, and balance in the water.

Fish
Streamlined **vertebrates** adapted to life in the water. Examples include hagfish, sharks, salmon, and coelacanth.

Fledgling
A young bird that has recently learned to fly.

Flora
The plant life of a particular region, geological period or special environment.

Fluke
In Cetaceans (whales, dolphins) and Dugongs, the flat, horizontal tail fins.

Forage
To search for food.

Fossil
The remains of dead organisms, or their imprint, which have been preserved in rocks. Fossils therefore reveal the history of life on earth in the fossil record. Palaeontology is the study of fossils and the fossil record.

Freshwater
Water that is not saline, as found in a river or lake.

Fusiform
Streamlined. Sometimes referred to as "torpedo-shaped." Cetaceans (whales, dolphins) are said to have fusiform-shaped bodies, aiding propulsion in water.

Gamete
A sex cell. When sexual **fertilization** takes place, the male sex cell or **sperm** fuses with the female sex cell or **ovum**.

Gelatinous
A substance having a jelly-like consistency.

Generalist
An animal that does not rely on specialized strategies for feeding or surviving, as distinct from a **specialist** animal that does.

Gene
A unit of **DNA** carrying hereditary information that is passed on from generation to generation. An assembly of genes make up a **chromosome**.

Genital
Pertaining to the genitalia, the reproductive organs.

Genus
A taxonomic rank superior to **species**, but subordinate to **family**.

Gestation
The period from conception to birth in mammals. Elephants have the longest gestation period of any animal, that is, 22 months.

Gills
Organs found in fish and other animals that are completely or mainly aquatic to obtain oxygen from the surrounding water. Consists of membranes through which exchange of oxygen and carbon dioxide takes place.

Grazers
Herbivorous animals that feed on grasses (if land-based) or other plant material, such as **algae** or plankton (if **aquatic**).

Gregarious
Sociable animals that often live in large groups, such as many species of **Old World** and **New World** monkey.

Guano
Phosphate deposits resulting from the accumulation of bird excrement or droppings.

Gut
Forming part of the **alimentary canal**, the gut is a hollow tube for the digestion and absorption of food, and for the elimination of waste material.

Habitat
The place or **environment** in which an animal or plant lives. Usually described in terms of the predominant vegetation of the area, and by its physical features and characteristics.

Harem group
A group of animals consisting of one dominant mature male and two or more breeding females. A common social arrangement among mammals.

Hen
A female bird.

Herbaceous
Pertaining to herbs; resembling leaves.

Herbivore
An animal that feeds mainly on plants, or parts of plants, for its source of energy.

Hermaphrodite
An animal which has both male and female sex organs, or which functions as both male and female at the same time. Some hermaphrodites alter their sex at different stages of their lives.

Herpetology
The scientific study of **reptiles** and **amphibians**.

Hibernation
A period of sleep-like inactivity for some mammals, reptiles, and amphibians, usually during winter. The animal reduces its normal physiological processes in order to minimize energy requirements.

Hierarchy
The pattern or structure of divisions within a social group or **population**, whereby some animals come to dominate others. Dominant individuals have control over the resources available in terms of access to food and mates.

Higher primate
The more advanced primates – monkeys, apes, and man – are also known as anthropoids.

Homing
The capability of an animal, or group of animals, to return to its original location following **migration**.

Hoof
The horny sheath that encases **digits** and bears the weight of certain **ungulate** mammals.

Hormone
A chemical substance produced by glands that regulates and controls many bodily functions, such as growth, digestion, and sexual development.

Host
The organism which a **parasite** organism lives on and receives food or shelter from.

Hybrid
The offspring resulting from crossbreeding two different species. Hybrids are often sterile;

the best known example is a mule, the result of crossbreeding a horse and a donkey.

Hyoid arch
One of the bony arches that supports the gills in primitive vertebrates.

Implantation
The process in which the early **embryo** becomes attached to the wall of the uterus in mammals, resulting in the development of the complex network of blood vessels linking the **embryo** to the mother's **placenta**.

Incisors
Chisel-shaped teeth in **carnivores**, used for cutting rather than tearing or grinding. In certain animals, such as rodents, the incisor teeth continue to grow throughout life as they are worn down by use.

Incubation
The period between the laying of eggs and their hatching. During incubation the eggs are kept warm by a parent.

Insectivore
An animal whose primary source of food is arthropods – insects and spiders. Not necessarily of the mammal order Insectivora.

Introduced
Species which are brought by man, either accidentally or deliberately, from regions where they occur naturally to other regions where they previously were not represented.

Intertidal zone
Intermediate area of shore that is exposed between high and low water marks.

Juvenile
The growth stage of development spanning the period between an infant and a full-grown **adult**.

Juvenile plumage
The plumage of a young bird, when it departs from the nest. Later replaced by **adult plumage**.

Keratin
A tough fibrous protein that produces an impervious outer layer in the **epidermis** of mammals, birds, amphibians, and reptiles. Thicker layers of keratin form the major part of hair, scales, feathers, nails, claws, and horns.

Kingdom
The second highest **taxonomic** category in the hierarchy of classification, one of which is Animalia – the animals.

Krill
Crustaceans that are an abundant source of food for marine mammals, particularly baleen whales.

Lactation
Discharge of milk from the mammary glands in mammals, occurring after the birth of young. Lactation is controlled by **hormones**.

Larynx
The upper part of the wind pipe which contains the vocal chords, used to produce vocal sounds.

Larva/Larvae
A pre-adult stage in species where the young of an animal has a completely different appearance and way of life from the adult. Amphibians and some fish have a larval stage.

Lek
A traditional "display ground," used year after year, where animals of one sex display themselves to members of the opposite sex in order to attract potential mates.

Lateral
On or toward the right or left side of the body.

Life cycle
The sequence of different stages in an animal's life. In **vertebrates**, the production of sex cells (**gametes**) is followed by fertilization and the development of an **embryo**, followed by birth or hatching, growth to adulthood, and repetition of the cycle.

Litter
A number of young produced by an animal at one time.

Longevity
A record or estimate of an animal's life span. May refer to the maximum recorded longevity or to the average life expectancy at birth.

Lower primate
A primitive primate known as a Prosimian.

Lung
An internal chamber, nearly always air-filled, used for the exchange of respiratory gases between the **environment** and the animal's body. The structure varies from a simple, unfolded chamber in some amphibians to the complex systems of tubes in mammals and birds.

Mammal
Vertebrate animals that are warm-blooded, breathe air using **lungs**, and give birth to live young. Mammals live in the air, land, and water. Examples include bats, monkeys, and dolphins.

Mammillae
Nipples or teats belonging to female mammals through which milk is passed to the young from the mother.

Mammary glands
The milk-producing organs in female mammals.

Mandible
The lower bone of the jaw, or the lower part of a bird's bill.

Mangrove forest
Tropical forests containing salt-tolerant trees and shrubs, located on the shores of **estuaries** and river deltas.

Marine
Living in the sea.

Marsupial
Unlike **eutherian** mammals, marsupial mammals such as kangaroos, wombats, and bandicoots have a very short gestation period, after which the immature young finish their development inside a pouch on the mother's belly.

Mating
Pairing of individuals for reproductive purposes.

Maturation
The attainment of sexual maturity, that is reaching reproductive age.

Membrane
Thin tissue covering or connecting organs and other bodily structures.

Metabolic rate
The speed at which chemical changes in the body occur.

Metabolism
The chemical changes in living cells by which energy is supplied for vital processes and other activities, for example, the production of protein from amino acids, and the extraction of energy from foods.

Metamorphosis
A transformation in the shape and structure (**morphology**) of an animal. For example, metamorphosis occurs when a tadpole is transformed into an adult frog.

Microplankton
Plankton so small they are not easily visible to the naked eye.

Migration
The seasonal movement of a population from one area to another – often over large distances – for the purpose of feeding or breeding.

Mimicry
A species development of a superficial similarity to another species or to natural objects in its environment, often for protective purposes.

Molar teeth
In mammals, cheek teeth used for crushing and chewing food. The biting surface is made up of a series of ridges and the teeth have several roots.

Monogamous
Having only one mate per breeding season.

Morphology
A branch of biology that deals with the structure and shape of animals and plants.

Moult
The shedding of fur, feathers, or skin. Reptiles shed their outer dead layers of skin when they grow; moulting in mammals and birds occurs seasonally.

Musk gland
A gland used for secreting musk, a strong smelling odor produced by animals such as badgers and musk deer. Such secretions usually occur during the breeding season.

Nasal plugs
Found in toothed whales, these are muscular flaps at the base of the nasal passage used to close the airway when diving. May be used to produce sounds.

Natal range
Home **range** into which an individual animal is born.

Natural Selection
The key evolutionary process whereby animals with the most appropriate **adaptations** are more successful at reproducing than others.

Nerve cell
Specialized cells which transmit information in the form of electrical signals. All types of animal behavior, from a blink of the eye to complicated body movements, are controlled by the action of the nerve cells.

New World
A term used to describe the western hemisphere, the Americas, and the animals from those regions, as distinct from the **Old World**.

Niche
Role of a **species** within its **community**, defined in terms of its lifestyle, that is, food, competitors, predators, and other resource requirements.

Nocturnal
Mainly active during the night.

Nomadic
Moving from place to place, not settled or resident in any particular area.

Nomenclature
A system used for naming and classifying animals and plants using **scientific names**.

Old World
A term used to describe the eastern hemisphere, Europe, Africa, Asia and Australasia and the animals from those regions, as distinct from the **New World**.

Olfactory
The sense of smell which relies on the receptors inside the nasal cavity.

Omnivore
An animal which feeds on both plant and animal material. The digestive system is specially adapted to cope with both sources of food.

Operculum
Any type of hard cover or flap used for protection of tissue, such as the flaps that protect fishes' **gills**.

Opportunistic
A type of feeding behavior. Many species of **carnivore** are opportunistic feeders, taking advantage of circumstances to exploit varied food resources.

Opposable
A finger or toe which can be used in conjunction with other **digits.**

Order
A **taxonomic** division superior to a **family**, but subordinate to a **class.**

Ornithology
The scientific study of birds.

Ovum
An egg or female sex cell (**gamete**). Develops into a new individual of the same **species** on **fertilization** by the male sex cell or **sperm.**

Oviduct
The tube between the ovaries and the uterus used to carry eggs. **Fertilization** and early development occur in the oviduct of mammals and birds.

Oviparous
Egg-laying animals. The young hatch outside the body of the female.

Ovoviviparous
An animal that produces eggs, but retains them inside the body until the release of the live young.

Pair-bond
Prolonged association between a mating pair of animals for breeding purposes. In some species, the association may last until the death of one partner.

Palaeontology
One of the earth sciences, a branch of geology which deals with the scientific study of **fossils** and the fossil record.

Palmate
Palm-shaped.

Pampas
Extensive grassland plain found in South America.

Parasite
A relationship between two organisms, whereby one, the parasite, obtains its food from the other, the **host.**

Passerine
In birds, where one toe is directed backward and the others are directed forward.

Patagium
A membrane found in bats and flying squirrels, situated along the sides of the body between the fore and hind limbs, that helps them glide through the air.

Pectoral fin
A pair of fins in fishes, situated immediately behind the head on either side of the body, which work in conjunction with other fins for swimming, turning, and balancing.

Pelvic fin
A pair of fins in fishes, situated in the pelvic region (on the underside of the body), which work in conjunction with the other fins for swimming, turning, and balancing.

Photophores
If fish, an organ which can produce **bioluminescent** light.

Phylogenetic
Pertaining to the **evolutionary** relationships within and between groups of animals.

Phylum
A **taxonomic** rank superior to a **class**, but subordinate to a **kingdom.**

Physiology
The scientific study of processes and metabolic functions of living organisms.

Pigment
The natural coloring of living tissue.

Placenta
The organ that develops inside the uterus, allowing the exchange of oxygen, food, and waste to and from the **fetus** in **eutherian** mammals during **gestation**. The placenta is discharged after birth.

Plankton
Tiny water-borne organisms, eaten by whales and some fishes.

Plastron
The lower section of the shell of tortoises and turtles, connected to the **carapace** by a bony bridge.

Plumage
The feather covering of birds.

Pod
Name for a family group of Cetaceans (whales and dolphins), which may remain together for life.

Polar
Pertaining to the north or south polar regions of the earth.

Polygamous
Mating of one male with several females or one female with several males.

Polygynous
Mating of one male with several females during the breeding season.

Polyandrous
Mating of one female with several males.

Population
A group of animals of the same **species** that live separately from other similar groups.

Pouch
Female **marsupial** mammals have a pouch on their abdomen in which the young complete their development, following a short **gestation** period.

Prairie
The grassland steppe of North America, treeless and flat.

Predator
Any animal which hunts for live prey to feed on. Predation is the killing of one **species** by another for food.

Prehensile
Capable of grasping or seizing, as in monkeys' or lizards' tails and the trunks of elephants.

Premolar teeth
The cheek teeth of mammals, in front of the **molars** and behind the **canine teeth**, which are normally preceded by milk teeth and are used for chewing and crushing food.

Primary forest
A mature forest that has lain undisturbed for a long period.

Primate
A member of the order of animals that includes lemurs, monkeys, apes, and humans. Primates have larger brains than other animals and their **digits** are adapted for grasping and holding.

Proboscis
A protruding organ used for sensing and food-gathering, such as an elephant's trunk.

Progeny
Offspring.

Protein
A long chain molecule made of amino acids, essential to all living organisms.

Protrusible
Capable of protruding, jutting out, as in the tongue of a lizard or other reptile.

Quadrumanous
An animal that uses both hands and feet for grasping or holding.

Quadruped
An animal that walks on four legs.

Rain forest
Tropical or subtropical forest that receives high levels of year-round rainfall and supports rich and diverse **flora** and **fauna.**

Race
A subgroup of a **species** in the hierarchy of classification of living things.

Range
Area in which an individual animal or a social group usually lives. The range may not be exclusive to the animal or group, and may overlap with the range of other animals or groups of animals. It typically contains regular areas for feeding and resting/sleeping.

Receptive
A female mammal that is ready to mate.

Regeneration
Having the capability to regrow an organ or limb after accidental loss.

Reingestion
The extraction of the maximum amount of energy from food by digesting it more than once. The animal brings up food from the stomach for further chewing.

Reproduction
The process by which living organisms produce other organisms similar to themselves by **sexual** or **asexual** means.

Reptile
Vertebrate animals that are **cold-blooded**, breathe air using lungs, and lay eggs. They need an external heat source to maintain their body temperature and are therefore found in the hotter regions of the Earth. Examples include lizards, snakes, and turtles.

Respiration
The system of breathing that involves the exchange of oxygen and carbon dioxide between an organism and its **environment.**

Retractile
Capable of being pulled back into the animal's body, for example, claws.

RNA
Ribonucleic acid, a long molecule that is used in several ways to carry out a cell's genetic instructions. RNA is chemically similar to **DNA**.

Rostrum
The upper jaw in Cetaceans or the forward projection of the snout in fish.

Rufous
Reddish-brown in color.

Ruminant
An animal, such as a camel or cow, with a complex stomach designed for chewing the cud, or regurgitating its food in order to chew it again.

Saddle
Distinctive markings on the back of whales and dolphins.

Salivary gland
A gland for the secretion of saliva that aids the digestive function.

Savanna
Grassland areas of the tropics and subtropics with few scattered trees and receiving seasonal rainfall. A transition zone from forest to open grassland.

Scales
Modified skin in the form of overlapping plates that serve as the outer protective covering in reptiles and fish.

Scavenger
An animal that feeds mainly on dead animal **carcasses**.

Scientific name
The precise Latin name of a **species** of animal, as distinct from its common name.

Scent mark
A place where chemical secretions from **scent glands** are left. Scent marks act as a form of communication between animals, often for breeding or territorial purposes.

Scent gland
Organs that secrete chemical "messages" to other animals.

School
A large number of fishes or Cetaceans (whales, dolphins) swimming together.

Scrub
A pattern of vegetation characterized by shrubs and low trees.

Sedentary
Animals that habitually remain in one place, or occupy a small range and do not migrate.

Sexual dimorphism
Differences between males and females of the same **species** in terms of size, color, and so on.

Sexual reproduction
The process by which living organisms produce new organisms similar to themselves by sexual means.

Siblings
Brothers and sisters, that is, animals who share one or both parents.

Simian
A monkey or ape, or having their characteristics; used colloquially to mean any of the **higher primates**.

Shoal
A large number of fishes swimming together.

Skeleton
The internal structure in an animal that provides support for the body and protects internal organs. In higher vertebrates, the skeleton consists of a system of bones.

Solitary
Animals which habitually live on their own, as distinct from social animals which live in family groups.

Sonar
Part of the facility of **echolocation** used by bats and some marine mammals to help them navigate.

Spatulate
Shaped like a spatula, that is, broad and rounded in shape.

Spawn
In **aquatic** animals, the act of producing and laying eggs.

Specialist
An animal that uses specialized strategies or techniques for feeding or surviving, as opposed to a **generalist**.

Species
A species is the basic **taxonomic** rank comprising a set of individuals having common attributes which can interbreed to produce fertile offspring. Related species are grouped together in a **genus**.

Sperm
The male sex cell (**gamete**), also known as spermatazoon (plural spermatazoa).

Spermatophores
A case enclosing the **sperm** in certain amphibians.

Sphagnum
Moss found in boggy areas in temperate regions, forming peat as it decays.

Steppe
Large areas of open grassland, known as **prairie** in North America; steppe lands receive low rainfall and may experience wide temperature variation.

Subfamily
A division of a **family**.

Suborder
A division of an **order**.

Subadult
Developmental stage between a **juvenile** and an **adult** animal.

Subspecies
A division of a **species**.

Swim bladder
A fish's gas-filled bladder that helps maintain buoyancy. Certain fish use them for breathing.

Taxonomy
The study of the classification of plants and animals. Animals that share common features are grouped together. The categories are: **species**, **genus**, **family**, **order**, **class**, **phylum**, **kingdom**; these can be divided further into subspecies, subfamily and so on.

Temperate
A climate that does not experience either hot or cold extremes.

Testis
The organ in which **sperm** are made in most mammals.

Tetrapod
Any **vertebrate** with four limbs.

Terrestrial
Living on the land.

Territory
An area defended from intruders by an individual or group of animals.

Thorax
In mammals, the chest or middle part of the body between the head and the **abdomen**.

Thermoregulation
The regulation and maintenance of body temperature in mammals.

Toxin
Any poisonous substance of animal or plant origin.

Trachea
The windpipe in air-breathing **vertebrates**, used to carry air from the throat to the bronchi.

Transluscent
Partially, but not completely transparent.

Tropical zone
Located between 15 and 23.5 degrees in the southern and northern hemispheres.

Tundra
A region of sparse vegetation and extremely low temperatures, where only lichens and mosses are able to grow.

Ultrasonic
Very high-frequency sound produced by some marine mammals, possibly as a form of communication.

Ungulates
Hoofed herbivorous mammals. Examples include horses, deer, cows, goats, and pigs.

Venom
A **toxic** secretion produced by some animals, used to kill their prey.

Vertebrate
Any animal with a backbone – mammals, birds, reptiles, amphibians, and fish. More than 40,000 species of vertebrates exist.

Vestigal
An organ which is no longer useful and is consequently diminished in size.

Viviparous
Giving birth to live young, as opposed to laying eggs.

Vocalization
The production of songs, calls and other vocal sounds by animals.

Warm-blooded
Animals that regulate body temperature independent of external temperature. Examples include mammals and birds.

Yolk sac
A sac containing the yolk of the egg, which contains food for the use of the **embryo**.

CLASSIFICATION

CLASS MAMMALIA: MAMMALS
Subclass Prototheria: Egg-laying Mammals

Order Monotremata: Monotremes
Family Tachyglossidae: Echidnas
Family Ornithorhynchidae: Platypus

Subclass Theria: Live-bearing Mammals
Infraclass Metatheria: Marsupials

Order Didelphimorpha
Family Didelphidae: Opossums

Order Paucituberculata
Family Caenolestidae: Shrew Opossums

Order Microbiotheria
Family Microbiotheriidae: Colocolo

Order Dasyuromorpha
Family Myrmecobiidae: Numbat
Family Dasyuridae: Marsupial Carnivores and Insectivores

Order Peramelemorpha
Family Peramelidae: Bandicoots and Bilbies
Family Peroryctidae: New Guinean Bandicoots

Order Notoryctemorpha
Family Notoryctidae: Marsupial Moles

Order Diprotodonta
Family Phascolarctidae: Koala
Family Vombatidae: Wombats
Family Phalangeridae: Phalangers
Family Potoroidae: Rat Kangaroos
Family Macropodidae: Kangaroos, Wallabies
Family Burramyidae: Pygmy Possums
Family Pseudocheiridae: Ring-tailed and Greater Gliding Possums
Family Petauridae: Striped and Lesser Gliding Possums
Family Tarsipedidae: Honey Possums
Family Acrobatidae: Pygmy Gliding Possum, Feather-tailed Possum

Infraclass Eutheria: Placental Mammals

Order Xenarthra: Edentates
Family Myrmecophagidae: Anteaters
Family Bradypodidae: Three-toed Sloths
Family Megalonychidae: Two-toed Sloths
Family Dasypodidae: Armadillos

Order Pholidota
Family Manidae: Pangolins

Order Lagomorpha
Family Ochotonidae: Pikas
Family Leporidae: Rabbits

Order Rodentia
Family Sciuridae: Squirrels
Family Geomyidae: Pocket Gophers
Family Heteromyidae: Pocket mice
Family Aplodontidae: Mountain Beaver
Family Castoridae: Beavers
Family Anomaluridae: Scaly-Tailed Squirrels
Family Pedetidae: Spring Hare
Family Muridae:
    Subfamily Sigmodontinae: New World Rats and Mice
    Subfamily Cricetinae: Hamsters
    Subfamily Calomyscinae: Mouse-like Hamster
    Subfamily Mystromyscinae: White-tailed Rat
    Subfamily Spalacinae: Blind Mole-rats
    Subfamily Myospalacinae: Eastern Asiatic Mole-rats
    Subfamily Rhizomyinae: Mole- and Bamboo Rats
    Subfamily Lophiomyinae: Crested Rats
    Subfamily Platacanthomyinae: Spiny Dormice
    Subfamily Nesomyinae: Madagascan Rats
    Subfamily Otomyinae: African Swamp Rats
    Subfamily Arvicolinae: Voles and Lemmings
    Subfamily Gerbillinae: Gerbils
    Subfamily Petromyscinae: Rock Mice, Swamp Mouse
    Subfamily Dendromurinae: African Climbing Mice
    Subfamily: Cricetomyinae: African Pouched Rats
    Subfamily Murinae: Old World Rats and Mice
Family Dipodidae: Jerboas and Jumping Mice
Family Myoxidae: Dormice
Family Ctenodactylidae: Gundis
Family Hystricidae: Old World Porcupines
Family Erethizontidae: New World Porcupines
Family Caviidae: Guinea Pigs
Family Hydrochaeridae: Capybara
Family Dinomyidae: Pacarana
Family Dasyproctidae: Agoutis
Family Agoutidae: Pacas
Family Chinchillidae: Chinchillas and Viscachas
Family Capromyidae: Hutias
Family Myocastoridae: Coypu
Family Octodontidae: Octodonts
Family Ctenomyidae: Tuco-tucos
Family Abrocomidae: Chinchilla-rats
Family Echimyidae: Spiny Rats
Family Thryonomyidae: Cane Rats
Family Petromuridae: Dassie Rat
Family Bathyergidae: African Mole-Rats

Order Macroscelidea
Family Macroscelididae: Elephant Shrews

Order Insectivora: Insectivores
Family Solenodontidae: Solenodons
Family Tenrecidae: Tenrecs
Family Chysochloridae: Golden Moles
Family Erinaceidae: Hedgehogs, Moonrats
Family Soricidae: Shrews
Family Talpidae: Moles, Desmans

Order Scandentia
Family Tupaiidae: Tree Shrews

Order Primates: Primates
Family Cheirogaleidae: Mouse Lemurs, Dwarf Lemurs
Family Lemuridae: Lemurs
Family Megaladapidae: Sportive Lemurs
Family Indridae: Indri, Sifakas, Avahi
Family Daubentoniidae: Aye-aye
Family Loridae: Lorises, Pottos
Family Galagonidae: Galagos
Family Tarsiidae: Tarsiers
Family Callitrichidae: Marmosets and Tamarins
Family Cebidae: New World Monkeys
Family Cercopithecidae: Old World Monkeys
Family Hylobatidae: Gibbons
Family Hominidae: Apes and Humans

Order Dermoptera
Family Cynocephalidae: Flying Lemurs or Colugos

Order Chiroptera: Bats
Family Pteropodidae: Fruit Bats
Family Rhinopomatidae: Mouse-tailed Bats
Family Emballonuridae: Sheath-tailed Bats
Family Craseonycteridae: Hog-nosed Bat
Family Nycteridae: Slit-faced Bats
Family Megadermatidae: False Vampire Bats
Family Rhinolophidae: Horseshoe Bats
Family Noctilionidae: Fisherman Bats
Family Mormoopidae: Moustached Bats
Family Molossidae: Free-tailed Bats
Family Phyllostomidae: New World Leaf-nosed Bats
Family Vespertilionidae: Evening Bats
Family Natalidae: Funnel-eared Bats
Family Furipteridae: Smoky Bats
Family Thyropteridae: Disc-winged Bats
Family Myzopodidae: Old World Sucker-footed Bat
Family Mystacinidae: New Zealand Short-tailed Bats

Order Carnivora: Carnivores
Family Canidae: Dogs, Foxes
Family Ursidae: Bears, Pandas
Family Procyonidae: Raccoons
Family Mustelidae: Mustelids
Family Viverridae: Civets
Family Herpestidae: Mongooses
Family Hyaenidae: Hyenas
Family Felidae: Cats

Family Otariidae: Sea Lions, Fur Seals
Family Odobenidae: Walrus
Family Phocidae: True Seals

Order Tubulidentata
Family Orycteropodidae: Aardvark

Order Artiodactyla: Even-toed Ungulates
Family Suidae: Pigs
Family Tayassuidae: Peccaries
Family Hippopotamidae: Hippopotamuses
Family Camelidae: Camels
Family Tragulidae: Mouse Deer
Family Moschidae: Musk Deer
Family Cervidae: Deer
Family Giraffidae: Giraffes
Family Antilocapridae: Pronghorn
Family Bovidae: Bovids

Order Cetacea: Whales
Family Platanistidae: River Dolphins
Family Phocoenidae: Porpoises
Family Delphinidae: Dolphins
Family Monodontidae: Narwhal, White Whale
Family Physeteridae: Sperm Whales
Family Ziphiidae: Beaked Whales
Family Eschrichtiidae: Grey Whale
Family Balaenopteridae: Rorquals
Family Balaenidae: Right Whales

Order Perissodactyla: Odd-toed Ungulates
Family Equidae: Horses
Family Tapiridae: Tapirs
Family Rhinocerotidae: Rhinoceroses

Order Hyracoidea
Family Hyracoidea: Hyraxes

Order Proboscidea
Family Elephantidae: Elephants

Order Sirenia: Sea Cows
Family Dugongidae: Dugong
Family Trichechidae: Manatees

CLASS AVES: BIRDS
Order Struthioniformes: Ratites
Family Struthionidae: Ostrich
Family Rheidae: Rheas
Family Casuariidae: Cassowaries, Emu
Family Apterygidae: Kiwis

Order Tinamiformes: Tinamous
Family Tinamidae: Tinamous

Order Craciformes: Curassows, Guans, Megapodes
Family Cracidae: Curassows, Guans, Chachalacas

Subfamily Fringillinae: Chaffinches, cardueline finches, Hawaiian honeycreepers
Subfamily Emberizinae: Buntings, wood warblers, tanagers, cardinals, icterids

CLASS REPTILIA: REPTILES
Order Chelonia: Turtles and Tortoises
Family Emydidae: Emydid Turtles
Family Testudinae: Tortoises
Family Trionychidae: Softshell Turtles
Family Carettochylidae: Plateless River Turtle
Family Dermatemydidae: Central American River Turtle
Family Kinosternidae: American Mud and Musk Turtles
Family Cheloniidae: Marine Turtles
Family Dermochelyidae: Leatherback Turtle
Family Chelydridae: Snapping Turtles
Family Pelomedusidae: Greaved Turtles
Family Chelidae: Matamatas

Order Sphenodontia
Family Sphenodontidae: Tuataras

Order Squamata: Lizards and Snakes

Lizards
Family Iguanidae: Iguanas
Family Agamidae: Agamid Lizards
Family Chamaeleonidae: Chameleons
Family Gekkonidae: Geckos
Family Pygopodidae: Scaly-footed Lizards
Family Dibamidae: Old World Burrowing Lizards
Family Gymnophthalmidae: Microteiid Lizards
Family Teiidae: Teiid Lizards
Family Lacertidae: Lacertid Lizards
Family Xantusiidae: Night Lizards
Family Scincidae: Skinks
Family Cordylidae: Girdled and Plated Lizards
Family Xenosauridae: Crocodile Lizards
Family Anguidae: Slow Worms and Alligator Lizards
Family Varanidae: Monitors
Family Helodermatidae: Gila Monsters

Amphisbaenians (Worm Lizards)
Family Bipedidae: Bipeds
Family Trogonophiidae: Trogonophiids
Family Amphisbaenidae: Amphisbaenids

Snakes
Family Leptotyphlopidae: Thread Snakes
Family Typhlopidae: Blind Snakes
Family Anomolepididae: Dawn Blind Snakes
Family Uropeltidae
Family Aniliidae: Pipe Snakes
Family Xenopeltidae: Sunbeam Snake
Family Loxocemidae: Loxocemid Snake
Family Boidae: Boas and Pythons
Family Boyleriidae: Round Island Snakes

Family Tropidophiidae: Neotropical Ground Boas
Family Acrochordidae: Wart Snakes
Family Atractaspidae: Burrowing Asps
Family Colubridae: Colubrid Snakes
Family Elapidae: Cobras and Sea Snakes
Family Viperidae: Vipers and Pit Vipers

Order Crocodilia: Crocodiles, Alligators and Gavial
Family Crocodylidae: Crocodiles
Family Alligatoridae: Alligators
Family Gavialidae: Gavial

CLASS AMPHIBIA: AMPHIBIANS
Order Anura: Frogs and Toads
Family Ascaphidae: Tailed Frogs
Family Leiopelmatidae: New Zealand Frogs
Family Discoglossidae: Discoglossid Frogs
Family Pipidae: Pipid Frogs
Family Rhinophrynidae: Mexican Burrowing Frog
Family Pelodytidae: Parsley Frogs
Family Pelobatidae: Spadefoot Toads
Family Centrolenidae: Glass Frogs
Family Heleophrynidae: Ghost Frogs
Family Bufonidae: Bufonid Toads
Family Brachycephalidae: Gold Frogs
Family Hylidae: Treefrogs
Family Pseudidae: Pseudid Frogs
Family Rhinodermatidae: Mouth-brooding Frogs
Family Leptodactylidae: Leptodactylid Frogs
Family Myobatrachidae: Myobatrachid Frogs
Family Sooglossidae: Sooglossid Frogs
Family Dendrobatidae: Poison-dart Frogs
Family Hyperoliidae: Reed Frogs
Family Microhylidae: Narrow-mouthed Frogs
Family Ranidae: True Frogs
Family Rhacophoridae: Rhacophorid Treefrogs

Order Caudata: Salamanders and Newts
Family Sirenidae: Sirens
Family Amphiumidae: Congo Eels
Family Plethodontidae: Lungless Salamanders
Family Rhyacotritonidae: Rhyacotritonid Salamanders
Family Proteidae: Olms and Mudpuppies
Family Salamandridae: Newts and Salamanders
Family Ambyostomatidae: Mole Salamanders
Family Dicamptodontidae: Dicamptodontid Salamanders
Family Cryptobranchidae: Giant Salamanders
Family Hynobiidae: Asiatic Land Salamanders

Order Gymnophonia: Caecilians
Family Rhinatrematidae: Rhinatrematid Caecilians
Family Ichthyophidae: Ichthyophid Caecilians
Family Uraeotyphlidae: Uraeotyphlid Caecilians
Family Scolecomorphidae: Scolecomorphid Caecilians
Family Caeciliaidae: Caeciliaid Caecilians
Family Typhlonectidae: Typhlonectid Caecilians

FISH
Class Myxini
Order Myxiniformes: Hagfishes

Class Cephalaspidomorphi
Order Petromyzontiformes: Lampreys

Class Chondrichthyes: Cartilaginous Fish
Order Heterodontiformes: Bullhead, Horn Sharks
Order Lamniformes: Sand Tigers, Goblin Sharks, Megamouth
Sharks
Order Carchariniformes: Cat Sharks, Hound Sharks, Requiem
Sharks
Order Orectolobiformes: Wobbegons, Nurse Sharks, Whale
Sharks
Order Squatiniformes: Angel Sharks
Order Hexanchiformes: Frilled Sharks, Cow Sharks
Order Squaliformes: Bramble Sharks, Sleeper Sharks, Dogfish
Sharks
Order Pristiphoriformes: Saw Sharks
Order Rajiformes: Rays, Skates, Sawfishes
Order Chimaeriformes: Chimaeras

Class Osteichthyes: Bony Fish
Subclass Actinopterygii: Ray-finned Fishes
Order Polypteriformes: Bichirs
Order Acipenseriformes: Sturgeons, Paddlefishes
Order Lepisosteiformes: Gars
Order Amiiformes: Bowfin
Order Osteoglossiformes: Bonytongues, Butterflyfish, Mooneyes
Order Elopiformes: Tarpons, Tenpounders
Order Albuliformes: Bonefishes, Halosaurs, Spiny Eels
Order Anguilliformes: Freshwater Eels, Moray Eels, Conger Eels
Order Saccopharyngiformes: Bobtail Snipe Eels, Swallowers,
Gulpers
Order Clupeiformes: Herrings, Anchovies
Order Gonorynchiformes: Milkfish, Beaked Sandfishes, Snake
Mudhead
Order Cypriniformes: Carps, Minnows, Loaches
Order Characiformes: Characins, Trahiras, Headstanders
Order Siluriformes: Catfishes
Order Gymnotiformes: Knifefishes, Electric Eel
Order Esociformes: Pikes, Mudminnows
Order Osmeriformes: Smelts, Slickheads, Noodlefishes
Order Salmoniformes: Salmon, Trout, Chars
Order Stomiiformes: Bristlemouths, Marine Hatchetfishes,
Lightfishes
Order Atelopodiiformes: Jellynose Fishes
Order Aulopiformes: Telescope fishes, Greeneyes, Barracudinas
Order Myctophiformes: Lanternfishes
Order Percopsiformes: Trout-perches, Cavefishes
Order Ophidiiformes: Carapids, Cuskeels, Brotulas
Order Gadiformes: Cods, Hakes
Order Batrachoidiformes: Toadfishes
Order Lophiiformes: Anglerfishes
Order Beloniformes: Flying fishes, Needlefishes, Halfbeaks
Order Cyprinodontiformes: Killifishes, Rivulines, Splitfins,

Pupfishes
Order Atheriniformes: Rainbow Fishes, Blueeyes, Silversides
Order Lampridiformes: Crestfishes, Oarfishes, Ribbonfishes
Order Stephanoberyciformes: Whalefishes, Gibberfishes
Order Beryciformes: Beardfishes, Lanterneyes, Squirrelfishes
Order Zeiformes: Dories, Oreos
Order Gasterosteiformes: Sticklebacks, Sand Eels, Tubesnouts
Order Synbranchiformes: Swamp Eels, Spiny Eels
Order Dactylopteriformes: Flying Gurnards
Order Scorpaeniformes: Scorpionfishes, Velvetfishes, Sculpins
Order Perciformes: Perchlike Fishes
Suborder Percoidei: Percoid Fishes
Suborder Elassomatoidei: Pygmy Sunfishes
Suborder Labroidei: Cichlids, Damselfishes, Wrasses,
Parrotfish
Suborder Zoarcoidei: Eelpouts, Wrymouths, Gunnels,
Wolffishes
Suborder Notothenioidei: Icefishes
Suborder Trachinoidei: Sand Lances, Weeverfishes, Stargazers
Suborder Blennioidei: Blennies
Suborder Icosteodei: Ragfish
Suborder Kurtoidei: Nurseryfishes
Suborder Acanthuroidei: Spadefishes, Scats, Rabbitfishes,
Surgeonfishes
Suborder Mugiloidei: Mullets
Suborder Scombrolabracoidei: Scombrolabracoid Fishes
Suborder Scombroidei: Barracudas, Mackerel, Tunas, Marlin
Suborder Stromateoidei: Medusafishes, Squaretails,
Butterfishes
Suborder Anabantoidei: Gouramis
Suborder Channoidei: Snakeheads
Order Pleuronectiformes: Flounders, Soles
Order Tetraodontiformes: Puffers, Triggerfishes, Porcupinefishes

Subclass Sarcopterygii: Lobe-finned Fishes
Order Ceratodontiformes: Australian Lungfishes
Order Lepidosireniformes: African and South American
Lungfishes
Order Coelacanthiformes: Coelacanth

INDEX

A

Aardvark 1:154
Aardwolf 1:140
Abramis brama 3:506
Abrocoma bennetti 1:69
Abudefduf saxatilis 3:561
Acanthisitta chloris 2:300
Acanthiza chrysorrhoa 2:320
Acanthocybium solanderi 3:568
Acanthodactylus boskianus 3:425
Acanthopthalmus kuhlii 3:509
Acanthurus coeruleus 3:566
Accentor, hedge 2:375
Accipiter cooperii 2:280
  gentilis 2:280
Acinonyx jubatus 1:145
Acipenser sturio 3:497
Acipenseriformes 3:496
Acontias sp. 3:426
Acris crepitans 3:466
Acrobates pygmaeus 1:27
Acrocephalus caffer 2:363
Acrochordus javanicus 3:441
Adalah 3:571
Addax 1:174
Addax nasomaculatus 1:174
Adder, puff 3:451
  saw-scaled 3:451
Adioryx xantherythrus 3:538
Aegithalos caudatus 2:355
Aegithina tiphia 2:336
Aegotheles cristatus 2:252
Aeoliscus strigatus 3:541
Aepyceros melampus 1:178
Aepyprymnus rufescens 1:31
Aeronautes saxatilis 2:244
Aethia cristatella 2:275
Aethopyga siparaja 2:372
African and South American
  lungfish order 3:581
African barbet family 2:223
African warbler family 2:361
Afrixales brachycnemis 3:469
Afropavo congensis 2:211
Agama agama 3:414
Agama, collared 3:414
Agamid lizard family 3:414
Agamid, Arabian toad-headed 3:415
Agamodon anguliceps 3:437
Agapornis roseicollis 2:240
Agile Mangabey 1:93
Agkistrodon halys 3:453
Agkistrodon piscivorus 3:453
Aglaiocercus kingi 2:247
Agonus acipenserinus 3:545
Agouti family 1:67
Agouti paca 1:67
Agriornis livida 2:306
Ailuropoda melanoleuca 1:126
Ailurus fulgens 1:126
Aix galericulata 2:217
Akepa 2:384
Akiapolaau 2:384
Akodon reinhardti 1:49
Alaemon alaudipes 2:371
Alauda arvensis 2:371
Albatross, light-mantled
  sooty 2:298
  wandering 2:298
Albula vulpes 3:499
Albuliformes 3:499
Alca torda 2:275
Alcedo atthis 2:232
Alcelaphus buselaphus 1:175
Alces alces 1:162
Alcippe poioicephala 2:366
Alectoris rufa 2:209
Alethe castanea 2:345
Alethe, firecrested 2:345
Alewife 3:502
Allactaga major 1:63
Alle alle 2:275
Allen's swamp monkey 1:97

Allenopithecus nigroviridis 1:97
Alligator mississipiensis 3:454
Alligator snapping turtle 3:408
Alligator, American 3:454
Alopex lagopus 1:121
Alophoixus flaveolus 2:359
Alopias vulpinus 3:489
Alosa fillax 3:502
  pseudoharengus 3:502
Alouatta caraya 1:90
  seniculus 1:90
Aluterus scriptus 3:577
Alytes obstetricans 3:454
Amandava amandava 3:380
Amazon, yellow crowned 2:243
Amazona ochrocephala 2:243
Amberjack, greater 3:551
Ambloplites rupestris 3:548
Amblyopsis spelaea 3:523
Amblyornis macgregoriae 2:316
Amblyrhynchus cristatus 3:412
Amblysomus hottentotus 1:74
Ambystoma maculatum 3:478
  mexicanum 3:479
  opacum 3:478
  tigrinum 3:479
Ameiva ameiva 3:423
American anteater family 1:32
American cuckoo family 2:236
American spiny rat family 1:70
Amia calva 3:497
Amiiformes 3:497
Ammodorcas clarkei 1:179
Ammodytes tobianus 3:564
Ammomanes deserti 2:370
Ammotragus lervia 1:183
Amphibolurus barbatus 3:415
Amphiprion percula 3:561
Amphisbaena alba 3:437
Amphisbaenid family 3:436
Amphistichus argenteus 3:561
Amphiuma means 3:474
Amytornis goyderi 2:317
Anabas testudineus 3:570
Anableps anableps 3:533
Anaconda 3:441
Anarhichas lupus 3:564
Anarhynchus frontalis 2:271
Anas clypeata 2:216
  platyrhynchos 2:216
Anastomus oscitans 2:293
Anathana elliotti 1:81
Anchovy, European 3:503
Andigena laminirostris 2:225
Anemonefish, clown 3:561
Angel shark order 3:492
Angelfish,
  imperial 3:560
  queen 3:558
Angler fish order 3:528
Anguilla anguilla 3:500
Anguilliformes 3:500
Anguis fragilis 3:433
Angwantibo 1:84
Anhinga 2:286
Anhinga anhinga 2:286
Ani, smooth-billed 2:237
Anilius scytale 3:439
Anis and guira cuckoo
  family 2:237
Anisotremus surinamensis 3:553
Anniella pulchra 3:433
Anoa, lowland 1:169
Anole, green 3:411
Anolis carolinensis 3:411
Anomalepis sp. 3:438
Anomalops kaptoptron 3:538
Anomalurus beecrofti 1:47
Anoplopoma fimbria 3:544
Anous stolidus 2:273
Anser anser 2:215
Anseranas semipalmata 2:214
Anseriformes order 2:214
Antbird, ocellated 2:310

  white-cheeked 2:310
Anteater, giant 1:32
Antechinus stuartii 1:22
Antechinus, brown 1:22
Antelope, beira 1:176
  four-horned 1:167
  roan 1:173
  royal 1:177
Antennarius multiocellatus 3:529
Anthops ornatus 1:111
Anthoscopus parvulus 2:354
Anthreptes singalensis 2:372
Anthus pratensis 2:377
  spinoletta 2:377
Antidorcas marsupialis 1:178
Antilocapra americana 1:165
Antilope cervicapra 1:178
Antpitta, chestnut-crowned 2:311
Antshrike, barred 2:311
  great 2:311
Antwren, streaked 2:310
Anura order 3:460
Aonyx capensis 1:133
Aotus trivirgatus 1: 88
Apalis flavida 2:361
Apalis, yellow-breasted 2:361
Ape family 1:102
Ape, barbary 1:92
Apeltes quadracus 3:540
Aphanius dispar 3:532
Aphyosemion australe 3:533
Aplodinotus grunniens 3:557
Aplodontia 1:46
Aplodontia rufa 1:46
Aplonis metallica 2:349
Apodemus sylvaticus 1:60
Apodiformes order 2:244
Apostlebird 2:324
Aprasia striolata 3:421
Aptenodytes forsteri 2:295
Apterygidae 2:205
Apteryx australis 2:205
Apus apus 2:245
Aquila chrysaetos 2:281
Ara macao 2:242
Aracari, curl-crested 2:225
Arachnothera robusta 2:372
Arapaima gigas 3:498
Aratinga solstitialis 2:242
Archerfish 3:557
Archilochus colubris 2:246
Archosargus probatocephalus 3:554
Arctictis binturong 2:136
Arctocebus calabarensis 1:84
Arctocephalus australis 1:148
Arctonyx collaris 1:131
Ardea cinerea 2:288
Aremus guarauna 2:260
Arenaria interpres 2:267
Argyropelecus aculeatus 3:521
Argyrosomus regius 3:557
Arius felis 3:515
Armadillo lizard 3:431
Armadillo, giant 1:34
  nine-banded 1:34
  pink fairy 1:34
Arripis trutta 3:559
Artamus leucorhynchus 2:332
Artamus superciliosus 2:332
Arthroleptis wahlbergi 3:473
Artibeus jamaicensis 1:115
Artiodactyla order 1:154
Aruana 3:498
Arundinicola leucocephala 2:303
Arvicanthis abyssinicus 1:60
Arvicola terrestris 1:55
Asellia tridens 1:111
Asian barbet family 2:223
Asiatic frogmouth family 2:252
Asiatic land salamander family 3:481
Asio otus 2:250
Asity family 2:301
Asp, bibron's burrowing 3:442
Ass, African 1:194

Asiatic wild 1:195
Astrapia mayeri 2:329
Astrapia, ribbon-tailed 2:329
Astrapogon stellatus 3:549
Astroscopus guttatus 3:565
Astyanax mexicanus 3:511
Atbene noctua 2:251
Ateles paniscus 1:90
Atelopus boulengeri 3:464
  japonicus 3:537
Atherina presbyter 3:535
Atheriniformes order 3:534
Atherinomorus stipes 3:534
Atherurus macrourus 1:64
Atilax paludinosus 1:138
Atlapetes albinucha 2:386
Atractaspis bibroni 3:442
Atrichornis clamosus 2:317
Auk, little 2:275
Auklet, crested 2:275
Aulacorhynchus prasinus 2:224
Aulopiformes order 3:522
Aulorhynchus flavidus 3:540
Auriparus flaviceps 2:354
Australasian robin family 2:321
Australian frogmouth family 2:252
Australian lungfish 3:580
Australian treecreeper family 2:315
Avadavat, red 2:380
Avahi laniger 1:83
Avocet, pied 2:270
Axolotl 3:479
Aye-aye daubentonia 1:83
Aye-aye family 1:83
Aythya marila 2:217

B

Babbler, blackcap mountain 2:368
  brown 2:367
Babirusa babyrousa 1:155
Baboon, chacma 1:94
  hamadryas 1:94
  olive 1:94
Babyrussa 1:155
Badger, American 1:131
  Chinese ferret 1:131
  Eurasian 1:130
  hog 1:131
  stink 1:131
Bagre marinus 3:515
Bagrus docmac 3:512
Baiji 1:184
Baillonius bailloni 2:224
Balaena mysticetus 1:193
Balaeniceps rex 2:291
Balaenoptera acutorostrata 1:192
  borealis 1:192
  musculus 1:193
Balearica pavonina 2:259
Balistes carolinensis 3:576
  vetula 3:576
Balistoides conspicillum 3:576
Ballyhoo 3:530
Bananaquit 2:392
Bandicoot family 1:24
Bandicoot, brown 1:24
  eastern barred 1:24
  rabbit 1:25
Bandicota indica 1:61
Bandy-bandy 3:449
Banteng 1:168
Barb, tiger 3:505
Barbastella barbastellus 1:117
Barbastelle 1:117
Barbel 3:505
Barber-eel 3:516
Barbet, coppersmith 2:223
  crimson-breasted 2:223
  double-toothed 2:223
Barbus barbus 3:505

tetrazona 3:505
tor 3:505
Barn owl family 2:248
Barracuda, great 3:567
Basiliscus plumifrons 3:412
Basileuterus culcivorus 2:393
Bass, giant sea 3:547
largemouth 3:548
rock 3:548
striped 3:546
Bassaricyon gabbii 1:127
Bat, Australian false vampire 1:109
American false vampire 1:114
big brown 1:117
common long-eared 1:116
Cuban flower 1:115
Egyptian free-tailed 1:113
Egyptian rousette 1:104
Egyptian slit-faced 1:108
fisherman 1:112
fish-eating 1:116
flower-faced 1:111
greater false vampire 1:108
greater fruit 1:104
greater horseshoe 1:110
greater mouse-tailed 1:106
hammerheaded 1:104
harpy fruit 1:105
heart-nosed 1:109
hog-nosed 1:108
Honduran disc-winged 1:119
Jamaican fruit-eating 1:115
large Malay leaf-nosed 1:111
leaf-chinned 1:112
lesser horseshoe 1:110
little big-eared 1:115
little brown 1:116
long-tongued 1:114
long-tongued fruit 1:105
mastiff 1:113
Mexican funnel-eared 1:118
New Zealand short-tailed 1:119
Old World sheath-tailed 1:107
painted 1:117
Persian trident 1:111
Philippine horseshoe 1:110
pipistrelle common 1:117
proboscis 1:106
Queensland blossom 1:105
red 1:117
short-tailed leaf-nosed 1:113
smoky 1:118
spear-nosed 1:114
sucker-footed 1:119
tent-building 1:114
tomb 1:107
trident leaf-nosed 1:111
tube-nosed fruit 1:105
two-lined 1:107
vampire 1:115
velvety free-tailed 1:113
white 1:107
Wroughton's free-tailed 1:113
yellow-winged 1:109
yellow-shouldered 1:115
Batagur 3:401
Batagur baska 3:401
Bateleur 2:278
Batfish 3:566
Batfish, shortnose 3:529
Bathyergus suillus 1:71
Batis minor 2:338
Batis, blackheaded 2:338
Batrachoidiformes 3:528
Batrachoseps attenuatus 3:477
Batrachostomus moniliger 2:252
Bdeogale crassicauda 1:138
Beaked whale family 1:190
Beamys hindei 1:59
Bear family 1:124
Bear, American black 1:125
Asiatic black 1:125
big brown 1:124
grizzly 1:124
polar 1:125
spectacled 1:124
sun 1:125
Beardfish, stout 3:539
Beaugregory 3:561

Beaver family 1:46
Beaver, American 1:46
Eurasian 1:47
mountain 1:46
Bee-eater family 2:231
Bee-eater, European 2:231
Bellbird, bearded 2:308
Belone belone 3:531
Belonesox belizanus 3:534
Beloniformes order 3:530
Belonion apodon 3:531
Beluga 3:496
Berardius bairdi 1:191
Berlepschia rikeri 2:313
Berrypecker and longbill family 2:375
Berrypecker, black 2:375
Beryciformes 3:537
Betta splendens 3:570
Bichir order 3:496
Bighorn, American 1:183
Binturong 1:136
Biped family 3:437
Bipes biporus 3:437
Bird-of-Paradise, blue 2:328
king 2:328
king of Saxony's 2:328
Bison bison 1:170
bonasus 1:170
Bison, American 1:169
European 1:170
Bitis arietans 3:451
Bitterling 3:506
Bittern, American 2:288
Blackbird, Eurasian 2:343
Blackbuck 1:178
Blackcap 2:369
bush 2:368
Blanus cinereus 3:437
Blarina brevicauda 1:76
Bleda syndactyla 2:360
Blennioidei 3:565
Blenny, redlip 3:565
Blind snake family 3:438
Bluebird, Asian fairy 2:321
eastern 2:344
Bluefish 3:550
Boa caninus 3:440
Boa, constrictor 3:440
emerald tree 3:440
rubber 3:440
Boar, wild 1:155
Boarfish 3:539
Boat-bill, yellow-breasted 2:335
Boat-billed heron 2:289
Bobcat 1:144
Bobolink 2:395
Bobwhite, northern 2:213
Boiga dendrophila 3:447
Bombina orientalis 3:461
Bombycilla garrulus 2:341
Bonefish 3:499
Bongo 1:167
Bonobo 1:103
Bontebok 1:175
Booby, brown 2:285
Boomslang 3:447
Bos frontalis 1:168
grunniens 1:169
javanicus 1:168
Boselaphus tragocamelus 1:167
Botaurus lentiginosus 2:288
Bothrops atrox 3:452
Bothus lunatus 3:572
Boulengerella lucius 3:511
Boutu 1:184
Bovid family 1:166
Bowerbird family 2:316
Bowerbird, MacGregor's 2:316
satin 2:317
Bowfin order 3:497
Boxfish, blue-spotted 3:578
Brachylagus idahoensis 1:39
Brachycephalus ephippium 3:465
Brachyistius frenatus 3:561
Brachylophus fasciatus 3:413
Brachypteracias leptosomus 2:230
Brachypteryx montana 2:344
Brachyramphus marmoratus 2:275
Brachyteles arachnoides 1:91

Bradornis pallidus 2:346
Bradypterus palliseri 2:364
Bradypus tridactylus 1:33
Brama brama 3:552
Branta canadensis 2:215
Bream, gilthead 3:555
ray's 3:552
Breviceps adspersus 3:470
Brevoortia tyrannus 3:503
Bristlebill, collared 2:360
Bristlehead, Bornean 2:332
Broadbill family 2:301
Broadbill, green 2:301
Brookesia spectrum 3:417
Bubalornis albirostris 2:379
Bubalus arnee 1:168
Bubalus depressicornis 1:169
Bubo virginianus 2:250
Bubulcus ibis 2:289
Buceros bicornis 2:227
vigil 2:227
Bucerotiformes order 2:226
Bucorvus cafer 2:228
Budgerigar 2:241
Budorcas taxicolor 1:182
Buffalo, African 1:170
bigmouth 3:509
Bufo americanus 3:464
bufo 3:465
calamita 3:465
marinus 3:464
viridis 3:465
Bulbul family 2:358
Bulbul, black Madagascar 2:359
garden 2:358
hook-billed 2:360
red-whiskered 2:359
white-throated 2:359
Bullfinch, Eurasian 2:383
Bullfrog 3:471
South African 3:472
South American 3:468
Bullhead 3:544
Bullhead shark order 3:488
Bullrout 3:544
Bummalow 3:522
Bunting, painted 2:391
reed 2:384
snow 2:385
Buphagus africanus 2:349
Burbot 3:525
Burhinus giganteus 2:269
oedicnemus 2:269
Burrfish, striped 3:579
Burrowing asp family 3:442
Busarellus nigricollis 2:280
Bush-shrike, gray headed 2:337
Bushbaby, greater 1:85
lesser 1:85
Bushmaster 3:453
Bushrunner, larklike 2:313
Bustard family 2:258
Bustard, black 2:258
great 2:258
Butcherbird, black 2:329
Buteo buteo 2:280
jamaicensis 2:281
Butterflyfish, copperband 3:558
forceps 3:558
foureye 3:558
Buttonquail family 2:218
Buttonquail, little 2:218
Buzzard, collared 2:280

C

Cabezon 3:545
Cacajao calvus 1:89
Cacatua galerita 2:239
Cacique, yellow-rumped 2:394
Cacicus cela 2:394
Caecilia ochrocephala 3:482
Caecilian family 3:482
Caecilian, Panamanian 3:482
Sao Tome 3:483
Seychelles 3:483
South American 3:483

sticky 3:482
Caenolestes obscurus 1:21
Caiman crocodilus 3:454
Caiman, spectacled 3:454
Cairina moschata 2:217
Calamus bajonado 3:554
Calandrella cinerea 2:371
California, thrasher 2:350
Callaeas cinerea 2:339
Callicebus moloch 1:89
Callichthys callichthys 3:517
Callimico goeldii 1:86
Callipepla californica 2:213
Callithrix argentata 1:87
Callorhinus ursinus 1:148
Callosciurus prevostii 1:41
Calypte helenae 2:246
Calyptomena viridis 2:301
Camel family 1:158
Camel, bactrian 1:159
Camelus bactrianus 1:159
Camelus dromedarius 1:159
Campephaga phoenicea 2:331
Campephilus principalis 2:219
Campethera abingoni 2:220
Campostoma anomalum 3:507
Campylorhamphus troshilirostris 2:314
Campylorhynchus brunneicapillus 2:352
Candirú 3:517
Cane rat 1:70
Cane rat family 1:70
Canis dingo 1:121
latrans 1:120
lupus 1:120
Canthigaster rostrata 3:578
Capra ibex 1:181
Capreolus capreolus 1:163
Capricornis sumatraensis 1:180
Caprimulgus europaeus 2:255
Caprolagus hispidus 1:37
Capros aper 3:539
Capuchin, white-fronted 1:89
Capybara family 1:67
Caracal 1:143
Caracal caracal 1:143
Caracara, crested 2:282
Caranx hippos 3:551
Carapus acus 3:524
Carassius auratus 3:505
Carcharhinus leucas 3:491
Carchariniformes 3:491
Carcharodon carcharias 3:490
Cardinal northern 2:391
Cardinalis cardinalis 2:391
Cardioderma cor 1:109
Carduelis carduelis 2:383
flammea 2:383
Caretta caretta 3:407
Cariama cristata 2:261
Caribou 1:163
Carnivora order 1:120
Carollia perspicillata 1:113
Carp 3:504
Carp, grass 3:507
Carpet shark order 3:492
Carpodacus purpureus 2:382
Cascadura 3:517
Casmerodius alba 2:289
Cassowary family 2:204
Cassowary, southern 2:205
Castor canadensis 1:46
fiber 1:47
Casuarius casuarius 2:205
Cat family 1:142
Cat, African golden 1:142
leopard 1:142
pale kangaroo pampas 1:142
Pallas's 1:144
wild 1:145
Catagonus wagneri 1:156
Catamblyrhynchus diadema 2:390
Catbird, gray 2:351
Catfish, African glass 3:513
Australian freshwater 3:516
blue 3:512
brown 3:512
electric 3:514
gafftopsail 3:515
glass 3:513

Mekong 3:514
pungas 3:514
sea 3:515
upside-down 3:515
walking 3:514
Catharacta skua 2:272
Cathartes aura 2:293
Catharus fuscescens 2:342
Catostomus commersoni 3:508
Caudata order 3:474
Cavefish, northern 3:523
Cavia tschudii 1:66
Cavy family 1:66
Cavy, rock 1:66
Cebuella pygmaea 1:86
Cebus albifrons 1:89
Celeus flavescens 2:221
Central American river
turtle family 3:405
Centrolenella albomaculata 3:463
Centropomus undecimalis 3:546
Centropus milo 2:236
Cephalopholis fulvus 3:547
Cephalophus dorsalis 1:171
silvicultor 1:171
Cephalopterus ornatus 2:309
Ceratodiformes 3:580
Ceratotherium simum 1:196
Cercocebus albigena 1:93
galeritus 1:93
Cercopithecus aethiops 1:96
Cercopithecus diana 1:96
erythrogaster 1:96
neglectus 1:96
Cerdocyon thous 1:122
Certhia familiaris 2:353
Cervus elaphus 1:163
Cerylid kingfisher family 2:233
Cetacea order 1:184
Cetatophrys cornuta 3:468
Cetomimus indagator 3:537
Cetorhinus maximus 3:489
Cettia fortipes 2:364
Chachalaca, plain 2:207
Chaenocephalus aceratus 3:564
Chaetodipus californicus 1:45
Chaetodon capistratus 3:558
Chaetorhynchus papuensis 2:336
Chaffinch 2:382
Chalcides bedriagai 3:426
Chamaea fasciata 3:379
Chamaeleo chamaeleon 3:417
dilepis 3:417
jacksonii 3:416
melleri 3:416
Chamaesaura aena 3:430
Chameleon family 3:416
Chameleon, European 3:417
flap-necked 3:417
Jackson's 3:416
Meller's 3:416
Chamois 1:181
Channoidei 3:570
Chanos chanos 3:504
Chanting-Goshawk, dark 2:279
Characiformes order 3:510
Charadrius hiaticula 2:271
Charina bottae 3:440
Charr, Arctic 3:520
Chauliodus sloani 3:521
Chauna chavaria 2:214
Cheetah 1:145
Chelmon rostratus 3:558
Chelonia mydas 3:406
Chelonia order 3:400
Chelonidae marine turtle family 3:406
Chelus fimbriatus 3:409
Chelydra serpentina 3:408
Chelydridae snapping
turtle family 3:408
Chersine angulata 3:402
Chevrotain family 1:160
Chevrotain, lesser Malay
water 1:160
Chickadee, blackcapped 2:355
Chicken, prairie 2:212
Chilomycterus schoepfi 3:579
Chimaera monstrosa 3:495
Chimaera order 3:495

Chimpanzee, 1:103
pygmy 1:103
Chinchilla 1:68
Chinchilla laniger 1:68
Chinchilla-rat family 1:69
Chinese Muntjac 1:161
Chionis alba 2:268
Chipmunk, eastern 1:42
Chirocentrus dorab 3:503
Chironectes minimus 1:20
Chiroptera order 1:104
Chiroxiphia pareola 2:309
Chitra indica 3:404
Chlamydosaurus kingii 3:414
Chlamyphorus truncatus 1:34
Chloebia gouldiae 2:381
Chlorocichla flaviventris 2:358
Chlorophonia occipitalis 2:388
Chloropsis aurifrons 2:321
Choloepus didactylus 1:33
Chrysochloris asiatica 1:74
Chrysococcyx cupreus 2:235
Chrysocolaptes lucidus 2:221
Chrysocyon brachyurus 1:122
Chrysolampis mosquitus 2:247
Chrysolophus pictus 2:210
Chrysopelea paradisi 3:447
Chrysophrys auratus 3:554
Chrysospalax trevelyani 1:74
Chub, Bermuda 3:559
Chuckwalla 3:411
Cicadabird, slender-billed 2:330
Cichlid, ring-tailed pike 3:560
Cicinnurus regius 2:328
Ciconia ciconia 2:293
Ciconiiformes, order 2:264
Cinclocerthia ruficauda 2:351
Cinclosoma cinnamomeum 2:324
Cinclus mexicanus 2:341
Circus cyaneus 2:279
Cissopis leveriana 2:387
Cisticola juncidis 2:361
Cistothorus palustris 2:353
Civet family 1:134
Civet, African 1:135
Congo water 1:135
Clarias batrachus 3:514
Clemmys insculpta 3:401
Clethrionomys glareolus 1:55
Climacteris picumnus 2:315
Clupea harengus 3:503
Clupeiformes 3:502
Clytoceyx rex 2:233
Cnemidophorus lemniscatus 3:423
Coati 1:127
Cobia 3:550
Cobitis taenia 3:509
Cobra and sea snake family 3:448
Cobra, king 3:448
Indian 3:449
Coccyzidae 2:236
Cocvyzus americanus 2:236
Cochlearius cochlearius 2:289
Cock-of-the-rock, Andean 2:308
Cockatiel 2:238
Cockatoo, sulphur-crested 2:239
Cod order 3:524
Cod 3:526
Antarctic 3:564
Baikal 3:545
trout 3:547
Coelacanth order 3:580
Coelops frithi 1:111
Coendou prehensilis 1:65
Coereba flaveola 2:392
Colaptes auratus 2:222
Coliiformes order 2:234
Colinus virginianus 2:213
Colius striatus 2:234
Colluricincla harmonica 2:325
Colobus angolensis 1:98
Colobus, Angolan black and
white 1:98
olive 1:98
red 1:98
Colocolo family 1:21
Colossoma nigripinnis 3:511

Coluber viridiflavus 3:444
Colubrid snake family 3:442
Colugo 1:79
Columba fisciata 2:257
livia 2:256
Columbiformes order 2:256
Columbina passerina 2:256
Comephorus baicalensis 3:545
Conchfish 3:549
Condor, California 2:292
Condylura cristata 1:79
Conebill, giant 2:389
Conepatus mesoleucus 1:132
Coney 3:547
Conger conger 3:501
Congo eel family 3:474
Connochaetes taurinus 1:174
Conolophus suberistatus 3:412
Conopophaga melanops 2:315
Conopophagidae 2:315
Contopus virens 2:305
Coot, American 2:263
Copsychus saularis 2:347
Coquette, frilled 2:247
Coracias garrulus 2:230
Coraciiformes order 2:230
Coracina novaehollandiae 2:330
tenuirostris 2:330
maxima 2:330
Cordon-bleu, red-cheeked 2:380
Cordylosaurus subtessellatus 3:430
Cordylus cataphractus 3:431
Coregonus lavaretus 3:519
Cormorant family 2:286
Cormorant, great 2:286
flightless 2:287
long-tailed 2:287
Corncrake 2:263
Coronella austriaca 3:446
Corvinella melanoleuca 2:322
Corvus brachyrhynchos 2:326
frugilegus 2:326
Coryphaena hippurus 3:552
Coryphistera alaudina 2:313
Corythaixoides concolor 2:248
Cotinga cayana 2:308
Cotinga, spangled 2:308
Cottonmouth 3:453
Cottontail, desert 1:38
Cottus gobio 3:544
Coturnix chinensis 2:315
coturnix 2:208
Coua cursor 2:236
Coua, running 2:236
Coucal family 2:236
Coucal, buff-headed 2:236
Courser, cream-colored 2:269
Cow and frill shark order 3:492
Cow-bird, brown-headed 2:395
Cowfish, scrawled 3:577
Coyote 1:120
Coypu family 1:68
Craciformes order 2:206
Cracticus quoyi 2:329
Crane family 2:259
Crane, black crowned 2:259
whooping 2:259
Cranioleuca erythrops 2:313
Craseonycteris thonglongyai 1:108
Crax rubra 2:207
Creeper, spotted 2:353
Crenicichla saxatilis 3:560
Crescentchest, elegant 2:315
Crested swift family 2:245
Crevalle Jack 3:551
Crex crex 2:263
Cricetomys emini 1:58
Cricetus cricetus 1:50
Crocidura miya 1:77
Crocodile, estuarine 3:455
Nile 3:455
West African dwarf 3:455
Crocodilia order 3:454
Crocodylus niloticus 3:455
Crocodylus porosus 3:455
Crocuta crocuta 1:141
Crossarchus obscurus 1:139
Crossbill, red 2:383
Crotalus adamanteus 3:452

Crotalus cerastes 3:452
Crotaphytus collaris 3:411
Crotophaga ani 2:237
Crow family 2:324
Crow, American 2:326
Cryptacanthodes maculatus 3:563
Cryptobranchidae 3:481
Cryptobranchus alleganiensis 3:481
Cryptoprocta ferox 1:137
Ctenodactylus gundi 1:63
Ctenomys talarum 1:69
Ctenopharyn godonidella 3:507
Ctenosaura pectinata 3:413
Cuckoo, African emerald 2:235
channel-billed 2:235
collared 2:234
drongo 2:235
striped 2:237
yellow-billed 2:236
Cuckoo-roller family 2:230
Cuckoo-shrike, ground 2:330
redshouldered 2:331
Cuculiformes order 2:234
Cuculus canorus 2:234
Cuiu-cuiu 3:515
Culicicapa helianthea 2:321
Cuon alpinus 1:122
Curassow family 2:207
Curassow, great 2:207
nocturnal 2:207
Curimbata 3:510
Curlew, stone 2:268
Currawong, pied 2:329
Cursorius cursor 2:269
Cusimanse 1:139
Cusk-eel, New Providence 3:524
Cutlassfish, Atlantic 3:567
Cyanerpes caeruleus 2:389
Cyanocitta cristata 2:327
Cyanocorax yncas 2:327
Cyclarhis gujanensis 2:323
Cycloderma frenatum 3:404
Cyclopes didactylus 1:33
Cyclorana cultripes 3:468
Cyclura cornuta 3:413
Cydopterus lumpus 3:545
Cygnus columbianus 2:215
Cynocephalus volans 1:79
Cynogale bennettii 1:137
Cynoglossus lingua 3:575
Cynomys ludovicianus 1:42
Cynoscion nebulosus 3:556
nobilis 3:556
Cyornis rubeculoides 2:346
Cyprinidon variegatus 3:532
Cypriniformes order 3:504
Cyprinodontiformes order 3:532
Cyprinus carpio 3:504
Cypselurus heterurus 3:530
Cypsiurus parvus 2:244
Cystophora cristata 1:153

D

Dab 3:573
Dace, 3:504
pearl 3:507
Dacelo novaeguineae 2:232
Dacelonid kingfisher family 2:232
Dacnis cayana 2:388
Dactylopteriformes 3:542
Dactylopterus volitans 3:542
Damaliscus dorcas 1:175
lunatus 1:175
Daphenositta chrysoptera 2:325
Darter family 2:286
Darter, orangethroat 3:549
Dassie rat family 1:71
Dasyatis americana 3:494
Dasycercus cristicauda 1:22
Dasypeltis scabra 3:444
Dasyprocta leporinii 1:67
Dasypus novemcinctus 1:34
Dasyuridae family 1:22
Dasyuromorpha order 1:22
Dasyuroides byrnei 1:23
Dasyurus viverrinus 1:23

Daubentonia madagascariensis 1:83
Dealfish 3:536
Deer family 1:161
   Chinese water 1:161
   pampas 1:164
   Père David's 1:162
   red 1:163
   roe 1:163
   tufted 1:161
   white-tailed 1:162
Degu 1:69
Delma nasuta 3:421
Delphinapterus leucas 1:189
Delphinus delphis 1:186
Dendroaspis angusticeps 3:448
Dendrobates auratus 3:466
Dendrocolaptes certhia 2:314
   ptinae 2:314
Dendrocopos major 2:219
Dendrocygna viduata 2:214
Dendrogale melanura 1:81
Dendrohyrax arboreus 1:197
Dendroica petechia 2:393
Dendrolagus lumholtzi 1:29
Dendromus mesomelas 1:58
Dendronanthus indicus 2:376
Denisonia devisii 3:448
Dermatemys mawii 3:405
Dermochelys coriacea 3:406
Dermogenys pusillus 3:530
Dermoptera order 1:79
Desman, Russian 1:79
Desmana moschata 1:79
Desmodus rotundus 1:115
Desmognathus fuscus 3:477
Dhole 1:122
Dibamus novaeguineae 3:422
Dibatag 1:179
Dicaeum hirundinaceum 2:374
Dicamptodon ensatus 3:479
Dicerorhinus sumatrensis 1:196
Diceros bicornis 1:197
Dickcissel 2:391
Diclidurus virgo 1:107
Dicrurus adsimilis 2:336
   paradiseus 2:336
Didelimorpha order 1:20
Didelphis virginiana 1:20
Dik-dik, Kirk's 1:177
Dingo 1:121
Dinomys branickii 1:67
Diodon hystrix 3:579
Diomedea exulans 2:298
Diploglossus lessorae 3:432
Diplomys labilis 1:70
Dipodillus maghrebi 1:56
Dipodomys deserti 1:45
Dipper family 2:341
Dipper, American 2:341
Diprotodonta order 1:25
Dipsas indica 3:443
Dipus sagitta 1:63
Disc-winged bat family 1:118
Discoglossid frog family 3:460
Discus fish 3:560
Dispholidus typus 3:447
Diver family 2:295
Diver, red-throated 2:295
Dog family 1:120
Dog, bush 1:122
   hunting 1:123
Dogfish, sandy 3:491
   spiny 3:493
Dolichonyx oryzivorus 2:395
Dolichotis patagonum 1:66
Dolphin family 1:186
Dolphin, bottlenose 1:186
   collared 1:186
   Ganges 1:184
   Indo-Pacific humpbacked 1:186
   Risso's 1:187
   striped 1:186
   whitefin 1:184
Dolphinfish 3:552
Dolphins 1:186
Dorcatragus megalotis 1:176
Dorcopsis veterum 1:30
Dormouse family 1:62
Dormouse, African 1:62

desert 1:62
edible 1:62
fat 1:62
Japanese 1:62
Malabar spiny 1:53
Douroucouli 1:88
Dove, blue-headed quail 2:257
   common ground 2:256
   mourning 2:257
   rock 2:256
Dovekie 2:275
Dracaena guianensis 3:422
Draco volans 3:414
Dragon, bearded 3:415
Drill 1:94
Dromaius novaehollandiae 2:204
Dromas ardeola 2:269
Dromedary 1:159
Dromiciops gliroides 1:21
Drongo, fork-tailed 2:336
   greater racquet-tailed 2:336
   pygmy 2:336
Drum, black 3:556
   freshwater 3:557
Dryoscopus cubla 2:337
Duck order 2:214
Duck, Falklands steamer 2:216
   mandarin 2:217
   muscovy 2:217
   ruddy 2:217
   white-faced whistling 2:214
Dugong dugon 1:199
Dugong family 1:199
Duiker, 1:171
   collared 1:171
   gray 1:171
   yellow 1:171
Dulus dominicus 2:341
Dumetella carolinensis 2:351
Dunnart, fat-tailed 1:23
Dunnock 2:375

E

Eagle, bald 2:278
   golden 2:281
   harpy 2:281
Eared-nightjar family 2:254
Echenis naucrates 3:550
Echiichthys vipera 3:565
Echidna catenata 3:500
Echidna family 1:18
Echidna, long-beaked 1:18
   short-beaked 1:18
Echinoprocta rufescens 1:65
Echinosorex gymnurus 1:75
Echis carinatus 3:451
Eclectus roratus 2:240
Edible-nest swiftlet 2:245
Eel order 3:499
Eel, conger 3:501
   electric 3:518
   European 3:500
   gulper 3:501
   rice 3:542
   sand 3:564
   spiny 3:542
   two-toed Congo 3:474
Egernia stokesii 3:428
Egret, cattle 2:289
   great 2:289
Egretta ardesiaca 2:289
Eider, collared 2:216
Eira barbara 1:129
Elaenia flavogaster 2:305
Elaenia, yellow-bellied 2:305
Elagatis bipinnulata 3:551
Eland 1:166
Elaphe obsoleta 3:445
Elaphodus cephalophus 1:161
Elaphurus davidianus 1:162
Eectrophorus electricus 3:518
Elephant family 1:198
Elephant shrew family 1:72
Elephant, African 1:198
   Asian 1:198
Elephant-snout fish 3:498

Elephant-trunk snake 3:441
Elephas maximus 1:198
Elk 1:162
Ellobius fuscocapillus 1:54
Elopiformes 3:499
Elops saurus 3:499
Emballonura monticola 1:107
Emberiza citrinella 2:385
   schoeniclus 2:384
Emoia cyanogaster 3:428
Emperor, sweetlip 3:555
   spangled 3:555
Empidonax traillii 2:304
Emu 2:204
Emydid turtle family 3:400
Emydura macquarii 3:409
Emys orbicularis 3:401
Engraulis encrasicolus 3:503
Enhydra lutra 1:133
Enhydris punctata 3:443
Enicurus leschenaulti 2:347
Ensatina eschscholtzi 3:477
Ensifera ensifera 2:246
Epinephelus itajara 3:547
Epixerus ebii 1:41
Epomops franqueti 1:105
Eptesicus fuscus 1:117
Eptonychotes weddelli 1:153
Equetus lanceolatus 3:556
Equus africanus 1:194
   burchelli 1:194
   grevyi 1:194
   hemionus 1:195
   przewalski 1:195
Eremias sp. 3:425
Eremophila alpestris 2:371
Eretmochelys imbricata 3:407
Erignathus barbatus 1:151
Erinaceus europaeus 1:75
Erithizon dorsatum 1:65
Erythrocebus patas 1:97
Erythrura trichroa 2:381
Eschrichtius robustus 1:192
Esociformes order 3:519
Esox lucius 3:519
Etheostoma spectabile 3:549
Eublepharius macularius 3:418
Eudynamys scolopacea 2:235
Eudyptula minor 2:294
Aramides ypecaha 2:263
Eumeces obsoletus 3:427
Eumetopias jubatus 1:149
Eumops perotis 1:113
Eunectes murinus 3:441
Euphonia minuta 2:388
Euphonia, white-vented 2:388
Eupleres goudotii 1:136
Eupodotis afra 2:258
Eurostopodus macrotis 2:254
Eurypharynx pelecanoides 3:501
Eurypyga helias 2:258
Euthynnus pelamis 3:568
Eutoxeres aquila 2:246
Evening bat family 1:116
Exocetus volitans 3:530

F

Fairywren and grass wren family 2:321
Fairywren, superb 2:317
Falco berigora 2:283
   peregrinus 2:283
   rusticolus 2:283
   subbuteo 2:283
   tinnunculus 2:282
Falcon family 2:282
Falcon, brown 2:283
   peregrine 2:283
Falconet, collared 2:282
Falculea palliataa 2:339
Falcunculus frontatus 2:325
Fallfish 3:508
False vampire family 1:108
Fanalouc 1:136
Fantail, rufous 2:333
   yellow-bellied 2:333
Felis silvestris 1:145

Fer-de-Lance 3:452
Ferret, black-footed 1:128
Feylinia cussori 3:427
Figbird 2:332
Fightingfish, Siamese 3:570
Filefish, planehead 3:577
   scrawled 3:577
Fimbrios klossi 3:442
Finch, bunting, and tanager
   family 2:382
Finch, gouldian 2:381
   plush-capped 2:390
   purple 2:382
   white-naped brush 2:386
   zebra 2:381
Finchbill, crested 2:359
Finfoot, African 2:260
Firefinch, red-billed 2:380
Fisherman bat family 1:112
Flamingo family 2:290
Flamingo, greater 2:290
Flatfish order 3:571
Flounder, peacock 3:572
   starry 3:573
   summer 3:572
   winter 3:574
Flowerpecker, crimson-breasted 2:374
Flycatcher, Asian paradise 2:334
   bar-winged shrike 2:331
   blue-throated 2:346
   citrine canary 2:321
   cliff 2:306
   gray silky 2:340
   ochre-bellied 2:302
   pale 2:346
   piratic 2:306
   royal 2:304
   rufous-tailed jungle 2:345
   scissor-tailed 2:302
   spotted 2:345
   tyrant 2:302
   vermilion 2:306
   white-tailed crested 2:334
   willow 2:304
Flying dragon 3:414
Flying gurnard order 3:542
Flying lemur family 1:79
Flyingfish 3:530
Flyingfish Atlantic 3:530
Football-fish 3:529
Forcipiger longirostris 3:558
Fordonia leucobalia 3:443
Forest falcon, barred 2:282
Forktail, white-crowned 2:347
Forpus conspicillatus 2:242
Fossa 1:137
Four-eyed fish 3:533
Fox, red 1:121
   Arctic 1:121
   crab-eating 1:122
   fennec 1:121
Francolin, red-necked 2:209
Francolinus afer 2:209
Fratercula arctica 2:274
Free-tailed bat family 1:112
Fregata magnificens 2:294
Friarbird, little 2:319
Frigatebird family 2:294
Frigatebird, magnificent 2:294
Fringilla coelebs 2:382
Frog, arum lily 3:469
   common 3:471
   corroboree 3:468
   Darwin's 3:467
   eastern narrow-mouthed 3:470
   glass 3:463
   gold 3:465
   gold spiny reed 3:469
   golden arrow-poison 3:469
   green and fold bell 3:467
   Hochstetter's 3:460
   horned 3:468
   marsh 3:472
   marsupial 3:467
   mottled burrowing 3:473
   Natal ghost 3:463
   northern cricket 3:466
   northern leopard 3:472
   parsley 3:462

Seychelles 3:469
sheep 3:470
South African rain 3:470
striped grass 3:472
termite 3:470
Wallace's flying 3:473
Frogfish, longlure 3:529
Frogmouth, Ceylon 2:252
Fruit bat family 1:104
Fruit bat, Franquet's 1:105
Fruiteater, barred 2:308
Fulica americana 2:263
Fulmar, northern 2:297
Fulmarus glacialis 2:297
Fulvetta, brown-cheeked 2:366
Funambulus palmarum 1:41
Fundulus heteroclitus 3:532
Funnel-eared bat family 1:118
Furipterus horrens 1:118
Furnarius rufus 2:312

G

Gadiformes 3:524
Gadus morhua 3:526
Gaidropsarus mediterraneus 3:525
Galago family 1:85
Galago senegalensis 1:85
Galaxias maculatus 3:519
Galbula ruficauda 2:226
Galbuliformes order 2:226
Galictis vittata 1:129
Galliformes order 2:208
Gallinago gallinago 2:267
Gallinula chloropus 2:262
Galliwasp 3:432
Galloperdix spadicea 2:209
Gallus gallus 2:210
Gannet family 2:285
Gannet, northern 2:285
Gar order 3:497
Gar, longnose 3:497
Garfish 3:531
Garrulax leucolophus 2:365
Garrulus glandarius 2:327
Gasteropelecus sternicla 3:511
Gasterosteiformes order 3:540
Gasterosteus aculeatus 3:540
Gastrophryne carolinensis 3:470
Gastrotheca marsupiata 3:467
Gaur 1:168
Gavia stellata 2:295
Gavial 3:454
Gavialis gangeticus 3:454
Gazella thomsonii 1:179
Gazelle, Thomson's 1:179
Gecko family 3:418
Brook's 3:419
green day 3:420
Kuhl's 3:419
leaf-tailed 3:420
leopard 3:418
marbled 3:419
tokay 3:418
web-footed 3:419
white-spotted 3:418
Gekko gekko 3:418
Gelada 1:95
Genet, small-spotted 1:136
Genetta genetta 1:136
Genypterus blacodes 3:524
Geocapromys ingrahami 1:68
Geochelone pardalis 3:403
nigra 3:402
Geococcyx californianus 2:237
Geocolaptes olivaceus 2:221
Geomys bursarius 1:44
Gerbil, fat-tailed 1:57
great 1:57
greater short-tailed 1:56
Indian 1:57
large North African 1:56
South African pygmy 1:56
Gerbillurus paeba 1:56
Gerbillus campestris 1:56
Gerenuk 1:179
Gerrhonotus multicarinatus 3:432

Gerrhosaurus flavigularis 3:431
Gerygone olivacea 2:321
Gerygone, white-throated 2:320
Ghost frog family 3:463
Giant salamander family 3:481
Gibbon, black 1:100
hoolock 1:101
Kloss's 1:100
lar 1:101
pileated 1:101
Gila monster family 3:435
Giraffa camelopardalis 1:164
Giraffe 1:164
Giraffe family 1:164
Girdled and plated lizard family 3:430
Glareola pratincola 2:273
Glass frog family 3:463
Glaucidium passerinum 2:251
Glaucomys sabrinus 1:43
Glider, greater 1:27
pygmy 1:27
Glirurus japonicus 1:62
Glis glis 1:62
Globicephala melaena 1:187
Glossophaga soricina 1:114
Gnatcatcher, blue-gray 2:354
Gnateater family 2:315
Gnateater, black-cheeked 2:315
Go-away bird, gray 2:248
Goat, mountain 1:180
Goatfish, spotted 3:557
Gobio gobio 3:506
Gold frog family 3:465
Golden mole family 1:74
Goldeye 3:498
Goldfinch, Eurasian 2:383
Goldfish 3:505
Gonolek, crimson-breasted 2:337
Gonorynchiformes order 3:504
Goose, Canada 2:215
graylag 2:215
magpie 2:214
Gopher, northern pocket 1:44
plains pocket 1:44
Gopherus polyphemus 3:402
Goral, common 1:180
Gorilla 1:102
Gorilla gorilla 1:102
Goshawk, northern 2:280
Gourami 3:570
Grackle, common 2:394
Gracula religiosa 2:349
Grallaria ruficapilla 2:311
Grallina cyanoleuca 2:335
Grampus griseus 1:187
Graphiurus murinus 1:62
Graptemys pseudogeographica 3:400
Grass snake 3:444
Grassbird, little 2:365
Grasswren, eyrean 2:317
Grayling 3:519
Greaved turtle family 3:409
Grebe family 2:284
Grebe, great crested 2:284
little 2:284
Greenbul, yellow-bellied 2:358
yellow-breasted 2:358
Greenlet, tawny-crowned 2:323
Greenling, kelp 3:544
Grenadier, rough-head 3:525
Gray whale family 1:192
Grison 1:129
Grosbeak, pine 2:383
rose-breasted 2:390
Ground antbird family 2:311
Ground-roller family 2:230
Ground-hornbill family 2:228
Ground-hornbill, southern 2:228
Grouper, black 3:547
Grouse, black 2:212
Gruiformes order 2:258
Grunion, California 3:535
Grus americana 2:259
Grysbok, cape 1:177
Guan, crested 2:207
Guanaco 1:158
Gudgeon 3:506
Guillemot 2:274
Guinea pig family 1:66

Guinea pig 1:66
Guineafowl family 2:213
Guineafowl, helmeted 2:213
Guitarfish, Atlantic 3:494
Gull and auk family 2:272
Gull, blackheaded 2:273
herring 2:273
ivory 2:272
Gulo gulo 1:130
Gundi family 1:63
Guppy 3:533
Gurnard, flying 3:542
tub 3:543
Gymnachirus melas 3:575
Gymnarchus niloticus 3:498
Gymnogyps californianus 2:292
Gymnophonia order 3:482
Gymnopithys leucaspis 2:310
Gymnorhina tibicen 2:329
Gymnotiformes order 3:518
Gymnotus carapo 3:518
Gypaetus barbatus 2:276
Gypohierax angolensis 2:278
Gyrinophilus porphyriticus 3:476
Gyrfalcon 2:283

H

Haartebeest 1:175
Haddock 3:527
Haematopus ostralegus 2:270
Haemulon album 3:553
Hagfish order 3:488
Hake, European 3:526
white 3:526
Halfbeak, wrestling 3:530
Haliaeetus leucocephalus 2:278
Haliastur indus 2:277
Halibut, Atlantic 3:572
California 3:572
Greenland 3:574
Halichoeres bivittatus 3:562
Halichoerus grypus 1:150
Hammerhead, smooth 3:491
Hammerkop family 2:290
Hamster, common 1:50
dwarf 1:50
golden 1:50
Hanuman langur 1:99
Hare, brown 1:36
hispid 1:37
snowshoe 1:37
spring 1:47
Hare-wallaby, spectacled 1:28
Harlequin fish 3:508
Harpactes erythrocephalus 2:229
Harpadon nehereus 3:522
Harpia harpyja 2:281
Harpyionycteris whiteheadi 1:105
Harrier, hen 2:279
northern 2:279
Hatchetfish 3:521
Hawk family 2:276
Hawk, African harrier 2:279
black-collared 2:280
Cooper's 2:280
red-tailed 2:281
Hawksbill 3:407
Hedgehog family 1:74
Hedgehog, desert 1:75
Western European 1:75
Helarctos malayanus 1:125
Heleophryne natalensis 3:463
Heliornis fulica 2:260
Hellbender 3:481
Heloderma suspectum 3:435
Hemicentetes semispinosus 1:73
Hemidactylus brookii 3:419
Hemigalus derbyanus 2:137
Hemignathus wilsoni 2:384
Hemiprocne longipennis 2:245
Hemipus picatus 2:331
Hemiramphus brasiliensis 3:530
Hemispingus atropileus 2:387
Hemispingus, black-capped 2:387
Hemisus marmoratum 3:473
Hemitragus jemlahicus 1:182

Heron family 2:288
Heron, black 2:289
black-crowned night 2:288
gray 2:288
Herpestes auropunctatus 1:138
Herring order 3:502
Herring, Atlantic 3:503
wolf 3:503
Heterandria formosa 3:533
Heterocephalus glaber 1:71
Heterodontiformes 3:488
Heterodontus portusjacksoni 3:489
Heterohyrax brucei 1:197
Heteromys anomalus 1:45
Heteropholis manukanus 3:420
Heterostichus rostratus 3:565
Hexagrammos decagrammus 3:544
Hexanchiformes 3:492
Hexanchus griseus 3:492
Hexaprotodon liberiensis 1:157
Hgpogeophis rostratus 3:483
Hillstar, Andean 2:247
Himantolophus groenlandicus 3:529
Himantopus himantopus 2:270
Hiodon alosoides 3:498
Hippocampus zosterae 3:541
Hippoglossoides platessoides 3:574
Hippoglossus hippoglossus 3:572
Hippopotamus amphibius 1:157
Hippopotamus family 1:157
Hippopotamus, pygmy 1:157
Hipposideros diadema 1:111
Hippotragus equinus 1:173
Hirundapus giganteus 2:244
Hirundinea ferruginea 2:306
Hirundo rustica 2:356
Histrio histrio 3:529
Hoatzin family 2:237
Hobby, Eurasian 2:283
Hog, giant forest 1:155
Hog-nosed bat family 1:108
Hogfish 3:562
Holacanthus ciliaris 3:558
Holocentrus ascensionis 3:537
Honey possum family 1:26
Honey-buzzard, European 2:277
Honeycreeper, purple 2:389
Honeyeater family 2:318
Honeyeater, brown 2:318
cardinal 2:319
fuscous 2:319
strongbilled 2:319
Honeyguide family 2:218
Honeyguide, black-throated 2:218
greater 2:218
Hoopoe family 2:228
Hoplomys gymnurus 1:70
Hoplosternum littorale 3:517
Hoplostethus atlanticus 3:538
Hornbill family 2:227
Hornbill, great Indian 2:227
helmeted 2:227
redbilled 2:227
Hornero, rufous 2:312
Horse family 1:194
Horse, Przewalski's wild 1:195
Horseshoe bat family 1:110
Houndfish 3:531
Howler, black 1:90
red 1:90
Huet-huet, chestnut-throated 2:315
Hummingbird family 2:246
Hummingbird, bee 2:246
giant 2:247
long-tailed Sylph 2:247
ruby-throated 2:246
ruby-topaz 2:247
sword-billed 2:246
Huso huso 3:496
Hutia family 1:68
Hyaena brunnea 1:141
hyaena 1:140
Hydrobates pelagicus 2:299
Hydrochaeris hydrochaeris 1:67
Hydrocynus goliath 3:510
Hydromys chrysogaster 1:59
Hydrophis cyanocinctus 3:449
Hydropotes inermis 1:161
Hydrosaurus amboinensis 3:415

Hydrurga leptonyx 1:152
Hyemoschus aquaticus 1:160
Hyena family 1:140
Hyena, brown 1:141
  spotted 1:141
  striped 1:140
Hyla arborea 3:466
  crucifer 3:466
  versicolor 3:466
Hylobates concolor 1:100
  hoolock 1:101
  klossii 1:100
  lar 1:101
  pileatus 1:101
  syndactylus 1:100
Hylochoerus meinertzhageni 1:155
Hylophilus ochraceiceps 2:323
Hynobius stejnegeri 3:481
Hyomys goliath 1:60
Hyperolius horstockii 3:469
Hyperoodon ampullatus 1:190
Hyphessobrycon flammeus 3:511
Hypocolius ampelinus 2:361
Hypocolius family 2:361
Hypocolius, gray 2:361
Hypopachus cuneus 3:470
Hypositta corallirostris 2:338
Hypothymis azurea 2:334
Hypsignathus monstrosus 1:104
Hypsipetes madagascarensis 2:359
Hypsiprymnodon moschatus 1:31
Hyracoidea order 1:197
Hyrax family 1:197
Hyrax, large-toothed rock 1:197
  small-toothed rock 1:197
  tree 1:197
Hystrix africaeaustralis 1:64

I

Ibex 1:181
Ibidorhyncha struthersii 2:271
Ibis family 2:290
Ibis, glossy 2:291
Ibisbill 2:271
Icefish 3:564
Ilchneumia albicauda 1:139
Ichthyomys stolzmanni 1:49
Ichthyophis sp. 3:482
Ictalurus furcatus 3:512
  nebulosus 3:512
Icterus galbula 2:394
Ictiobus cyprinellus 3:509
Idiurus zenkeri 1:47
Iguana family 3:410
Iguana iguana 3:410
Iguana, common 3:410
  Fijian banded 3:413
  forest 3:411
  Galápagos land 3:412
  Madagascan 3:413
  marine 3:412
  rhinoceros 3:413
  spiny-tailed 3:413
Impala 1:178
Indicator indicator 2:218
Indri indri 1:83
Indri, avahi and sifaka family 1:83
Inia geoffrensis 1:184
Insectivora order 1:72
Irena puella 2:321
Isoodon obesulus 1:24
Ispidina picta 2:232
Istiophorus platypterus 3:568
Isurus oxyrinchus 3:490

J

Jacamar family 2:226
Jacamar, rufous-tailed 2:226
Jacana family 2:265
Jacana spinosa 2:265

Jacana, American 2:265
  northern 2:265
Jack rabbit, black-tailed 1:36
Jackknife-fish 3:556
Jaguar 1:146
Jaraqui 3:510
Jay, blue 2:327
  Eurasian 2:327
  green 2:327
  Tibetan ground 2:326
Jerboa, great 1:63
  northern three-toed 1:63
Jewfish 3:547
John dory, 3:539
  American 3:539
Jollytail 3:519
Jolthead porgy 3:554
Jumping mouse and jerboa
  family 1:62
Junco hyemalis 2:385
Junco, dark-eyed 2:385
Jungle runner 3:423
Junglefowl, red 2:210
Jynx torquilla 2:219

K

Kagu family 2:261
Kakapo 2:240
Kangaroo family 1:28
Kangaroo, red 1:30
  Umholtz's tree 1:29
Kangaroo-rat, desert 1:45
Kauai O-o 2:318
Kea 2:239
Kelpfish, giant 3:565
Kerivoula argentata 1:117
Kerodon rupestris 1:66
Kestrel, common 2:282
Ketupa zeylonensis 2:249
Killifish, common 3:532
  least 3:533
Kingbird, eastern 2:303
Kingfisher family 2:232
Kingfisher
  African pygmy 2:232
  belted 2:233
  common 2:232
  common paradise 2:233
  mangrove 2:233
  shovel-billed 2:233
  white-collared 2:233
Kinglet family 2:360
Kinglet, golden-crowned 2:360
Kingsnake, common 3:446
Kinixys erosa 3:403
Kinkajou 1:127
Kinosternidae mud and musk
  turtle family 3:405
Kinosternon flavescens 3:405
Kite, Brahminy 2:277
  everglade 2:277
  red 2:277
  snail 2:277
Kittiwake, black-legged 2:273
Kiwi family 2:205
Kiwi, brown 2:205
Klipspringer 1:176
Knifefish, banded 3:518
Koala family 1:26
Kob, Uganda 1:172
Kobus ellipsiprymnus 1:172
  kob thomasi 1:172
  leche 1:172
Koel, Asian 2:235
  common 2:235
Kogia breviceps 1:188
  simus 1:188
Kokako 2:339
Komodo dragon 3:434
Kookaburra, laughing 2:232
Kowari 1:23
Kryptopterus bicirrhis 3:513
Kudu, greater 1:166
Kyphosus sectatrix 3:559

L

Labrus bergylta 3:562
Lacerta muralis 3:424
  iridis 3:424
  vivipara 3:424
Lacertid lizard family 3:424
Lachesis muta 3:453
Lachnolaimus maximus 3:562
Lactophrys quadricornis 3:577
Ladyfish 3:499
Lagocephalus lagocephalus 3:578
Lagomorpha order 1:36
Lagonosticta senegala 2:380
Lagopus mutus 2:212
Lagorchestes conspicillatus 1:28
Lagostomus maximus 1:68
Lagothrix lagotricha 1:91
Lake trout 3:520
Lalage sueurii 2:331
Lama guanicoe 1:158
Lammergeier 2:276
Lamna nasus 3:490
Lamniformes 3:489
Lampern 3:488
Lampetra fluviatilis 3:488
Lamprey order 3:488
Lamprey, river 3:488
  sea 3:488
Lampridiformes 3:536
Lampris guttatus 3:536
Lamprolia victoriae 2:335
Lampropeltis getulus 3:446
Lamprotornis superbus 2:349
Lance, sand 3:564
Land tortoise family 3:402
Langur, snub-nosed 1:99
Laniarius atrococcineus 2:337
Lanius excubitor 2:322
Lanternfish 3:523
Lanthanotus borneensis 3:435
Lapwing, northern 2:271
Lark family 2:370
Lark, redcapped 2:371
  bifasciated 2:371
  clotbey 2:370
  desert 2:370
  greater hoopoe 2:371
  greater short-toed 2:371
  horned 2:371
  shore 2:371
  singing 2:370
  thick-billed 2:370
Larus argentatus 2:273
  ridibundus 2:273
Lasiurus borealis 1:117
Lates niloticus 3:546
Latimeria chalumnae 3:580
Laughingthrush, white-crested 2:365
Lavia frons 1:109
Leafbird family 2:321
Leafbird, gold-fronted 2:321
Leaffish, Schomburgk's 3:559
Leaflove 2:358
Leatherback 3:406
Lechwe 1:172
Legatus leucophaius 2:306
Legless and alligator lizard
  family 3:432
Leiolopisma infrapunctatum 3:429
Leiopelma hochstetteri 3:460
Leiothrix lutea 2:367
Leiothrix, red-billed 2:367
Leipoa ocellata 2:206
Lemming, Norway 1:54
  southern bog 1:54
Lemmiscus curtatus 1:54
Lemmus lemmus 1:54
Lemur catta 1:82
Lemur family 1:82
Lemur, Philippine flying 1:79
  ring-tailed 1:82
  ruffed 1:82
  woolly 1:83
Leontopithecus rosalia 1:87
Leopard 1:146
Leopard, clouded 1:145
  snow 1:147
Leopardus pardalis 1:144

Lepidochelys olivacea 3:407
Lepidosiren paradoxa 3:581
Lepidosireniformes 3:581
Lepisosteiformes 3:497
Lepisosteus osseus 3:497
Lepomis gibbosus 3:548
Leporillus conditor 1:61
Leptailaurus serval 1:144
Leptodactylid frog family 3:468
Leptodactylus pentadactylus 3:468
Leptosomus discolor 2:230
Leptotyphlops humilis 3:438
Lepus americanus 1:37
  californicus 1:36
  europaeus 1:36
Lethrinus chrysostomus 3:555
  nebulosus 3:555
Leuciscus leuciscus 3:504
Leuresthes tenuis 3:535
Lialis burtonis 3:421
Lichenostomus fusca 2:319
Lichmera indistincta 2:318
Limanda limanda 3:573
Limpkin and sungrebe family 2:260
Ling 3:526
Ling, New Zealand 3:524
Linophryne arborifera 3:529
Linsang, African 1:134
  banded 1:134
Liomys irroratus 1:45
Lion, 1:146
  mountain 1:143
Lionfish 3:543
Lioptilus nigricapillus 3:368
Liparis liparis 3:545
Lipophrys pholis 3:565
Lipotes vexillifer 1:184
Litocranius walleri 1:179
Litoria cydorhynchus 3:467
Lizard, basilisk 3:412
  Bosc's fringe-toed 3:425
  Caiman 3:422
  California legless 3:433
  collared 3:411
  desert night 3:425
  eastern fence 3:410
  Essex's mountain 3:425
  Florida worm 3:436
  frilled 3:414
  girdled 3:431
  green 3:424
  imperial flat 3:430
  plated 3:431
  southern alligator 3:432
  Texas horned 3:411
  two-legged worm 3:437
  viviparous 3:424
  wall 3:424
  white-bellied worm 3:437
  worm 3:437
  red 3:522
Loach, coolie 3:509
  spined 3:509
  stone 3:509
Lobodon carcinophagus 1:151
Lobotes surinamensis 3:553
Locustella naevia 2:363
Loddigesia mirabilis 2:247
Longbill, pygmy 2:375
Longclaw, yellow-throated 2:376
Longtailed tit family 2:355
Lookdown 3:551
Loon, red-throated 2:295
Lophiiformes 3:528
Lophiomys imhausi 1:52
Lophius piscatorius 3:528
Lophornis magnifica 2:247
Lora, common 2:336
Lorikeet, rainbow 2:238
Loris family 1:84
Loris tardigradus 1:84
Loris, slender 1:84
  slow 1:84
Lorius lory 2:238
Lory, black-capped 2:238
Lota lota 3:525
Lovebird, peach-faced 2:240
  rosy-faced 2:240

Loxia curvirostra 2:383
Loxodonta africana 1:198
Loxops coccineus 2:384
Lucifuga spelaeotes 3:524
Lumpsucker 3:545
Lungfish, African 3:581
    Australian 3:580
    South American 3:581
Lungless salamander family 3:476
Lutjanus analis 3:552
Lutra lutra 1:132
Lybius bidentatus 2:223
Lycaon pictus 1:123
Lynx 1:143
Lynx lynx 1:143
    rufus 1:144
Lyrebird, superb 2:316
Lyretail, Cape Lopez 3:533

M

Mabuya 3:428
Mabuya wrightii 3:428
Macaca arctoides 1:92
    fuscata 1:92
    radiata 1:93
    sylvanus 1:92
Macaque, bonnet 1:93
    Japanese 1:92
    stump-tailed 1:92
Macaw, scarlet 2:242
Maccullochella macquariensis 3:547
Machaerirhynchus flaviventer 2:335
Mackerel, Atlantic 3:567
Macroclemys temmincki 3:408
Macroderma gigas 1:109
Macrodipteryx longipennis 2:255
Macroglossus minimus 1:105
Macronyx croceus 2:376
Macropodus opercularis 3:570
Macropus rufus 1:30
Macroscelides proboscideus 1:72
Macrotis lagotis 1:25
Macrourus berglax 3:525
Macrozoarces americanus 3:563
Madoqua kirki 1:177
Magpie goose family 2:214
Magpie, Australian 2:329
    black-billed 2:327
    Ceylon 2:327
    common 2:327
Magpie-lark 2:335
Mahseer 3:505
Makaira nigricans 3:568
Mako 3:490
Malachite, scarlet-tufted 2:373
Malaclemys terrapin 3:400
Malaconotus blanchoti 2:337
Malapterurus electricus 3:514
Malkoha, small greenbilled 2:236
Mallard 2:216
Malleefowl 2:206
Malocochersus tornieri 3:402
Malurus cyaneus 2:317
Mamba, eastern green 3:448
Man-o'-war fish 3:569
Manakin, blue-backed 2:309
    wire-tailed 2:309
Manatee family 1:199
Manatee, American 1:199
Mandi 3:516
Mandrill 1:95
Mandrillus leucophaeus 1:94
Mandrillus sphinx 1:95
Mangabey, white-cheeked 1:93
Manis gigantea 1:35
    tricuspis 1:35
Manta birostris 3:495
Manta, Atlantic 3:495
Manucode, crinkle-collared 2:328
Manucodia chalybata 2:328
Manushi 3:453
Mara 1:66
Margate, black 3:553
Marlin, blue 3:568
    striped 3:569
Marmosa Robinsoni 1:20

Marmoset and tamarin family 1:86
Marmoset, Goeldi's 1:86
    pygmy 1:86
    silvery 1:87
Marmota monax 1:43
Marsupial mammals 1:20
Marsupial mole family 1:25
Marsupial mole, Southern 1:25
Marten, American 1:129
Martes americana 1:129
Martes zibellina 1:129
Martin, purple 2:357
    sand 2:357
    white-eyed river 2:356
Massasauga 3:452
Mastacembelus armatus 3:542
Mastigure, princely 3:415
Matamata 3:409
Meadowlark, eastern 2:395
Medaka, Japanese 3:531
Meerkat 1:139
Megaceryle alcyon 2:233
Megaderma lyra 1:108
Megalaima haemacephala 2:223
Megalurus gramineus 2:365
Megapode family 2:206
Megapodius freycinet 2:206
Megaptera novaeangliae 1:193
Megasorex gigas 1:76
Melanocharis nigra 2:375
Melanochlora sultanea 2:355
Melanogrammus aeglefinus 3:527
Melanopareia elegans 2:315
Melanotaenia fluviatilis 3:535
Meleagris gallopavo 2:212
Meles meles 1:130
Melidectes princeps 2:319
Melidectes, long-bearded 2:323
Melierax metabates 2:279
Melithreptus validirostris 2:319
Mellivora capensis 1:130
Melogale moschata 1:131
Melomys cervinipes 1:61
Melopsittacus undulatus 2:241
Melospiza melodia 2:387
Menhaden, Atlantic 3:503
Menura novaehollandiae 2:316
Mephitis mephitis 1:132
Merganser, red-breasted 2:217
Mergus serrator 2:217
Merlangius merlangus 3:527
Merluccius merluccius 3:526
Merops apiaster 2:231
Mesite family 2:261
Mesite, white-breasted 2:261
Mesitornis variegat 2:261
Mesocricetus auratus 1:50
Mesoplodon bidens 1:191
Mexican burrowing toad
    family 3:462
Micrastur ruficollis 2:282
Micrathene whitneyi 2:249
Microbiothera order 1:21
Microcebus rufus 1:82
Microdipodops pallidus 1:45
Microgale longicaudata 1:73
Microhierax caerulescens 2:282
Micromesistius poutassou 3:527
Micromys minutus 1:60
Micronycteris megalotis 1:115
Micropsitta bruijnii 2:239
Micropterus salmoides 3:548
Microtus pennsylvanicus 1:55
Micrurus fulvius 3:449
Midshipman, Atlantic 3:528
Milkfish 3:504
Milvus milvus 2:277
Mimus polyglottos 2:350
Minivet, scarlet 2:331
Minnow 3:507
Minnow, sheepshead 3:532
Mionectus oleaginus 2:302
Miopithecus talapoin 1:97
Mirafra cantillans 2:370
Mirounga angustirostris 1:152
Mistletoebird 2:374
Mniotilta varia 2:392
Mockingbird,
    Charles 2:350

    Galápagos 2:350
Moho braccatus 2:318
Mola mola 3:579
Mole family 1:78
Mole salamander family 3:478
Mole, cape golden 1:74
    European 1:78
    giant golden 1:74
    hairy-tailed 1:79
    hottentot golden 1:74
    Pacific 1:78
    star-nosed 1:79
Mole-rat family 1:71
Mole-rat, cape dune 1:71
    lesser 1:51
    giant 1:51
Mole-vole, southern 1:54
Moloch horridus 3:414
Molossus ater 1:113
Molothrus ater 2:395
Molva molva 3:526
Momotus momota 2:231
Monacanthus hispidus 3:577
Monachus monachus 1:153
Monarch, black-naped 2:334
    spectacled 2:335
Monarcha trivirgatus 2:335
Monasa nigrifrons 2:226
Mongoose family 1:138
Mongoose, banded 1:138
    bushy-tailed 1:138
    Indian 1:138
    marsh 1:138
    white-tailed 1:139
Monitor lizard family 3:434
Monitor, earless 3:435
    Gould's 3:435
    Nile 3:434
Monkey, black spider 1:90
    common woolly 1:91
    De Brazza's 1:96
    Diana 1:96
    night 1:88
    patas 1:97
    proboscis 1:99
    red-bellied 1:96
    vervet 1:96
    woolly spider 1:91
Monkfish 3:492
Monocentris Japonicus 3:537
Monodelphis brevicaudata 1:21
Monodon monoceros 1:189
Monopeltis capensis 3:436
Monopterus alba 3:542
Monotremata order 1:18
Monticola rupestris 2:342
Montifringilla nivalis 2:379
Moonrat, 1:75
    mindanao 1:75
Moorhen, common 2:262
Moorish idol 3:566
Moose 1:162
Moray, 3:500
    chain 3:500
Morelia argus 3:441
Mormoops megalophylla 1:112
Mormyrus kannume 3:498
Morus bassanus 2:285
Moschus chrysogaster 1:160
Motacilla alba 2:377
    flava 2:377
Motmot family 2:231
Motmot, blue-crowned 2:231
Mouflon 1:183
Mountain beaver family 1:46
Mouse, African climbing 1:58
    American climbing 1:47
    Californian pocket 1:45
    deer 1:48
    eastern shrew 1:59
    fat 1:58
    forest spiny pocket 1:45
    four-striped grass 1:60
    golden 1:49
    harvest 1:60
    hopping 1:61
    meadow jumping 1:63
    Mexican spiny pocket 1:45
    mosaic-tailed 1:61

    northern birch 1:63
    northern grasshopper 1:49
    silky pocket 1:44
    South American field 1:49
    western harvest 1:47
    wood 1:60
Mouse-lemur, russet 1:82
Mouse-tailed bat family 1:106
Mousebird family 2:234
Mousebird, speckled 2:234
Moustached bat 1:112
Moustached bat family 1:112
Mouth-brooding frog family 3:467
Mouthbrooder, nile 3:560
Moxostoma macrolepidotum 3:508
Mudpuppy 3:475
Mugil cephalus 3:567
Mulgara 1:22
Mulleripicus pulverulentus 2:220
Mullet, red 3:557
    striped 3:567
Mullus surmuletus 3:557
Mummichog 3:532
Mungos mungo 1:138
Muntiacus reevesi 1:161
Muraena helena 3:500
Murray 3:547
Murre, common 2:274
Murrelet, marbled 2:275
Mus musculus 1:61
Muscicapa striata 2:345
Musk deer family 1:160
Musk deer, forest 1:160
Muskrat 1:55
Musophagiformes order 2:248
Mustela erminea 1:128
    nigripes 1:128
    nivalis 1:128
    putorius 1:128
Mustelid family 1:128
Myadestes ralloides 2:344
Mycteroperca bonaci 3:547
Myctophiformes order 3:522
Myctophum punctatum 3:523
Mydaus javanensis 1:131
Myioborus pictus 2:393
Myiopsitta monachus 2:243
Myiornis ecaudatus 2:305
Myliobatis aquila 3:495
Myna, hill 2:349
Myobatrachid frog family 3:468
Myocastor coypus 1:69
Myosorex varius 1:77
Myotis lucifugus 1:116
Myoxida 1:62
Myoxocephalus scorpius 3:544
Myrmecobius fasciatus 1:24
Myrmecophaga tridactyla 1:32
Myrmotherula surinamensis 2:310
Mystacina tuberculata 1:119
Mystomys albicaudatus 1:52
Myxine glutinosa 3:488
Myxiniformes 3:488
Myzomela cardinalis 2:319
Myzopoda aurita 1:119
Myzornis pyrrhoura 2:367
Myzornis, fire-tailed 2:367

N

Naja naja 3:449
Nandinia binotata 1:135
Narrow-mouthed frog family 3:470
Narwhal 1:189
Nasalis larvatus 1:99
Nasica longirostris 2:314
Naso lituratus 3:567
Nasua nasua 1:127
Natalus stramineus 1:118
Natrix natrix 3:444
Neacomys guianae 1:47
Nectarinia johnstoni 2:373
    jugularis 2:373
    sperata 2:373
    superba 2:373
Necturus maculosus 3:475
Needlefish, freshwater 3:531

Needletail, brown-backed 2:244
Nemichthys scolopaceus 3:501
Nemorhaedus goral 1:180
Neoceratodus forsteri 3:580
Neodrepanis coruscans 2:301
Neofilis nebulosa 1:145
Neophoca cinerea 1:149
Neophocaena phocaenoides 1:185
Neophron percnopterus 2:276
Neoseps reynoldsi 3:427
Neotoma albigula 1:49
Neotragus pygmaeus 1:177
Nesolagus netscheri 1:39
Nesomimus trifasciatus 2:350
Nesomys rufus 1:52
Nestor notabilis 2:239
New World barbet
  and toucan family 2:224
New World leaf-nosed bat family 1:113
New World porcupine family 1:65
New World vulture
  and stork family 2:296
New Zealand frog family 3:460
New Zealand short-
  tailed bat family 1:119
New Zealand wattlebird family 2:339
New Zealand wren family 2:300
Newt family 3:480
  eastern 3:481
  great crested 3:480
  rough-skinned 3:481
  warty 3:494
Nicator chloris 2:360
Nicator, common 2:360
  yellow-spotted 2:360
Night lizard family 3:425
Nightjar, Eurasian 2:255
Nightjar and nighthawk
  family 2:254
Nightjar, great eared 2:254
  lyre-tailed 2:254
  standard-winged 2:255
Nilgai 1:167
Noctilio leporinus 1:112
Noctule 1:117
Noddy, brown 2:273
Noemacheilus barbatulus 3:509
Nomeus gronovii 3:569
Northern wheatear 2:346
Notacanthus chemnitzii 3:499
Notharchus macrorhynchos 2:226
Nothocrax urumutum 2:207
Notomys alexis 1:61
Notophthalmus viridescens 3:481
Notornis mantelli 2:266
Notoryctemorpha, order 1:25
Notoryctes typhlops 1:25
Nothothenia coriiceps 3:564
Notropis cornutus 3:508
Noturus gyrinus 3:512
Numbat family 1:24
Numenius phaeopus 2:266
Numida meleagris 2:213
Nunbird, black-fronted 2:226
Nuthatch family 2:351
Nuthatch, coral-billed 2:338
  redbreasted 2:351
Nutria coypu 1:69
Nyala 1:167
Nyctalus noctula 1:117
Nyctereutes procyonoides 1:123
Nyctea scandiaca 2:250
Nycteris thebaica 1:108
Nyctibius griseus 2:253
Nycticebus coucang 1:84
Nyctidromus albicollis 2:255
Nyctimene major 1:105
Nycticorax nycticorax 2:288
Nymphicus hollandicus 2:238

O

Oarfish 3:536
Oceanites oceanicus 2:299
Oceanodroma hornbyi 2:299
  melania 2:299
Ocelot 1:144

Ochotona alpina 1:36
Ochrotomys nuttalli 1:49
Octodon degus 1:69
Octodont rodent family 1:69
Ocyurus chrysurus 3:553
Odobenus rosmarus 1:149
Odocoileus virginianus 1:162
Odontaspis taurus 3:489
Oedistoma pygmaeum 2:375
Oenanthe oenanthe 2:346
Ogcocephalus nasutus 3:529
Oilbird family 2:253
Oilfish 3:545
Okapi 1:165
Okapia johnstoni 1:165
Old World burrowing
  lizard family 3:422
Old World cuckoo family 2:234
Old World monkey family 1:92
Old World porcupine family 1:64
Old World sucker-footed
  bat family 1:119
Olingo 1:127
Olm and mudpuppy family 3:475
Onager 1:195
Oncifelis colocolo 1:142
Oncorhynchus nerka 3:521
Ondatra zibethicus 1:55
Onychogalea fraenata 1:30
Onychognathus morio 2:348
Onychomys leucogaster 1:49
Onychorhynchus coronatus 2:304
Opah 3:536
Openbill, Asian 2:293
Ophicephalus striatus 3:571
Ophidiiformes order 3:524
Ophioblennius atlanticus 3:565
Ophiophagus hannah 3:448
Ophisaurus apodus 3:433
Opisthocomus hoazin 2:237
Oplurus sp. 3:413
Opororonis philadelphia 2:393
Opossum, water 1:20
  pale-bellied mouse 1:20
  short-tailed 1:21
  Virginia 1:20
Orang-utan 1:102
Orcinus orca 1:187
Oreamnos americanus 1:180
Orectolobiformes 3:492
Oreochromis niloticus 3:560
Oreomanes fraseri 2:389
Oreotragus oreotragus 1:176
Oreotrochilus estella 2:247
Oribi 1:176
Oriole, golden 2:332
  northern 2:394
Oriolus oriolus 2:332
Ornithorhynchus anatinus 1:19
Oropendola, chestnut-headed 2:394
  wagler's 2:394
Ortalis vetula 2:207
Orthotomus sutorius 2:365
Orycteropus afer 1:154
Oryctolagus cuniculus 1:39
Oryx leucoryx 1:174
Oryx, Arabian 1:174
Oryzias latipes 3:531
Oryzomys peninsulae 1:47
Oryzorictes hova 1:73
Osbornictis piscivora 1:135
Osmeriformes order 3:519
Osmerus eperlanus 3:519
Osphronemus goramy 3:570
Osprey 2:276
Osteoglossiformes 3:498
Osteoglossum bicirrhosum 3:498
Osteolaemus tetraspis 3:455
Ostracion tuberculatus 3:578
Ostrich family 2:204
Otis tarda 2:258
Otocolobus manul 1:144
Otolemur crassicaudatus 1:85
Otomops wroughtoni 1:113
Otomys irroratus 1:53
Otter, African clawless 1:133
  Eurasian 1:132
  giant 1:133
  sea 1:133

Otter-civet 1:137
Otus asio 2:249
Ourebia ourebi 1:176
Ovenbird and woodcreeper family 2:316
Ovenbird 2:393
Ovibos moschatus 1:182
Ovis canadensis 1:183
  orientalis 1:183
Owl family 2:249
Owl, barn 2:249
  brown fish 2:249
  burrowing 2:251
  eastern screech 2:249
  elf 2:249
  Eurasian pygmy 2:251
  great horned 2:250
  little 2:251
  long-eared 2:250
  northern hawk 2:251
  oriental bay 2:248
  snowy 2:250
Owlet-nightjar family 2:252
  Australian 2:252
Ox, musk 1:182
Oxpecker, yellow-billed 2:349
Oxybelis fulgidus 3:447
Oxydoras niger 3:515
Oxyruncus cristatus 2:307
Oxyura jamaicensis 2:217
Oystercatcher, common Eurasian 2:270
Ozotoceros bezoartieus 1:164

P

Paca family 1:67
Pacarana family 1:67
Pachycephala pectoralis 2:325
Pachyptila vittata 2:296
Pachyuromys duprasi 1:57
Pacu 3:511
Padda oryzivora 2:380
Paddlefish 3:496
Pademelon, red-legged 1:28
Pagellus bogaraveo 3:555
Pagophila eburnea 2:273
Pagophilus groenlandica 1:150
Paguma larvata 1:134
Painted snipe family 2:265
Palila loxioides 2:396
Palm civet, African 1:135
  banded 1:137
  masked 1:134
Palmatogecko rangei 3:419
Palmchat 2:341
Palmcreeper, point-tailed 2:313
Pan paniscus 1:103
  troglodytes 1:103
Panda, red 1:126
  giant 1:126
  lesser 1:126
Pandion haliaetus 2:276
Pangasianodon gigas 3:514
Pangasius pangasius 3:514
Pangolin family 1:35
Pangolin, giant 1:35
  tree 1:35
Panthera leo 1:146
  onca 1:146
  pardus 1:146
  tigris 1:147
Panurus biarmicus 2:368
Papio anubis 1:94
  hamadryas 1:94
  ursinus 1:94
Paradisaea rudolphi 2:328
Paradisefish 3:570
Paradoxornis guttaticollis 2:368
Paraechinus aethiopicus 1:75
Parakeet, monk 2:243
  rose-ringed 2:241
  sun 2:242
Paralichthys californicus 3:572
  dentatus 3:572
Parascalops breweri 1:79
Pardalote family 2:320
Pardalote, spotted 2:320
Pardalotus punctatus 2:320

Pareas sp. 3:443
Parotomys brantsii 1:53
Parrot family 2:238
Parrot, eclectus 2:240
  gray 2:240
  owl 2:240
  yellow-headed 2:243
Parrotbill, bearded 2:368
  spot-breasted 2:368
Parrotfinch, blue-faced 2:381
Parrotfish, blue 3:563
  rainbow 3:562
  stoplight 3:563
Parrotlet, spectacled 2:242
Partridge, crested 2:209
  red-legged 2:209
Parula americana 2:392
Parula, northern 2:392
Parus atricapillus 2:355
  fringillinus 2:355
  major 2:355
Passer domesticus 2:378
  griseus 2:378
Passerculus sandwichensis 2:385
Passeriformes order 2:300
Passerina ciris 2:391
Patagona gigas 2:247
Paucituberculata order 1:21
Pauraque 2:255
Pavo cristatus 2:211
Peacock-pheasant, gray 2:210
Peafowl, blue 2:211
  Congo 2:211
  Indian 2:211
Pearlfish 3:524
Peccary family 1:156
Peccary, chaco 1:156
  collared 1:156
  white-lipped 1:156
Pedetes capensis 1:47
Pedionomus torquatus 2:265
Peeper, spring 3:466
Pegasus volitans 3:541
Pelagodroma marina 2:299
Pelea capreolus 1:173
Pelecanoides urinatrix 2:297
Pelecanus occidentalis 2:291
  onocrotalus 2:291
Pelican and shoebill family 2:291
Pelican, brown 2:291
  great white 2:291
Pelobates fuscus 3:462
Pelodytes punctatus 3:462
Penduline-tit, yellow 2:354
Penelope purpurascens 2:207
Penguin family 2:294
Penguin, emperor 2:295
  Galápagos 2:295
  little 2:294
Peppershrike, rufous-browed 2:323
Peprilus triacanthus 3:569
Peramelemorpha order 1:24
Perameles gunnii 1:24
Perca fluviatilis 3:549
Perch 3:549
Perch, climbing 3:570
  kelp 3:561
  nile 3:546
  ocean 3:543
Perchlike fish order 3:546
Percopsiformes 3:523
Percopsis omiscomaycus 3:523
Pericrocotus flammeus 2:331
Perissodactyla order 1:194
Pernis apivorus 2:277
Perodicticus potto 1:84
Perognathus flavus 1:44
Peromyscus maniculatus 1:48
Petaurista petaurista 1:43
Petauroides volans 1:27
Petaurus breviceps 1:27
Petrel albatross and storm
  petrel family 2:296
Petrel, black storm 2:299
  common subantarctic diving 2:301
  European storm 2:299
  mottled 2:297
  ringed storm 2:299
  white-faced storm 2:299

Wilson's storm 2:299
Petrogale xanthopus 1:29
Petroica phoenicea 2:321
Petromus typicus 1:71
Petromyzon marinus 3:488
Petromyzoniformes 3:488
Petronia petronia 2:378
Phacochoerus aethiopicus 1:154
Phaenicophaeus viridirostris 2:236
Phaenostictus mcleannani 2:310
Phaethon rubricauda 2:284
Phalacrocorax africanus 2:287
carbo 2:286
harrisi 2:287
Phalaenoptilus nurtallii 2:254
Phalanger family 1:26
Phalarope, red 2:267
Phalaropus fulicarius 2:267
Pharomachrus mocinno 2:229
Phascolarctos cinereus 1:26
Phasianus colchicus 2:211
Pheasant, common 2:211
golden 2:210
Pheasant, grouse, and
turkey family 2:208
Phelsuma vinsoni 3:420
Phenacostethus smithi 3:535
Pheucticus ludovicianus 2:390
Philemon citreogularis 2:319
Philentoma velata 2:338
Philentoma, maroon-breasted 2:338
Philetarius socius 2:379
Philomachus pugnax 2:267
Phoca vitulina 1:151
Phocoena phocoena 1:185
Phocoenides dalli 1:185
Phodilus badius 2:248
Phodopus sungorus 1:50
Phoebe, eastern 2:303
Phoebetria palpebrata 2:298
Phoenicopterus ruber 2:290
Phoeniculus purpureus 2:228
Pholis gunnellus 3:563
Photoblepharon palpebratus 3:538
Phoxinus phoxinus 3:507
Phrynocephalus nejdensis 3:415
Phrynomerus bifasciatus 3:470
Phrynosoma cornutum 3:411
Phyllastrephus scandens 2:358
Phyllodactylus porphyreus 3:419
Phyllomedusa appendiculata 3:467
Phyllomedusa, Lutz's 3:467
Phyllonycteris poeyi 1:115
Phyllopteryx taeniolatus 3:541
Phylloscopus trochilus 2:364
Phyllostomus hastatus 1:114
Physailia pellucida 3:513
Physeter catodon 1:188
Physignathus leseueri 3:415
Phytotoma rara 2:307
Pica pica 2:327
Picathartes gymnocephalus 2:340
Piciformes order 2:218
Piculet, rufous 2:222
white-barred 2:223
whitebrowed 2:222
Picumnus cirratus 2:223
Picus viridis 2:220
Pig family 1:154
Pig, bearded 1:155
bush 1:154
Pigeon family 2:256
Pigeon, band-tailed 2:257
Rock 2:256
Pika family 1:36
northern 1:36
Pike, northern 3:519
Pilchard 3:502
Pimelodus blodii 3:516
Pimelometopon pulchrum 3:562
Pinecone fish 3:537
Pinicola enucleator 2:383
Pipa pipa 3:461
Pipe snake family 3:439
Pipefish, greater 3:541
Pipid frog family 3:461
Pipilo erythrophthalmus 2:386
Pipistrellus pipistrellus 1:117
Pipit, golden 2:376

water 2:377
meadow 2:377
Pipra filicauda 2:309
Pipreola arcuata 2:308
Pipromorphinae mionectine 2:302
Piranga olivacea 2:386
Piranha, red 3:510
Pirarucu 3:498
Pitangus sulphuratus 2:303
Pithecia monachus 1:88
Pitohui ferrugineus 2:325
Pitohui, rusty 2:325
Pitta family 2:300
Pitta brachyura 2:300
granatina 2:301
Pitta, garnet 2:301
Indian 2:300
Pituophis melanoleucas 3:446
Pityriasis gymnocephala 2:332
Pizonyx vivesi 1:116
Plaice 3:573
Plaice, American 3:574
Plains-wanderer 2:265
Plains-wanderer family 2:265
Planigale maculata 1:22
Planigale, pygmy 1:22
Plantcutter, rufous-tailed 2:307
Platacanthomys lasiurus 1:53
Platanista gangetica 1:184
Platax pinnatus 3:566
Plateless river turtle family 3:405
Platichthys stellatus 3:573
Platycercus elegans 2:241
Platypus family 1:19
Platyrinchus platyrhynchos 2:305
Platysaurus imperator 3:430
Platysteira cyanea 2:338
Platysternon megacephalum 3:408
Plecostomus commersonii 3:517
Plecotus auritus 1:116
Plectrophenax nivalis 2:385
Plegadis falcinellus 2:291
Plethodon cinereus 3:476
glutinosus 3:476
Pleurodeles waltl 3:480
Pleuronectes platessa 3:573
Pleuronectiformes 3:571
Plotosus lineatus 3:516
Plover and avocet family 2:270
Plover, crab 2:269
Egyptian 2:269
ringed 2:271
American golden 2:271
Pluvialis dominica 2:271
Pluvianus aegyptius 2:269
Poacher, sturgeon 3:545
Pocket gopher family 1:44
Pocket mouse family 1:44
Podargus strigoides 2:252
Podica senegalensis 2:260
Podiceps cristatus 2:284
Podicipediformes order 2:284
Podocnemis expansa 3:409
Podogymnura truei 1:75
Poecilia reticulata 3:533
Pogonias cromis 3:556
Poiana richardsoni 1:134
Polecat, western 1:128
Polioptila caerulea 2:354
Pollachius virens 3:527
Pollock, walleye 3:527
Polyboroides typus 2:279
Polyborus plancus 2:282
Polycentrus schomburgkii 3:559
Polychrus gutterosus 3:411
Polymixia nobilis 3:539
Polyodon spathula 3:496
Polyplectron bicalcaratum 2:210
Polypteriformes 3:496
Polypterus weeksi 3:496
Pomacanthus imperator 3:558
Pomacentrus leucostictus 3:561
Pomatomus saltatrix 3:550
Pompano, Florida 3:551
Pongo pygmaeus 1:102
Poorwill, common 2:254
Porbeagle 3:490
Porcupine, Asian brush-tailed 1:64
crested 1:64

Indonesian 1:64
long-tailed 1:65
North American 1:65
tree 1:65
upper Amazon 1:65
Porcupinefish 3:579
Porichthys porosissimus 3:528
Porphyrio mantelli 2:262
Porpoise family 1:185
Porpoise, common 1:185
dall's 1:185
finless 1:185
harbour 1:185
Possum, brush-tailed 1:27
honey 1:26
Potamochoerus porcus 1:154
Potamogale velox 1:73
Potoo family 2:253
Potoo, common 2:253
Potoroo 1:31
Potorous tridactylus 1:31
Potos flavus 1:127
Potto 1:84
Pout, ocean 3:563
Powan 3:519
Pracheirodon innesi 3:511
Prairie dog, black-tailed 1:42
Pratincole family 2:269
Pranticole, collared 2:269
common 2:269
Primates order 1:82
Prinia gracilis 2:361
Prinia, graceful 2:361
Priodontes maximus 1:34
Prion, broad-billed 2:296
Prionace glauca 3:491
Prionailurus bengalensis 1:142
Prionochilus percussus 2:374
Prionodon linsang 1:134
Prionops plumata 2:338
Prionotus carolinus 3:543
Pristiophorus cirratus 3:493
Pristiophoriformes 3:493
Pristis pectinata 3:494
Proboscidea order 1:198
Procavia capensis 1:197
Prochilodus platensis 3:510
Procnias averano 2:308
Procolobus badius 1:98
verus 1:98
Procyon lotor 1:127
Profelis aurata 1:142
Progne subis 2:357
Promerops cafer 2:374
Pronghorn family 1:165
Pronolagus crassicaudatus 1:37
Propithecus verreauxi 1:83
Proteles cristatus 1:140
Proteus anguinus 3:475
Protopterus aethiopicus 3:581
Protoxerus stangeri 1:40
Prunella modularis 2:375
Psalidoprocne pristoptera 2:357
Psammodromus algirus 3:425
Psammomys obesus 1:57
Psarocolius wagleri 2:394
Psettodes erumei 3:571
Pseudobranchus striatus 3:474
Pseudochelidon sirintarae 2:356
Pseudohydromys murinus 1:59
Pseudonaja textilis 3:449
Pseudophryne corroboree 3:468
Pseudoplatystoma fasciatum 3:516
Pseudopleuronectes americanus 3:574
Pseudopodoces humilis 2:326
Pseudotriton ruber 3:477
Pseudupeneus maculatus 3:557
Psittaciformes order 2:238
Psittacula krameri 2:241
Psittacus erithacus 2:240
Psophia crepitans 2:259
Psophodes olivaceus 2:324
Ptarmigan 2:212
Pteridophora alberti 2:328
Pterodroma inexpectata 2:297
Pteroglossus beauharnaesii 2:225
Pterois volitans 3:543
Pteronotus parnielli 1:112
Pteronura brasiliensis 1:133

Pterophyllum scalare 3:560
Pteroptochos castaneus 2:315
Pteropus giganteus 1:104
Ptilocercus lowi 1:81
Ptilogonys cinereus 2:340
Ptilonorhynchus violaceus 2:317
Ptychadena porosissima 3:472
Ptychocneilus oregonensis 3:507
Ptychozoon kubli 3:419
Pudu mephistophiles 1:164
Pudu, northern 1:164
Puffback, black-backed 2:337
Puffbird family 2:226
Puffbird, white-necked 2:226
Puffer, bandtail 3:578
sharpnose 3:578
Pufferfish 3:578
common 3:578
Puffin, Atlantic 2:274
Puffinus puffinus 2:296
Puma concolor 1:143
Pumpkinseed 3:548
Pycnonotus barbatus 2:358
Pygmy gliding possum family 1:27
Pygmy parrot, red-breasted 2:239
Pygmy-tyrant, short-tailed 2:305
Pygopus nigriceps 3:421
Pyononotus jocosus 2:359
Pyrocephalus rubinus 2:306
Pyrrhula pyrrhula 2:383
Python and boa family 3:440
Python molurus 3:441
Python, carpet 3:441
Indian 3:441
Pyxicephalus adspersus 3:472

Q

Quail, California 2:213
common 2:208
painted 2:208
Queen triggerfish 3:576
Quetzal, resplendent 2:229
Quiscalus quiscula 2:394
Quokka 1:29
Quoll 1:23

R

Rabbit and hare family 1:36
Rabbit, brush 1:38
European 1:39
pygmy 1:39
Sumatran short-eared 1:39
swamp 1:38
Raccoon family 1:126
Raccoon-dog 1:123
Racerunner 3:425
strand 3:423
Rachycentron canadum 3:550
Rail family 2:262
Rail, water 2:263
giant wood 2:263
Rainbowfish, crimson-spotted 3:535
Raja batis 3:494
Rajiformes 3:494
Rallus aquaticus 2:263
Ramphastos toco 2:225
Ramphocelus carbo 2:389
Ramphocoris clotbey 2:370
Rana catesbeiana 3:471
pipiens 3:472
ridibunda 3:472
temporaria 3:471
Rangifer tarandus 1:163
Raphicerus melanotis 1:177
Rasbora heteromorpha 3:508
Rascasse 3:542
Rat, African grass 1:60
Arizona cotton 1:49
armoured 1:70
Baja California rice 1:47
bamboo 1:50
black 1:60

brown 1:61
crested 1:52
fat sand 1:57
fish-eating 1:49
giant pouched 1:58
gliding spiny 1:70
greater bandicoot 1:61
karroo 1:53
long-tailed pouched 1:59
Madagascan 1:52
Norway 1:61
rough-tailed giant 1:60
spiny rice 1:47
stick-nest 1:61
swamp 1:53
white-tailed 1:52
Rat-fish 3:509
Rat-kangaroo family 1:31
Rat-kangaroo, musky 1:31
rufous 1:31
Ratel 1:130
Rattlesnake, eastern diamond back 3:452
Rattus norvegicus 1:61
rattus 1:60
Ratufa bicolor 1:41
Ray, Atlantic torpedo/electric 3:495
eagle 3:495
Razorbill 2:275
Recurvirostra avosetta 2:270
Redfish 3:543
Redhorse, northern 3:508
Redpoll, common 2:383
mealy 2:383
Redshank, common 2:266
Redstart, painted 2:393
Redunca arundinum 1:173
Reed-warbler, long-billed 2:363
Reedbuck, southern 1:173
Reedling 2:368
Regalecus glesne 3:536
Regulus satrapa 2:360
Reindeer 1:163
Reinhardtius hippoglossoides 3:574
Reithrodontomys megalotis 1:47
Remizinae penduline 2:354
Remora 3:550
Remora remora 3:550
Requiem shark order 3:491
Rhabdomis, stripe-sided 2:369
Rhabdomys pumilio 1:60
Rhabdornis mysticalis 2:369
Rhacophorid treefrog family 3:473
Rhacophorus nigropalmtus 3:473
Rhampholeon marshalli 3:417
Rhea americana 2:205
Rhea family 2:205
Rhea, greater 2:205
Rhebok 1:173
Rhincodon typus 3:492
Rhinecanthus aculeatus 3:577
Rhineura floridana 3:436
Rhinobatos lentiginosus 3:494
Rhinoceros family 1:196
Rhinoceros unicornis 1:196
Rhinoceros, black 1:197
Indian 1:196
square-lipped 1:196
Sumatran 1:196
white 1:196
Rhinoderma darwinii 3:467
Rhinolophus ferrumequinum 1:110
hipposideros 1:110
philippinensis 1:110
Rhinomyias ruficauda 2:345
Rhinophis blythii 3:439
Rhinophrynus dorsalis 3:462
Rhinopithecus roxellana 1:99
Rhinopoma microphyllum 1:106
Rhipidomys venezuelae 1:47
Rhipidura hypoxantha 2:333
leucophrys 2:333
rufifrons 2:333
Rhodeus sericeus 3:506
Rhombomys opimus 1:57
Rhynchonycteris naso 1:106
Rhynochetos jubatus 2:261
Rhizomys sumatrensis 1:50
Ricefish 3:531

Ridley, Pacific 3:407
Rifleman 2:300
Right whale family 1:193
Ring-tailed and greater gliding possum family 1:27
Riopa sundevalli 3:426
Riparia riparia 2:357
Rissa tridactyla 2:273
River dolphin family 1:184
Roach 3:506
Roadrunner and ground-cuckoo family 1:237
Roadrunner, greater 1:237
Robin, American 2:343
flame 2:321
northern sea 3:543
oriental magpie 2:347
Roccus saxatilis 3:546
Rock-jumper and rockfowl family 2:340
Rockfowl, white-necked 2:340
Rockhare, greater red 1:37
Rockling, three-barbed 3:525
Rockthrush, cape 2:342
Rodentia order 1:40
Roller family 2:230
Roller, European 2:230
short-legged ground 2:230
Rollulus rouloul 2:209
Romerolagus diazi 1:37
Rook 2:326
Rorqual family 1:192
Rosella, crimson 2:241
Rostrhamus sociabilis 2:277
Roughie 3:538
Rousettus aegyptiacus 1:104
Ruff 2:267
Runner, rainbow 3:551
Rupicapra rupicapra 1:181
Rupicola peruviana 2:308
Rush-tyrant, many-colored 2:304
Rutilus rutilus 3:506
Rynchops niger 2:272
Rypticus saponaceus 3:548

S

Sable 1:129
Sablefish 3:544
Saccopharyngiformes 3:501
Saccopteryx leptura 1:107
Sagittarius serpentarius 2:281
Saguinus imperator 1:87
nigricollis 1:87
Saiga 1:180
Saiga tatarica 1:180
Sailfish 3:568
Saimiri sciureus 1:89
Saithe 3:527
Saki, black-barred 1:88
monk 1:88
Salamander, amber-colored 3:481
Asian 3:481
California slender 3:477
dusky 3:477
fire 3:480
marbled 3:478
Pacific giant 3:479
red 3:477
red-backed 3:476
sharp-ribbed 3:480
slimy 3:476
spotted 3:478
spring 3:476
Texas blind 3:476
tiger 3:479
yellow-blotched 3:477
dicamptodontid 3:479
Salamandra salamandra 3:480
Salano 1:139
Salanoia concolor 1:139
Salmo gairdneri 3:520
salar 3:521
trutta 3:520
Salmon order 3:519
Salmon, Atlantic 3:521
Australian 3:559

sockeye 3:521
Salpinctes obsoletus 2:353
Salpornis spilonotus 2:353
Saltador, buff-throated 2:390
Saltator maximus 2:390
Salvelinus alpinus 3:520
namaycush 3:520
Sand racer, Algerian 3:425
Sand-smelt 3:535
Sandgrouse family 2:264
Sandgrouse, Pallas's 2:264
Sandpiper family 2:266
Sapsucker, yellow-bellied 2:222
Sarcophilus harrisii 1:23
Sarcoramphus papa 2:292
Sardina pilchardus 3:502
Sardine 3:502
Sardinha 3:511
Sargassumfish 3:529
Sasia ochracea 2:222
Sassaby 1:175
Sauromalus obesus 3:411
Saury 3:531
Sawfish, greater 3:494
Saxicola torquata 2:346
Sayornis phoebe 2:303
Scaly-tailed squirrel family 1:47
Scalyfoot lizard family 3:420
Scalyfoot, hooded 3:421
Scandentia order 1:80
Scapanus orarius 1:78
Scaphiopus hammondi 3:463
Scarus coeruleus 3:563
guacamaia 3:562
Scat 3:566
Scatophagus argus 3:566
Scaup, greater 2:217
Sceloporus undulatus 3:410
Schistometopum thomense 3:483
Scincella lateralis 3:429
Scincus philbyi 3:427
Sciuridae 1:40
Sciurus carolinensis 1:40
vulgaris 1:40
Scolecomorphus kirkii 3:482
Scolopax minor 2:266
Scomber scombrus 3:567
Scomberesox saurus 3:531
Scophthalmus aquosus 3:571
maximus 3:571
Scopus umbretta 2:290
Scorpaena porcus 3:542
Scorpaenichthys marmoratus 3:545
Scorpaeniformes 3:542
Scorpionfish order 3:542
Screamer family 2:214
Screamer, northern 2:214
Scrub bird, noisy 2:318
Scrubfowl, common 2:206
Scrubwren, white-browed 2:320
Sculpin, shorthorn 3:544
Scup 3:554
Scutisorex somereni 1:77
Scyliorhinus canicula 3:491
Scythebill, red-billed 2:314
Scythrops novaehollandiae 2:235
Sea bream, red 3:555
Sea lion family 1:148
Sea lion, Australian 1:149
California 1:148
steller 1:149
Seabass, white 3:556
Seadragon, weedy 3:541
Seahorse, dwarf 3:541
Seal family 1:150
Seal, bearded 1:151
common 1:151
crabeater 1:151
gray 1:150
harp 1:150
hooded 1:153
leopard 1:152
Mediterranean monk 1:153
northern elephant 1:152
northern fur 1:148
South American fur 1:148
Weddell 1:153
Seatrout, spotted 3:556
Sebastes marinus 3:543

Secretary bird family 2:281
Seedsnipe family 2:264
Seedsnipe, least 2:264
Seicercus castaniceps 2:363
Seiurus aurocapillus 2:393
Selene vomer 3:551
Selenidera maculirostris 2:225
Selevinia betpakdalaensis 1:62
Semaprochilodus insignis 3:510
Semnopithecus entellus 1:99
Semotilus corporalis 3:508
margarita 3:507
Sergeant major 3:561
Sericornis frontalis 2:320
Seriema family 2:261
red-legged 2:261
Serinus canaria 2:382
Seriola dumerili 3:551
Serow 1:180
Serpent eagle, crested 2:279
Serpophaga cinerea 2:307
Serrasalmus nattereri 3:510
Serval 1:144
Setonix brachyurus 1:29
Setornis criniger 2:360
Shad, twaite 3:502
Shanny 3:565
Shark order 3:489
Shark, basking 3:489
blue 3:491
bluntnose six-gilled 3:492
bull 3:491
common saw 3:493
Greenland 3:493
Port Jackson 3:489
thresher 3:489
whale 3:492
white 3:490
saw 3:493
Sharksucker 3:550
Sharpbill 2:307
Shearwater, manx 2:296
Sheath-tailed bat family 1:106
Sheathbill family 2:268
Sheathbill, snowy 2:268
Sheep, barbary 1:183
Sheepshead 3:554
California 3:562
Shelduck, common 2:215
Shield-snout, South African 3:438
Shieldtail snake family 3:439
Blyth's landau 3:439
red-blotched 3:439
Shiner, common 3:508
Shoebill 2:291
Shortwing, blue 2:344
whitebrowed 2:344
Shoveller, northern 2:216
Shrew family 1:76
Shrew opossum family 1:21
Shrew, armored 1:77
feather-tailed tree 1:81
giant Mexican 1:76
giant otter 1:73
long-tailed 1:73
madras tree 1:81
masked 1:76
mountain tree 1:80
mouse 1:77
Philippine tree 1:81
pygmy white-toothed 1:77
short-eared elephant 1:72
short-tailed 1:76
Sri Lankan long-tailed 1:77
Shrike family 2:322
Shrike, black-faced cuckoo 2:330
great gray 2:322
long-crested helmet 2:338
magpie 2:322
northern 2:322
white helmet 2:338
Shrike-thrush, gray 2:325
Shrike-tit, crested 2:325
Shrike-vireo, chestnut-sided 2:323
Shrimpfish 3:541
Sialia sialis 2:344
Siamang 1:100
Sicista betulina 1:63
Sickle-billed vanga 2:339

Sicklebill, 2:339
    white-tipped 2:246
Sidewinder 3:452
Sifaka, Verreaux's 1:83
Siganus virgatus 3:566
Sigmodon arizonae 1:49
Silktail 2:335
Siluriformes order 3:512
Silurus glanis 3:513
Silver-eye 2:362
Silverside, hardhead 3:534
Siphonops annulatus 3:483
Siren family 3:474
Siren lacertina 3:474
Siren, dwarf 3:474
    greater 3:474
Sirenia order 1:199
Sistrurus catenatus 3:452
Sitella, varied 2:325
Sitta canadensis 2:351
Sittasomus griseicapillus 2:314
Skates and ray order 3:494
Skimmer, black 2:272
Skink family 3:426
    brown 3:429
    Florida sand 3:427
    great plains 3:427
    legless 3:426
    prickly forest 3:429
    round-bodied 3:426
    spiny-tailed 3:428
    sundeval's 3:426
    western blue-tongued 3:429
Skua, great 2:272
Skunk, striped 1:132
    hog-nosed 1:132
    western spotted 1:132
Skylark, common 2:371
    Eurasian 2:371
Slider, pond 3:400
Slippery dick 3:562
Slit-faced bat family 1:108
Sloth, three-toed 1:33
    two-toed 1:33
Smalltooth 3:494
Smelt 3:519
Sminthopsis crassicaudata 1:23
Smoky bat family 1:118
Snail, sea 3:545
Snake, banded sea 3:449
    common garter 3:445
    De Vis's banded 3:448
    eastern brown 3:449
    eastern coral 3:449
    egg-eating 3:444
    false coral 3:439
    glass 3:433
    gopher 3:446
    mangrove 3:447
    paradise tree 3:447
    rat 3:445
    red-bellied 3:445
    Schlegel's blind 3:438
    slug 3:443
    smooth 3:446
    snail-eating 3:443
    spotted water 3:443
    sunbeam 3:439
    vine 3:447
    western blind 3:438
    white-bellied mangrove 3:443
    whip dark-green 3:444
Snake-lizard, Burton's 3:421
Snakehead 3:571
Snapper 3:554
    mutton 3:552
    yellowtail 3:553
Snipe, common 2:267
    greater painted 2:265
Snipe-eel 3:501
Snook 3:546
Snowcock, Himalayan 2:208
Snowfinch, white-winged 2:379
Soapfish 3:548
Softshell turtle family 3:404
Sole 3:575
    long-tongue 3:575
Solea solea 3:575
Solenodon cubanus 1:78

Solenodon family 1:78
Solenodon, Cuban 1:78
Solitaire, Andean 2:344
Somateria mollissima 2:216
Somniosus microcephalus 3:493
Sooglossid frog family 3:468
Sooglossus sechellensis 3:469
Sorex cinereus 1:76
Sousa chinensis 1:186
Spadebill, white-crested 2:305
Spadefoot toad family 3:462
Spadefoot, European 3:462
    western 3:463
Spalax leucodon 1:51
Sparisoma viride 3:563
Sparrow, chipping 2:386
    gray-headed 2:378
    Java 2:380
    rock 2:378
    savannah 2:385
    song 2:387
Sparus aurata 3:555
Spatuletail, marvellous 2:247
Speirops leucophoeus 2:362
Speirops, Principe Island 2:362
Speothos venaticus 1:122
Speotyto cunicularia 2:251
Sperm whale family 1:188
Spermophilus tridecemlineatus 1:42
Sphecotheres viridis 2:332
Sphenisciformes order 2:294
Spheniscus mendiculus 2:295
Sphenodon punctatus 3:410
Sphenodontia order 3:410
Sphoeroides spengleri 3:578
Sphyraena barracuda 3:567
Sphyrapicus varius 2:222
Sphyrna zygaena 3:491
Spiderhunter, long-billed 2:372
Spilogale gracialis 1:132
Spilornis cheela 2:279
Spinachia spinachia 3:540
Spinefoot, blue-lined 3:566
Spinetail, red-faced 2:312
    stripe-breasted 2:312
Spiny-eel 3:499
Spiza americana 2:391
Spizella passerina 2:386
Spizixos canifrons 2:359
Springhare family 1:47
Springbok 1:178
Spurdog 3:493
Spurfowl, red 2:209
Squaliformes 3:493
Squalus acanthias 3:493
Squamata order 3:410
Squatina squatina 3:492
Squatiniformes 3:492
Squawfish, northern 3:507
Squeaker, bush 3:473
Squirrel family 1:40
Squirrel monkey 1:89
    African giant 1:40
    African ground 1:42
    African palm 1:41
    Beecroft's flying 1:47
    black giant 1:41
    European red 1:40
    gray 1:40
    Indian striped palm 1:41
    northern flying 1:43
    Prevost's 1:41
    red giant flying 1:43
    thirteen-lined ground 1:42
    Zenker's flying 1:47
Squirrelfish 3:537
Stargazer, northern 3:565
Starling and mockingbird family 2:348
Starling, metallic 2:349
    red-winged 2:348
    shining 2:349
    superb 2:349
Starnoenas cyanocephala 2:257
Steatomys krebsii 1:58
Steatornis caripensis 2:253
Stenella coeruleoalba 1:186
Stenotomus chrysops 3:554
Stephanoberyciformes order 3:537
Stereolepis gigas 3:547

Sterna hirundo 2:273
Sternotherus odoratus 3:405
Stickleback, fifteen-spined 3:540
    four-spined 3:540
    three-spined 3:540
Stilt, blackwinged 2:270
Stingray, southern 3:494
Stizostedion lucioperca 3:549
Stoat 1:128
Stomiiformes order 3:521
Stonechat, common 2:346
Stonefish 3:543
Stoneroller 3:507
Storeria occipitomaculata 3:445
Stork, white 2:293
Strepera graculina 2:329
Strigiformes order 2:248
Strigops habroptilus 2:240
Striped and lesser gliding
    possum family 1:27
Strix aluco 2:251
Struthidea cinerea 2:324
Struthio camelus 2:204
Struthioniformes order 2:204
Sturgeon order 3:496
Sturgeon, common 3:497
Sturnella magna 2:395
Sturnira lilium 1:115
Sturnuslgaris 2:348
Sucker, white 3:508
Sugar glider 1:27
Sugarbird, cape 2:374
Sula leucogaster 2:285
Sunbeam snake family 3:439
Sunbird, flowerpecker, and
    sugarbird family 2:372
Sunbird, crimson 2:372
    olive-backed 2:373
    purple-throated 2:373
    red-tufted 2:373
    ruby-cheeked 2:372
    superb 2:373
    wattled false 2:301
    yellow-backed 2:372
Sunbittern family 2:258
Suncus etruscus 1:77
Sunfish, ocean 3:579
Sungrebe 2:260
Surfperch, barred 3:561
Suricata suricatta 1:139
Surnia ulula 2:251
Surniculus lugubris 2:235
Surubim 3:516
Sus barbatus 1:155
    scrofa 1:155
Swallow family 2:356
Swallow, bank 2:357
    barn 2:356
    golden 2:357
    white-browed wood 2:332
    white-breasted wood 2:332
Swallow-tanager 2:390
Swan, tundra 2:215
Swift family 2:244
Swift, African palm 2:244
    common 2:245
    crested tree 2:245
    gray-rumped tree 2:245
    white-throated 2:244
Swordfish 3:569
Swordtail 3:534
Syconycteris australis 1:105
Sylvia atricapilla 2:369
Sylvicapra grimmia 1:171
Sylvilagus aquaticus 1:38
    audubonii 1:38
    bachmani 1:38
Sylviorthorhynchus desmursii 2:313
Symphurus plagiusa 3:575
Symphysodon discus 3:560
Synallaxis cinnamomea 2:312
Synanceia verrucosa 3:543
Synaptomys cooperi 1:54
Synbranchiformes 3:542
Synceros caffer 1:170
Syndactylus 1:100
Syngnathus acus 3:541
Synodontis nigriventris 3:515
Synodus synodus 3:522
Syrrhaptes paradoxus 2:264

T

Tachuris rubrigastra 2:304
Tachybaptus ruficollis 2:284
Tachycineta euchrysea 2:357
Tachyeres brachypterus 2:216
Tachyglossus aculeatus 1:18
Tachyoryctes macrocephalus 1:50
Tachyphonus luctuosus 2:387
Tadarida aegyptiaca 1:113
Tadorna tadorna 2:215
Tadpole madtom 3:512
Taeniopygia guttata 2:381
Tahiti reed-warbler 2:363
Tahr, Himalayan 1:182
Tailed frog family 3:460
Tail-less leaf-nosed bat 1:111
Tailorbird, common 2:365
    longtailed 2:365
Takahe 2:262
Takin 1:182
Talapoin 1:97
Talpa europaea 1:78
Tamandua, northern 1:32
Tamarin, black and red 1:87
    emperor 1:87
    golden lion 1:87
Tamandua mexicana 1:32
Tamias striatus 1:42
Tanager, magpie 2:387
    paradise 2:389
    scarlet 2:386
    silver-beaked 2:389
    white-shouldered 2:387
Tandanus tandanus 3:516
Tang, blue 3:566
Tangara chilensis 2:389
Tanysiptera gala tea 2:233
Tapaculo family 2:315
Tapera naevia 2:237
Taphozous longimanus 1:107
Tapir, Brazilian 1:195
    Malayan 1:195
Tapir family 1:195
Tapirus indicus 1:195
    terrestris 1:195
Taraba major 2:311
Tarentola annularis 3:418
Taricha granulosa 3:481
Tarpon 3:499
Tarpon atlanticus 3:499
Tarsier family 1:85
Tarsier, western 1:85
Tarsipes rostratus 1:26
Tarsius bancanus 1:85
Tasmacetus shepherdi 1:191
Tasmanian devil 1:23
Tatera indica 1:57
Tauraco erythrolophus 2:248
Tautog 3:562
Tautoga onitis 3:562
Tawny frogmouth 2:252
Tawny owl 2:251
Taxidea taxus 1:131
Tayassu pecati 1:156
    tajacu 1:156
Tayra 1:129
Tegu, common 3:422
Teiid lizard family 3:422
Teius teyou 3:423
Tench 3:505
Tenrec ecaudatus 1:72
Tenrec family 1:72
Tenrec setifer setosus 1:72
Tenrec, streaked 1:73
    rice 1:73
    tail-less 1:72
    greater hedgehog 1:72
    long-tailed shrew 1:73
Terathopius ecaudatus 2:278
Tern, common 2:273
Terpsiphone paradisi 2:335
Terrapene carolina 3:401
Terrapin, diamondback 3:400
    river 3:401
Tersina viridis 3:404
Testudo graeca 3:403
Tetra, flame 3:511
    Mexican 3:511

neon 3:511
Tetracerus quadricornis 1:167
Tetrao tetrix 2:212
Tetraodon cutcutia 3:578
Tetraodontiformes 3:576
Tetraogallus himalayensis 2:208
Tetrapturus audax 3:569
Teyu 3:423
Thamnophilus doliatus 2:311
Thamnophis sirtalis 3:445
Thecurus sumatrae 1:64
Theragra chalcogramma 3:527
Therapon jarbua 3:559
Theropithecus gelada 1:95
Thick-knee family 2:268
Thick-knee, beach 2:268
Thinocorus rumicivorus 2:264
Thomomys talpoides 1:44
Thornbill, yellow-rumped 2:320
Thorny devil 3:414
Thread snake family 3:438
Three-toed sloth family 1:50
Threskiornithidae 2:290
Thrush, austral 2:343
   cinnamon quail 2:324
   island 2:343
   olive 2:343
   white's 2:342
Thrush, Old World flycatcher,
   and chat family 2:342
Thryomanes bewickii 2:353
Thryonomys swinderianus 1:70
Thunnus albacares 3:568
Thylogale stigmatica 1:28
Thymallus thymallus 3:519
Thyroptera discifera 1:119
Tichodroma muraria 2:351
Tiger 1:147
Tiger, sand 3:489
Tigerfish, 3:559
   giant 3:510
Tiliqua occipitalis 3:429
Timetothylacus tenellus 2:376
Tinamou family 2:206
Tinamiformes order 2:206
Tinamou, great 2:206
Tinamus major 2:206
Tinca tinca 3:505
Tit family 2:354
Tit, great 2:355
   longtailed 2:355
   red-throated 2:355
   sultan 2:355
Titi, dusky 1:89
Tmetothylacus tenellus 2:376
Toad family 2:464
Toad, African clawed 3:461
Toad, American 3:464
   Boulenger's arrow poison 2:478
   common 3:465
   giant 3:464
   green 3:465
   Mexican burrowing 3:462
   midwife 3:460
   natterjack 3:465
   oriental fire-bellied 3:461
   Surinam 3:461
Toadfish order 3:528
Tockus erythrorhynchus 2:227
Toco toucan 2:225
Todirhamphus chloris 2:233
Todirostrum cinereum 2:302
Todus todus 2:231
Tody family 2:231
Tody, Jamaican 2:231
Tody-flycatcher, common 2:302
Tonguefish, blackcheek 3:575
Topaza pella 2:247
Topaz, crimson 2:247
Torgos tracheliotus 2:277
Tortoise, African pancake 3:402
   bowsprit 3:402
   Galápagos giant 3:402
   gopher 3:402
   leopard 3:403
   serrated hingeback 3:403
   spur-thighed 3:403

Torpedo nobiliana 3:495
Toucan, plate-billed mountain 2:225
Toucanet, emerald 2:224
   saffron 2:224
   spot-billed 2:225
Towhee, rufous-sided 2:386
Toxostoma redivivum 2:350
Toxotes jaculator 3:557
Tragelaphus angasii 1:167
   eurycerus 1:167
   strepsiceros 1:166
Tragopan temminckii 2:210
Tragopan, Temminck's 2:210
Tragulus javanicus 1:160
Tree shrew family 1:80
Tree shrew, Bornean
   smooth-tailed 1:81
   common 1:80
Treecreeper, brown 2:315
   common 2:353
   Eurasian 2:353
Treefrog family 3:466
Treefrog, common gray 3:466
   European Green 3:466
Trembler, brown 2:351
Tremarctos ornatus 1:124
Triaenops persicus 1:111
Trichechus manatus 1:199
Trichiurus lepturus 3:567
Trichoglossus haematodus 2:238
Trichosuruslpecula 1:27
Trichys fasciculata 1:65
Triggerfish, black-barred 3:577
   clown 3:576
   gray 3:576
   Sargassum 3:577
Trigla lucerna 3:543
Triller, white-winged 2:331
Tringa totanus 2:266
Trionyx spiniferus 3:404
   triunguis 3:404
Tripletail 3:553
Triportheus elongatus 3:511
Trochiliformes order 2:246
Trochocercus albonotatus 2:334
Troglodytes aedon 2:352
   troglodytes 2:352
Trogon, copperytailed 2:229
   elegant 2:229
   red-headed 2:229
Trogon elegans 2:229
Trogon family 2:229
Trogoniformes order 2:229
Trogonophiid family 3:437
Tropic bird family 2:284
Tropic bird, red-tailed 2:284
Tropidophorus queenslandiae 3:429
Tropidosaura essexi 3:425
Trout, rainbow 3:520
Trout-perch 3:523
Trumpeter, gray-winged
   common 2:259
Trout 3:520
Trout-perch order 3:523
True frog family 3:471
Trumpeter family 2:259
Tsessebi 1:175
Ttagelaphus oryx 1:166
Tuatara family 3:410
Tuatara, Cook Strait 3:410
Tubesnout 3:540
Tubulidentata order 1:154
Tuco-tuco 1:69
Tuco-tuco family 1:69
Tuna, skipjack 3:568
Tuna, yellowfin 3:568
Tupaia glis 1:80
Tupaia montana 1:80
Tupinambis teguixin 3:422
Turaco family 2:248
Turaco, red-crested 2:248
Turbot 3:571
Turdoides plebejus 2:367
Turdus falklandii 2:343
   merula 2:343
   migratorius 2:343

   olivaceus 2:343
Turdus poliocephalus 2:343
Turkey, common 2:212
Turniciformes order 2:218
Turnstone, ruddy 2:267
Turtle, Arrau river 3:409
   big-headed 3:408
   Central American river 3:405
   common musk 3:405
   Eastern box 3:401
   European pond 3:401
   false map 3:400
   flapshell Zambesi 3:404
   green 3:406
   loggerhead 3:407
   Murray River 3:409
   snapping 3:408
   softshell Indian 3:404
   softshell Nile 3:404
   softshell spiny 3:401
   softshell Zambesi 3:404
   wood 3:401
   yellow mud 3:405
Turnix sylvatica 2:218
Tursiops 1:187
Two-toed sloth family 1:33
Tylosaurus crocodilus 3:531
Tympanuchus cupido 2:212
Typhlomolge rathbuni 3:476
Typhlonectes compressicauda 3:483
Typhlops schlegelii 3:438
Typical antbird family 2:310
Typical waterfowl family 2:214
Tyrannus forficata 2:303
   tyrannus 2:303
Tyrant family 2:302
Tyrant, white-headed marsh 2:303
Tyranulet, torrent 2:307
Tyto alba 2:249

U

Uakari, bald 1:89
Umbrella bird, Amazonian 2:309
Uncia uncia 1:147
Unicornfish, striped-face 3:567
Upupa epops 2:228
Upupiformes order 2:228
Uraeginthus bengalus 2:380
Uria aalge 2:274
Urocissa ornata 2:327
Uroderma bilobatum 1:114
Urogale everetti 1:81
Uromastyx princeps 3:415
Uropeltis biomaculatus 3:439
Urophycis tenuis 3:526
Uroplatus fimbriatus 3:420
Uropsalis lyra 2:254
Ursus americanus 1:125
   arctos 1:124
   maritimus 1:125
   thibetanus 1:125

V

Vampyrum spectrum 1:114
Vandellia cirrhosa 3:517
Vanellus vanellus 2:271
Vanga curvirostris 2:339
Vanga, hook-billed 2:339
Varanus gouldi 3:435
Varanus komodensis 3:434
Varanus niloticus 3:434
Varecia variegata 1:82
Veery 2:342
Verdin 2:354
Vermicella annulata 3:449
Vermivora chrysoptera 2:392
Vicugna vicugna 1:158
Vicuña 1:158
Vidua paradisaea 2:381
Vieja 3:517
Viper 3:442
Viper and pit viper family 3:450
Viper, Asiatic pit 3:453

aspic 3:451
   common 3:450
   desert sidewinding 3:450
   gaboon 3:451
   horned 3:450
Vipera ammodytes 3:450
   aspis 3:451
   berus 3:450
   gabonica 3:451
   peringueyi 3:450
Viperfish, Sloane's 3:521
Vireo family 2:322
Vireo, olivaceus 2:322
   red-eyed 2:322
Vireolanius melitophrys 2:323
Viscacha and chinchilla family 1:68
Viscacha, plains 1:68
Viverra civetta 1:135
Vole, bank 1:55
   European water 1:55
   meadow 1:55
   sagebrush 1:54
Vombatus ursinus 1:25
Vulpes zerda 1:121
Vulpes vulpes 1:121
Vulture, bearded 2:276
   Egyptian 2:276
   king 2:292
   lappet-faced 2:277
   palm-nut 2:278
   turkey 2:293

W

Wagtail, forest 2:376
   pied 2:377
   white 2:377
   yellow 2:377
wahoo 3:568
Wallabia bicolor 1:31
Wallaby, bridled nail-tailed 1:30
   New Guinea forest 1:30
   swamp 1:31
   yellow-footed rock 1:29
Wallcreeper 2:351
Walrus 1:149
Walrus family 1:149
Wapiti 1:163
Warbler family 2:362
Warbler 2:364
   black-and-white 2:392
   Ceylon bush 2:364
   chestnut-crowned 2:363
   chestnut-headed 2:363
   golden-crowned 2:393
   golden-winged 2:392
   grasshopper 2:363
   mourning 2:393
   willow 2:364
   yellow 2:393
Wart snake family 3:441
Warthog 1:154
Water dragon, eastern 3:415
   Soa-soa 3:415
Water rat, Australian 1:59
Waterbuck, common 1:172
   Defassa 1:172
Wattle-eye, brown-throated 2:338
   common 2:338
Waxwing family 2:340
Waxwing, bohemian 2:341
Weasel, least 1:128
Weaver and grass finch
   family 2:375
Weaver, sociable 2:379
   white-billed buffalo 2:379
   lesser 3:565
Wels 3:513
Whale, Baird's beaked 1:191
   blue 1:193
   bowhead 1:193
   Cuvier's beaked 1:190
   dwarf sperm 1:188
   Greenland right 1:193
   gray 1:192
   humpback 1:193
   killer 1:187

long-finned pilot	1:187	Woodchuck	1:43	**X**		Zebra, common	1:194
minke	1:192	Woodcock, American	2:266			Grevy's	1:194
northern bottlenose	1:190	Woodcreeper, barred	2:314	*Xantusia vigilis*	3:425	Zeiformes	3:539
pygmy sperm	1:188	long-billed	2:314	Xenarthra order	1:32	*Zenaida macroura*	2:257
sei	1:192	olivaceous	2:314	*Xenopeltis unicolor*	3:439	*Zenopsis ocellata*	3:539
Shepherd's beaked	1:191	Woodhoopoe family	2:228	*Xenops minutus*	2:312	*Zeus fiber*	3:539
Sowerby's beaked	1:191	Woodhoopoe, green	2:228	Xenops, plain	2:312	*Ziphius cavirostris*	1:190
sperm	1:188	Woodpecker family	2:218	*Xenopus laevis*	3:461	Zitting cisticola	2:361
white	1:189	Woodpecker, blond-crested	2:221	*Xenosaurus* sp.	3:432	*Zonosaurus* sp.	3:431
Whalefish	3:537	Eurasian green	2:220	*Xerus erythropus*	1:42	*Zoothera dauma*	2:342
Whimbrel	2:266	golden-backed	2:221	*Xiphias gladius*	3:569	*Zosterops japonicus*	2:362
Whipbird, eastern	2:324	goldentailed	2:220	*Xiphophorus belleri*	3:534		
Whistler, golden	3:331	great slaty	2:220				
Whistling duck family	2:214	great spotted	2:219				
White whale family	1:189	greater flame-backed	2:221				
White-eye family	2:362	ground	2:221	**Y**			
White-eye, gray-backed	2:362	ivory-billed	2:219				
Japanese	2:362	Woodrat, white-throated	1:49	Yak, wild	1:169		
Whiting	3:527	Worm, slow	3:433	Yapok	1:20		
Whiting, blue	3:527	Wrasse, ballan	3:562	Yellowhammer	2:385		
Whydah, paradise	2:381	Wren	2:352	*Yuhina gularis*	2:366		
Wildebeest, blue	1:174	Bewick's	2:353	Yuhina, stripe-throated	2:366		
Willie wagtail	2:333	cactus	2:352				
Winged dragon	3:541	long-billed marsh	2:353				
Wire-tail, Des Murs'	2:313	rock	2:353				
Wolf, gray	1:120	Wren, treecreeper and		**Z**			
maned	1:122	gnatcatcher family	2:353				
Wolf-fish, Atlantic	3:564	Wren, winter	2:352	*Zaglossus bruiini*	1:18		
Wolverine	1:130	Wrentit	2:369	*Zalophus californianus*	1:148		
Wombat family	1:25	Wrybill	2:271	*Zanclus cornutus*	3:566		
Wombat, common	1:25	Wrymouth	3:563	Zander	3:549		
Wood peewee, eastern	2:305	Wryneck, Northern/Eurasian	2:219	*Zapus hudsonius*	1:63		

ACKNOWLEDGEMENTS

The Publishers received invaluable help during the preparation of the Animal Encyclopedia from: Heather Angel, who lent us reference slides, Angus Bellairs, who gave advice, Dr H. G. Cogger, who lent us reference slides; Rosanne Hooper and Zilda Tandy who assisted with research, Dr Pat Morris of Royal Holloway College, London and Dr Robert Stebbings of the Institute of Terrestrial Ecology, Huntingdonshire, who both helped with reference on the Mammal section, Ed Wade, who helped with reference on the Fish section, the staff of the Herpetology Department of the British Museum (Natural History), London, particularly Colin McCarthy and Barry Clarke, who allowed us access to specimens and reference, the staff of the Ornithology Department of the British Museum (Natural History) outstation at Tring, particularly Peter Colston, who gave assistance with the specimen collection, the staff of the Science Reference Library, London, the IUCN Conservation Monitoring Centre, Cambridge, England, for data on threatened species, and the Zoological Society of London, which allowed us to reproduce information from its *International Zoo Yearbook*.

We acknowledge the contribution of Professor Carl Gans in his book *Reptiles of the World* (Bantam 1975).